Exiled Memories

Exiled Memories

Stories of Iranian Diaspora

Zohreh T. Sullivan

TEMPLE UNIVERSITY PRESS

PHILADELPHIA

Temple University Press, Philadelphia 19122
Copyright © 2001 by Temple University
All rights reserved
Published 2001
Printed in the United States of America

⊗ The paper used in this publication meets the requirements of
the American National Standard for Informational Sciences—Permanence
of Paper for Printed Library Materials, ANSI Z39.48-1984

Library of Congress Cataloguing-in-Publication Data

Sullivan, Zohreh T.
   Exiled memories : stories of Iranian diaspora / Zohreh T. Sullivan.
      p. cm.
   Includes bibliographical references and index.
   ISBN 1-56639-842-8 (cloth : ack. paper) — ISBN 1-56639-843-6 (pbk. :
   alk. paper)
   1. Iranian Americans—Interviews.   2. Immigrants—United
States—Interviews.   3. Exiles—United States—Interviews.   4. Iranian
Americans—Ethnic identity.   5. Iranian Americans—Social conditions.
6. Iran—History—Revolution, 1979—Personal narratives.   I. Title
E184.15 S85 2001
973'.04915—dc21
                                                      00-041195

For Mahin,

Taimur and Kamran,

and all our families

Made You Mine, America

America
in the poems of Walt Whitman
Langston Hughes
Allen Ginsberg
the songs of Woody Guthrie
and Joan Baez
I made you mine

rushing to you
at night and daybreak
by air and water—
on the land
getting a social security number
in the year nineteen hundred seventy
working the grave-
yard shift for ITT
a teenager four levels below the ground
a cashier in a three-by-eight booth
under the Denver Hilton Hotel
sheltering derelicts
who slept on beds
of cardboard and newspaper
pillows of shoes
my young body luring
late-night prostitutes and transvestites
hip to my accent

the midnight thief
pouring Mace in my eyes
escaping
up the long ramp

passing through barbed wires
and waiting for hours in the INS lobbies
facing grouchy secretaries
overwhelmed by the languages
they can't speak and accents
they can't enjoy
becoming naturalized
in the year of bicentennial celebration

the migration of my parents
to your welfare state
of millions living
in tenement housing
reeking with the smell of urine
and cheap liquor

traveling
the US of A
as large as Whitman's green mind
white beard and red heart
from the Deadman's Pass rest area
on the old Oregon Trail
to the Scenic Overlook at the Mason-Dixon line, Maryland
from Mountain Home—Idaho
to Rockford—Illinois
as large as Mark Twain's laughter and irony
from the YMCA's casket-sized single rooms
in Brooklyn
Chicago
San Francisco
to Denver's Republic Hotel
the home of broken old men
and women subsisting on
three hundred sixty-four dollar

social security checks

waiting on
Denver oilmen in the Petroleum Club
nights of jazz at El Chapultepec
the Larimer of the past
where Arapahoes lived in their
teepees and now sleep
on the sidewalks
with battered lips
and broken heads

going door to door on Madison Avenue, Seattle
selling death insurance
for American National
servicing houses of bare minimum—
a TV and a couch
drunken men and women
lonely ailing old African
women making quilts
selling each
for fifty dollars

marrying a teacher
a third-generation auto worker
whose parents shared crops
in Caraway, Arkansas

fathering two tender boys
born in America
with their blue and brown eyes

substituting
for teachers
baby-sitting bored middle school children
driving them
home in a school bus
teaching your youth
to write English
and speak Persian

loving
your children
daughters
sons
mothers
fathers
grandmothers
grandfathers
hating your aggression
you aligned yourself with the worst
of my kind
exiled my George Washington—
Dr. Mohammad Mosaddeq—
helped Saddam bomb my birthplace
destroy the school of my childhood
his soldiers swarming the hills of Charzebar
where as a child I hunted
with my grandfather
sold arms to warmongers
who waged battles on grounds
on which my great-grandfather made
fifteen pilgrimages on foot
to Karbala

now I lay claim
to your Bill of Rights
and Declaration of Independence.

I came to you
not a prince
who had lost his future throne
not a thief finding
a cover in the multitudes
of your metropoles
hiding behind your volumes of law
not a merchant dreaming of exploiting
your open markets
not a smuggler
seeking riches overnight
but a greenhorn seventeen-year-old

with four hundred dollars
after Dad sold his prized Bretta rifle
and Mom some of her wedding jewelry
with a suitcase of clothes
and books—
Hafez
Rumi
Shakespeare
Nima
Forugh
and a small Qu'ran—
my grandmother's gift
not to conquer
Wall Street
Broadway
or Hollywood
I came to you to study
to learn
and I learned
you can't deny me parenthood
I lost my grandparents
while roaming your streets
traveling across your vastness
you can't turn me down
I gave you my youth
walking and driving Colfax nights long
I came with hate
but now
I love you
America.

"Made You Mine, America" by Ali Zarrin appeared in Persis M. Karim and Mohammad Medhi Khorrami, *A World Between: Poems, Short Stories, and Essays by Iranian-Americans* (New York: George Braziller, 1999). Reprinted with permission.

Contents

Photographs follow page 122

Preface, or, How I Started Story Gathering

> I feel I am the wandering Jew who has no place to which she belongs. I thought I could settle down, but can't imagine staying. Whenever I bought a bar of soap and two came in the package, I thought there would be no need to buy a package of two because I would never last through the second. Why? Because I knew I was returning to Iran—tomorrow. So too, I would buy the smallest size toothpastes and jars of oil. Putting down roots here is an impossibility.

Spoken at my dining table in Champaign-Urbana in 1989, these words were part of one woman's meditations on exile and on her resistance to diasporic assimilation, part of a conversation with me, now her closest Iranian friend, who had once been her teacher in Damavand College, Tehran, Iran, from 1970 to 1972. I resumed a long-time friendship with this woman (I shall call her Pari) after she found herself stranded in the United States, exiled by the revolution that led to her coworkers being killed and her brother being locked in solitary confinement. The recognition of the different challenges we faced in locating ourselves, combined with my own troubled relationship to nations and nationality, provoked the greater part of this inquiry.

I met Pari as a student in Iran in 1970 when she had decided, even though she was professionally established, that she wanted a degree in English literature. Ten years later, in 1980, her daughter also sat as a student in my class on the British Novel, except that I was now a revolution and continents away at the University of Illinois in the middle of Midwestern cornfields. Pari's visit to her daughter in Illinois coincided with the revolution that separated her from Iran for ten years. She had worked in Iran as a writer of children's books, as an editor, as a translator, and as an assistant director in a ministry in charge of the women's literacy campaign in villages. Her arrival out of Iran was much the same as that of any other new immigrant, but what she chooses to remember articulates significant moments of transition.

She remembers the first words she heard at the airport, words inflected beyond intention by U.S. immigrations officials: "Why have you come here? How much money do you have? Who will support you? Why are you traveling alone? How long do you plan on staying in this country?" Her recollection echoed that of so many others; yet refracted through Iranian eyes that had just seen a national revolution, even generic questions about money, aloneness, support, and change of country were now charged with a particular history of revolution and loss. She was then interrogated for two hours at the airport, asked more questions about matters she considered private and intimate, and lost her luggage because the immigrations officer had held her up so long. Away from the comforting chaos and litter of Tehran streets, she felt she did everything wrong. There were anti-littering signs everywhere, and she was faced with the silent codes of the big city. When she tipped the cabby who drove her in from the airport, he cursed all foreigners. When she threw her cigarette butt on the city street, her daughter picked it up and silently carried it to a garbage can.

Once she realized that she could not return home, she struggled daily to cope with life first in a university town, and then in Los Angeles, suffering what she perceived to be recurring failures interrupted by breakdowns. On those occasions she felt as if she were in some undefined hollow space that threatened her equilibrium. Some days she said her panic took on the configuration of a landscape where she was balanced on the edge of a huge black hole about to swallow her; other days she felt she had lost her self. She thought that perhaps the problem could be solved if she set down roots, if she bought a house and owned a piece of space she could turn into solid ground. But then she wondered how she could buy a house when she couldn't buy a tube of toothpaste without paralyzing anxiety and ambivalence.

In the polarity between "here," where one does not belong, and "there," the romantic point of departure and return, lies the imagined territory of exilic identity and of all identity formation. Although the dichotomy seems simple—there and here, nation and enemy, home and exile—its separateness is blurred by an entangled dialectical relation. *There, nation,* and *home*—often defined by what they are *not*—also become the charged spaces that constitute "identity" and "culture" reorganized by memory in exile.

Pari's daughter, Maryam, once made her the subject of a five-minute film in which each shot showed her mother locked outside a door—first the door to her car, then the door to a neighbor's house, and finally the door to her own apartment whose outer walls were covered with anti-Iranian graffiti. My interest in recording stories and memories of displaced Iranians began with my friend's palpable grief at her loss of identity, work, home, language, family, and country, then evolved into an interest in the differences between our attitudes toward the past, toward nation, language, identity, and culture. In Iran, Pari's last name would announce her past, her family, and her "identity" to most educated and literate Iranians. The language—Persian—in which she wrote short stories and children's books and into which she translated English texts was one of her key sources of power. To me as a hybridized outsider, her house in Tehran had once represented a fantasy space that reconstructed the imagined and idealized spaces of the East (the domed ceilings, the vast stone floors jeweled with Kerman carpets, the garden, the courtyard) and the conspicuous spaces of the West (the sauna and the swimming pool). Now she lived in either student flats or a small rented room in someone else's house; she couldn't master the grammar or spelling of the language she had studied for years; and she had a name no one could pronounce.

The violent anxiety Pari and others faced in displacement provided the impetus for a series of interviews with emigrés and exiles that started in 1990, eleven years after the Islamic Revolution. "I know you have lost much," I said to her on one particularly dreary Champaign afternoon. "Let's not lose your memories of that loss." We then started to record her narrative. The need to raise those memories was predicated on the conviction that Pari's voice was part of the contemporary history of Iran, of dislocation, and of migration, and that somewhere in the links and gaps between my voice and hers and those of the other interviewees we could stitch together fragments of what had been omitted from other stories of identity, gender, and history.[1]

I started talking about this project to Pari in 1989 when I thought of centering my sample of storytellers in a group of exilic women Pari met with once a month in Los Angeles. This group included at least one woman whose family had been arbitrarily shot after the revolution because she had welcomed into her home for one night an unknown guest—Bani Sadr, the ex-president, fleeing for his life from the regime's displeasures.[2] But Pari returned to Iran before I could fly out to California. She visited the United States for two months in the spring of 1990 when she joined me in interviewing some twenty Iranians in Illinois and in California, and then she immediately returned to Tehran. Pari returned to the United States for short visits in 1992 and 1994. Her narrative is woven out of several conversations I taped during those visits.

Except for one informant who was interviewed in November 1999, the other forty-four informants were interviewed between 1990 and 1995. From various ethnic and religious backgrounds, their ages ranged from thirteen to eighty-eight; they lived in Canada; Illinois; Boston; Washington, D.C.; San Francisco; and Los Angeles. Although thanks to a study grant in a second discipline I took time off to learn what I could of anthropology and ethnography, it was the spirit of oral history that inspired me more than its specific quantitative methods. While I had no scientifically chosen sample, I focused on those whose voices evoked stories beyond their own.[3] I knew that I wanted to provide narrative documents and representations of a diversity of Iranians—Muslims, Zoroastrians, Baha'is, Jews, and Christians—life histories unavailable in books and in the media. I chose those stories that were most compelling, most resonant, and demanded an audience. Out of the sixty-five recorded transcripts, although I made some effort to represent differences in class, religion, ethnicity, and professions, I did not entirely succeed. Because most of those who managed to leave Iran were usually lower-middle to upper-middle class, I recorded only one clearly lower-class male. And then, because the few Christian Iranians I interviewed planned to return and therefore wanted their narratives deleted, I exclude an important minority Iranian voice. The types of work my informants did varied: several worked in offices as accountants, secretaries, or computer programmers. Some were academicians of all stripes—from departments of film, history, sociology, anthropology, comparative literature, political science, and women's studies. Some worked as waitresses; others worked as salespersons in department stores. A few were high school students. Some were undergraduates. Two were graduate students. One was an editor of children's books, another a private scholar who ran an Iranian research and education center; one is a well-known California journalist and radio personality; some were housewives. My youngest informants left Iran when they were toddlers of two or three years old, while the oldest left Iran when they were in their sixties and seventies.

I met my informants with a tape recorder, no questionnaire, and no list of set questions. I told them they could speak in Persian, English, or both. Following anthropological advice, I interviewed people where they chose and where they admitted to feeling most comfortable. I met them in their homes, in cafes, in their offices, or in my house. Four of my informants came to Champaign and stayed in my house, one for several weeks, one for two weeks, another for a week, and one for two days. Each interview lasted for at least two hours, after which, except in seven cases, I followed up with another interview. On the problem of identities, several informants felt that pseudonyms contributed to the invisibility suffered by Iranian immigrants and at least one refused to participate if my book contained such nameless presences. I have, however, given pseudonyms to those who asked that their identities be protected and to those who I felt needed their identities protected.

At the start of our interviews, I described the project as a gift of stories to the next generation. I began the conversation with a statement that allowed for multiple channels of entry: "Start anywhere you like, but give a sense of who you are, of who made you, what it means to be Iranian, why you are here rather than there, and whether you see yourself as an exile or an emigré. What you say will allow us ways to understand similarities and differences between Iranians who left their homes after (or because of) the revolution." I returned to these and other key questions about gender, class, family, politics, and dislocation throughout the interview. If we faced initial silence (this seldom happened), I expanded with a further suggestion: "If you were to make a film of your life, what moment or image would you choose to start with? How would you shape your story?" Narrative revealed the process through which memory reorganizes the past, predicating identity on events that center on national affiliation, resistance, and loss. For some of my interviewees, early stories of childhood were orchestrated in safe images of creativity preparing them for later accomplishments. Others read childhood experience as the personal wound whose cultural implications prepared them for the later violence of history. The image of the wound, however, does not feed into the romanticizing of exile as deprivation and loss. Rather, I recall Edmund Wilson's *The Wound and the Bow* where the wound is the image of unimaginable strength resulting from, and inseparable from, disability in exile.[4] Many saw the revolution as the moment when long repressed power struggles exploded into history, and as a fall into fragmentation and loss of self- and national identity. Distinctions between exile and diaspora emerged between those who waited to return and those who gradually embraced their new condition of diasporic assimilation.

I told each interviewee that I planned to remove most of the question/answer format because we were having a conversation rather than an interview. As I divided each narrative into three parts—There, Revolution, and Here—and as I cut the original book from twelve hundred pages to its current form, I sometimes reduced entire stories to one part and deleted the rest. In organizing each section, I often pair two who have shared work, religious, ethnic, or gender similarities in order to highlight contrast.

My book is conceptually different from empirical sociological studies of Iranians in America and, by extension, the important Iranian oral history projects being conducted by Mahnaz Afkhami (Foundation for Iranian Studies), Habib Lajevardi (Harvard Oral History Project), and Homa Sarshar (Iranian Jewish Oral History Project). It speaks to the reconstruction of memory and identity through diasporic narratives, to the conjuncture of the Americas and not to Iran itself. Also, unlike other books on emigrés, many of my informants are fairly well known figures in the United States who spoke to me on the condition that their narratives were not subjected to the anonymity endemic to the immigrant condition. Except for those who said they felt no need to see the transcript, I sent each interviewee the translated, transcribed, and edited version for further editing; I included a cover letter or made a phone call to let the interviewee know that I would assume that no returned transcript meant they had no objections. Several asked me to correct their flawed English so they didn't "sound stupid"; in addition to shortening their narratives, and cutting most of my conversational questions, I have corrected grammar and omitted repetitions and speech-tics. One, Mohamad Tavakoli, took my transcript and wrote a new version taking control, he said, of his own self-representation. Susan Bazargan, who translated most of the tapes, preferred, she said, to respond to the other narratives by writing her own. The others made more minor changes. At first everyone wished to be identified, but as the climate overseas changed between 1990 to 1998, I found myself giving more pseudonyms to protect identities. Seven asked to have their interviews entirely removed. I do not presume to have a representative sample of anything other than a fortuitous group of Iranians with whom I happened to come in contact, who were part of or extensions of a circle of friends. Where I have chosen one voice to stand in for others, I selected the most evocative. No selection could do justice to the many eloquent and splendid people who agreed to speak with me.

This book makes modest claims. It does not intend "truths" about Iranians, exiles, or Iranian culture. In the clashes, connections, sympathies, and resistances that make up the "connective tissue" of migratory culture, it recognizes "culture's in-between."[5] The narratives that follow are intended (borrowing Michael M. J. Fischer's phrase) to provide necessary "touchstones, reminders, and access" to others, not in order to universalize their humanity, but rather to illuminate difference and relationality that open up new worlds of local knowledge (Fischer 1990). Not only, in other words, are diasporas different from each other, but, as Avtar Brah reminds us, power configurations differentiate diasporas internally (Brah 1996, 183). This is particularly important for a culture often represented monolithically over the past twenty years and therefore remembered in terms of *fatwas* (religious decrees), hostages, and terrorism. The stories included in this book show how one accidentally chosen group of Iranians in the United States remembers the past, produces a discourse about their lives, and negotiates the troubled transitions from one culture to another after the revolution.

Acknowledgments

This book would not exist were it not for the friends who inspired me to write it, the Iranian communities who participated in it, and the colleagues, friends, relatives, and anonymous readers for the press who read and responded to its many versions. To each of them I owe an abundant and inexpressible debt. Now to be more specific. I am grateful for the unflagging friendship of Mahdokht Sanati who, refusing to be daunted by thousands of pages of manuscript, saw me through uncertain years. From the start of this project I have been extraordinarily lucky with the critical and loving advice of other friends who have read either all or parts of this manuscript—sometimes repeatedly: Evelyne Accad, Susan Bazargan, Michael Bérubé, Tim Brennan, Libby-Ann Dunseth, Janet Eldred, Usha Gandhi, Alma Gottlieb, Stephanie Foote, Philip Graham, Keya Ganguly, Jim Hurt, Kwaku Korang, the Nelsons-all, Robert Parker, Soheyl Parviz, and Richard Powers. I am grateful to Michael M. J. Fischer for his heroic willingness to respond to a rough early section—a gesture that emboldened a fledgling ethnographer. Special thanks to Yvette Koepke-Nelson whose sharpness and diligence as a final reader saved me from many mishaps. I have been fortunate too in my artist and mapmaker Mehran Nasser-Ghodsi, and in three gifted and skillful translators—Susan Bazargan, Forough Minoo-Archer, and Soraya Paknazar. Forough Minoo-Archer translated and transcribed Mrs. Ghandsaz's interview; Soraya Paknazar translated and transcribed the interview with Soheyl; and Susan Bazargan translated and transcribed interviews with Zia Ashraf Nasr, Mehrdad Haghighi, Ramin Sobhan, Mandana, Professor Ali, and several others whose narratives I did not include.

I thank the Ragdale Foundation for three fellowships when I was allowed the privilege of its magical retreat to transcribe, edit, and write parts of this book undisturbed by the ordinary world. My research in the early 1990s was supported generously by the Research Board of the University of Illinois, which granted funds that allowed—along with travel—the help of Ann Moore and Lauri Harden. At Temple University Press, I am deeply grateful for the patience and support of Doris Braendel, Tamika Hughes, and Jennifer French. I also appreciate the intelligent editing skills of Yvonne Ramsey.

This book is dedicated to Mahin and to my sons Taimur and Kamran who continue to make the world into a home—with a little help from the transformative powers of their exceptional families that include Emma and Ali; Batul, Shahnaz, Vida, Keyhan, and Soheyl; Mojdeh, Mandana, Mona, Mahnaz, and Hamid; Mana, Bijan, and Daryoosh; Christopher, Sara, and Tom; Jason, Jared, and Sheila; Mehran and Keyvan; Mary Ann, Cart, Liza, Margie, and John; Mehri, Ron, Mitra, and Mark; Zahra and Hadi; Fouri and Darius; and Jim, Rick, and Allison.

Iran and the United States:
A Chronology

1848   Nasirudin Shah ascends the throne; visits Europe in 1873 and 1889.

1856   United States establishes diplomatic relations with Persia; not until 1944 does it send its first ambassador to Iran.

1870s and 1880s
  Start of American missionary activity and Christian schools.

1880s   Archaeologists from the Universities of Chicago, Pennsylvania, Michigan, and Yale begin research and digs in Iran. Samuel G. W. Benjamin, author of *Persia and the Persians*, is appointed minister to Persia.

1890   Tobacco concessions granted to a British company.

1891   Religious leaders start opposition to tobacco concessions through a boycott of tobacco.

1896   Nasirudin Shah assassinated by Mirza Reza Kirmani.

1901   Oil concessions that allow for sixty-six years of oil exploitation granted by Qajar king Muzaffarudin Shah to D'Arcy, an English banker.

1906–1909
  The Constitutional Revolution produces the first modern constitution in 1906, overthrows the monarchy (the Qajar king Mohammad Ali Shah), unyokes the control of foreign corporations over Iranian resources, and executes leading cleric Sheikh Fazlullah Nuri for opposing what he perceived to be a constitutional movement contaminated by the West.

For many of the details in this chronology I am indebted to David H. Albert's "Twentieth Century Iranian History: A Chronology," in *Tell the American People: Perspectives on the Iranian Revolution*, ed. David H. Albert (Philadelphia, Pa.: Movement for a New Society, 1980), to Mohamad Tavakoli chronology in his forthcoming *Vernacular Modernity* (London: Macmillan, St.Anthony Series), and to Shaul Bakhash's indispensable *The Reign of the Ayatollahs* (New York: Basic Books, 1990).

1907   Rivalry between competing world powers divides the country into three zones of influence with Russia taking the North, Britain the South, and the center remaining nominally Iranian. Oil has already been known to lie beneath the lands in the South.

1911   Women's groups confront Parliament (with guns beneath chadors) on the loss of Persian independence to foreign countries. Czarist Russia and Britain cooperate in dissolving the constitutional government. An American financier, W. Morgan Shuster, is invited by the Majlis (the national assembly) to organize the chaotic Iranian tax system and replenish the treasury.

1914   After World War I begins, Iran is occupied by the British, the Russians, and the Ottomans.

1917   Russian Revolution and change in overt Russian imperial designs on Iran.

1919   Britain sets up the Anglo-Persian Treaty of 1919.

1921   Military coup; Reza Pahlavi crowns himself Shah.

1930s   Reza Shah counters Soviet and British power in Iran by courting Germany.

1935   Persia is renamed Iran by royal decree.

1941   Soviets and British occupy Iran and force Reza Shah to abdicate. His son, Mohamad Reza Pahlavi, becomes Shah.

1942–1944
       United States establishes military bases in Iran; thirty thousand soldiers under the command of General Clarence Ridley and Colonel H. Norman Schwartzkopf. Also, the start of the Marxist Tudeh Party in Iran. U.S. oil companies open discussions for oil concessions.

1947–1948
       Rio Conference in September and the Inter-American Conference at Begota in March 1948 see the beginnings of the Investment Guarantee Program that encouraged investment in underdeveloped countries.

1949   Truman inaugurates the Point Four program designed to (a) spread scientific and industrial knowledge and (b) aid in the establishment of new markets and new sources for raw materials.

1951   Charismatic leader of the social-democratic National Front, Prime Minister Mohamad Mossadeq, nationalizes the oil fields. Britain's retaliatory economic blockade weakens Iranian economy, encourages the Tudeh Party to make gains, and feeds into U.S. fears of creeping Communism.

1953   At U.S. insistence, Shah attempts to dismiss Prime Minister Mossadeq. Mossadeq resists. Shah flees. The CIA, directed by Allen Dulles, in a mission led by CIA operatives Kermit Roosevelt and H. Norman Schwartzkopf, helps organize the coup with pro-Shah generals. Mossadeq is overthrown and the Shah returns to power. Commercial rights over oil fall to British Petroleum (40 percent) and the rest to U.S. oil companies.

1954   Eisenhower sends direct aid to Iran. U.S. companies are encouraged to operate in Iran.

1957   The secret police SAVAK formed and trained by British, U.S., and Israeli intelligence.

1961–1962

Shah cuts relations with the Arab League, builds relations with Israel, and visits the United States to ask for more aid. Kennedy agrees to aid contingent on American interests.

1963   Shah's White Revolution that called for land reform, literacy, and human rights. Peasants lose their function in a known system; their new money takes them toward cities that get progressively overcrowded; the number of villages declines from forty thousand in 1963 to ten thousand in 1978. The establishment of such American companies as Dow Chemical, Bank of America, John Deere, and Royal Dutch Shell.

March 1963

A little known cleric, Ayatollah Khomeini, protests against the Shah's White Revolution.

June 5, 1963

Thousands of unarmed citizens are killed by the Shah's commandos in the streets and bazaars of Tehran, Qum, Shiraz, and other cities. The day is now celebrated as "the 15th of Khordad." Khomeini is arrested and then driven into exile.

August 1963

U.S. military advisors given diplomatic immunity.

1964   Dr. Ali Shariati, philosopher and ideologue of revolutionary Islam, returns to Iran from Paris; he is arrested but later freed to teach at the University of Mashhad.

1965–1967

Shah orders squadrons of F-4 fighter-bombers. Shah orders attacks on the Qashqai tribes of southern Iran.

1968   Establishment of *Kanun-i Nivisandegan-i Iran* (Writers' Association of Iran).

January 1969

Fourteen artists and writers are sentenced by the military court and tortured in prison.

January 1969

SAVAK starts operating in the United States.

1971   The Mujahedin (radical Islamic nationalist) and the Feyayeen (anti-Soviet Marxist-Leninist) become active guerrilla movements.

October 1971

Nixon's vice president, Spiro Agnew, is one of the guests at the spectacle in Persepolis in celebration of 2,500 years of Persian monarchy. Cost of event: over $60 million.

May 1972

Students protest Nixon's visit to Tehran. Shah buys, among other items, Boeing radar patrol planes, Grumman F-14 jet fighters, McDonnell-Douglas antiship missiles, deep-strike fighter bombers, and Lockheed ocean surveillance planes. Iran agrees to defend U.S. interests in the Middle East. U.S. sales of military equipment to Iran go from $519 million in 1972 to $5.8 billion in 1977.

1973 Arab-Israeli War. Iran raises oil prices. Richard Helms, former head of the CIA, is named ambassador to Iran.

March 2, 1975

Shah forms the single party, *Hezb-i Rastakhiz* (National Resurgence Party of Iran).

1977 Jimmy Carter presses human rights issue after Amnesty International finds that no country in the world has a worse record than Iran and after the International Commission of Jurists in Geneva hears reports of torture by former prisoners of SAVAK.

June 1977

Ali Shariati, imprisoned and tortured by SAVAK and forced into exile, dies in London.

June 12, 1977

Shapur Bakhtiar, Karim Sanjabi, and Daryoosh Forouhar, leaders of the National Front, write an open letter to the Shah calling for the end of "despotism in the guise of Monarchy" and for the restoration of constitutional and political liberty.

October 1977

Fifty-nine members of the Writers' Association of Iran start a series of poetry readings and lectures at Tehran's Goethe Institute.

November 22, 1977

The Karaj Road Incident, when SAVAK and the Iranian army combine to break up a holiday gathering at the home of Daryoosh Forouhar—a moderate middle-class intellectual. (Forouhar and his wife are stabbed to death by right-wing "rogue" intelligence officers of the Islamic Republic of Iran in November 1998.)

October 1977

Ayatollah Khomeini's son dies (suspiciously) in Iraq.

December 1977

U.S. Department of Defense reports to Congress the presence of 7,674 Americans on military contracts working in Iran, more than thirty paramilitary organizations, and corporations with military contracts such as Bell International, Hughes Aircraft, Computer Sciences Corp., Harsco, TRW, Rockwell International, GTE, Lockheed, and Harris Corp.

January 7, 1978
    Curious attack on Ayatollah Khomeini in a government-controlled Tehran newspaper as a result of which huge protests are staged by the clergy in Qum. Police fire on unarmed demonstrators, killing many.
1978   Ritual periods of mourning follow killings; strikes, marches, and demonstrations in all major cities.
September 8, 1978
    Black Friday "17th of Shahrivar." Troops open fire on hundreds of thousands of demonstrators in the streets of Tehran. Three thousand dead.
October 6, 1978
    Khomeini expelled from Iraq; finds refuge in Paris.
October 31, 1978
    Oil workers' strike shuts down the oil fields.
November 28, 1978
    Government bans all processions and demonstrations.
December 1978
    Iranians defy the ban on demonstrations in all major cities. Army fires on unarmed demonstrators, killing more than seven hundred.
January 16, 1979
    Shah leaves Iran.
February 1, 1979
    Khomeini returns in triumph.
Spring 1979
    Known as the Spring of Freedom; culminates in the establishment of the Islamic Republic.
February 12, 1979
    Jimmy Carter recognizes and proposes cooperation with the new Iranian regime.
March 1979
    The women's march on International Women's Day in protest against new Islamic rules and codes.
April 1979
    Ayatollah Taleghani debates political differences with Khomeini.
May 1, 1979
    Ayatollah Motahheri, liberal member of the revolutionary council, assassinated by commandos.
September 1980
    Iraq attacks Iranian military bases and invades Iran on September 23, starting the ten-year Iran-Iraq war.
October 22, 1979
    Former Shah flies to New York for cancer treatment.
November 4, 1979
    Students storm the U.S. embassy seizing ninety hostages, sixty-three

of whom are Americans; start of the Hostage Crisis. All black and female hostages are released on November 28.

November 6, 1979

Bazargan government resigns.

January 25, 1980

Bani-Sadr elected first President of Iran.

July 27, 1980

Former Shah dies in Egypt.

January 20, 1981

Fifty-two American hostages are released.

February 5, 1981

Start of a new operation designed to destroy the "insurrections" in Kurdestan.

June 1981

The fall of Bani-Sadr's government and his flight from Iran.

1981–1982

Mass executions of such leading figures as Farrokhru Parsa, former minister of Education, and relatives of other informants.

June 3, 1989

Death of Ayatollah Khomeini.

Exiled Memories

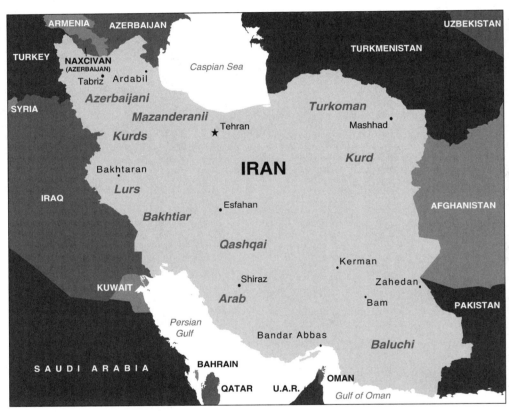

Map of Iran showing major ethnic groups.

CHAPTER I

Introduction: Fabricating Identity

To articulate the past historically does not mean to
recognize it "the way it really was" . . . . It means to seize
hold of a memory as it flashes up at a moment of danger.
—Walter Benjamin

The purpose of this book is to read history through the remembered pasts of
diasporic Iranians in the United States. As our storytellers weave their identities across two nations—Iran and the United States—the memories recovered
in these narratives, part of a constellation formed with earlier images from
legend, nation, and everyday life, link the palimpsest of autobiography and
identity to that of diasporic history. It is true that colonization, decolonization,
revolution, and diasporas have long destabilized the idea of unified identity
and nation. Nonetheless, we see witnesses to the stubborn persistence of
nations and nationalisms generally understood as the "historical expression of
the fundamental unity of any people, transcending the specific social conflicts
that threaten to disintegrate civil society."[1] Diaspora, however, complicates
that imagined unity by forging new postessential, postterritorial, and postnational realignments that sometimes crack open the fault lines of ethnic,
religious, class, and gender difference repressed by ideologies of sacrosanct
national unity. Unlike the sudden shift of exile or forced deterritorialization
that clings to the dream of return and gradually evolves into the larger diaspora,[2] the displaced emigré can be defined by contingency, indeterminacy, and
moveable identity.

My ethnographic interest in splintered diasporic identities stems from an
early awareness of being "not-quite" and Othered wherever I was, and of difficulties with "belonging" and "home." The war, unemployment, and family

illness provoked a move from my earliest home in Tehran to other more temporary ones in India—Lucknow and Calcutta. The partition of 1947 provoked others. Before I turned seventeen I had moved from Tehran to Lucknow to Calcutta to Madras to Dacca to Karachi to Lahore. Although each move carried predictably mundane loss and estrangement, shortly after I settled into the University of Illinois in the early 1970s I knew I would never return to any of my former "homes." I had carried my adjustable backpack with me when I left childhood's countries: Iran, India, Pakistan—places that seemed to demand allegiances I could not give. Baggaged with lifelong ambivalence toward the troubling signposts of my pasts defamiliarized by history, I felt that the changing spaces I created around myself in the spacious Midwest constituted my chosen unhomely "home."[3]

In contrast to an exile's forced separation from an inaccessible homeland, my journeys were a continuation of a late nineteenth-century Persian diaspora—a voluntary displacement, a scattering of Iranians through India, Burma, Pakistan, and Bengal in search of trade. The communities I lived in saw no contradiction between their efforts to remain a separate group and their accommodation to the new postpartition Pakistan. Colonial culture had already taught this Persianized enclave the strategies required to straddle fences, the ways to occupy dual contact zones between the colonizer and the colonized and not belong to either.

Thus it was that when I returned to Tehran in the spring of 1997 after an absence of twenty-five years, I could find no place that I looked for and I recognized nothing—not the landmark squares and fountains that populate the city, not the college where I once taught, not even the street where I once lived.[4] I wrote in my journal: "I remember something I don't remember. I remember loss and anxiety. I am reminded of the poet to whom the city felt like a body with phantom limbs—spaces lost and amputated and yet present." I have lived halfway between many a "here" and a "there," sometimes fearing, sometimes cherishing fragments of the past—but always negotiating a space that kept me slightly outside its embrace. In the midst of an evening during that 1997 return, surrounded by a circle of women holding hands in meditative unity, I suddenly recognized in my multiple dislocation and discomfort an uncanny alienation from such culturally exclusive circles of intimacy. While I wanted to record the event and hear the women's stories, I wanted even more fiercely to flee my unnameable fears.

It is that repeated flight I try to counter with this book. Through the many voices that speak of home-in-exile, this book writes and unwrites mutilated memory, negotiating the troublesome boundaries between home and not-home. And as a work of memory, it tries to remember what I have forgotten. I use fragments of my own story of migration as frame not to identify with the trauma of recent postrevolutionary diaspora but rather to suggest a range of diasporic experience, and to contrast my ambivalence towards home and nation[5] with the nostalgia in some of the stories I record.

For me, "home" became the Midwest not only because it was the space within which I raised my children and studied and taught for more than half my life, but also because it is a place where I am allowed to construct my own imagined community.[6] As the convergence of economic, personal, political, and cultural specificities inscribed in the shifting lines drawn on alienating maps, childhood's homes were always spaces of anxiety—unexpected new locations subject to rapid geographic and emotional change amidst an ever-expanding set of extended families. My earliest sense of home was complicated by a ghostly other home elsewhere—someplace we were not. Although they were places in which I was welcome, the word "home" has no single originary source, no single center, no monolithic associations with childhood's stability or with the privilege of belonging and ownership. Neither do the words "country" or "patriotism."[7] In part, this is because growing up female in the subcontinent in the 1950s taught me early lessons in the gendering of authority, sexuality, and power inflected through the Persian community's certainty of and desire for difference, first from Hindu, then from Indian and Pakistani culture.

Reading a History and Geography of Authority: Rites of Passage, Gender, and Problems of Self-Fashioning

My emotional life—centered around a blind, saintly Persian grandmother, who saw her first eight children die in early childhood, who thought that suffering was the destined lot of women, and who taught me to read the Qur'an—was, in part, formed around ideas of religious propriety, purity, dirt, and danger; and around the word *najis* (unclean) that served as both warning and admonition. More generally, I knew that to be Muslim was to be pure, that Hindus were impure, and that girls were pure until they had a period.

I earned my way into adulthood and definition in Pakistan at the age of fourteen when, during *Moharrum*, I could lead a recitation (*Nowheh*) and beat my chest into impassioned shades of purple and blue. *Moharrum*, the month of mourning for Imam Husain, the prophet's grandson, was the favorite month for us as children because the entire Persian community (an "imagined community" in more ways than we knew) collected together to mourn but also, more importantly, to eat (or so it seemed) constantly. The idea of community filled a gap created by our fragmented pasts. It convinced us that we centered around rituals that would protect us (it certainly nourished us) against all that threatened in the outside world. It was a month of togetherness when we all wore black and intensified communal ties by attending the same houses of mourning and by dressing so as to distinguish us from the Sunnis. The first month of the Islamic year, it was devoted to ritual lamentations over the death of Husain at the hands of Yazid and his men on the battlefield of Karbala in A.D. 680. The conflict was over the succession to the Caliphate that Shiia Islam believes should rightfully pass from Mohammad to Ali to Husain and the rest of the twelve Imams—the last of whom remains hidden. During this month, Husain was a living part of our daily lives: we wore black for the first ten days, during which we heard repeated stories (*Rowzeh*) and mourned the loss of each member of Husain's martyred family: his journey to Kufa (that had, we were told, invited him to preserve Shiite Islam from the tyranny of Moawiya and his son Yazid) was interrupted on the plains of Karbala where the first death, that of his assistant Hazrat Moslem, was followed by those of Husain's two infant sons Ali Akbar and Ali Asgar, of Abbas his half-brother, of his nephew Qassim whose marriage to Husain's daughter turned into a funeral, and of all the other men in the party.

My favorite *Nowhehs* (hymnlike chants, or choral laments) were about the deaths of the children, Ali Akbar and Ali Asgar. Our role in the gatherings we called the *Majlis* was to chant the repetitions in the choral lament, to repeat the scene of lamentation of the women at each death culminating in the death of Husain on *Ashura,* the tenth day, when his head was cut off by Shimr, the hated leader of Yazid's army. Religious leaders in Iran in the 1960s and 1970s defied authority during this particular month by identifying the Shah as the contemporary Yazid, and *rowzeh khans* (rhapsodic preachers) would evoke the themes of Karbala—the loss of the ideal Islamic community and government—to point to Pahlavi injustice. Among the revolutionary slogans in 1979 (derived from Ali Shariati's writings) was "Every Day Is Ashura: Every Place Is Karbala." As a minority Shiia community in Sunni Pakistan in the innocent 1950s, we associated the rituals of *Moharrum* with the lost land of origins most of us had never seen.

Looking back on my memories of Moharrum, I see how it taught us to link adult identity with mourning, with a perpetual state of loss to which the child was immune. The fact that I could not weep over Imam Husain but could over Mrs. Henry Wood's *Evelyne* or anything by Charles Dickens was a source of puzzlement to me. Tears over Imams implied a state of "*savab*" (divine merit). Depth of character was associated with the ability to feel and give expression to grief. Adulthood, we felt, would arrive automatically equipped with the ability to empathize totally with the grief of the families of Imam Hasan, Husain, Ali, Fatima, and Zainul Abedin who eternally mourned their loss. But the ability to publicly mourn the deaths of Imams did not translate into the practice of everyday life. Even though we assumed a connection between the public and the private, we knew that our inner emotional lives were sources of confusion, secrecy, and mystery.

When I was twelve and took my first pilgrimage to the holy cities of Karbala, Najaf, and Samereh, we stopped in Baghdad to visit my grandmother's

sister and her family. Her turbaned and long-robed husband was Sayyid Mohamad Sadr—a leading figure in politics, parliament, and the court. The
gendered geography of the house was split between outer porches and open
rooms for men (birun) and the enclosed insides (andarun) with a courtyard centered around a little pond surrounded by balconied rooms occupied
by women.

But the magical figure in that household was the lone male turbaned figure robed in a dark mantle (abba) who walked silently outside, sometimes
venturing into the women's andarun (inner quarters) but for the most part
staying in his own outer quarters where he and his male friends would smoke
perfumed water pipes and talk politics, beaded tasbih (prayer beads) in hand,
in a grape arbor from which I was warned away. My mother said girls were
to remain inside, that the garden was only for men. When I turned my plea
toward my great-aunt, she agreed to let me out because, she said, I was young
enough for my presence not to disturb the men. Unknown to me, between
the warning to stay in and the permission to go out, the unstable status and
identity of a prepubescent Muslim girl was the issue at stake.[8] Of that entire
trip to Iraq, those moments in the garden fringed by the symbolic mantle of
Sayyid Sadr are most vivid in my memory, perhaps because, at an age when
I was most uncentered, they introduced me to the mysteries of another's
authenticity and to the power of male authority. The ordering of everyday
experience, I soon learned, was one in which the world of women was an
enclosed world whose activities had little to do with the world of men who
(to my childish envy) went out unchaperoned, studied abroad, worked and
earned money, ruled the land and made the laws, and had the right to be
served by women.

The layered house, the courtyard with its andarun for women, the garden
and the birun (outside) for men finally made visible the geography of my
grandmother's stories of the extended family whose enclosures were layered
with religion, food, and ritual. Because she was blind, veiled, and frail, and
her religiosity so unobtrusive, I chose to ignore the centrality of religion in
her life and in the political life of her extended family. Decades later in a
heathen continent I discovered that her sister had been married to Sheikh
Fazlullah Nuri, the ferociously conservative cleric publicly executed in 1909
for his opposition to the first Constitutional Revolution, after which his
family went into exile to Iraq. That figure of Sheikh Fazlullah returned from
the repressed to haunt the revolution, and, in a minor key, the margins of
this book.

Although Sheikh Fazlullah has been celebrated by the Islamic Revolution
in drama and verse, his granddaughter Zia Ashraf Nasr (born 1903), whom
I interviewed in 1990, expressed little sympathy with the revolution. As
a woman who occupies an important position midway between privilege
and persecution, between belonging and exile, Zia Ashraf Nasr seems to

span the century, to embody its history of muted achievement and loss. Her temperament and life were formed in the crossfire of tradition and change, at a time when women began their activities through the formation of secret organizations, the opening of girls' schools, and the publication of women's periodicals. The beginnings of the women's movement in Iran were provoked by the inhumane exercise of patriarchal authority, through marriage laws that made girls of nine marry men of sixty, that allowed women no rights over their bodies, their finances, or their children.

Zia Ashraf attended the first girls' school in Iran, established in her home in Tehran by Tuba Azmudeh in 1907. Education for women, considered undesirable and unnecessary in a patriarchal society structured on the myth of benevolent protection of one sex by the other, began to become a reality at the turn of the century. The American Presbyterian Missionary School, established in Iran in 1874, enrolled about 120 women by 1909. There were fifty schools for girls by 1910. The clergy were opposed to girls' schools, which they characterized as fertile ground for the breeding of future prostitutes.

As a woman from a conservative family, Zia Ashraf Nasr surprises and refutes the monolithic image of the repressed "Islamic woman" constructed by the West. Not that there is no basis to that image—all stereotypes inevitably contain a minute element of truth. But masculine categories of power, action, and work are not synonymous with female categories of the same and often fail to account for the complex variations of power available to women in Middle Eastern societies.

Zia Ashraf had seen the beginnings of the long struggle for women's rights in Iran from the forcible removal of the veil to the hard-won right to vote. The same Constitutional Revolution that saw the death of Nasr's grandfather also saw the beginnings of women's secret societies that opposed foreign powers and supported the revolution. In 1911, when it was rumored that some of the members of Parliament (Majlis) were giving in, again, to Russian demands, the women's groups took action. Three hundred women in chadors with guns beneath their skirts entered the buildings, confronted the leader of Parliament, tore aside their veils, and threatened the group with their decision to kill their husbands, sons, and then themselves if the independence of the Persian people were again given away.[9] Many other nonviolent protests by women took place between 1912 and 1980. Faranak, Afsaneh Najmabadi, Fereydoun Safizadeh, and Tahereh all took part in the women's demonstration on International Women's Day. We will hear their voices later.

To be born female was to start life with a disadvantage. Afsaneh Najmabadi was born, as she tells the story, into darkness. At hearing that her daughter had given birth to her third female child, her maternal grandmother ordered all the lights of their house to be turned off. Afsaneh's mother, however, compensated for this dark birth through the most enlightened upbringing available for her girl child. When male children were born into

Shusha Guppy's family, her father congratulated her mother with lines from
Ferdowsi's *Shahnameh:*

> Sufficient unto women is the art of
> Producing and raising sons as brave as lions.

When a daughter was born, she was welcomed as "such a pretty girl."[10]
Tahereh was subjected first to the surveillance and veiling common to girls
in her particular class; then to a loveless, arbitrary, and arranged marriage;
then to taunting mockery when she was accepted into Tehran University.
"Congratulations," said her aunt to her parents. "Your daughter has been
accepted into the institute of prostitution." Mandana's brothers offered to pay
her the same wages as her job if she would agree to stay home and not go out to
work. Mohamad Tavakoli's father feared that his son's training in gymnastics
would result in terminal loss of masculinity, that he would become (in this
order) a dancer, a drinker, and a sodomist.

Female networks of cooperation and mutual support were not necessarily
opposed to male spheres of domination. In Tahereh's family, her father's liberal
stance toward his daughter was opposed by her mother's insistence that he
prove his manhood by enforcing stricter rules, by removing his daughter from
the presence of her young love, and by teaching her the perils of transgression
by subjecting the child to an unwarranted and humiliating gynecological
exam. Women were a precious commodity to be kept intact until they were
bartered as brides. Education, like the loss of virginity, was, in some families,
a liberation to be feared. Virginity, therefore, was a girl's most valued property
and modesty her most prized virtue.

Yet as these narratives will show, public and private are not necessarily
analogous to power and powerlessness, and gender roles in these families are
seldom stable or predictable. Gendered variations in familial authority and
power are made evident in the contrast between the narratives of the men and
women in the following chapters. They vary, for instance, between country
and city. Mrs. Kazemi, a country Azari, grounded her understanding of gender
equality in her early awareness of men and women working together on farms
and not in separate private and public spheres.

Identifying the Collective:
Exile and the Antinomies of Belonging

If, from a remembered perspective, gender and self-identification were problematic, the "we" of collective identification was no less so. I was a child in
Calcutta during the 1947 Partition that saw more slaughter in the name of
religion and national self-determination than any other comparable event in
recent history; I went through middle school, high school, and three years of

college in East and then West Pakistan during its adolescent imaginings of Islamic nationhood.

In contrast to postcolonial Iranians on the subcontinent who were the result of nineteenth-century expatriate economic turmoil, postrevolutionary Iranians in the United States were the result of political violence (and therefore often exiles). Both diasporic groups, however, had one thing in common: they carried a portable ideology that set up alternate cultural spaces in their new homelands. My interest therefore lies in diaspora and exile as ways in which identity is played out, as an entry into notions of self-definition and loss of self-representation, and as a particular case of how we define ourselves against others, of how any group consolidates homogenous selfhood and structures of feeling as defense against the anxieties of division and against lost attachments. My premise here is that cultural and national identities are narrative myths that not only underlie the major political upheavals of our time, but sustain those displaced by such upheaval. Just as American national formation relied, particularly in times of economic stress, on the exclusion of less desirable Others like Native Americans, African Americans, Hispanics, Irish, Asian Americans, Arabs, Vietnamese, and Iranians, so too Iranian diasporic identity after the revolution, responding to historic, economic, and cultural stress, has sometimes relied on constructing an imagined unity that ironically reinscribes the exclusions that fueled the "people's" revolution.[11]

As a rather confused child, I thought happiness meant a return to an imaginary country—Iran—where life was always rich with loving relatives and saffron-scented rice. We were a migrating family who had moved (before my birth) from Isfahan to Rangoon to Calcutta to Tehran; then after my birth to Lucknow, Calcutta, Madras, Dacca, Karachi, and Lahore. Somewhere between Dacca and Karachi in the mid-1950s when I was fourteen and my father lost his job, my parents moved back to Iran (Abadan). I did not. I was expected to attend high school and live with relatives in Karachi (Pakistan). Those points of time and place, spiraling around the problematic midnight of India's 1947, constituted the first of many looms on which my identity was woven.

Even when our extended families had materially and ideologically integrated with the newly formed Islamic state of Pakistan, they insisted on their difference from the Other—the native, the Bengali, Pathan, Punjabi, or Sindhi. That "difference" was a confusing and curious space that seemed occupied by unexamined certainties about identity, by the implicit assumption of a distinction between cultural and national identity that in practice meant that one could hold a Pakistani passport, wear Pakistani clothing, speak Urdu, and be loyal to the idea of the newly formed nation, yet retain a distinctly "Persian" cultural identity within it.

In Dacca, between 1951 and 1954, we lived in an enclave defined by its Persian name—"Ispahani Colony." Isfahan was the magic city of our imagination; we associated with it bright blue beads, enameled mosques, and ancient sayings. I remember two. *"Isfahan/Nesf e Jahan"* (Isfahan is half the world) was one, and the other was a rhyming verse:

> *Arab dar biyabann malakh mikhorad,*
> *Sag-e Isfahan ab-e yakh mikhorad.*

> The desert Arab must feed on locust
> Yet even the dogs of Isfahan feast on ice water.

Far from being the blue-domed originary city, Ispahani Colony in Dacca was a way of appropriating, resisting, and reterritorializing an alternative enclave of imagined unity amidst what we saw as chaos. In fact, the language and the word "Bengali" were, for the Anglophile/Persian enclave, synonyms for chaos. All the houses in the colony (I recall about fifty and have not sought to confirm my childhood memory) were rented or owned by near, distant, and imaginary relatives of the wonderfully generous Pater Familias, Mirza Ahmad Ispahani—the old man Ispahani as he was called—who protected those vaguely Iranian refugees who had escaped from Burma after the war by finding them homes and jobs in his new tea and jute industries in Bengal. We referred to everyone in the colony and to anyone vaguely related to anyone we knew as "community." I think we felt no uncertainty about its abiding value. It was a matter of concern and interest whether or not "our girls and boys" married inside or outside "the community." This "original" Ispahani was—like so many others in India and Pakistan (the Shirazis, the Nemazis, and the Kashanis)—an Iranian by "blood," by proxy, by association, by metonymy. Somewhere in the distant past, Ispahani's grandfather had migrated to Burma or India and then found himself, like the rest of us, inventing and reinventing imaginary connections to lost origins. Those imaginary connections, however, produced real people who combined their portable culture with postpartition ideology and the material realities of Bengal. Our sense of permanence and stability was provided by these heads of families, the "old man" Ispahani, or the other elder, G. H. Shirazi—names grounded in resonant places like Isfahan and Shiraz that provided scaffolding to our community, a net for us to fall into at the worst of times, and food always awaiting us at the best and worst of times. The Shirazis and Ispahanis gradually migrated to West Pakistan by the end of the 1950s, except for Mirza Ahmad Ispahani who refused, even during the 1972 war, to abandon Dacca and the Bengal to which he had developed a fierce loyalty.

Among the ways we celebrated ourselves as a community, food of course was one of the most delicious. There were an endless host of *Eids* or Feast Days, those celebrated in Iran (like *Norooz* or the pre-Islamic New Year) and those particular to the Muslims in the subcontinent—*Eid-ul-Fitr, Eid-e-Qorban, Eid-i-Qadir,* and *Eid-i-Mabbas.* We confirmed our identities in the course of gatherings on such *Eids,* during *Ramazan* when we broke our fasts at one another's homes, and during the month of *Moharrum* when the Majlis ritualized our mourning. We visited every single house during *Eid* and ate at every single table, potatoes and chickpeas soaked in tamarind, spices, and fresh coriander; *samosas* stuffed with cumin, coriander, tumeric, onions, garlic, vegetables, shrimp, or meat; silver-coated *rasmallai*; almond and milk *barfis*; cardamomed *gulab jamuns*; and saffroned *Gajjar* (carrot) halva. Of the foods I remember, only two were Persian in origin—*Sholleh Zard* (a saffroned pudding) and *Shir Berenj* (a creamed rice). Those gestures toward an originary cuisine were happily hybridized with subcontinental foods and articulated with other celebratory practices like the *sofreh* (a ritual meal; literally "table" or "tablecloth") and the *Rowzeh Khuni* (impassioned sermonizing) that were more or less specifically Iranian, and the *Kunda* (another occasion for ritual eating) that was subcontinental.

In the colony where we spoke English to each other, Urdu or Bengali to the servants, and Persian to some of the elders, where we attended Catholic convents, memorized Walter de la Mare and Shakespeare, acted in *Alice in Wonderland*, celebrated Pakistan Day, and imagined ourselves Iranian, some homes out-Persianed others by setting out the *Norooz Haftsin* with its traditional foods said to bring good luck in the year ahead. The "Haftseen" was a ritual table set with seven (*haft*) items starting with the letter *sin* that symbolized rebirth, health, wealth, and love. In addition to the Qur'an, a mirror, and a candle, we had green sprouts (*sabzi*), garlic (*siir*), apples (*sib*), sumac, coins (*secce*), and wheat paste (*samanu*), and, in place of unavailable hyacinths (*sombol*), we placed local fruit starting with the magic letter. We waited for the *Tahvil*—the moment of the spring equinox—and prayed and kissed everyone around. The *Norooz* meal to which my mother always invited others was rice with green herbs (*sabzi pulow*) and fish (*mahi*). As children, we knew that there was a hierarchic though invisible difference between those who had "been-to" and those who relied on past or blood connections with the imaginary homeland.

When I was a student at Kinnaird College in Lahore, my occasional weekends away from the enclosed and fortified college (located on Jail Road) would be spent at the always open home of Mirza Ahmad Ispahani's daughter—Mehrangiz—who had married her first cousin, a Shirazi. The servants (Muslim, of course) were "family servants" who had lived with these unalterable cornerstones for generations. The patriarchs educated their servant's children who then went on to leave the "compound," to go abroad, to return for visits, to become part of the outer circles that, like the rest of us, always knew (or imagined) there was a reliable or symbolic center to which to return—even if that mobile "center" dispersed from Dacca to Karachi to Lahore to Tehran. The community gathered together not only during feast days, but during Moharrum, weddings, and funerals. Sometimes a servant chose to follow a family from Burma to Iran. Elahi left his wife and children and followed my

maternal uncle's family to Abadan—to a land where he was the Other, a lonely
alien who looked different, who was unable to speak the language (Persian), yet
believed that this was his "family" of choice and that his immediate family
deserved his money more than his presence. Or, at least, that is what my
uncle's family chose to think, and to say when asked, that Elahi believed. The
assumption, I suspect from this distance, was always that servants were lesser
breeds who felt less strongly about family. And so our families continued in
their cultural complicity with economic values denying the predication of one
upon the other.[12]

That lost land of Iran, however, in the context of the newly formed Pakistan,
was a Janus-faced entity—both preserver of the original Shiia theocracy and its
destroyer. We learned that what differentiates Islam from other major world
religions was its "unity," its "Oneness," its consistent denial of separation between God and Caesar, mosque and state. No flirtations for us with ambiguity
or with gods that were "three in one." Yet we were expected to understand and
accept the splitting of Iranian "nationhood" between its "authentic past" and
modern Westernized present. That authentic past was of course again split
between the secular and spiritual. Its pre-Islamic secular culture was glorified
in centuries of epic and lyric poetry, or in such central culturally observed
traditions as the *zurkhanah* (House of Strength where youth or *pahlavans*
train to combat national foes) and *Norooz* (the Persian new year). Its spiritual
component was split between a generic Muslim history and a Shiia past that
saw its essential self as part of a continuum beginning with Ali (husband
to Fatima, daughter of the Prophet) and proceeding through twelve Imams,
direct descendants of the Prophet who needed to protect their faith against the
Sunni majority through *Taqiyya* (secrecy, dissimulation). (In another context
and time, James Joyce would make his artist Stephen Dedalus valorize secrecy,
silence, exile, and cunning.) So too in Pakistan, this small colony of hybridized
Iranians sought to build a distinct culture within a newly formed nation, to
deny the effects of history, politics, partition, or time on the timeless truths
of Shiia Islam or on the originary myth of Iranian selfhood.

When I argued with anyone about anything, my father would admonish
me by saying, "Don't be such a Bengali," and, if I raised my voice, "Don't
be an Arab." His model of idealized behavior and identity was constructed
out of a multitude of received cultural models from Gandhi to Churchill,
from "The Boy Stood on the Burning Deck" (which he had to memorize in a
Rangoon High School) to the governess in *The Sound of Music*, to my blind,
pious, submissive grandmother, and, later, to Mother Teresa. My paternal
uncle, another "Ispahani-born" Pakistani, born and raised in the colonies and
educated by the British in Burma, thought most natives, particularly Bengalis,
were weak and consequently dark-skinned, that his children should marry into
the dispersed yet singular Persian community to avoid mongrelization, that
Pakistanis could be hierarchically divided from the smaller and darker tribes

to the taller, fairer, and stronger Baluchis, Punjabis, and Pathans. The closer to Iran the tribe, the stronger the breed. His sense of "identity," "difference," and "Other" was narrated within terms made familiar both by Iranian romantic racism and by the Western Imperial imaginary, by the unacknowledged presence of the subcontinental caste systems, and by the dominant historical discourse made available by colonial education that split humanity according to power and color into the strong and the weak, that cast Jews, Hindus, and most natives, particularly the Bengalis, into undifferentiated, stereotyped, and vaguely degenerate Others.

Diasporic Iranians in America: Discontinuities with Subcontinental Patterns

If the subcontinental patterns my autobiographical account sets up are illustrative of patterns in a long-settled diasporic community, the subjects of this study, interviewed while their memories of revolutionary upheaval were still fresh, reveal some of the dangerous flash points of a community unsettled by the actual and remembered trauma of recent upheaval and violence.

Of the sixty-plus Iranians who participated in this study, seven were children of exiles and expatriates. I was particularly struck by these children, who, for the most part, have no memory of Iran but nonetheless seem to have a fairly clear idea of something essential and different that has been lost and of a nebulous something that must be preserved, that must not simply melt into the generic melting pot of homogenous Americanness.

The children I spoke to articulated most clearly the difference between their postexilic condition and that of other ethnic groups. Their concern was with the representation of Iranians in a media that alienates them from what they imagine to be a larger Iranian community from which they already feel excluded (Sullivan 1992). The response to nonbelonging alternates between clinging more fiercely to family, language, and culture, and a rejection of bonds to a culture that hurts their present. Their fantasy, sometimes, is that of all refugees, expatriates, and exiles who wish to affirm a continuation with a past that they soon discover is lost in reification. The media mutilates what time has already distorted and what history has already revised. Consequently, among the stresses mentioned most often by exiled Iranians and their children are those caused by monolithic representations of Iranian culture and history by a media that seemed, for the decade following the revolution, to persist in reproducing the same images of frenzied crowds in black beating their chests and burning American flags. But that stress is complicated by the shame many express at the recognition that behind the simplified media images, some awful, unnameable, unfilmable destruction was being unleashed in a country that they imagined as devouring its own youth.

Homa Sarshar's son, Houman, told me that although he has no actual memories of Iran, he has been compelled into actions that make him defend a constructed memory of what Iran means: "As a thirteen-year-old, I had to fight my classmates who implied that my father was a terrorist or an exploiter of the masses in Iran." Houman went on trying to explain how he experienced his Iranianness in America in terms of a story. (This too is part of characteristic Iranian conversational behavior: you ask a question and you get a story in response to illustrate an implied answer.)

> Let me tell you about Bijan Mofeed's play—*Shahre Qesseh*—about an elephant who enters the land of the camels, jackals, and monkeys, none of whom has ever seen an elephant before. But they try to make him fit into their society. So they cut off his trunk and pull out his teeth and try to fix smaller parts of his anatomy onto his head. But it doesn't work. The elephant is no longer an elephant; neither is he anything else. It's that loss of identity the Iranian fears in America.

Houman's mother, the Iranian journalist Homa Sarshar, had been a successful reporter and translator for Iranian newspapers and magazines for years until 1979, when she was told that she could no longer translate the stories about the Ayatollah because she made the news *najis* (unclean). The fact that she was Jewish was never explicitly named as a reason for disallowing her to translate the news. It was then that to avoid the fate of the elephant in her son's story, she knew she would have to turn in her resignation and leave the country.

I spoke to a Kurd whose village had been destroyed who said, suddenly and unexpectedly at the end of a long narrative, "Maybe Iran is a country that no longer exists." Perhaps in that summary statement is the recognition that the instability of exile is partly caused by separation from a nation and culture that memory has reconstructed first as unity and then as difference. But for the Kurd in Iran, the nation is always "the zone of occult instability," which they have been repeatedly dispossessed of by the whims of regimes who either accept or deny their very existence.[13] A Baha'i who had been compelled into flight after the purge of Baha'is in Shiraz said that the United States was to her a prison from which she longed to escape—to Iran.

What, I wondered, were the sources of nostalgia that collapsed the complex, the different, and the many into one? What was the source of the yearning for the lost land, culture, and people? Why, in a culture that so rigidly splits classes, genders, ideologies, and architectural and personal spaces, should distance effect such a collapse in boundaries? Why would Pari's return to a land divided by war and revolution heal her exilic anxiety and melancholy? What was it in the voices and eyes of the Iranian Hezbollahis that satisfied for a moment the Iranian Baha'i's desire and alleviated the violence of her exile? Why, during the period when the Pahlavi dynasty was on the verge of disintegration, did so many Iranians turn to spirituality and parlor Sufism? Why were my California cousins taking evening classes in the *Shahnameh*?

Where and how and at what points does cultural dispersion hook invisibly and silently into the dream of symmetrical identity? What turns the many into one?[14]

Cultural Difference: The Many in the One

The self-identity of the Iranians to whom I spoke was often announced in terms of, first, ethnic affiliation and subculture, then family, religion, and country: "I am not a Persian," said Jahan, "I am a Kurd and an Iranian." "We are Azaris," said Abbas Kazemi, "and the language we speak at home and joke in is Turkish, not Farsi." The nostalgia for Iran, however, produced a discourse of unity and shared values in spite of frequent reminders that Azaris, Kurds, Baha'is, and others were groups whose distinctions were blurred in the construction of the nationalist imaginary. Almost all seemed to assume that what connected Iranians to each other and separated them from Americans was, in diaspora, more important than their ethnic differences. While their sense of difference is essentialized, their understanding of differences between Iranians is complex.

What some find more difficult to articulate is the multiplicity of identity interiorized from conflicted and changing cultural, national, and religious sources. Yet many of my subjects (Pari, Mohamad Tavakoli, Tahereh, and Kambys Shirazi, for example) said that rethinking their lives in the course of telling their stories exposed the link between such conflicted origins and the multiple fault lines within their immediate families. Most defined themselves oppositionally or in terms of an *agon*, a struggle—against secular or religious patriarchal authority, or against a particular history, culture, religion, and sense of nation. "Our family culture," said Hamid Naficy, is and continues to be in "opposition to whatever the current regime might be." Many of my informants and their families were harassed or incarcerated by both the Pahlavi and Khomeini regimes. The Azaris and Azarbaijanis directed more hostility toward their Soviet and Russian antagonists than toward the Iranian government; the Kurds directed their anger toward the central state government that has denied them tribal and ethnic rights to identity.

The difference between cultural and national affiliation occurred significantly in several postrevolutionary stories. One that I include is Afsaneh Najmabadi's contrast between the cultural complexity of recognizing, during the Iranian women's march of 1979, the collapse of "Iranian woman" as category, and a later simpler moment of "national shame" when, during the hostage crisis, she encountered a woman wearing a button that read "Let my people go." Memory construes as both whole and one "culture" that is multiply rent, even as Najmabadi unified woman-as-category, but, in her moment of epiphany, saw what she had imagined as whole to be fragmented. Her shock at recognizing the unexpected fusion between class and religious rage also opened a new space for difference and exile *within* her own culture.

Far from being homogenous, the revolutionary class was a fractured category split between such symbolic points as the conservative Right (the bazaar) and the radical Right (Jalal Al-e-Ahmad in one of his phases); the Islamic Left (Mojahedin, Ayatollah Taleqani, and Ali Shariati) and the Islamic Right (Hezb Jomhoori Islami, the Ayatollahs Shariat Madari and Khomeini); and finally, a three-way split among the nationalist Right (the Shah), the nationalist Left (Fadayaan, the National Front), and the nationalist Islamics (Mehdi Bazargan and Ayatollah Taleqani).[15]

"We need fathers to follow," said one exile, "but, as in the *Shahnameh*, fathers betray their sons." Iranian people, she said, have often looked to saviors to deliver them from the chaos of history. The twentieth-century figures mentioned most often by my interviewees were those who helped constitute the contradictory and conflicted national imaginary—figures as varied as Sheikh Fazlullah Nuri, Reza Shah, the writer Jalal Al-e-Ahmad, the popular prime minister Mossadeq, or the philosopher and sociologist Ali Shariati. Each of these figures is a paradox whose heroism lies in the charismatic links he creates between the secular and the religious, between selfhood and selflessness, combining anticolonial, sometimes nationalist desires for autonomy with mystic Sufi celebrations of ascetic transcendence. Some are figures whose deaths have been directly caused (Nuri) or indirectly suspected to have been caused (Shariati) by the State.

The Untranslatability of Cultural Difference

When I asked one of the younger Iranians, Houman Sarshar, what it meant to be "Iranian," what made him different from other groups in the United States, he described it as "a way of caring for others. . . . which brings up a whole series of concepts in Persian culture which are untranslatable—concepts like *ta'arof* and *roodarvarsi*." Every foreigner who has lived in Iran is alternately bewildered and charmed by certain modes of social behavior, the most elaborate and striking of which is *ta'arof*. A word impossible to translate and therefore perhaps a key to the untranslatability of culture, the Urdu version is *takallof*. *Ta'arof* refers to the unwritten laws of elaborate civility in which words and behavior relate metaphorically to meaning. It is used when one greets friends and strangers. It refers to the kind of courtesy in which no guest, no matter how unwelcome, can feel anything but welcome in your house. It means that you will greet guests with a ritual set of verbal gestures that imply your deference to the status of the guest; these include such statements as "please place your feet upon my eyes." "The guest," says a Persian proverb, "is God's beloved" (the Sanskrit variation says "The Guest *is* God"). It therefore means that any house you enter will always welcome you with at least a cup of tea and something sweet (if only *nabaat*), that you will at first refuse and then, when coaxed, accept.

Michael Fischer tells the postrevolutionary story of Nurullah Akhtar-Khavari placing a piece of *nabaat* (rock sugar) in the mouths of each of the villagers who broke into his house before taking him to prison during the roundup of Baha'is in Shiraz, and of him placing a piece of *nabaat* into the mouth of his executioner thanking him for what he was about to do (Fischer and Abedi 1990, 249). His gesture too may be read as *ta'arof,* its aim to insist on civility in a situation that was unimaginably barbaric, unjust, and cruel. *Ta'arof* means that a beggar eating a piece of bread will offer it to you with the simple word *befarmayid,* and it means that you will with equal courtesy say *noush-e-jan* ("may it nourish your soul") and imply refusal. It means that we understand the process of civilization to be a series of gestures toward the impossible—toward connection, restraint, cohesion, and communication, that the reality of actual connections is hard, but that these gestures, accessible to all because the phrases are metaphoric and figural, allow us, if only for a moment, to feel part of a recognizably familiar configuration, and therefore safe.

It also means that it can take longer for two people to pass through a simple doorway in Iran than in most other parts of the globe. And gift-giving is part of the complex unarticulated code of *ta'arof.* Awkward social problems therefore occur when a newcomer into that society doesn't know the rules: at Damavand College for Women where I taught, we needed to warn new teachers from the United States to watch out for the consequences of compliments. We told them urban legends of Americans walking into Iranian tea parties and walking out with priceless Persian rugs. One teacher walked into class the first day and came out with a new pair of earrings—the result of telling a student she liked the earrings. She had yet to learn that in the art of *ta'arof,* the instant Persian response "please take them, they're really yours," requires an equally graceful response that in the course of complimenting the wearer rejects the offer.

My narrative of *ta'arof,* however, like that of Houman's, was chosen to produce a unifying series of stories. But *ta'arof* is much more complicated than I have made it appear. *Ta'arof* and *roodarvasi* (a self-abnegating reticence)—the two terms flagged by Houman to describe Iranian identity—are also codes of behavior produced by a class-conscious, hierarchical society that celebrates certain forms of repression and concealment, and therefore may be read as the manifest level of denied anger and aggression. Clearly there is an alternate way of reading the story of Nurullah Akhtar-Khavari's courteous acceptance of his outrageous arrest and execution. Does one offer ceremonious tokens to the storm troopers coming to arrest you? Can one read *ta'arof* and *roodarvasi* against the grain, as gestures produced by a privileged social class and "naturalized" by the underclass for the preservation of the upper class? To what degree do such formal gestures of courtesy collaborate in the worst excesses of the state? Paul Vieille, the French sociologist, tells me of living in an Iranian village where villagers used the convoluted courtesy of *ta'arof* to block official designs for development. One of the reasons Iranians take so long to adjust to any other culture, he added, is that they can't apply the same modes of everyday conduct in everyday life. *Ta'arof*, therefore, is more than civility; it is also a multipurpose strategical conduct often designed (unconsciously perhaps) to keep the other at bay, to imprison the other in the gift/countergift exchange, and to impose one's superiority on the other by the enormity of a reception impossible for the other to reciprocate.

When I returned to Iran in 1997, I was led to expect a change in postrevolutionary courtesy: "We have all changed utterly, and that includes our old patterns of hospitality," said a friend. But when I started to pay taxi drivers, every one of them responded with the words "Nothing, thank you, my cab is worth nothing," and then (before the final precise amount) "pay me next time," or, "anything you desire." The revolution had not, as I expected, erased everyday *ta'arof*.

Remembering Iranian Differences in a World Context

In exploring narrations of displacement, migration, diaspora, and exile, I am interested in the tensions between remembered unity and homogeneity and the changes my informants experience over time in the United States. Our question "What does it mean to be an Iranian?" (*Irooni boodan chi hast?*) raised a series of responses that seemed to announce, as it were, phases in historical consciousness. Their ruminations on continuities between the "essential" past and modernity ranged from those who valorized cultural rituals and cultural cohesion through poetry, history, and geography to one who read racial difference as a sign of elitist, national consolidation and identity, to those who interpreted the constructedness of all identity formations in terms of the fluidity within specific categories of discourse.

To cite an example, in spite of the recurring references to the love of poetry "essential" to Iranian identity, even that passion for poetry has not passed unchallenged within its culture.[16] Among the critiques Ahmad Kasravi (the anticlerical intellectual assassinated in 1946 by the Fadayaan-Islami) made on Persian cultural and poetic practice was his *Hasan Is Burning His Book of Hafez*, in which he satirizes the Persian's everyday use of poetry and poetic references as anesthetic against thought. Kasravi, an historian, a jurist, a linguist, and a social reformer, was part of a tradition of intellectuals and moderate theologians who in seeking new ways to open Iran to the West and to modernization grew impatient with cultural obstacles to such "progress." In Persian poetry, for instance, he saw the celebration of human and political characteristics that he despised. Why waste time with fictions and fabrications when there was work to be done? He therefore organized book-burning festivals at the winter solstice. In place of what he perceived to be the reactionary fatalism of a poetry that celebrated a hierarchy and monarchy of oppression, he preferred to seek secular, social, and political solutions to Iranian cultural problems; the title of one of his pamphlets, *The Best Form of Government Is Constitutional* (Mottahedeh 1985, 104ff), testifies to that practical ideal.

Some of my subjects read the cultural politics of Iranian "difference" in the context of world history—the result of world powers producing difference. During the World War II, for instance, after the Germans had invaded Russia in 1941, the chief alternate route into Russia was through Iran. When the Allies insisted on Iran expelling Germans and entering their war, Reza Shah chose connections with the Germans and abdication (some say he was forced) over occupation. Two of my interviewees still idealized the Aryan bond between Persians and Germans, and one (Soheyl) recalled seeing pictures of Nazi leaders decorating the walls of his cousin's bedroom. The combination of geography and the history of successive invasions also accounts, some claimed, for the country's defensive and xenophobic character.

Other narratives read the trauma of twentieth-century Iran as the troubled birth of a modern nation in spite of theocratic resistances to secular modernization. The story of Reza Shah, who was both cherished and hated for his despotic rule and for his autocratic insistence on modernization and independence, is, for most of those with whom I spoke, a paradigm of the contradictory needs of the Iranian people. But when the national ideals of Reza Khan are translated into individual terms, then we see that the "people" too wanted "independence" and freedom from his autocratic will that commanded them, for instance, to drop the veil. The imposition of power from above gave the people the leader they craved, yet necessarily stunted the potential for self-reliance. Although Reza Shah was valorized for his initiative and power (he built roads, hospitals, and schools; purified water; and made trains run on time), it was after his fall that a civil state structure seemed to be in the making.[17]

Reza Shah's son, Mohammad Reza Shah, was read by most of my interviewees as the weak son of a strong father. Centering political power in the court, he instituted many economic and educational reforms; witnessed the growing distrust of the clergy, the students, and the nonurban masses; and catered to the pretty reading of Iranian history as a seamless tradition of 2,500 years of monarchical rule. This was yet another fiction of coherence to contain what was a turbulent and fragmented society divided between religions, languages, tribes, classes, and ideologies. The central government and monarchy in Iran relied on that illusion of an essential monolithic unity—on the symbolic power of anthems, pageantry, and pomp—to transcend the fissures in Iranian society. Gradually, however, in its quest for transcendent symbols, the monarchy severed itself from the very social groups that had given it power and in so doing claimed a symbolic divinity (the Shah in his celebration of 2,500 years of Persian monarchy) that doomed it to terminal isolation and to revolt by the very masses that once supported it.

If revolution can be read as the return of the repressed, what the Shah's government repressed consistently were two groups—the clergy (both traditional and radical) and the Left. Isolated, the clergy looked for support and found it in the many leftist organizations that had well-articulated principles of revolt. The naiveté of the Left (and Hannah Arendt may be cited as one of its Western theorists[18]) lay in its conviction that revolution was inevitably secular. The unlikely forces, whose distinctions were strategically blurred, that came together to form the revolution were not only the Left and the clergy, but the radical and the conservative positions (respectively) of Ali Shariati and Ayatollah Khomeini. I will have more to say about Shariati in my introduction to Chapter 3, Revolution.

The discourse of the radical and liberal philosophers and theologians that led up to the Islamic Revolution, by providing a counterdiscourse, replaced one set of myths, one idea of nation for another. But the hybridized audience that constituted the apparently unified black-robed marchers on the streets of Tehran, according to my friends who were among them, were anything but unified in their understanding of what the revolution represented. The face of the revolution—as witnessed by the changing stamps produced weekly in Iran—was the changing face of Iran's many heroes from the progressive Ali Shariati and Mossadeq to the conservative Sheikh Fazlollah Nuri. The revolution became a *tabula rasa* on which could be mapped all manner of fantasy and desire.[19]

Like the revolution and the nation that changed continually, so too our narration of self is a mediated story always in a state of improvisation, "fictions that we employ," as Rosemary George puts it, "to feel at home" (1996, 170). This is particularly true of identities in exile or diaspora whose relation to homeland and their new nation shifts with the multiple channels on the evening news, as new histories and new social movements transform reformers into reactionaries, allies into adversaries, and the exiled into the exalted. Twelve years after the revolution, exiled playwrights and filmmakers in California began to protest film festivals from the Islamic Republic with marches and counterfestivals as the exiles took it upon themselves to contest the politics of art that, in its very production, sanctified the brutalities of the Republic. At the same time Iranian newsletters published in the United States through the 1990s headlined "The Exile Iranian Political Opposition as the Endangered Species" by publishing lists of assassinated Iranian leaders of that opposition. And as the meaning of exile has been transformed on domestic and foreign ground, so too has it been contested in virtual space as the internet opens a new place for the homeless to find homes and for Iranians to contest diverse positions on *vatan parasti* (homeland worship), *vatan doosti* (love of homeland), or *vatan foroushi* (betrayal/selling of homeland).[20]

We live our lives, as the Bible reminds us, as a tale told, and the tales we tell have to do with fashioning a gendered self as part of or in opposition to a collective unit. The process of telling who we are, however, changes when people are suddenly removed from the group. When the received story of relation between the self and the collective breaks down, the process of telling who we are continues in a new circumstance. Although some forge identities out of the debris of loss, my narrators suggest that all stories of new belonging are not told from positions of powerlessness and alienation, that sometimes new stories are told to recapture new power interests, newly-imagined alternative gender and national identities, or multivoiced artistic expressions (comedic plays, films, and journals) that challenge, reconfigure, and subvert traditional cultural affiliations. What follows are the interrupted narratives of self, nation, and belonging, new stories that begin to be told in the new circumstance of exile, migration, or diaspora when we see people knitting the story of themselves with the story of the collective after it has been torn apart.

CHAPTER 2

There:
Remembering Home

Zia Ashraf Nasr

Born in 1903, Zia Ashraf was eighty-seven years old when I interviewed her in February 1990 at her son's house in Virginia, and then again for a week in October 1990 at my house in Champaign. Her life begins and ends in revolution and exile—the first Constitutional Revolution of 1906 and the recent Islamic Revolution of 1979, both of which sent her family into exile. A tall and handsome woman with short gray hair, gray eyes, and light olive skin, her easy laughter and remarkable memory shape the past with jokes, anecdotes, meditations, and stories. She is suspicious of politics ("it knows neither father nor mother") and therefore wanted me to omit all her sharp comments on the subject—impossible because her family maps the divisions in the Constitutional Revolution of 1906 between the Reformists (Mashruteh) who supported the Constitutional Revolution and the Conservative theocrats (Mashrueh) who opposed it. Her older son, Hossein Nasr, is a prominent theological scholar now in exile in the United States. Her younger son, Mehran Nasr, is a businessman whose oldest son studies theology and philosophy. She spoke in Persian.

If the story of my life were to be written, it should be called "From the *Kajaveh*[1] to the Jet." I remember all my journeys. Our family goes back twenty-five generations to a man called Kiamarz. That's where the name Kia comes from. His grave is in *Nur* [light]; hence our family name Kia-Nuri. My grandfather was Nuri. My uncle took the name KiaNuri, but my father crossed out the Nuri; he named us Kia.

Here is the story of our family: Once a father had eight sons and three daughters. They were a wealthy family. But one of the sons left his father in Iran, went to Najaf, studied and gradually became a *Mojtahid* [a theologian qualified to interpret *Sharia* and the Qur'an]. His name was Mohammad Taghi Allameh Nuri. He was the great-great-grandfather. These are our family roots. Haj Mirza Hosein Nuri, your [Zohreh's] great-grandfather and my grandfather, was the son of Allameh Nuri, and his studies were in theology in Iraq. When he finished his studies, he stayed there.

My father married at twenty and studied to become a *Mojtahid*—as hard as getting a Ph.D. today in theology. I was the third child in the family. He lived in Najaf for nine years. My mother's family was Tabatabaii, which means that my mother's uncle was a leader of *Mashruteyat* [the Constitutionalists]. They were a large family and had many *dowrehs* [family gatherings] where I had a great time. My father's family also had such *dowrehs,* especially while my grandmother was alive. After my cousin got married and left my grandmother's house, it was I who was responsible for setting the *sofreh* [table] and serving the guests during such family gatherings.

Do you have memories of Sheikh Fazlullah?
I remember him through something that happened during the long journey from Iraq to Iran. I remember a story that will tell you the kind of man my grandfather was.

When I was seven and my father decided to return with his family to Tehran, we traveled on *kajaveh.* A journey that took us two months then today would take an hour. In those days there was no security on roads, so people traveled in groups of five or ten families. The group in which we traveled from Karbala to Tehran was large—maybe ten families.

The *kajaveh* was a kind of "room" with dimensions of 60 × 70 centimeters attached to the back of a mule. It was made of light wood. It was latticed on the top. On the bottom was a mattress and pillows where one would sit and cover oneself. On our first journey from Iraq to Iran we traveled in two *kajavehs.* My father and mother sat in one, tied together and put on top of a mule—mules are stronger than donkeys you know; my mother had a baby she carried in her arms. In the other, my older brother and I sat on one side, and a female servant and my sister Ghamar on the other. We had eight or nine mules, two for the *kajavehs,* two for our servants, and the rest for our luggage and my father's books.

Before reaching Kermanshah, we got to a place called Balatagh—dangerously located behind the mountains. The next morning the caravan was to be leaving at 4:00 a.m. My father said, "No, I won't wake up my children so early in the morning. You go on and I'll catch up with you later." So we left at 6:00 a.m., two hours after everyone else had left on the caravan. On the way, before we reached a resting place called *Caravansarai Shah-Abbasi* built by Shah Abbas [in the seventeenth century], one of the servants said, "I see some figures in the distance." My father stopped and told them to go and look. The group that traveled in the caravan that had left at 4:00 a.m. had been attacked and robbed. The men and the cattle had been taken; women and children were left. So we gave them rides to get to the *Caravansarai.* When we arrived there—we were supposed to spend the night—my father prepared to get off the *kajaveh.*

Standing by, however, was a group of men on horses carrying guns. One of them asked, "Who is this gentleman?" My father used to wear an *amameh* [turban worn by clergy] at the time. They told the man that my father was the son of the late Sheikh Fazlullah Nuri. The man on horseback said, "Really?" He then came forth and bent down and offered his knee to my father and asked my father to step on his knee. When my father stepped down he asked the man who he was and why he was being so kind to him.

The man said, "I am a robber, a bandit. These men are also robbers and I am their leader." My father asked, "Then why are you so courteous to me?" The man replied, "Well, it is said that what you give with one hand you take away with the other. A long time ago I was an outcast in Tehran. People wouldn't let me in anywhere; I had been a robber. Then in one street I saw a house. I entered that house. I was welcomed; no one asked me who I was. I sat in a room and they brought me tea; at noon they brought me lunch. At night they brought me dinner. So I stayed there for a week, ate and slept. Then I asked, 'Whose house is this?' They said that it was Sheikh Fazlullah's house. It was in your father's house in which I ate and slept! So now I'll return the kindness to you. Stay here, have the children eat lunch, and then we'll accompany you because we have friends [robbers] who are waiting behind those mountains. We'll get you to Kermanshah safely." And they did this.

My father was very grateful. We have a poem that says, "Do a good deed and fling it in the *Dajleh* [Tigris River] / God will return it to you in the desert." This was exactly what happened in our lives.

The bandits accompanied us to Kermanshah. There the governor who was Farmanfarma came to greet my father and asked us to be his guests for a few days. When we left Kermanshah we continued our journey from one resting place to another. We would dismount from our *kajavehs* so that the mules could rest. My father would give each of us an onion and tell us to eat it. They said that onions were good when you traveled from one place to another; now the West has discovered what we always knew—that it would keep you from getting sick. We didn't get sick on the way.

When our *kajavehs* finally brought us to Tehran, the door of my grandfather's house, the *birun* [outer quarter], was closed. [Once it had been open to all.] Behind it they had stashed garbage. The family used a narrow corridor that led to the *andarun* [inner quarters] where my grandmother and uncle lived. There were two or three courtyards. When we finally arrived at their house, I remember that when our mules reached the passageway, a child appeared in front of the door and cried, "There they are!" As they kissed and hugged us tears poured from my grandmother's eyes like rain, and yet she kept hugging us.

My grandfather was a great personality, well known in Iran. Five secretaries worked in his house to deal with the family's marriages, divorces, estates, problems. It was as though there were a court of justice inside his house. And they took this man to his martyrdom and looted the entire house. Even the servants turned out to be thieves. He had enemies within the family. Even my aunts turned out to be married to men who were against my grandfather.

Do you remember your earliest schooling in Iraq?
I remember that since childhood I had always been fascinated by any kind of writing. The printed word, any word in any work, would catch my eye and I would stare at it. The Qur'an for instance: I would open it and look at the script. At the age of four they put me in a *maktabkhaneh* [traditional school]. No, it wasn't a real school. It was a room where children of all sorts would gather. One might be a beginner, another a good reader. We sat in a circle on the floor and each of us had her Qur'an in front of her on the floor. We began with the *Alhamdolallah* [Praise be to God] and the smaller verses in the Qur'an until we got more skills and could read the longer ones. I was four years old. Our teacher was paralyzed in her legs. Her daughter would help her sit in her place and she was a very good woman. She paid a lot of attention to me and I learned to read very fast. I read the entire Qur'an in a year.

It was a tradition then in Iraq that when a child had completed a first reading of the Qur'an, there would be a ceremony of celebration for her. This ceremony involved a street procession with the children in line, each with her Qur'an, with the child who had completed the Qur'an in front dressed in nice new clothes; and then they would sing. They celebrated me—it was great fun—we went out and marched through a few streets and then returned. I remember—because I was so small, I was only four or five—how they put me in front of the line. My mother kept saying, "She's too young. Don't take her very far." I was dressed in rose-colored clothes. This is a very sweet memory of those times that I'll never forget. I learned to write later when I was about seven—in Iran. There in Iraq I only learned to read.

I wasn't taught writing then, only reading. No, girls generally weren't allowed to learn writing, and I doubt if my tutor knew how to write either. I did a little writing on my own. I would copy what was in the book.[2]

Tell us about some of the women who most influenced you.
Our family is well known for having strong will, for breeding powerful women who are decisive and purposeful. If they decide on something they stick to it. Look at the number of strong women in our family who have doctorates in medicine, literature, and other fields. My aunt, Houra Khanum, was the first Iranian woman to go to the American school and learn English. The family was against girls going to school. But my uncle was the first man who let his daughters go to school—to the American Missionary School!

As a child I spent a lot of time with my grandmother. She was a very powerful woman whose authority over her family taught me what it meant to be human [*insaniat*]. Her actions and her stories taught me that women can and should have power. All the work I did in Iran for fifteen years was for the enhancement of women, to honor women, to empower women. Of course I worked in organizations with others, not alone. But I was always at the forefront. But to return to my grandmother. I spent a lot of time with her, I did household chores, went on family outings. But no school. As I said earlier, in Iran in those days, it was customary not to send girls to school. They hired tutors for us who were usually the daughters of close relatives.

Until I was fourteen I was my grandmother's close companion because she was alone, and so at night I'd go to her and she would tell me stories about the family, about my grandfather's martyrdom. At times I would accompany my grandmother to [the shrine of] Hazrat Abdol Azim where I would read the *Ziyarat Nameh* (a prayer) for her because she had weak eyes. Because of all this, I was very close to grandmother.

Tell us about your later education and your marriage to Valiullah Nasr.
It was only after my grandmother died that I went to school. By then (1918) I was about fourteen or fifteen years old. I realized then that I needed to know more than just the Qur'an. The others in my family didn't want to cooperate with my idea of going to school. But I had an aunt, Khanum Monir-Zaman. I asked her if she would go to Madrisseh Namoos (the first Muslim's girl's school founded in 1907) with me. We went. They tested me in the school and said "second grade," because I knew no math or any of the new subjects like geography. But I was blessed with a good memory. In six months after entering the second grade officially, I not only finished the fifth grade, I also got the sixth grade certificate. Reading was very easy for me. I had only to read a book twice to have it entirely memorized.

My high school education led to my marriage. After high school, there was no further school in Iran for girls. I taught in the same school where I had studied for a year. *Namoos* was a school to which many well-known families and wealthy aristocrats sent their daughters. After that year, the government opened a school called *Dar-ul-Moallemat*—"a teachers' training school." The principal was from France and the school included the higher grades and teacher-training courses. We took turns going to an elementary school where we did student teaching, where we would be observed and graded on our performance.

After I finished the three years and received my diploma I became a teacher at the same place—at the *Dar-ul-Moallemat*. I was chosen by the French principal who recommended me to the ministry. I taught in that school for four years, every day of the week. During summers I sat on the board of examiners.

One day I was sitting with a gentleman colleague on the jury for exams on theology and the Qur'an. It was the end of the session and only a few students remained. Then the door opened and the assistant to the Minister of Education, Valiullah Nasr, entered the room. He used to visit schools from time to time and lecture to us, the first group of trained women teachers in the country, about *akhlagh* [ethics/psychology]. I used to enjoy his lectures. Yes, so he entered the room. He was holding a rose blossom in his hand and he placed it on the desk. He asked about the students, the exam. My colleague said to him that they were good. After we finished our work and were about to close the office and leave, my male colleague said to me, "Khanum Kia, this flower that the doctor left on this desk is for you because the Aga doesn't usually give me flowers." [She laughs.] I was really embarrassed and picked up the flower and went into the school office to sign and leave. When I entered the office I saw that this same assistant to the minister, Dr. Valiullah Nasr, was there. He said, "Miss Kia, I would like to see you in my office at the Ministry. When can you come?" I said, "Tomorrow, after the exams are over here, I'll come and see you." I left the school.

The next day I went to visit him and I thought he wanted to discuss my teaching; maybe there was something wrong with it. When I came in he told the servant, "I won't see any more visitors. Let Miss Kia come in." I wondered why he was seeing me alone. I went in and all his conversation, I realized, had nothing to do with the Ministry of Education or with teaching or with lessons. He was talking about his family. And I kept wondering why he was telling me all this. At the end he said, "I think I tired you with my talk. My purpose was not to talk about my family or about myself or about my earlier marriage in my youth. But you should know I told you all this because I want to ask you to marry me."

In those days a man would not ask such a question of a woman, so I naturally was somewhat embarrassed. I said, "Aga Doctor, the things you talked to me about, these are usually discussed among the family. I have a father, a family. I can't answer you right now. You know what family traditions are. You have to ask my father." He said, "I know. I'll come to see your father. But first I wanted to know what you thought." He immediately called on my father. My father said he had no objections. My father said to the doctor, "There's no opposition on my part. I would be honored to be related to you. But my daughters are free. Ashraf herself should answer."

I didn't give an answer for two months. I thought about it constantly. I would be ready to accept the proposal, but then my sister would change my mind. She would say, "He's too old for you. You'll get old if you become his wife." There was a huge age difference—thirty-five years—between us. I was twenty-four and he was about sixty. After two months he called my brother and said, "I haven't heard from your sister. I am waiting for an answer." When my brother asked me why I hadn't answered, I said, "Invite him over. I'll answer." He came, we talked, I was still doubtful, I gave the answer, and our marriage took place. At that time I was writing a book on home economics. Then later I gave this manuscript away to someone else to use as part of her work. This is the story of my marriage. We had two children. I benefited a lot from his knowledge and understanding, and he from me. We lived together for almost fourteen years and then he had an accident. A bicycle hit him and broke his pelvis; he was such a good man that he told the man who apologized for hitting him, "Don't stop here and look after me—they will arrest you. Go, go on." They carried him home on their backs. He was bedridden for two years until his death.

That's when I sent my son Hossein to America because my brother thought he should go there. At first my husband didn't agree. But then he said, "It would be good to send him to your brother Emad Kia because I don't want Hossein here when I am dying." No, I don't know if this was the right thing to have done. He thought his death would leave a bad impression on him. But in fact it left an impression mainly because he was absent. For some time he was sad because he said, "Why wasn't I there when my father died?" A few months after the funeral, I brought my younger son Mehran to America.

Could you recall memories of veiling?
I remember when the veil was first lifted by Reza Shah. And yes, of course I wore the veil—not in Iraq where we were very free. I was seven in Iraq and didn't wear the *chador* there. There I wore a long dress and didn't even cover my head. But when we came to Iran we saw that even the small children in my father's and mother's families wore the veil.

As long as my grandmother was alive (until 1918), to respect her I wore the *chador.* But of course other Iranians wore the *chador* also until there was a change in the monarchy and Reza Shah ordered the lifting of the veil (1936). I have very strong memories of this: my aunts did not like to leave the house without the *chador* and many women simply did not leave the house at all after the order. My mother-in-law went out one day and they forcibly removed her *chador;* so she went into a store and waited for someone to came from the house with a covering for her head before she walked on. I remember the first party given by Reza Shah for the foreign minister of Turkey when the order went out that ladies who came with their husbands should not be veiled. That was the first party I recall to which our women came with their hair done, wearing elegant Western clothes, and, instead of veils, hats. That night we went out without the *chador.* When we left the house, everyone on the street came out to stare at us.

Reza Shah did a lot for the people—he was a strong man. When he took over, Iran was a very poor country controlled by foreign powers. Its exports were controlled by one country, its imports by another, another country took its taxes, another its oil. Each province was run by a governor who fancied himself an independent ruler. And the Qajar Shah was a child and couldn't do anything. The country was in poverty and misery. There was illness and famine. But when Reza Khan came to power [and became Shah], he fought with the governors in the provinces until he united Iran under a central government. When he took power, Iran was in debt to everyone. There was no money in the treasury or in banks in spite of our natural wealth. He refused to bow to foreign powers. That's why the Allies sent him into exile. In the middle of the war when Iran was occupied he refused to allow our foreign minister to visit other embassies; he refused to accept a visit from the British ambassador or any ambassador because he feared they were planning on taking over Iran. He loved Iran.

When poverty-stricken Iran became rich, it was he who built hospitals, roads, dams, and brought us electricity. We used to light lanterns before that. He brought us new technology. All that is in history books. I can only tell you about what I saw and remember. We lived in the Sangelaj district. The water in Sangelaj was always polluted and I myself was infected with typhoid at the age of thirteen (1917). I was dying. In that neighborhood, twenty-five people got typhoid. We had no piped water. Everything was thrown into the water passing through the street's open drains. This same water was used as drinking water in the homes. All this changed under Reza Shah. It was he who brought clean mountain water into our homes. His son was weak, not a bad person, but weak and indecisive; he let others take advantage of him. And it was his weakness that left the land in Khomeini's hands.

Tell us about your awareness of and involvement in women's movements.
I remember the start of women's groups such as the *Jameyat Banovan*, a charity organization. But a major memory for me is the return of Khanum Siddiqeh Dowlatabadi from Europe. She was a very important figure for women in our history. I was then about fifteen years old, in high school at Namoos School (ca. 1918). Because the subject of women's liberation was always on my mind, I was very excited one day to hear that Khanum Dowlatabadi, the progressive leader of women's liberation in Iran, had returned from abroad and was giving a lecture in town. I asked to accompany some of our teachers. We went early and waited for her to arrive in this huge hall with balconies. She entered looking very dignified dressed in white. She greeted a few people, went behind the desk, and began her lecture. There was silence as she began. But suddenly from the balcony a large pomegranate was thrown at her which landed on the lecture desk and exploded, splashing all its juice on her face and clothes. But Khanum Dowlatabadi was so collected and well composed that she did not pause; she continued as if nothing had happened. From that day on, I was won over and became devoted to this woman. Whenever she gave a lecture, I tried to attend. We became more aware of each other as I started to work in the Women's Organization. When she got ill, I would often go to visit her. Her grave was desecrated after this revolution.

After she described the work she did as supervisor of Iranian students in Boston—forming social clubs, arranging Norooz festivities, taking care of sick and homesick students, and facilitating admissions into schools—I asked if she felt sufficiently rewarded for her work without pay.

Yes, of course. I saw the results. All I got from the government when I returned from the United States was an official letter of thanks.

When I returned to Iran I was asked to write an article about the students. I had wanted to do that myself. So I wrote an essay called "Tikke hai Jigar" [literally "Lobes of the Liver," or, less literally, "Our Beloved Wandering Ones"] in which I urged Iranians not to send their very young children abroad. I raised questions about the reasons why they thought sending a child away from the family was good for the child. The article was published in *Etela'at*.

A little after this article came out, Princess Ashraf invited fifty women to establish the Women's Organization and I was asked to be the first general secretary (*Dabir*). She chose Mrs. Yeganegi to be the second secretary and asked us to decide on our program. We decided we should do social work, charity work. Our organization was called *Shoraye Alee Zan* [High Council for Women]. I was in charge of the Committee for Small Cities and took over the province of Mazandaran and set up its committees.

Another group I belonged to was one that Mrs. Masoodi (of the *Etela'at*) asked me to help with. This group connected to the newspaper set up a journal called *The Journal for Banovan and Dooshezegan* [married and unmarried women]. You became a paying member for five tomans [then about twenty-five cents] so anyone could join. They wanted me to be president of this organization, to bring about some order, so I set up classes in literacy, in sewing, in foreign language, in hair and beauty. I also set up lectures because these women, who were from underprivileged classes, from places like Molavi Street and Esmail Bazzaz Street at the end of the bazaar, these women didn't know anything about their rights—for instance, the right not to be beaten by men. The women who joined our group were mostly illiterate, and therefore the work we did through them had an important effect on society. For fifteen years I worked with this organization and with another Committee for Small Cities. We did this years before the government set up its Family Protection Plan.

We worked especially hard during crises—during the Bo-in Zahra earthquake and the floods of Varamin (1960s). We worked in hospitals. For instance, a worker had fallen, broken his leg, was confined to a wheelchair, and couldn't work. I found him a place in the organization serving tea. Another woman was widowed and without a job. We bought her a sewing machine with which she earned enough money to send her children to school. Another woman with many children came and told us she was destitute because her husband left her for another woman. We enrolled this woman in a typing class so she could have a skill, then we found the husband, brought him to the organization, and talked to him. I told him that when children aren't brought up with fathers and mothers, they become vagrants. He let go of the other woman and returned to his family. We had many such cases.

Then I chose about fifty or sixty women and formed a central committee with two secretaries and branch committees—one for education, another for charity, and another for family problems. How many demonstrations we had then! I was the head of this committee. We went to the *Majlis* [Parliament]; we held up the flag saying that women had to have the right to vote. We demonstrated so much, yelled and screamed so much that one day all women, not just our group, but all the groups started marching with us. The Shah of course wanted women to have the right to vote, but he had to take the *akhoonds* [clerics] into consideration. The women even tied themselves to the front of the *Majlis* while protesting for their right to vote, until finally the *Majlis* passed the bill in February 1963.

Yes, much work was done to advance and strengthen women. But what was the use? All the work we did for women—for their advancement, for their rights—was destroyed by this revolution. It washed everything away, and some of those great women who were in the Senate were later put into prison. Many, many women were killed. We have lost much.

Pari

Pari (pseud.)—teacher, writer, translator, and friend—has been introduced earlier. Born in 1936 in Isfahan, some thirty-two years after Zia Ashraf Nasr, Pari belongs to a generation of women activists who experienced the effects of liberation and foreign education in the early 1960s. In spite of the difficulties of introspection, she insisted on recalling memories she was culturally trained to repress, but which she had learned to confront and articulate during her years in the United States. She spoke of her troubled childhood with much difficulty over several sessions. She spoke with pride of her work as writer, translator, and teacher in the villages. I interviewed her first in 1990, and then again in 1992 and 1994. The last time I talked through a rough draft of this manuscript, she wanted to add more details about the constellation of other women—her grandmother and great-aunt in particular—who had in some part been responsible for who she is today. Pari's mother was the last Azali or Babi in the family. Her aunt was one of Iran's most famous feminists, Siddiqeh Dowlatabadi. For Pari's mother, the Azali movement is light and the Baha'i movement is darkness.[3] Pari spoke in English with occasional lapses into Persian.

The very first memory that I have of my childhood is this: I was put outside the door and I was banging on the door, wanting to get inside and was kept outside. I was sitting on the floor and I must have been about two or three years old. I remember that the ground that I was sitting on was wet. It is customary in Iran to sprinkle water and then sweep the floor, because it is earth, so that the dust will not rise. It was in the morning perhaps before lunch time. I remember I had done something wrong at home and my mother put me out and I was trying to get back into the house.

I must say that I had a very difficult childhood because when I was about six months old my parents got divorced. I stayed with my mother. After her divorce, she moved to Isfahan and we lived with my grandmother. Then sometime soon we moved to Tehran. Later, during the Second World War, I was sent back to Isfahan without my mother, because the war was getting too complicated for Tehranis and they thought that it would be safer for me if I went to Isfahan to live with my grandmother. And all these early memories are mixed up with lots of child abusers.

Mother, being single and pretty with many modern (*Babi*) ideas of men and women as equal, was leading a life freer than the ordinary sheltered life led by most Iranian women. In my grandmother's house there was another lodger and that young man used and sexually abused me. That time I must have been five. Then we came to Tehran and my grandfather had died and my father had left the house and I was staying with my two brothers and my mother and we had a servant and I remember I was going to school then, which means I must have been about six years old and this servant also used and abused me.

The effects are permanent. You are a child and you wonder what is going on and you think that all you are good for is to give pleasure to men. And when you are older you still think that is your only meaningful role in life. I know in my head that I am capable of more than what my previous self thought possible. My achievement in writing books and succeeding at my jobs should tell me that, but I am always filled with doubt, fear, and depression. I must tell you that even now when something of mine gets published I think that some man must have put in a word for me because he liked me. The first time my friend in England sent one of my stories to outside readers for a magazine and it got accepted, though I knew that no man with designs on me had accepted it, still I doubted myself.

I remember that in my father's house there was constant fighting between my two brothers, my two older brothers—a house filled with terror. Then, I'm all mixed up, remembering a series of abusers—different people, whoever was close to my mother. The abusers were sometimes my mother's lovers, but not exclusively my mother's lovers. Other relatives. Then I remember that, after we moved to another house with my uncle and his wife, the brother of my uncle's wife also molested me. My sexual abuse continued off and on until I left Iran. My abusers all made sure that they didn't destroy my virginity. They knew its value. But for the one being abused, it was a very scary thing to have, on top of everything, the fear of losing my virginity.

All girls of all Iranian classes have to be virgins and at least in my generation they had to keep their virginity until marriage. Part of the bride price, virginity was a sign of *Ismat*, honor, chastity. And the sign of this virtue is the handkerchief that was stained with blood on the night of the wedding.

I have no nostalgia for childhood. A lot of tension and a lot of fear. The fear of telling, of somebody finding out this shame in my life and the fear of me not being a perfect girl, which meant an obedient daughter, of not being a virgin, the fear that my father would come and take me back. Because as you know in Iran mothers cannot keep their children after divorce—they lose that right—and by the time that the child is seven, the father can claim the female child. And that happened to me, too.

The hidden agenda of our society for children is to make them obedient. That, I think, is a horrible system. That kind of obedience makes children into slaves—now slaves of parents, later slaves of husbands, finally slaves of society, any society.

One day I turned seven and my father wanted me back and so I was taken back to my father for the first time. I had always thought that going to my father would be the end of me, because the picture that my mother had drawn of my father was extremely fearful. I was sent to live with my father during the Second World War, and I was terrified. I now had a stepmother and I thought that stepmothers killed children, that she would hurt me or do something terrible. In fact she is one of the most pleasant and understanding women I know. She later told me that she was as frightened by me as I was of her because she was afraid that I would kill her daughter.

I didn't eat at all for about a week—the whole week that I was with my father—and so his wife persuaded my father to send me back because she thought I would die of starvation. I knew that I was going to die there sooner or later, so why not starve and make my death come sooner. So my father sent me back. All through this journey back to Isfahan, the tires on the car kept going flat at least two hundred times and each time they had to mend a tire. Each time it took at least an hour and it postponed forever my getting back to Isfahan to where I thought of as home. And yet, when I got home it was not much better than in Tehran.

At that time I think my mother got married again. But somehow this fact was not told to me by my mother, so I gathered it from other people and they kept on asking me, "What's going on? Do you hear, do you see your stepfather? Is he staying with you in the evenings?" And as a child it was very traumatic because I didn't know what was going on and I needed to have some sort of knowledge, or some sort of solid ground to live on but I didn't have it. Then my mother and this man left for Tehran because he was going to be a new prophet and claim that he was the Twelfth Imam. I stayed with my grandmother.

The man involved with my mother wasn't a Babi or Baha'i. He just wanted to have my mother and because my mother had this religious drive, he thought that the way that he could have her would be to say he was the hidden Imam. He went to Shah Abdul Azim in Rey, the most religious shrine around Tehran, and in broken Arabic in the *sahn* [courtyard around the shrine], he held out his arms and declared himself to be the Twelfth Imam. Of course he was taken to prison to be interrogated. And of course he said, "I take back my words." And of course the marriage then dissolved.

I had a year with my grandmother in Isfahan. That was a good year. I often wonder what sort of person I would have become if my grandmother's unconditional love had not been there. In my life and work I have tried to emulate my grandmother. She was illiterate, from a lower class, and got married when she was nine to a man who was seventy. She was the daughter of my grandfather's secretary, and as a nine-year-old would carry tea into his sitting room. One day he asked her, "Do you like me?" "But of course," the child answered innocently. Haji Mirza Hadi, then seventy years old, ordered a marriage between himself and the nine-year-old girl. Marzieh Khanum found herself suddenly moved from a lower working-class position to the wife of the *Aga*. She became pregnant before having her first period. The young girl grew so confused during labor that she didn't know whether to stand or lie down. She decided to hang on the rafters to ease the pain. A relative came in and finding her in this position, eased her down, helped her deliver the baby, and cut the umbilical cord. As long as she nursed the baby, she was well; the moment she stopped, the old man again impregnated her. This time she gave birth to my mother.

After this birth, my grandfather fell ill and died, leaving my grandmother a widow at the age of fifteen. The seven children from my grandfather's first wife decided my grandmother must marry, and they found an old man to whom they gave the still-young girl. My grandfather's family already looked at her as a lower-class interloper who had come to the family, so that we who descended from her felt sort of inferior to the rest of the family.

Tell about your early involvement with politics.
I was very young, about ten or twelve, and I was in Isfahan, a worker's town, and I remember a huge demonstration. My brother was involved in organizing *Hezb Tudeh* [the Communist Party]. My other brother was active in the streets, in making demonstrations, collecting people, talking, shouting—things like that. The secret party meetings took place in our house and I knew all the top members of the *Hezb Tudeh*. Sometimes they would give me a piece of paper—I never knew what it was—and ask me to take it from one place to another. But when I came back I would get a pat on the back from my brother. And that was what I really wanted.

All this was about 1945 when I was about twelve years old. Never, never did any of these political men make any sexual overtures towards me; none of them touched me—which has been good for my relationship to politics. Most of the men who abused me as a child were religious—people who were making a new religion, people on my mother's side.

Did you understand what the Tudeh Party meant?
Yes. Not how I understand Marxism now, but then it meant that men and women were equal, that there was a way to bridge the gap between the upper class and lower class. And I think the reason that I was supporting it so whole-heartedly without really knowing what was going on was the fact that I knew we were the descendants of a secretary of a very rich man my grandmother married. Both my brothers were politically active. The older educated me with books. My younger brother was very kind but very irrational. He would

be loving and buy me presents and the next moment, with no provocation, would beat me severely.

Growing up for me involved politics, sexual abuse, physical abuse, insecurity because I never knew when I might lose the family I had. And I couldn't tell anyone. The only person that I could have told was my grandmother, whom I trusted and I loved. But she was away, and I couldn't. Of course I couldn't.

Yet perhaps this also was what gave me the incentive to fight for the underdog, to want to get rights for people who had no power, who are underdogs and who are oppressed.

I turned seventeen in 1952. This was the time that Iran became a unified group against the British, thanks to Mossadeq, and that was really something. We felt that finally we as a country had achieved an identity, a pride. And when the Shah left Iran, I remember we threw big parties to celebrate. Standing on our balcony, my brother yelled out and invited everybody—the neighbors, the laborers and anyone on the streets—to come to our house. But the Shah's abdication didn't last very long; the CIA brought him back, and after a few days we were terrified that my brother would be jailed, and in fact he fled.

I went to Tehran University when I was seventeen years old, and once again there I was exposed to all the political activities in *Hezb Tudeh* against the Shah. I wanted to take part by carrying, for example, the forbidden *Mardom* Papers [People's Papers] to the university, and I wanted to risk distributing something for which death was the penalty if I got caught. When I fell in love with a boy my brother didn't approve of, he sent me to England when I was eighteen to get me away from this boy and from my political involvement at Tehran University. Why didn't my brother approve? It was power. I wasn't supposed to choose my involvement with politics or with men. He needed to control that choice.

The problem of "control" for you is tied with the inefficacy of formal education.

Of course. Did I ever learn anything from my diplomas? No. I would like another life without the education but with the experience. All Iranian parents are willing to sell their last belongings to give their children an education, either in Iran or abroad. The Western parent would not understand such sacrifice. Education in Iran is a way to bridge classes. Before the Constitutional Revolution in 1906, an education was the sole prerogative of the upper classes. After the Constitutional Revolution, modernization, and Westernization, everyone wanted their children educated but Iran was not ready for all these educated people. Our universities had limited seats; students had to pass severe entrance exams. Even if they passed, they were not free to choose their fields or their subjects. They had to enter the field in which their *Conkur* [university entrance exam] scores were highest.

But when they came out of the university, they weren't prepared for anything except the civil service, which was already overfilled. If they weren't hired by the government, they were considered failures. No longer could they participate in their father's family business—a sweet shop or cloth shop; the father wouldn't want his university-educated son to work there. That would be like saying that his son had not progressed farther in life than himself.

My formal education was similarly pointless—first radiography, which I studied for two and a half years in England, but which I was forbidden to practice when I returned to Iran. Why? Because my husband, my brother, and my mother told me it might damage my health by making me infertile. Although I have been trained in many fields and have various diplomas, none of them were chosen by me. But things have changed. After the revolution, people read much, much more than before the revolution. Now reading and learning have some practical use. Iranians need to learn that all classes have to control their lives, and not to leave things to God.

I wonder about the cultural constraints on such control in a land where life is usually in the control of a God or a Shah or an ayatollah or a father, and whether you find that phase of Western "enlightenment" celebrating individual control over oneself a desirable goal.
These are questions I share. The most revealing moment for me took place with a therapist in the United States when I was suffering a breakdown at the age of fifty. She was trying to help me understand the idea of control over one's own life. That very idea was alien to me: I, a Marxist, assumed that God was really behind the scenes, in control of our lives! I argued with this therapist, "Surely you aren't in control of your life either. What if you discover that your husband is having an affair with someone else?" She laughed and said that I had not heard her correctly. She was in control of her life, not that of her husband's, and his affair was part of his life and out of her control. That was a real lesson to me. In Iran we have not reached this sort of enlightenment. One reason why we get so depressed as a nation is that when our children, exposed to Western culture, are no longer subject to our control, we are lost as parents and as human beings.

It seems as if your loyalties, like that of the country at various points, have been divided and defined by the two most important men in your life—your brother the Marxist and your husband the royalist.
Yes, that's right. And my closest friend at that time was a person who was very actively involved in *Hezb Tudeh;* she was a political activist and my husband did not like her. I would have loved to see her every day. But she refused to come even to my wedding. She disapproved of my marrying a royalist. Yet both my husband and I compromised in our marriage, because—I must give him credit for this—he too stopped supporting the Shah openly as I stopped

supporting the *Hezb Tudeh* openly. But it was the beginning of SAVAK getting very strong, and it was painful to know that I could not trust anyone. Nobody.

This is now about 1960. Because a few years after the Shah returned (after the CIA coup), the Israelis came and started to build up the SAVAK. But I remembered even at home as a child when we had secret meetings, we ran the water taps while we talked for fear of SAVAK spies.

Do you want to talk about your work history?
I started working for a children's journal, *Paik,* in 1962 and stayed with them for seven years. They decided that if they wanted to do something for illiteracy, they had to start in the villages. The usual practice had been to have uniform texts for all Iran. Central to this part of my work was Franklin, an American organization, that controlled the largest cartels in Iran. It owned, among other things, a paper mill and a shopping center, and it began to monopolize the production of all primary school books, which they gave free to students. Now, Franklin Publications knew of a United States journal called *Scholastic* and asked some Americans to come and help realize a similar project for children in villages. At first this was a low-profile journal, published every two weeks on the cheapest possible paper and costing two *rials* [at that time, about a nickel]. But as soon as it appeared and the Ministry of Education saw it, they raised a fuss; they started by complaining that there were no roads to many villages. Then they said, "City children have no such magazine; why should village children have it?"

Getting my first job required investigation by SAVAK. They asked me to come to the SAVAK Center and sit in an office and talk. I had to hide all my beliefs and once again got very scared. I wanted to get out in one piece. But again I knew that with my brother there, I'd be safe because the head of SAVAK was always dining with him.

I'm surprised. After his history, how could this possibly be?
Well, my brother probably convinced him that though he had once been a Communist, he was no longer. He now worked for the Americans. And Franklin, the Shah, my brother, and SAVAK were all taking money from the Americans. My brother went to the Shah and said, "Just as soldiers need ammunition and clothing, so too the kids need books." So my brother was made head of the literacy campaign. That's why he was one of my models and why I admired him. But I also saw him as dangerous and saw the need to keep a distance.

SAVAK and their spying made me miserable. I had two kids who didn't know why I got so angry, so depressed, so out of control—I didn't know what to believe and I didn't believe in myself. I didn't trust anyone and I couldn't create a trusting atmosphere for the children, who knew I was trying to hide something from them—my political self and my emotional self.

And around this time, in 1971, the Shah's celebration of 2,500 years of monarchy happened. I was very angry. I wrote a children's story in reaction to the celebration.

The story was about a little bird in a prison who wants to get out of the prison. She flies to a castle, sees friends and rooms and a wealth of things, and flies out of the castle where she finds illumination and lights and music and festivity, and yet the people are dying of hunger. And the bird sickens and wants to return to its prison. Because at least in the prison she doesn't see people dying of hunger.

So my brother, who was in charge of Franklin Publications, suggested I work for children's periodicals. But my future friend and boss Lily said no nepotism. After three applications, she still said she could see nothing for me to do. But when Lily saw some of my translations from English into Persian, she quickly changed her mind. She said I had a great ability to write for children and that I had good eyes to pick up on the right stuff for children. She suggested that I become her assistant.

Franklin asked Lily and me to prepare a four-volume anthology of children's literature to use in the classroom. That's how I got involved with children's literature. After I started writing for children, Lily asked me to teach some of her courses at the university.

After Franklin I worked for the Persian literary scholar, Ehsan Yarshatar, for one year. Then I studied for my M.A. exams and started once again working for my brother. My job was to prepare directions instructing chicken farmers how to run their farms. I did not find this interesting.

In the mid-1970s, a friend introduced me to *Vezarat Taavoon* [the Ministry of Agriculture and Rural Affairs], where I was supposed to run ten centers for educating village girls who would be expected to return to their villages after training. In these ten centers the girls were supposed to write books about their village, and I was to edit and publish their work. While still working for Franklin Publications, I had started teaching at the Teacher's College. I also taught in *Sepayan Engelab* [the Civil Corps] and also taught teacher-preparation courses at Farah Pahlavi University.

Because of my experience in writing books for children, I was at first hired to edit books that village girls had written. The literacy campaign had staffed centers for educating village girls for one-and-a-half years to become "agents of development" and return to the villages to effect change. When I got this position as editor of their books, I met with the writers, recognized their problems, and started to address their wishes to make these centers more like home and less like Western boarding schools. These six centers were outside villages in beautiful buildings that looked like English boarding schools. Most of these girls had never seen a Western-style toilet, or showers, or beds in their own village. And here they were having baths and showers, and sleeping for the first time in a bed. They would fall off their beds in the middle of the night. They were given bunk beds and the woman on the top was tied to her bed with her *chador*. The problem was that after being exposed to this life they could not readjust easily to life in the villages.

When I wrote about this and brought it to the attention of those in charge of the centers and said that this was defeating our purpose, I was asked to write a proposal with solutions. My proposal, indebted to the philosophy of Paulo Freire, was that the ministry hold classes and address problems *in* the village, that we make each village with a center into a sample for other villages, to show others how villagers working together could make life more productive and pleasant. For instance, they could develop group projects in childcare, in handicrafts, and in village hygiene. Each village's program varied from the next, and therefore the whole project shifted, at my suggestion, from these isolated, fake Western boarding schools to programs inside the villages.

I became the director of this entire project for all Iran. Many good people in my office were volunteers helping in this project. Only later did I find out that all of my volunteer assistants were strongly political. Some had been imprisoned by the Shah and were either *Fadayaan-i-Khalq* or *Mojahedin*. This project appealed to them because it involved work with the *Mardom,* the "People."

I started with four villages south of Kerman. Within six months the results were so good that the literacy campaign wanted to spread centers all over Iran. I would live in one village for twenty-five days and watch the development of projects. One of my pet projects was teaching reading and writing. The girls who came from the surrounding villages were required to have at least five years of elementary school; all were older than seventeen or eighteen and had experience living in villages. All worked hard and had a passion to help develop their communities. But although my project sounded good, it generated unexpected problems.

It was too much to take a young girl of eighteen, train her, put her in charge of some aspect of village life, and to promise her a position of authority in place of, say, her father. The women I worked with were subsequently beaten by their fathers and their husbands. The men could not tolerate the fact that someone from outside the village would come and ask to speak to a woman and not to a man. So I think it was all premature, the way the Shah operated, and the way I as his agent tried prematurely to promote village women's status. The men should first have learned to trust the government agent, to see that I could do something well and benefit them.

I later found out that when I wasn't present, the women I worked with would ask permission from their fathers, brothers, and husbands for the smallest thing. And they would do nothing without the men's permission. Then I would reappear and treat the women as if they were the people responsible for doing the work. And I would anger the men. We moved too fast in the villages. We taught, for instance, women's rights: how women should not allow themselves to be beaten or abused sexually.

I first realized our naiveté on a day after my project had been going on for six months when I went to the village and asked to see one of the girls, but was refused. It was only when I was leaving the village that someone came and told me that this girl had been beaten. I struggled with my conscience. Should I put pressure on her father and interfere, or keep quiet? I decided on the second choice, telling myself that next time I returned to the village I would not ask for her; instead I would ask for her father and request his permission to take his daughter to the hospital.

By the end of the Shah's rule, the government was trying to pretend that Iran was on its way to becoming a progressive industrial country with equal rights for men and women. They were pushing women to perform and act in society and government. But, their flaws and shortsightedness were no different from my own: like me when I went to work in the villages, the government too didn't know what they were doing.

So this is what I did in the villages from 1976 to 1978. They were glad to hear me say, "Look, I am divorced, I am single, and I am making a living. There is a life other than staying at home and being a mother." Because of my background, I was able to make them trust me, to confide how they had been abused physically and sexually by their grandfathers, stepfathers, or others. The revolution happened during a trip when I had gone to Europe in 1978 to see my daughter. And these same village girls with whom I had worked very nicely told the *akhoonds* that Khanum Pari had told them that they should not be beaten. "Who," the *akhoonds* demanded, "was this Khanum Pari? The Qur'an has said that a man is allowed to beat his wife." And that is why I have never returned to those villages.

I get very upset when I think of those girls whom I treated as my daughters. They must miss me and they cannot find me and don't know where this woman is who came from the city with a car, with a helicopter, and with all sorts of power and treated them as they had never been treated before, and then suddenly disappeared.

No, Zohreh, I haven't changed anyone's life for the better. I might have changed their lives by introducing multiple possibilities and newness, but not really. There was this girl with damaged eyes who was the daughter of a beggar. She got interested in me and in my way of speaking to them. Finally she said, "I don't talk myself because my father is a village beggar. I, too, have been a servant, but now I want to do something different." This woman passed the entrance exam to Tehran University. I told her that degrees wouldn't teach her as much as she could learn by working within her villages. Here she might get a job. She accepted my word. Of course I don't know what happened to this girl. I'll never know.

Mohamad Tavakoli

Now a professor of history at Illinois State University, Mohamad Tavakoli, born in Tehran in 1955, left Iran for the United States on a gymnastics scholarship in 1975. He returned briefly to Iran for four months in 1979 to celebrate the revolution. Although he is one of several Iranian academicians I interviewed, his working-class background in Chaleh Meidun provides a different culture and locality from that of the others. That site of struggle became also the site of affiliation and compulsive contemplation. He recalls childhood and family, the 1963 anti-Shah bazaar riots, a historical prelude for the later Islamic Revolution, work during childhood and adolescence, and his eventual strategy of escape from privation through athletics.

I sent him an edited version of our conversations in 1994. He asked to rework the interview and edit it himself. The version that follows is therefore Mohamad's spoken words, revised by him. I place his story next to Pari's because although one lived in the north and the other in the south of Tehran, both choose to define their beginnings in terms of child abuse, a practice they read as metonymy for an authoritarian, patriarchal culture.

The story that I am about to tell you is important because it has shaped my views on gender issues and Iranian cultural politics. Between the ages of four and eight, I was subject to sustained molestation, rape, and physical abuse. Growing up male in a phallocratic society, although different, is as painful and oppressive as growing up female. Virgin women are emblems of family honor [abiru], so boys often became the easily accessible objects of adult male desire.

It is not uncommon for young boys to have their first sexual experiences by the age of five. In my own case, I was four when a cleric renting a room in our house lured me to his apartment with the promise of sweets. Once there he lifted me onto his lap, gave me the sweets, and holding my hand guided it up and down a big thing between his legs. As he kissed me I felt him ejaculate. The sheikh's pleasure was brought to an abrupt end by my mother's voice inquiring after me. I looked up and saw my mother in the doorway of the sheikh's room where she found her son on the cleric's lap. She immediately began to beat the cleric on the head with her shoe, calling him *lavvat* [sodomist]. She then sought the help of other neighbors to evict him, and before the day's end she had thrown all his belongings onto the street. The incident puzzled me for years and it was never mentioned again. My mother never responded to my questions, "What is a *lavvat*?" or "Why is the sheikh being thrown out?" The beating that I received that day was a clear message that I had done something never to be repeated.

He was the first of several men who abused me. Until the age of eight I was repeatedly tricked into dark rooms by older men who covered my mouth tightly with their hands, forced my pants down, and sodomized me. These planned entrapments were usually initiated by the trusted men of the community. My severe pain seemed to give them pleasure. My resistance to their actions always led to severe beatings. I was slapped, punched, and hit with leather belts. If I cried, they threatened to choke me. If I said I would tell my mother, they threatened to kill me.

These childhood physical violations taught me to run fast, to strengthen my body for self-protection, and never to be alone with another man. I also developed the habit of covering my ass by leaving my shirttail out of my pants in public. Like a woman's veil, my shirttail diverted the male gaze and kept men's desiring hands off my body.

I did not recognize these early violations as sexual. I was not a desiring sexual subject in those early years. Becoming a man meant the end of physical violence and the beginning of a time when other men could not impose themselves on me. My fear of penetration during my early years translated into strong homophobia in later life. My own experiences led me to identify pedophilia with homosexuality and shaped my views of same-sex relations among males.

This is a culture in which child abuse is a pervasive yet unspoken practice. Breaking the silence surrounding sexual abuse in a community that defines itself as pious is a violation of its most sacred codes. For a long time I denied the trauma of my childhood. Like other Iranian children, I internalized cultural codes of silence and learned that breaking such codes could lead to further abuse. In a sexual hierarchy where active sexuality is seen as masculine and passive sexuality as feminine, it was common for men to brag about "fucking" a child who was seductive and cheeky [*por rooh*; literally, full of spirit]. Once a boy is identified as "passive," he becomes the object of desire and subject to harassment.

To protect myself against the aggression of men, I sought comfort among women. On occasions after being abused, I frequently sought comfort beneath the veils of women relatives who opened their arms to me without question. Male relatives objected to my crying and therefore contributed to my silence. Among women I had no need to guard my body. It was with women that I always felt safe.

It is probably that early identification with women as protectors that accounts for my interest in gender issues and women's issues today. "Veiling" my buttocks taught me something about women's veiling and about unrestrained and unchanneled sexual desire. The veil, for me, has become a symbol of Iranian/Islamic culture's inability to speak the truth about sexuality, sodomy, abuse, pedophilia, rape, and violence.

How do you understand the connection between place and identity, or the link between you and the parts of Tehran that formed you?
Before I learned to pronounce my last name, I introduced myself as *Chaleh Maiduni* [the one from the Ditch]. My identification with the Ditch predated my identification with Iran; my local patriotism preceded and outlasted my Iranian nationalism.

The Ditch was Tehran's most notorious neighborhood known for its drug dealers, gangsters, and street gamblers. It was the home of Tehran's *Haft Kachaloun* [the Seven Bald Brothers], of Nasir Jigraki and Tayib, who organized the anti-Shah uprisings in June 1963. They were my childhood heroes. I learned about them by listening to adult conversations on street corners and in Ali Gulah's coffee shop where my father spent most of his time in the bazaar.

The Ditch received its name, *Chaleh Maidun,* in the nineteenth century when the area was dug out to provide material for the construction of the Wall of Tehran. Adjacent to the Bay al-Haramain Bazaar between two shrines, it also served as a dumping ground for the city's garbage. As Tehran expanded in the twentieth century, the Ditch grew into a center of commercial activities. Part of it became a donkey-sellers' market [*Maidan Malfurusha*] and another became a junkyard [*Maidan i Kuhnah*] where enthusiastic customers found used and stolen things ranging from empty aluminum Nivea containers to car engines. Many years later, I felt a connection with the much smaller version of Tehran's junkyard in Chicago's Maxwell Street Market.

My birthplace was located strategically at the intersection of the dumping ground to the east, the junkyard to the north, and the donkey-sellers' market to the south. By the time I was born, in the mid-1950s, only two houses had survived the appetite of the bazaar for more storage space and shops. To enter our house, one had to pass through the donkey-sellers' market or cut through the dump. Every morning beasts of burden from neighborhood stables were auctioned in front of our house. Auction time meant that the neighborhood would be packed with sellers, buyers, blacksmiths, tea vendors, storytellers, and entertainers who would narrate and perform stories about heaven and hell. When braying donkeys interrupted those performances, the audience would laugh uncontrollably. By afternoon, however, my neighborhood would be transformed into a site for gambling, drug users, drug dealers, and many fistfights. During those hours children were forbidden to go out, but we found that a rooftop perch provided the best view of the market.

My family shared a house with ten other families, a few solitary individuals, and the wicked preacher I mentioned earlier. The men in these families worked in the bazaar as artisans, vendors, and laborers. The women stayed home and worked on commissioned assembly jobs. During financially diffi-cult times, my mother (*Maman*) sewed for a local futon maker in addition to tending the house. During this time my father (*Baba*) lost most of his possessions in one of Tehran's major fires at the wheat silo [*Anbar Gandum*]. His little shop in the Sayyid Ismail bazaar had nothing left to sell but a small supply of quilts that interested no one.

By 1963, our neighborhood changed even more. Mr. Samadi, our Baha'i neighbor and friend and a well-respected bazaari, died. His family sold the house to a broom-seller who used it for storage. When our landlord tried to sell the house in which we lived, my mother objected. So he arranged for the city garbage truck to unload at our front door. We learned to overcome this problem by getting in and out of our apartment through a ladder from the street into the courtyard. Finally, however, all the other families left the house, and so did we. This move was the first in a long and frequent series of displacements. A few years later, my old home and dumping ground was turned into a parking lot for the modernized bazaaris who had replaced their old bicycles with new automobiles.

The move from my birthplace, or so my mother believed, put a curse on the family. It was the start of our pauperization. My father's business went from bad to worse, and when I was in the second grade he was jailed for failure to pay the rent. After he spent two months in jail (Qasr Prison), my maternal grandmother sold some of her land to post his bond. Evicted from our second house, we moved to Pachinar in the heart of the bazaar and adjacent to the Friday Mosque. This house, which my mother disliked intensely, was much smaller than the first. To get to it we had to pass through a long and pitch-black tunnel. It terrified my brothers. But I was happy there. I played on the rooftops of the bazaar and in the inner courtyard of the mosque, whose janitor allowed us to feast on the fruit from its mulberry trees. Our play at night included reenactments of the drama of Husain, Kurd-i-Sahbistari, the Shiite equivalent of the Iranian Rustam. I remember a Chinar tree into which we disappeared while playing *Gurgam be hava*, or hide and seek.

When I got into the third grade, we had to move again into the southernmost part of Tehran, beyond even the gravestone maker's street, in the notorious *Shotorkhun* neighborhood well known for its serial child rapists and murder-ers. The house lacked water and electricity, and the three years we spent there were the most bitter part of my childhood. My parents fought constantly. Part of the tension was caused by the class difference between my parents. My mother came from a village where her family were landowners, and visits from her family were a constant source of shame and stress.

When we finally moved to a more respectable neighborhood near Khurasan Square, and found a house between a mosque and a sports stadium, that stadium soon shaped my future as a top-ranking gymnast.

Tell about your understanding of work as you grew up, about your family's work. How did a boy from your particular neighborhood and class end up a gymnast?

I had always worked, even as a child. Before the first grade I used to tend a vending stand in the junkyard. I would sell plastic combs and funnels in the bazaar, and I always worked after school. During elementary school all the way to high school, I worked respectively as shoemaker, plastic molder, biscuit maker, butcher, tailor, brass molder, welder, and finally as a maker of welding equipment. With the help of my other brothers, we occasionally auctioned shoes and shirts; sometimes we sold steamed beans [*baqali*] and roasted corn.

During my father's imprisonment in 1964, my two older brothers, Ahmad and Mahmoud, dropped out of school. One of them started his own business, and I became his sibling slave. I showed up at his shop by 4:30 every afternoon. Playing after school or arriving late at work often cost me severe physical punishment. This pattern changed in 1970.

Baba (my father) was very conservative. He thought that radio and television were Satan's boxes and on a number of occasions he smashed radios bought by my brothers. Music and movies were both forbidden to us. He was a devoted follower of Aga Khomeini, soon to be the architect of the Islamic Republic. For every action, father sought the advice of Aga Qaravi, a leading Mujtahid in the bazaar and a confidant of Khomeini during his years in exile. We concealed from him the fact that my brother Reza planned on going to the United States to study. He was informed of his departure only a few days before the event. As predicted our house was turned into a *Sahra-i-Karbala* (a place of mourning and lamentation) over Reza's departure. He was certain that Reza would convert immediately to Christianity and marry a *zanbur* (literally, a bee, or a blond woman). Reza left promising Baba that he would keep his fasts and prayers and, in the shrine of Shah Abdul Azim, swore not to marry a Christian woman. He even sealed a promise on the Qur'an to marry his cousin, and although I had never seen him pray, somehow he kept all his promises to Maman and Baba.

Once Reza, the family's despotic disciplinarian, left for the States, my freedom increased. I could wander around the neighborhood without fear of punishment. One day, walking to Ahmad's shop, I discovered the sports stadium in southern Tehran. I watched boxers and wrestlers and gymnasts. Although unfamiliar with gymnastics, I had learned to walk on my hands and do a handspring on a pile of pillows. I got interested in the stadium and particularly in gymnastics and pleaded with my mother to allow me to join. She came up with the registration fee, but once again we had to agree to keep this a secret from Baba and from Ahmad.

After three months of training I won a gymnastics costume at a competition. On the night of that competition, I returned home late and was met by an outraged Ahmad and Mahmoud. They swore at me and chased me with a leather belt, threatening to kill me. They came at me accusing me of stealing the outfit: *"In ra az kuja bardashti?"* ["Where did you lift this from?"] I responded with pride, *"As jayi bar nadashtam. Burdam!"* ["I didn't take it. I won it!"] My two brothers greeted my triumph differently: Mahmoud came to watch me perform and became a fan, but Ahmad became a sworn enemy. Gradually, with Mahmoud's help, I refused to work for Ahmad and began training six times a week. Things changed further when brother Mahmoud also decided to leave for the United States. His motivation was specifically political: in 1972 he had been beaten severely by plain-clothed SAVAK agents for *fuzulying* [meddling] in the affairs of a *bandah-i-khuda* [servant of God] who had been attacked by a group. For this intervention, Mahmoud had been beaten and detained for three days in prison. This was his second beating, and this time he wanted no more. *"Gur-i-pidar-i in mamlikat"* ["To hell with this country"], he said and left.

My career as a gymnast in the meantime, though still a secret from my father, was catching fire. *Keyhan Varzishi*, a weekly sports magazine, did a feature story on me. On the evening of that publication I went home with a big smile on my face that did not last long. My father had heard of the picture from Mashd Musayib, whose son was a pretentious *kushtigar* [wrestler], and who hoped that Baba would stop me from my deviant path. Mashd Musayib therefore told my father that gymnasts end up working in cabarets, drinking alcohol, and sleeping around with whores. Eventually, he warned my father, *kuni mishand* [they become sodomites]. And the picture of me in my shorts was proof to my father of the truth of Mashd Musayib's claim. In bazaar culture, men dressed with modesty and not in shorts. My father cursed me for tainting his *abiru* [honor]. He cut my daily allowance, which was worse than any physical punishment. That allowance had enabled me to go to Amjadiyeh Stadium and observe the training of the national team.

My mother felt that Mashd Musayib's tales to my father were caused by his *hasudi* [jealousy]. She recalled other occasions when, to quote her, *"Baba ra tir kardeh bud"* ["He had agitated Baba"] against Mahmoud, claiming, for instance, that he had seen him in a whorehouse. In the fight that followed between my Maman and Baba, my mother shouted *"akheh ahmaq* [you stupid man], what do you suppose the honorable source of this story against my son was doing in the whorehouse himself?" The feature story in the sports magazine solidified my father and brother Ahmad's opposition to my gymnastics career. Things got even worse when my younger brother, Ali, decided to also take up gymnastics.

My career changed radically when a new Japanese coach was hired to work with the Iranian team for the Seventh Asian Games to be held in Tehran in 1974. When I was asked by the head of the Iranian Gymnastics Federation to train with the national team, I was stunned. But I worried about the effect it would have on my old coach, Pahlavan. I was right to worry. He was hurt and angry and accused me first of *khudfurushi* [self-selling] and then of being *Mamali-i Khain* [Mohamad the Traitor]. These were serious accusations against a child of Chaleh Meidun. Was I really selling myself to a foreigner? This question haunted me for months.

These words *khudfurush* and *khain* took me back to an earlier time; they reminded me of a famous historic incident that took place on June 5, 1963. I had been six years old and working as an assistant to a vendor on the edge of Sayyid Ismail's *ab anbar* [water storage]. That day, while playing with an imaginary car, I noticed a crowd attacking governmental properties across the street belonging to the Imperial Organization for Social Services. I thought it was a fight. But Baba came and lifted me up and raced toward the house. On the way we passed the bazaar. There we saw a crowd dressed in black shirts marching toward us shouting "*Khomeini, Khomeini, to farzand Husain-i*" ["Khomeini, Khomeini, you are the son of Husain"]. That day, the day of the bazaar riots, I heard for the first time of *Shah-i Khain* [the Traitor Shah]. That day was the first time I remember shooting; I saw soldiers' tanks in the bazaar. I remember hiding behind a funnel-shaped speaker on the top of Nasir Jigaraki's shop. And the next day, I remember Reza reporting that Nazir Jigaraki and two others in his shop had been killed by the firing. In the days that followed, Ahmad and Mahmoud, who usually sold nothing more glamorous than plastic combs and handkerchiefs, made a killing selling glossy photographs of Aga Khomeini. My mother kept his picture in her shroud with all her other valuables.

I remember another time when I heard the word *khain*. It was on my very first day of elementary school when students were lined up in class columns. After reciting the national anthem, we were supposed to shout the words *javid Shah*, or long live the Shah. One of the sixth-grade students shouted instead "*shashid Shah*" ["the Shah pissed"]. This student was pulled out of line, his feet were tied to a bar, and the school prefect [*nazim*] whipped him for a long time. I cried. I later told my brother Reza that my first school lesson had been not to say *shashid Shah* when I was supposed to say *javid Shah*.

Gymnastics also liberated me by allowing me to move out of South Tehran and into other Irans. I traveled to Shiraz, Isfahan, Rasht, Tabriz, and Ahvaz. I met people quite different from those I had known in my childhood localities. In this newly discovered Iran, people listened to music, danced, drank, and went to the movies. It was the Iran that Baba feared, and it was the Iran that I grew to enjoy. Baba was, after all, right. Gymnastics separated me from my childhood world of daily prayers, from recitations of the Qur'an, of the *hadiths,* and of *Nahj al Balaghah* [the sayings of Ali]. I used to attend, before my days in the stadium, the lectures by such popular preachers as Falsafi, Kafi, and Ansari. I had learned about the "Wahabi teachings of Ali Shariati," the theoretician of the Islamic Revolution. But both Kafi and Ansari had been core enemies of Shariati's version of Islam. One of my brothers called these preachers *adam khar kun* [those who turn people into donkeys]. I defended these preachers. Gradually, however, I moved away from my father's religious positions. I saw the *hadith* being misused. I found Aga-i Gharavi's problem-posing during the *masalahguyi* to be unethical. I found Baba's views forbidding radio and television unbearable, as I did the focus on ritual [*qusl*] in religion. Even the recitation of the Qur'an in Arabic bothered me. In protest I began to pray in Persian. As I quietly revolted against my father's world, his views were in fact gaining currency with the future revolution and the promise of the Islamic Republic.

What most confused me while growing up were words like *khain* and *khudfurush,* and people like the Shah and Khomeini, or symbols like *kishvar* [nation] and *parcham* [flag]. These words shifted in value depending on where you were. In school, the Shah was good and Khomeini was bad. But among Baba's friends the Shah was bad and Aga Khomeini was good. But yet, I was never supposed to repeat this in school. Likewise, the flag was raised every day in school, but never in the bazaar. One day, quite unknowingly, I planted the Iranian flag by Baba's shop in the Bazaar of Sayyid Ismail. Baba slapped me hard when he found out that I had done that. I still feel the weight of my father's hand across my face whenever I look at the Iranian flag. After the beating, Baba told me that "we" never raise the flag because that would mean we were *dowlati* [believers in the State].

The distinction between "we" and the *dowlat* was something that I reflected on years later, after the Islamic Revolution, while writing a history dissertation at the University of Chicago on the revolutions of 1906 and 1979.

Lily

I interviewed Lily in a restaurant in Chicago in 1992. I met her through Pari with whom she had worked in Tehran in the 1960s and 1970s. Born in 1930 in Tehran, Lily has worked as a teacher, a writer, and a translator. One of many women who worked within the system to change the education of teachers and of children from reinforcing a unitary model of ethics and class identity to educating Iranians in their difference, Lily hired Pari at Franklin Publications and then helped her through her early work with children's literature. Lily speaks of her childhood, her family, her schooling and move to Moscow, her education, her marriage, and the politics of work and censorship in the 1960s and 1970s. Because Lily predicated her rewriting of texts and teaching methodology on questioning the "submission" demanded by the dictates of the State, her style of education would have met with disapproval under the Shah or the current regime. She continued to write books after she left Iran in 1979. She currently lives and teaches in the United States.

I was born into an Iranian family privileged with highly educated men and women. What made my paternal family elite was not wealth but education. My mother was Russian. She came to Iran at the end of the First World War to marry the man she loved, my father. My father, who had finished his higher education in political science at Moscow University, was the third child of a large, traditional Persian family. He was a fervent nationalist and believed that to serve Iran and its people was our most sacred duty. Although we were brought up as Muslims, we were not a very religious family. We were taught respect for other people's religions and beliefs.

My mother, a Christian, became a believing Muslim by her own wish. Try to imagine yourself as a young Russian woman seventy-five years ago, coming to Iran, a young woman who had completed her studies at the music conservatory of Moscow and St. Petersburg in singing and piano, and who, because of the war, had become a trained nurse as well. This educated, European girl in her mid-twenties had decided to become a Muslim because to her there was only one God, and different religions were simply a matter of difference of rituals.

She used to say, "It doesn't matter to God how we pray to Him or in what language." She felt that if becoming Muslim would make her more accepted in a new culture and in a new family, she should do that. But she did not do it out of hypocrisy. She really became a Muslim. Her most sacred vow was *"Be Ali, or Be Hazrat Abbas"* ["I swear on Ali or St. Abbas"].

She had many stories of her early days in Iran. This is one of my favorites. Once, when she was still nursing her firstborn, my aunts took her for pilgrimage to a religious shrine. While encircled by other women in the shrine, suddenly, her *chador* slipped off, revealing a bit of her golden hair. An angry mullah ran up to them and said, "Who is this *farangi* [foreigner]?" My mother said, "I am not a *farangi*, I am a Muslim." The astonished mullah said, "Well, if you're a Muslim, throw a stone on that rock you see over there. If you are truly a Muslim the stone will stick to the rock, and if not, we will tear you to pieces because you have soiled this sacred place." My mother was scared to death as she knew that a stone was not going to stick to a rock. So she said, "God, you know that I did not lie, that I have become a Muslim, and that I'm here with all my faith. So, please, do something so that the stone will stick to the rock." Then she picked up a stone, closed her eyes, threw it. And it stuck! Screams of joy filled the air. The women were trying to tear her chador to pieces, as an omen of good luck. Later on, she went to see what had made the stone stick to the rock. She noticed that the rock surface was one on which candles had been lit; the stone had stuck to the wax.

I was the youngest child of our family. I saw very little of my always-busy father, who died before I was seventeen, yet I have wonderful memories of him. He was very strict, very moral, and very loving. Every Friday I was expected to recite a Persian poem to him. Regardless of his demanding schedule, he would find time to read poetry with us and sit and talk. My mother, too, was an extremely loving woman with a very lively mind. All our friends loved her company. Her open house on Tuesdays was always filled with young people. And they used to say, "We didn't come to see you, we came to see Maman"—our mother. She was the second person who became a member of the Philharmonic Society in Iran. We all started our music lessons with her. My childhood memories are of her playing piano and singing for us, but then in the Iran of those times, public performance was not acceptable for ladies from good families.

My father, however, respected her talent and got her a piano even then, sixty-five years ago, and she respected the customs of the land. This is an example of how our family combined traditional and modern Persian ways—modern, in a good sense of the word, not *Gharbzadegi* [Westoxification], which my father hated. He felt that if we adopted something from the West, we should know why and understand its implications within our culture.

My father was twice in prison. Having a Russian wife in an Iran afraid of Communism was not an asset. Furthermore, he was a politically outspoken person. Nevertheless, he occupied high positions in the government. He was governor of Fars, minister of the cabinet, and an ambassador. He was also asked to become prime minister, but he declined the offer.

When did you first became aware of difference and of minorities in Iran?
I remember how I was introduced to the treatment of minorities as a child. Once when I was a child in primary school—I attended a Zoroastrian school— I became suddenly aware that some of the schoolchildren were singing ugly and obscene songs about Baha'is. I would see the Baha'i girls crying but not saying anything. One day I went to my father and I told him, "In school, the children are singing very dirty songs about a man called Abbas Effendi and there are a group of children who cry when they hear this. Who is this man and why are the children crying?" He told me, "Now remember two things. Never repeat those songs and never befriend those children who sing them." He never told me who Abbas Effendi was! What my father taught me that day was reverence toward other people's feelings. A lot of issues that now are public issues of human rights, I learned to address through family experiences.

I remember the third of Shahrivar, 1320 (1941) when Reza Shah was forced to abdicate. I was eleven. My father was Minister of Justice. And I remember the news of the invasion; we heard the bombing. It was the end of the summer of 1941. We were in Zargandeh, high on the slopes of hills from where we could see flashes. We were always worried during the bombings because we never knew whether my father was all right. And then I remember my father calling from work one day and saying, "It is finished. He is leaving. *He* is leaving." That meant Reza Shah. And there was a lot of whispering among the adults that I couldn't understand. Later, on the twenty-fifth of Shahrivar, the young Shah—Mohamad Reza Pahlavi—was supposed to be sworn in. By that time we were back in Tehran from Zargardeh. That day, I remember as if it were yesterday, father came back from the parliament, his face drawn and completely tired. I was a child and full of excitement. I ran to him and said, "Well, congratulations with the new king," and he answered, "Yes, yes, yes, let's hope that it will be an era for congratulations." After all, the young king was only twenty-five. And when we were at table that evening, my mother asked, "Why are you so worried?" He said, "You know, he's a very kind-hearted man, but he's very weak. And the future of Iran depends on who his entourage is going to be. If he surrounds himself with people who only flatter him, we can forget about it." That's what happened.

When were you first politicized?
It was during the period after Reza Shah that I started being politicized. I became all eyes and ears. I read a lot and I listened. I listened to foreign news. I knew three languages—French, Russian, and Persian. And I was really alert to what was going on in the world. The war, the persecution of the Jews. At that

time I was in the seventh grade and I was twelve years old. It was the fashion of that time to be pro-German because the Germans were against Britain and Russia, and because Hitler played with the Iranian need for racial superiority. My father was much against this and told us there was no such thing as "race," that when people used the term, it was really politics they were talking about.

Who do you believe most influenced you in your later love for books?
First, there was our storytelling cook, Ali Akbar, who knew the *Shahnameh* by heart. I remember, I had a little stool that I would take with me into the kitchen to listen to his stories while he cooked. In addition to those fascinating times in the kitchen, I also had a great storyteller in my *naneh* (nanny)—the greatest storyteller in the world—and all the old Iranian folktales I now know come from her. And then, of course, I had my mother who was an avid reader herself. I well recall that we had a huge walnut wood trunk that was always filled with books from which my mother would find wonderful things to read to us. My first storybooks were Russian storybooks because during my childhood till I was about ten or eleven, there were no printed Persian books for children. So my introduction to literature came from Russian, then French, and then gradually Persian books.

When I was thirteen my father became ambassador to the USSR. I finished my high school in the Soviet Union with honors at the age of sixteen and entered the Institute for Foreign Languages. After the war, in 1946, we came back to Iran, and a week later I lost my father. My whole life changed.

Tell us about your education and work history.
The Moscow years were very important in teaching me the value of education. Because my father was an advocate of women's rights and observed the work of women in the USSR, I came to appreciate my identity as a woman. From being a girl whose only ideal was to become just a good mother, I have become a person with social ideals. After my father's death, I tried to study medical sciences, but didn't like it. So I transferred to the study of philosophy and education, and that's where I met my husband, Iraj.

I finished with honors and I got a degree that also qualified me to work as a teacher. After a year of teaching, I went to London, and after a few months Iraj and I got married. I left London University and went to Edinburgh where Iraj was a student of psychology. I started work towards a Ph.D. in child psychology. But then the crisis over the nationalization of oil happened (1952), and we were forced to return to Iran before completing our studies.

Because Iraj was a Baha'i, it was not easy for him to find a job in the Ministry of Education or in any educational field. A few years later, Iraj got a grant to pursue his Ph.D. in the United States. So we came to the United States where I worked and Iraj completed his Ph.D. in psychology and management. After he completed his Ph.D., he suggested that now it was his turn to work and for me to complete my Ph.D. But I decided not to. I said, "What will I need a Ph.D. for? What would I do with it?" I did not wish to teach at the university. I was more interested in educating children. In fact, I believed that the fewer degrees you had, the better your chances for getting things done in Iran, because then one was not alienating others. I also felt that having two Ph.D.s in a family may cause difficulties. I did not wish conflicts to arise where I might hear myself saying, "But why did I get the doctorate?" After Iraj completed his Ph.D. we returned to Iran with our two daughters in 1956.

It was during my work for the Ministry of Education that I discovered corruption and how superfluous all the so-called reforms were. For instance, our department would set up a counseling program, but the administration would make it impossible for a teacher to spare time for counseling. We developed educational files in which student records should have been entered. But nobody entered the necessary material into the files. We worked at standardizing tests that I discovered were never used.

I resigned and looked for another job. About the same time the Ministry of Education and the Ford Foundation and Franklin Publications started a project to send educators to study the preparation of textbooks in different fields for elementary and secondary schools. I was chosen as a member of that group. This completely changed my life.

We were to modify the content and methodology of teaching in schools. Our main goal was to make the students think, to help them become creative. That is why we developed careful teachers' guides to accompany the textbooks. But when we found out that our teachers' guides were not getting to the teachers, we decided to beat the system. Samineh Baghcheban and I, with no reimbursement from the Ministry of Education, initiated three teacher-training courses. In teacher-training institutes we trained teacher-trainers, and in our methodology classes we insisted on the importance of critical thinking.

But, we were a nation of followers instead of a nation of thinkers and decision makers. This was a source of our cultural weakness. And this is what I wished to change.

Unfortunately, what we learned from Islam was blind submission and obedience. This suited both the government and the clergy. They needed to keep the people ignorant and in need. The logic was that society had politicians and religious leaders to do our thinking and the masses simply had to follow the rules. But my mission as a writer and teacher-trainer was to change this and to make people think. I remember that even as a young history teacher I used dialectical approaches to history. Then reports reached the Minister of Education that this strange teacher doesn't make children memorize facts and dates about kings. Instead she asks why the events happened the way they did. Fortunately nobody reacted badly to such reports.

I have followed this educational commitment throughout my career as an author of children's books as well as a teacher. After working at the

Textbook Institute, in 1964 I brought into life a new and beautiful project—
Paik magazine—that later was developed by a dear friend, Iraj Djahanshahi. I
did not stay long with this project—the stress of editing periodicals was too
much. I left to join the Committee for Literacy Campaign, and there I spent
the last fifteen years of my working life in Iran.

I am always thankful for this period in my life because I felt that, finally, I
was in some ways in real contact with the people of my country, Iran. This
was a wonderful experience to know that I was not only working in Tehran. In
Tehran I always felt uneasy writing books in a big city for unseen children who
lived behind the hills in small towns and villages far away. It was ridiculous, I
thought, to have one text for a country as big and as diverse as Iran. But I never
got anywhere with my argument because the administrators in the Ministry
of Education did not understand or did not care to realize that having different
textbooks did not mean having different standards of education. They were
hiding behind the fear that, by using different books in rural and urban areas,
they would be accused of using a lower standard for rural education.

I argued that you can't address a child in Kurdistan or in Baluchistan who is
part of a nomadic tribe with the same language and stories that you use for a
child brought up in the suburbs of Tehran. No one was interested. Certainly we
could use stories from our common heritage—like the *Shahnameh* or *Kalileh
and Dimneh*—for both rural and urban schools. But we also made sure that
the children in the books were not all given modern, fashionable names like
FiFi and FuFu. Instead, they were called Ahmad and Kobra. I wanted so much
to have Baluchi stories and Kurdish tales for the children. I wanted to talk
about the nomads of Iran. This was not possible in the Ministry of Education
textbooks. But just a few years before the revolution, the Committee for
Literacy Campaign was finally able to achieve this goal.

This is where I should mention the name of that wonderful writer Samad
Behrangi. It was through Jalal Al-e-Ahmad that I got to know him in the 1960s;
I asked him to help us write the book for Azari children, and he did. But
when the book was ready, he unexpectedly said, "I cannot give it to you." The
reason was this: he could not compromise his political integrity to include
the required prefatory tribute to the Shah—the rule for all textbooks.

Early in our work we had decided to compromise, so that in the first reader
we would introduce the Shah in the course of teaching the letters of the
alphabet. "Iran has a Shah. The Shah loves the people. Iran has a Queen."
Nothing more. I asked Behrangi to accept this to avoid trouble. He refused. I
was very upset because I saw a dream shattered on some political whim. A
few months later, Samad met his tragic death.[4] Only then was that textbook
for Azari children published. We dedicated the book to Samad Behrangi.

This book, however, got me into trouble with SAVAK—because I had to
answer to lots of questions. Why a special book for Azarbaijanis? Why was it
dedicated to Samad? They questioned me every two or three weeks at their

headquarters. In the Committee for Literacy Campaign I also worked with about forty students, most of whom were revolutionaries. When officials brought the "book" of the Rastakhiz Party to be signed, I told them, "Feel free. If you want to sign, sign—if you don't want to sign, do not sign. I myself will not. The book I wrote is a sign of my love for my country, its people and constitution. But I do not want to become a member of the Rastakhiz Party." I was warned that I might lose my job, but I didn't. This is what was different under the Shah; we finally did not have to step on our own principles. We had some choice.

Later we published different texts for rural children, women, and men. But it was too late. The revolution came with all its force.

Tell about any memories of the end of Pahlavi rule.
The Shah's last masquerade was the celebration of 2,500 years of monarchy. Everything was superficial. An example: our Committee for Literacy Campaign decided not to do anything flashy for the occasion. The decision we made was to build twenty-five hundred schools in twenty-five hundred villages where there were no schools. They built the schools, but they were so flimsily constructed that after two or three years they began to disintegrate. The gesture toward twenty-five hundred schools was done in a way to say that we've done it. And God knows who got the money saved in the construction project.

In 1977, I learned that I was appointed by a royal decree to become a member of the Imperial Commission for Education. At first I was furious, as I did not want to have any connections with the court and I wished to resign. I learned that one could not resign a post given by royal decree. So I told the Minister to the Shah that at least I needed the freedom to say what I had to say. This commission headed by the Shah and Farah met only two times, and those were both very memorable meetings. Fortunately the sessions were taped and should still exist. In those meetings I spoke openly about our educational problems and about corruption in the system. The last time I saw the Shah he looked very strange. He was extremely tense and bad-humored. I did not know that he had cancer. It was during that session that I had the chance to reveal to him the story of the twenty-five hundred schools. The Shah kept saying, "This is not what they told me." I said, "Your Majesty, don't believe whatever you're told." "Does your Majesty know," I asked, "that the opening of schools has been delayed because of the lack of desks and chairs? Why do we need chairs and desks as long as we have a teacher and children? Please ask them to open the schools." And the Shah asked, "But where are the children going to sit?" I said, "Where do they sit when they are at home?" He said, "You mean for them to sit on the floor?" I said, "Sure, what problem could there be with sitting on the floor? Let them each bring a mat to sit on if you don't want them to sit on the floor. You surely must know that our children live in dust everywhere." He said, "Yes, but they may catch rheumatism." And I looked at him and said, "Rheumatism? In Yazd and Baluchistan where you cannot find a trickle of water?" And he got up and left the room in anger. And Farah ran behind him and then she came and said, "His Majesty doesn't feel good." That was in the autumn of 1978.

We left Iran in 1979. I saw the Shah leave. I experienced the Spring of Freedom. It was a very strange feeling. I was not young enough to share the ecstasy of youth. But I was not old enough to lose my faith in the people and say that all our life depends on the king and that we would be lost without him. I had grown angry with the Shah toward the end and was very much in favor of some sort of radical change.

Hamid Naficy

Pari and I interviewed Hamid Naficy in his apartment in Venice Beach in March 1990. He was then teaching film studies at UCLA and completing his dissertation. Born in Isfahan in 1944, educated in Iran and in the United States, he is the author of many studies including The Making of Exile Culture: Iranian Television in Los Angeles *(1993). He currently teaches media studies at Rice University in Houston. Although Pari and Hamid Naficy are from the same class and the same town—Isfahan—their recollections of childhood, of home, of family, and of adjustment to the United States are quite different. Yet his stories of books and the family magazines made Pari remember that she too had participated in such ventures in childhood. But as in the cases of Pari, Tahereh, Rebwar, and others, the repressive state apparatus produced the desire for what it denied. It became the source of the erotics of knowledge and of a secret life that, as Hamid tells it, is characteristically Persian—hermeneutically intense and constantly subject to interpretation. This part of Hamid's story is also revealing of the possibilities available, for the first time, to innovative educators in the 1970s during the Pahlavi regime.*

I think more than anything else what made me was first the culture of the family. I was born in Isfahan. Our family was a large, extended family like most families in Iran but it was also very diversified in terms of class structure and outlook, religious training, Westernization, and professionalism. The immediate family—my parents and their immediate families, my aunts and uncles on both sides and their children and so forth—formed a unit that constituted or produced its own culture that was different from the culture of the country.

Our family culture was essentially oppositional and has continued to be so. It was and is a family culture in opposition to whatever the dominant ideology might be. It was not only a secular intellectual family but, I must add, a religiously intellectual family. We always created things. From childhood on we created, for example, handwritten magazines for and by all the children in the family. I was one of the editors.

The magazine would include editorials; it would include a few stories and relevant illustrations. It would include excerpts from books we had read and found interesting. It would include pages of jokes and items of comedy, sketches and so forth. Then this magazine would be passed around from member to member in the family. Our work on this family magazine also involved certain other activities—establishing a library, a family library, not just a private library within the individual families, but a sort of communal family library. And ours had about three thousand books in it. And remember, all this was done by children under the age of eighteen.

Who encouraged us to do this? It was there. In the beginning was the library, like in the beginning was the word. It was there from, from as long as I can remember.

My father is a physician and my mother is a housewife; my father's father was a teacher and my mother's father was a doctor and a businessman in the bazaar. My father's family goes back to Kerman and my mother's goes back to Isfahan. We have had eight generations of physicians in my father's family.

My idea of family is not of a nuclear family; it includes uncles, aunts, cousins, children, and grandparents. And I suppose most people use their own family subconsciously as a model for their new family and I probably do that. I try to repair some of what I saw as problems with my original model—with my parents. My father was very busy because as a medical man he was always in demand to make house-calls, and so he was not around during the week. But during the weekend he was. And I, because I was a boy, was part of his world. I went out with him and his friends on outings. Every Friday morning, before the sun came up, we'd go to the mountains for a walk.

This outing with the men ended around 9:00 a.m. Then he would go out with his family— his wife and kids and other extended family members— who would all get together to go to some garden or place in the country. So on weekends there were two outings.

The library was set up basically at my grandmother's house by my father's brothers. He had eight brothers, one of whom was younger than me. My uncles and myself and a couple of other family members were involved in the creation of this library, and also even earlier than that we were involved in creating a minigovernment—for ourselves. One person would be the Minister of Roads—I occupied that position—somebody else would be the Minister of Education, and so on. My grandmother's house was huge. So we would set up miniature models of schools that we would actually build with mud. We would build roads and construct our own cars out of cardboard or wood. The older members of this group, my uncles, would do that for the younger ones; in those days plastic and model cars were not available. So we were creative not only in making things but also in manufacturing imaginary institutions and magazines, which, when we grew up, we passed on to the younger kids in the family. And there was not only one magazine. Several magazines evolved. The names changed according to who was in charge at the time.

Our legacy was not the magazine itself but rather the idea of actually doing something for and within the family. It also included outings, children's group outings to the countryside on bicycles. Our library, very well organized, charged a small fee for borrowed books, but whatever money we got went back into the library to replenish itself. We made a long list of our collection of books in a notebook—pretty organized!

With the intensification of surveillance by SAVAK we basically had to disband the library. Because any such organization seemed at that time to be oppositional, revolutionary, or against the establishment. In some ways it was, but it was not a directly political opposition. It was a way of creating our own culture that was clearly opposed to the culture of spectacle that the Shah at the time was trying to inculcate—the kind of cultural spectacle represented by the celebration of 2,500 years of Iranian monarchy, by his coronation, by the year-long celebration of the fiftieth anniversary of the Pahlavi dynasty, and various other efforts at creating an official ideology. In a way this library and what it stood for was opposed to that because it encouraged people to read, to read the literature of the world in translation and also a lot of Iranian books. It became the focus for plays that we put on, some of which were written by us kids, and some of which were plays that others had written like Bahram Beizaii's *Char Sandoq* [Four Boxes].

Adults were not involved in our projects other than as spectators. They would be invited to come to the theater show and we would have some eighty people in attendance watching their kids or their family members perform. We also had exhibits, art exhibits, in someone's house where the artwork of the kids of the family was set up on the walls. So this is the kind of family culture important in my formation.

I sensed my family's openness to everything we did. I recall very clearly how they came to our theater performances, how they clapped at the end and how I really savored all the attention and all that was happening. And of course part of this family culture has to be understood in terms of its elitism. Their encouragement of our theatrics was also a way to discourage us from going outside the family for culture and entertainment.

I lived in Isfahan from 1944 to 1962. During this period I became fascinated with film and cinema and have published a theorized account of my relation to cinema in *Emergences*.

When did you first become aware of politics and its complexities? Could you trace its stages?
Very early. I remember the Mossadeq era very clearly. I remember how we used to pass around those little ten *shais* [coins] that had engraved on them *Zindebad Mossadeq* [Long Live Mossadeq]. SAVAK was formed in 1957, post-

Mossadeq. I think SAVAK became important and increasingly visible and threatening in the 1960s after the Shah's White Revolution. But because we were involved with literature and with poetry and because I and one of my brothers who was a poet were involved with poetry and literary circles in Isfahan and Tehran, which were outside the family, we knew a lot about the kinds of pressures SAVAK exerted on writers and artists.

The effect of SAVAK on our family life began when one of my brothers was arrested. And it's at that point that we decided to disband the library. He had been charged with passing leaflets against the Shah. So we divided up the library among family members. It was a sad disintegration and dis-memberment. The log book of our library, which included a list of who had borrowed what and when, was buried in someone's garden so nobody could see the list because it could become a very dangerous hit list. And I burned in the mid-1970s fifteen years of my letters to my parents from England and America, which they had received and kept in Iran. I burned them because I wanted to have nothing left for anybody to use against the family, because when you write letters you don't necessarily censor yourself politically. And you talk about people. For all I know SAVAK may have seen those letters in transit through the postal system and not said anything about them. I mean this is a part of the treachery of state censorship, both before and after the revolution, that leads to self-censorship. But in retrospect, it's a shame that that happened. On the other hand, at the time there was a lot of fear. And fear was what SAVAK tried to inculcate in the people—the sense that they were monolithic and everywhere, and that you couldn't do anything about it.

But they were not as monolithic as they might have wished because they operated within an Iranian context and were necessarily subject to all the complexities and blind spots of Iranian society and culture. And so the idea that you would have a super-efficient system operating in an inefficient society was ludicrous—and this fallacy was exposed later. People claimed that SAVAK had one hundred thousand members; we later learned that three thousand was perhaps closer to the figure.

Politicization for me was a continuous process. Politicization came with books and with associating with those who read books. We would read books that are innocuous now, but in those days, reading Jack London's books, *The Iron Heel*, for example, was a banned activity. However, we read and exchanged his books clandestinely among friends. The same was true about *The Grapes of Wrath*. The first translation of *The Grapes of Wrath* was banned and we exchanged that, too, under the table among ourselves. So politicization was a process that involved or maybe began with books.

This is the 1950s we're discussing. Mohammad Masoud was a famous editor of a newspaper called *Mard-e Imruz* [Man of Today] and he was a rabble-rousing journalist who tried to expose the corruption of the government and royal family. There were friends of ours who were jailed because they were either close to a *Tudehi* or were themselves *Tudehi* or were reputed to be *Tudehi* or had been *Tudehi*. There were also certain poets who wrote poetry in ways that needed decoding. The poems would be read differently by different people. Ahmad Shamlu's poetry was read by my poetry group very intensely. To use the language of today, we engaged in a deconstruction of the official culture. We became skilled interpreters. All Iranians, in fact, are skilled interpreters. That is a characteristic of our culture that makes our lives hermeneutically very intense. We don't usually take anything at face value. There's always a subtext we learn to read from childhood on. It creates problems of its own, but in terms of hermeneutic strategies Iranians are very good at interpretation and that's why they're also good conspiracy theorists.

Tell me about the history of your work in Iran.
When I first left Iran I was eighteen years old. I went to England for about eight tough, cold months to a boarding school in Lancaster. From 1964 to 1973, I was in the United States getting a B.A. and an M.F.A. in film and television. I was intimately involved in the U.S. counterculture movement; I lived in a commune; and I produced and directed film and television programs for Group W Cable in Los Angeles.

I returned to Iran in 1973 and I came out in 1978. During these years, I was helping to establish a new university called the Free University of Iran—*Daneshgah-e Azad-e Iran*. The idea for this university was the result of a study conducted by an Iranian scholar—Abdolrahim Ahmadi, one of the translators of the banned *Grapes of Wrath*—to explore the possibility of creating a university that was based in part on the Open University in England. And perhaps to some extent on the Free University in Berlin.

The prime minister at the time, Amir Abbas Hoveyda, liked the idea, liked Ahmadi's written evaluation of the open university system, and asked him to develop a proposal for Iran. I was asked to help. The planning project was set up by five people. It took us three years to draw up the plans for the university, to have it approved by the Prime Minister and the Shah, and to get the go-ahead to go into the execution phase. We did. And the university was established in 1975. It took in its first students in 1978. It was a very unusual experiment in Iran because it was not a residential university. It didn't have any campus as such to which students had to come. It was a multimedia university. Its academic core consisted of course teams comprising faculty members in different fields—educational technologists, film and TV producers, and book editors. It was a group-oriented project. Existing textbooks were not used; rather, members of these course teams sat down together, designed a course, and allocated which aspect of it would be carried in print, which aspect would be done as television or radio programs, and which aspect would require a kit to be designed for scientific experiments at home.

To accomplish these goals, the university established a sophisticated print-ing plant and a kit manufacturing plant. It had a television, radio, and film center that I headed and that worked with the Iranian National Radio and Television to produce and broadcast those shows. Some very interesting books were also created by these course teams. The university also established some twenty centers across the country, mostly in small towns, where students could go for counseling purposes and for taking exams. There they would find copies of TV and radio programs, reference books, as well as a larger laboratory for more elaborate experiments. Those students taking science courses would receive a kit though the mail that allowed them to carry out experiments in their home kitchens.

So, you see, it was a very elaborate system requiring interconnection among a range of organizations external to the university. For example, it required that the post office be responsible and accountable. For the first time in the country we conducted our entrance examination nationally, in twenty centers, and not in Tehran alone. The idea was basically to decentralize, to avoid bringing everybody to the capital or to the central cities for their education. The idea was to democratize education, to take education to where people lived, thereby reducing immigration from rural areas to urban centers. This would allow the man who is needed on the farm to work on it during the day, and at night to educate himself, to read his textbooks, or to watch the television programs. Ideally, it was a revolutionary experiment. But when the revolution of 1978–79 came, it was closed down as an emblem of untoward Western influence. It was combined with some other educational units to create new universities, such as Allameh Tabatabai University in Tehran. They retained the name *Daneshgar-e Azad* but changed the Iran in the title to Islami—a change emblematic of postrevolutionary change. But the new *Islamic Free University* was not the same as the *Free University of Iran.* It was basically a second-rate correspondence school. But then a few years later, they started a new *Nur* University (The University of Light), which, I am told, is patterned on the original idea of the Free University.

Although four out of five of the original planners are all out of the country now, there were many others the new regime could draw upon. By the time I left Iran, we had some seven hundred people working at the university.

I left Iran in 1978 because I had asked for a sabbatical two years earlier and it was approved to start at just about the time the tanks were coming to the streets, and I left because of that. I had no idea of staying abroad for a long time. After a year I would have returned.

Mehrnaz Saeed-Vafa

I talked with Mehrnaz Saeed-Vafa in February 1992 in her office at Columbia College in Chicago where she teaches at the department of Film and Video. After receiving her MFA in Film from the University of Illinois at Chicago in 1987, she taught at the school of Television and Cinema in Tehran from 1978 to 1983. Among her many short films screened in several festivals are "The Silent Majority," "Ruins Within," "Far from Home," and her award-winning documentary, "A Tajik Woman." Currently at work on a book entitled Home in Exile *on film director Abbas Kiarostami, she has been artistic consultant of the Iranian film festival at the Film Center in Chicago and has written and lectured extensively on Iranian cinema. She came to the United States in 1983. I started with the usual question about the forces of family, religion, and culture responsible for her early formation.*

I belong to a generation of confused children. Confused because I was born during the time of the Pahlavi—the last Shah—and because my mother was a professional woman, a doctor. I wasn't born into what might be considered a traditional family. It was a divided family. On one hand it was traditional in terms of its expectations of female roles. On the other I was encouraged by the family to be educated, to be professional, and to further my studies outside Iran. I received consistently mixed messages. Women, I was told, had to be highly educated, but women also had to be subservient. Women had to be educated, but women had to get married very young so that they could start having children young and get used to being subservient to their husbands. But because I could see the stupidity of many husbands, I couldn't see why my entire life should be determined by a man whose wisdom was at best unreliable. My confusion started at this point.

I was also confused by the rigidity of values dictated by our society—the way women had to look, entertain, and dress. Westernization seemed to be admired, but not Westernized clothing or such Western behavior as mixed-sex schools or socializing between the sexes. So, caught in a double standard,

I was expected magically to negotiate both standards of values and behavior, and maintain both.

That dual standard was both public and private—something I saw first within my own household. My mother experienced my father's double standards. He didn't want her to work outside the home, but he enjoyed her income and the lack of responsibility it afforded him. He didn't see the value in her work—that my mother was needed, wanted, and appreciated by her patients. She worked in a free clinic in the south of Tehran—Naziabad—as a gynecologist. Her patients loved her, not only because they would not go to a male doctor, but also because they couldn't afford another doctor. Her treatment was free. My mother also educated her patients by showing them films and by training nurses. So the women simply worshiped her. Her conflict was this: Should she conform to my father's will and wishes, or should she take care of her patients?

On the other hand—and here's the double standard—my father was the kind of man who flirted casually and easily with other women. Not so casually really, because eventually after thirty-four years [of marriage] and four children he divorced my mother and married his secretary, who was thirty years younger than him.

This was the pain of the double standard—he was forcing my mother to give up her job to stay home so that he could go and marry someone else.

My mother understood that and said to him, "If you want to flirt with other women or get married, go ahead and do that, but I will not leave my job." Yet he chose to divorce her and did. My understanding of this double standard began then in childhood—I understood that men, my father, worshiped women who were intellectual, educated, and professional; yet at the same time they were afraid of them. My father was a bank accountant, certainly not as satisfying a job as my mother's, and he was jealous of my mother's job, of her importance, of her being wanted by her patients. Yet I witnessed and suffered with my mother as she endured the years of my father's mistreatment of her.

So for me the question as I was growing up was this: Is it better to have a successful private life with a man, or to be a successful professional woman in the service of people? I understood then that it was impossible to have them both together. Women who were pursuing ambition and talent were feared by husbands who could not control them. Sometimes they would split up. They would not have a "normal" Iranian family life. But I also saw a lot of women wishing to be like my mother, to have four kids and a "good" husband. I never saw a role model, a woman, who had both. In fact, to this day I have not met an Iranian man who sincerely desires a woman who is aware, professional, and independent. They may like such a woman as a friend, but when it comes to a wife, then they want someone they can control, either a very young woman they can mold like my stepmother, or a woman who doesn't know much. They can't deal with women of ambition.

Why can't Iranian men deal with this? The habit has five thousand years of history behind it. There is a great fear of women who might be economically independent and emotionally independent. There is a great fear that if a woman is not dependent, she might leave you. I have experienced this in my own field—that men feel safe as long as you are flirting with them. But if you don't define yourself within a pattern of seductive cuteness, or if you threaten them with serious professionalism, you will be seen as a rival and be given a hard time.

Did religion play a significant part in your family or in your life? Were there contradictions in religion that bothered you growing up?
As a child I was very religious. Even as an eight-year-old I covered my head. Although my father discouraged me from praying and fasting, saying I was stupid, I continued to do so until I was a teenager. But I soon gave up on it—I saw too much hypocrisy. I needed religion as a child as the only sanctuary from the insanity inside my family. And I developed a religious spirituality that saved me.

But recently I feel a need to return to my old spirituality, to connections that could be tapped. Part of my attraction is to the rituals, but part of that is an attraction to a larger connection, to a larger spirituality, and perhaps for me filmmaking is a version of that sort of connection, a kind of spirituality.

My problem with the Islam that I grew up with is that, as in Iranian households and culture, it fails to encourage you to be responsible for your own life; it denies power to women and gives control once again to men. In the household, the father decides for everyone else. Now if Islam welcomed women and allowed us positions of power within religion, I would be the first in line. Everything for me starts in the family—the father is supposed to be the figure of authority, but when he is crazy himself, that leaves a huge need.

How did you grow to understand gender roles within your particular family structure and within the career choices you eventually made?
My father was also very strict with us girls in other ways [besides religion]: he refused to allow us to go out with our brother to places where there might be boys, and he refused to let us go out with girls. This was from about 1969–74, throughout my teenage years. So I gave up. He felt that daughters should be protected within the home, that the outside was dangerous and dirty, that people would gossip, that men were dirty and should not be trusted. And because my father was a very frightening man, my mother didn't dare to contradict his stance. So I painted and studied in my room at home—but that displeased him, too. He would get worried at my staying within closed doors. The point is that I was totally controlled by this man. What I have experienced, despite coming from an open-minded middle-class family, is that I could do only what was totally approved of by men who were assumed to be wiser. My

father would advise us to dress modestly, never to go out, only to be seen by guests who came into our house. Society, he said, was dirty. But I saw other families with different standards.

I have stories to tell about how I grew up, about how I arrived where I now am, and that story and struggle would be important for other Iranian women going through the same thing. The obstacles and problems were many. In high school, for instance, I wanted to study Iranian literature and I loved art and painting. But my father discouraged me. He said that this was not a worthwhile field, not lucrative. And my mother said that if I wished to succeed as a woman in Iranian society, I should be a doctor. Only then, she said, will you be both needed and respected. They felt that I would be miserable and unwanted as an artist, that I would get joy only out of being wanted and needed. Unfortunately, I was not cut out to be a doctor. I went with my mother to her clinic where the women could not afford painkillers and I heard women scream until they delivered their babies, and the combination of blood and screaming made me sick. My mother loved it and I would faint. My brother, however, became a doctor. And my sister is a nuclear physicist.

So I thought there was nothing I could study, nothing I was good for, that I was useless, that there was nothing I could amount to. My father suggested that I enter economics and business. I did and hated it although I passed the courses.

But I was dead for four years. As a teenager I had memorized three thousand poems/verses. I knew and loved art—but my father would destroy my paintings. He would discourage me from reading books—if you read books, he said, you will become introverted, sad, and depressed. Do something simple, study business, work, and get married.

I felt that life was hopeless, that I was nothing, that I didn't wish to marry any of the men who formally proposed for me to my family. And because of my mother's problems with my father, I also lost hope in married life. I thought that even if you were beautiful, talented, loyal, and professional, and an excellent housewife—which my mother was—that none of it worked, that men could still leave you and betray you at any age. And still you could be miserable. So very early I decided not to get married. I didn't want another man like my father to control my life.

I wanted to find something I couldn't find—work I liked—until by chance I took a class in the school of Film and Television recently opened in Tehran and suddenly I was so happy and wondered, is this serious work or is this a hobby? It seemed like too much fun to be serious work or study. When teachers gave over a few classes to me I suddenly realized that four years of my life had been wasted in hell—in business and economics. I started studying film at the age of twenty-three, and after a few months there was a revolution within me that made me revolt against my father and my family, who finally gave in and sent me to England.

There I attended the London Film School. Now in Iran I couldn't have imagined being a film director—that, I thought, was a job for men. I thought, well, okay, I'll be a film editor. But then I got an opportunity to make my first student films and both films won awards. The first was called "The End of a Dream" and was about an Iranian immigrant family in London who, pressured by their illegal status, are divided by the husband's corruption and by the wife's unhappiness. It ends with their young daughter lost and abandoned on the streets of London. This won the Best Student Film award and was sent to such places as Melbourne, Australia, for showings. I made another film called "Rooms" about a boardinghouse with housemates who lead parallel lives, who come and go and don't ever know each other. But one of the tenants has a heart attack, is taken to the hospital, and returns to find that someone else (he finds women's clothes and underwear) has occupied his place. This was a story of displacement.

After this success (1974–75) I gained self-confidence, broke into film, started writing about film, was employed by Iranian TV, started to teach at the School of Cinema and Television, and wrote scripts. I realized how hungry and thirsty my students were for the courses I taught and how much this field was needed and appreciated. After the revolution, the only woman kept at this school was me. They kept me because I had been a successful teacher, because I was a serious and hardheaded woman.

But then everything broke. As the revolution and the war broke over Tehran, so too my marriage broke apart after a few months. A very rough time when I was all alone, unable to confide in anyone because a woman in revolutionary Iran could not live alone, unwilling to tell my mother who was ill in the United States. So while the bombs were falling over Tehran, I was all alone in my house going though the difficulties of divorce and work that had its own trials.

Afsaneh Najmabadi

I talked to Afsaneh Najmabadi over a period of a few weeks in June, July, and August of 1991 and taped most of our conversation during three days in August when she stayed with me in Champaign. Born in Tehran in the late 1940s, educated in Iran, the United States, and England, one of the founders and editors of the leading Persian feminist journal **Nimeye Digar** *(the Other Half), Najmabadi has authored several books and articles, most recently on the gendered history of Iranian modernity. Her narrative about growing up female shows the range of models of womanhood and possibilities available to girls from her particular class and background before the revolution. She returned to Iran in September 1978 to be part of the revolution and left in the summer of 1980. She currently teaches women's studies at Barnard College. Afsaneh starts by describing her neighborhood and family.*

We lived in the Sheikh Hadi neighborhood near what used to be the Serah-i-Shah [Crossroads of Shahs] but now it's Serah-i-Inqelab [Crossroads of the Revolution]. I love that old neighborhood. Its main street (Sheikh Hadi) is named after Sheikh Hadi Najmabadi who is the grandfather of my grandmother. As with many old Tehran families, most of the neighborhood was populated by my large extended family. The neighborhood hospital was built on a trust left to Sheikh Hadi and his male descendants, and in addition to producing religious scholars, our family produced many male and female doctors and engineers.[5]

Many stories grew around Sheikh Hadi: one is that Reza Kermani who assassinated Nasirudin Shah was a disciple of his and actually went and asked Sheikh Hadi's permission to assassinate Nasirudin Shah. My grandmother's version is that Sheikh Hadi neither forbade nor encouraged him. Another part of family lore is that he was a hidden [secret] *Azali* or *Babi* [precursor to Bahaullah and the Baha'i movement]. Highly respected locally and nationally as a model of a liberal family patriarch, he was among the constitutionalist clergy to whom there are references in histories of the Constitutional Revolution.

One of his sons, Sheikh Mahdi, was my grandmother's father who lived in the neighborhood when I was a child. Although considered religiously tolerant, he was intolerant of such things as music. When I was about nine years old, my father decided to get my sister, Farzaneh, and me a music teacher and teach us to play the *santoor*. But this was never told to him. The fact that his great-granddaughters were learning music had to be kept a secret. If anyone spotted him walking down the road to visit our house they would come and tell us, and we would stop the music and hide our instruments.

Until I left for the United States, for the first twenty years of my life we lived near Bombast-i-Najmabadi [the blind alley of the Najmabacis]. We lived on Kucheh Orfi, off Sheikh Hadi Street on which every other house was a Najmabadi house. The *Maqbareh* [tomb] of Sheikh Hadi was located in the cul-de-sac. There is actually a library in the building that houses Sheikh Hadi's tomb. Within the Najmabadi clan, some families were much richer than others. I recall feeling that our house was tiny and dilapidated. My neighborhood was a mixed neighborhood, perhaps less cohesive than a lot of other neighborhoods because ours bordered one area that was Armenian and another that was Jewish. Near our butcher was a *kashir*, or a kosher butcher. Across from the local public elementary school, *Firuzkuhi*, was a Jewish school, *Kurush*. And behind *Kurush* was the Armenian school, *Maryam*. For many years on Saturday mornings my sister and I (this was the tradition in orthodox homes) lit the stove for an old Jewish lady who lived in a *kahgeli* (mud-thatched) house. As a child I had friends who were Jewish, Armenian, Baha'i, Muslim, and Zoroastrian. Further down the road was an Armenian family who rented their ground floor to Russian emigrés. Next door to the Russians lived a Zoroastrian family who later converted to Baha'ism. My paternal relatives also lived around us and every other house was occupied with some relative. But even as I and my generation grew up, people started constructing houses north of Tehran and started moving out. This was modernization, a sort of upward mobility out of the old traditional quarters.

Tell about your understanding of gender roles—perhaps through your parents. How did you grow to understand class, labor, and economics?
Because my father was a minor government employee who could hardly afford setting up separate households, we lived with his parents. Because my mother never had her own household, she always felt under my grandmother's supervision. And she resented it. We had one room in the family house where my parents, my sister, and I slept. When I was eight or nine years old we rebuilt the house, modernizing it into a brick instead of a *kahgel* house.

The strongest emotional memory of my childhood is of protection by my mother. One of the earlier generations of women who worked, who grew up going to school, and having a job—she had several jobs. She had wanted to study medicine and become an obstetrician. But when she contracted trachoma and couldn't continue, her older sister and husband found her a job as a secretary where they worked in the Ministry of Education. All this was in the '30s. When she married in 1941 she was thirty years old. It was a late marriage for an Iranian woman. But she had this very strong sense that she wanted to marry a man she loved and not have an arranged marriage. Remarkable determination and conviction for a woman of her generation. I don't have any memories of ever being punished by her. When I was about four, my mother went back to work. She was probably going crazy in that household. She felt she was doing nothing, feeling totally wasted, so she got a job as an elementary schoolteacher. Perhaps because there were no brothers in my family, both my parents brought us up just as they would have brought up a boy—to be educated. And in a way I guess I was brought up gender-neutral. I never felt I was being given a female education. I never grew up thinking I was going to grow up and get married and have children.

The strongest emphasis in our family, generally in the Najmabadi family, at that time of my life was education as the secret to the good life. I therefore never felt the pressures of female roles imposed on me. And I was never expected to behave in any particular way that would make me conscious I was a girl and not a boy. I (and my sister) studied mathematics and physics and made all these "unfeminine" choices.

Within our household the divisions of labor were blurred. For instance, my mother was not necessarily the person who cooked, because my grandmother did [the cooking]. My mother went to work and came back at lunchtime. There was no clear-cut division, then, between my mother and my father because it was quite evident that the survival of our household depended on both their incomes.

Even with two incomes, we were always in debt. For instance, we bought our groceries on credit from the local grocer. When my parents got paid at the end of the month, they would clear the accounts, but, by the tenth of each month, we would run out of cash and start running up credit at the local grocery. I lived with this unreal fear that one of these days the grocer wouldn't give us food anymore because we had run out of credit.

If I had to name our "class" I would call it lower-middle class in the sense that, first of all, we were always short of money. I always had a very small allowance, which would maybe buy me one snack a week. I know my mother's salary was less than a thousand tomans a month [about $100]. She kept a little bit of it for her own expenses; the rest of it went for groceries. And my father probably earned about two or three thousand tomans a month. Later on, with the rising oil revenues, the government employees' salaries went up and both of them had higher salaries. I don't remember exactly how much but we always felt it wasn't enough.

I felt this class difference especially when I went to high school. When I went home with a friend in elementary school (a public school) her house was more or less like my own. In high school, however, I felt class difference because, for the first time, I went to a private high school—*Hadaf*—highly regarded because its graduates were known to pass the university entrance exam. I got in because of a good tuition scholarship.

When I went to visit other children's houses, I saw that they were substantially different from mine. They were bigger, some had swimming pools, and there suddenly I felt a bit isolated. I knew I couldn't feel comfortable inviting them to my house.

The other major event I should mention in describing my family, and perhaps this contributed towards feeling the outsider, is that sometime in the '40s my father became a Baha'i. That made him the odd person in the family. Our family, which had produced several leading Muslim religious figures, suddenly had this aberration—although my father claimed that his own father may have been a secret Baha'i and even Sheikh Hadi may have been a Baha'i without anyone's knowledge; he proceeded to invent his own Baha'i pedigree.

I know you have written on women's education. Could you tell us more about the schools you attended and your education?

Before going to the university there was school. An important memory I have is of my elementary school, one of the earliest girls' schools in Tehran, that was set up in Serah Salsabiel. Its name matters—*Dabestan i Efaf* [School of Chastity]. It was quite far from our house and we used to take this rickety bus in the morning back and forth. I laugh because now I'm reading these early twentieth-century newspapers on the opening of girls' schools. In working on the emergence of the "woman question" in Iran, I notice that the names of the early girls' schools have to do with female honor and propriety—names like *Efaf* and *Effat* [chastity], *Namoos* [honor], *Esmatieh* [innocence], *Hejab* [the veil]. So I would take a rickety bus each day to this school in Serah Salsabiel, which was in more of a lower-class neighborhood than our own house was. The school was an old house turned into a school.

My strongest memory of both my elementary school and high school was that my sister and I were expected to be, and were, very good students. So I was praised, and that praise continued to feed itself. I had several crushes on female teachers. One of these was my physics teacher, and I know that's why I decided to study physics. People kept asking, "Why physics?" After all I had the highest university entrance scores and could have entered any field. I couldn't tell them that my choice had nothing to do with anything other than a teenage crush. And I know most of my decisions in life have been shaped by these sorts of contingencies, by completely "irrational" moments. For a long time physics shaped my life.

I entered Tehran University in the fall of 1964. I was seventeen. I stayed only two years because, extremely single-minded, I knew I wanted to become a world-class physicist. After the first year, dissatisfied at seeing the same teaching methods used at the university as in high school, learning by rote and doing petty experiments, I realized there was no way I was going to become a Nobel Prize physicist in that place! And I said, "I'll have to go to America. That's the only place to go to study physics. And win a Nobel."

The problem, however, was that of course my family couldn't possibly send me abroad on their meager salaries. Again here as always, I was lucky. I went to the Near East Foundation after my first year at Tehran University. A kind lady took my transcripts, got them translated, and said she would send them to a number of universities for placement. She called me after a few months and said I had two acceptances to the University of Michigan and Radcliffe College, which I hadn't heard of. Radcliffe was giving me full tuition plus two thousand dollars a year pocket money. I was very upset because Radcliffe College was a women's college I'd never heard of. I said, "I want to go to a university, not a women's college." But when she told me that Radcliffe would be almost like going to Harvard I felt a bit better and agreed to go.

But the next problem was how to buy a ticket. I told her there was no way I could find money to buy a ticket to the United States. Could she get me a scholarship? By this time I had become very aggressive at finding other people to pay my way—to my Nobel Prize, right? So she said yes, she knew people in the Rotary Club of Iran who, after a really bizarre luncheon, approved my ticket to the United States. A one-way ticket. It turned out to be a one-way ticket in more ways than one.

Tahereh

Pari and I spoke to Tahereh (pseud.) in her office at the University of Southern California in 1991. She was then teaching sociology and women's studies at four different campuses in Los Angeles. Born in the early 1950s and educated in Tehran and in the United States, she has written widely on women's issues. She left Iran the first time in the mid-1970s to do graduate work in the United States. She returned in 1978 to participate in the revolution, but left Iran again after the establishment of the Islamic Republic in 1979. In her struggle for personal liberation, we can see private dimensions in the making of the later public activist. The oppressions and conflicts she experienced as a girl and a woman are particular to the intersection of class, religion, and gender in a specific lower-middle-class neighborhood near the Tehran bazaar. As with several of the other interviewees, books—literature, translations, philosophy, and poetry—played a crucial part in her identity formation. As is the case in cultural circumstances where sexuality is heavily proscribed, she is the survivor of an early tragic relationship reminiscent of medieval forbidden courtship, after which she escaped an unconsummated arranged marriage, survived a self-initiated divorce at twenty, and finally married a man of her own choosing in 1984 after graduation. She spoke in both English and Persian.

My father was a high-school teacher. I owe my zeal for learning to him. He taught me my first words, how to read, how to write. Although my mother encouraged us, she had only an elementary school level of literacy. My father tried to influence her to become less religious, to become more open-minded—to even, for example, remove her *chador* when she could, not to cover her face.

My father was open-minded and rebellious, particularly noteworthy because he was raised to become a mullah. Both my grandfathers in Tabriz were senior mullahs—*Hojjatul Islam*. My father left Tabriz after divinity school, came to Tehran, and continued his studies at Tehran University in religion, theology, and philosophy. Then, like Kasravi, he rebelled against the clergy as an institution. Like Kasravi, who thought of the clergy as obstacles to God, he too was against the mullahs. So one day he took off his turban and his robe, a very rebellious act, after which he was made into an outcast. His father literally cast him out and never talked to him. And this is a strong childhood memory. You know how extended the family was, especially in our area, so the break between my father and his father was very important. We always wondered why our grandfather never visited us.

When did you start wearing the chador and how did you feel about it?
I didn't have to for the first three years of elementary school when we were in Sananjan and separated from the religious pressure of family. But once I went to Tehran, I had to wear the veil right after the start of middle school. I was twelve years old—1963. Back in Tehran and closer to the location of my grandfather and grandmother on my mother's side, I was now considered a grown woman. I am twelve years old and I have to cover myself.

I was the first woman in my family—my extended family—who broke out of *chador,* who removed her veil, who went to university. When a cousin called me the Jeanne d'Arc of our family I didn't know what he meant. But being Jeanne d'Arc was very difficult. I had to fight my own mother not to wear the *chador.* As the first child of a large family, seven siblings, I was always expected to behave like a responsible helpmate to my mother. And never allowed to be a child.

By the time I got to the eighth grade, I was fifteen years old, and the pressure mounted to veil—particularly through my grandfather, a Mojtahid in the Tehran bazaar, who was stopped by his supporters on the street and told, "Your granddaughter is going to high school and doesn't wear a veil. We're not going to stand behind you in prayer." Another day my grandfather was stopped by his followers in the bazaar and accused of having a TV in his house: "You have this *Sheeshe Shaitoon"* (they called it the "devil's glass"); he denied it. I remember him coming home rapping his *assaa* [cane] on the door, angry because he realized something terrible had happened. Where is this "devil's glass," he asks, wanting to break it. My uncle calmed him by assuring him that the purpose of TV was only to hear the news and not, God forbid, for entertainment. Eventually our family had to move out because it wasn't possible to have a television in that house, in that place.

This was now the 1960s when, along with the introduction of TV, came other kinds of modernization. The government started a new housing project for teachers, so while we waited for the house to finish, we had to stay with our grandfather. So in my grandfather's house, what did I do about my veil? Every day I wore my veil up to the end of the alley [*we all laugh in recognition of a familiar scene*] and then took it off, folded it, and hid it in my school bag before arriving at school because I was embarrassed to wear it in front of my peers and my teachers. Then one day, one of my teachers, herself a religious woman but in a more modern, liberal way, noticed that I had hidden my veil. She asked, "Why are you hiding it? I too wore *chador* when I was a child and what you are doing is perfectly okay." So she removed my shame at *chador* being a sign that we were old-fashioned or lower class.

I got conflicting messages from my parents, from my family, from my social environment, from my school, and from my peer group who were not as religious as my family was. I began to see other differences: many of my schoolmates appeared to be wealthy. My father was a schoolteacher and you know how poor teachers are.

How poor?
His exact salary was not talked about but I always lived under the pressure of not having enough money, not being able to pay for even my books. Even now I feel pained when I think of that poverty. We were of a class that wished to be part of the middle class, but knew it was not. He simply did not make enough money. Especially with seven kids. Why is this so painful? Because I was always the top student with the highest grades (*shagerd aval*), and therefore very noticed by teachers, but at the same time I never could take my books to the classroom because they were so old and torn and secondhand. Embarrassed to take them to class, I copied just enough of the text to prevent my friends from seeing my books as evidence of my poverty.

Tahereh then responded to a series of questions about her later formation, about the influence of books, TV, politics, and role models.
My role models were my teachers. Although the books I read included romances—typically about the oppression of women by deceiving men, or about the dilemmas faced by women whose families want them to marry the old rich man and they want to marry the poor young man. But this was also exactly the same time that I started reading philosophical books that my father gave me. I was very fond of Maeterlinck, who questioned the meaning of life and who helped me with thinking through the existence of God, and also with the conflicting messages that I was getting from my father and from my grandparents.

Because my father was a philosopher, he wanted me to understand philosophy, so I learned Plato and Aristotle. My father taught me how to read *Kalileh and Dimneh*, Saadi and Khayyam. He would interpret their philosophical and political messages, tell me how anticlerical Khayyam was, and how and why mullahs were against him. I memorized all the poems of Khayyam. I remember also reading Charlotte Brontë, Victor Hugo, Charles Dickens, *Uncle Tom's Cabin*, and even Jack London whom we read though he was forbidden. This was high school, this was age fourteen, and we got these forbidden books from our special teachers. I knew I had to always act adult, not read too many romances, and not fall in love.

Tahereh's first transgression—first love.

Despite all this I fell in love. I was in the ninth grade. I was fifteen, yes, and this was when I fell in love with the son of my neighbor. This is a separate story and a very crucial and painful time in my life, because you see this love was so romantic, so nonphysical, and so abstract.

My neighbor's son was nineteen. We wrote to each other and my sister would deliver the letters. We were never alone. The second time that we—my sister and I—went out with this boy, we went to a movie. All this was done under the cover of going to a friend's house. But we were seen in the theater by another neighbor and we knew that they would tell my father. So when I came home I told my father. Because I felt closer to my father and because he read a lot of poetry, I thought my father would be more understanding about my falling in love. My mother would, I thought, be scared and fearful of the shame on her daughter. So I said to my father, "Tonight I went out with this boy to a movie. We haven't even touched." And this was the truth. We hadn't even allowed our hands to touch each other's.

My father's reaction was simple. He thought that he was winning my trust and my love more than my mother and he responded by saying, "Okay, not a big deal. I understand, everybody falls in love, but I know that you value your education, so of course you are not going to marry this boy are you?" And I said, "No, but can't we get engaged and I could continue my education and after I finish high school we could marry?" He thought we were both too young—I was fourteen, he nineteen and jobless. I didn't know and I didn't care.

This boy and I exchanged books. He had given me romantic books like *Anna Karenina, Yadi Doost*—short stories by Hooshang Mostofi. My sister would carry these presents between us. But the same night, once my mother returned home and after my father talked to her, everything changed. My mother must have got angry and shamed him: "What kind of man are you that your daughter doesn't dare to tell me of her doings, but she tells you? It shows what a non-man you are, that even your daughter manipulates you." And she probably so attacked his masculinity that he needed to prove to her that he really was a man and could control me.

So the next day he said, "You will not go to school anymore." When I asked why, he answered, "Because if you go to school you will meet this boy again. We can't trust you anymore. Your mother thinks you have been influenced by your friends. We must forget this boy."

And then the worst thing happened. They took me to a gynecologist. My mother couldn't believe me anymore because (I think in retrospect) she felt so hurt that she was not the first one I confided in. She said, "How do I know how close your relationship was with him?" Concerned only with reputation and family honor, she took me to a gynecologist to check my virginity and I cried. This was so humiliating, because at that time it meant that I was a *jende*—a whore— horrible. I was fifteen, and only one year after I had my period. Just awful. Then they sent me to live in my grandparents' house so I wouldn't see this boy again. For one month I was restricted to the house and not allowed to go to the school that had been everything to me. Every night I cried myself to sleep.

When this boy noticed my absence, his parents tried to come with an official proposal. But my parents would not even accept a visit. But this boy was himself very romantic. He was reading Sadeq Hedayat and Freud. Freud actually was first introduced to me by him. He grew depressed. He was sensitive, complex, and young. I think he couldn't stand all those pressures that included the pressure of his work and living with his older brother. So to make this story short, he committed suicide. He killed himself.

I'm still going to be very emotional because it's very hard to talk about it. It's a terrible burden. Especially when you get blamed by the entire neighborhood.

I was living, you remember, in my grandfather's house. One day my father came for me in a taxi—unusual for him; he never used taxis. On the way he started to speak: "You know, I told you this boy is crazy. How can he fall in love with a person like you—such a talent? How can you lower yourself to fall in love with such a stupid person? He's crazy. And after all this you know what he does? He kills himself." That's how my father said it. This boy who has already caused us so much trouble now kills himself to cause more.

First I was shocked and then I felt this was a trick to make me forget him. Until somehow I found the newspaper. This was, if you remember, that time when several people killed themselves by throwing themselves from the top of the Elghanian building, one of the first high-rise buildings in Tehran—and the newspaper printed his name, described how he killed himself, and how a letter he had written showed he was in love with a girl whose family prevented their marriage.

After his death, my parents had to leave that neighborhood. I remember from then on they thought that the only way to save me from my bad reputation and prove to everybody that I was a virgin and therefore save their honor, was for me to get married to a decent man.[6]

So, now who's going to arrange this marriage? Before this incident, when a man's family came with a proposal for me, my father always said, "Oh no. My daughter is too young. She is still studying and cannot marry while she is in school." But then he changed and agreed to a marriage. And so they forced me to marry a man I hated. I even hated his looks, let alone other parts of him, so when I resisted, they insisted.

The story that follows is one that Tahereh narrated to me on the telephone on June 23, 1994. She called me after reading the transcript of her earlier interview and my opening chapter, and apologized for leaving out what she now realized was an important yet painful part of her story, saying, "Something was missing from my earlier interview—a certain integrity was not there. What I am going to tell you reveals something important within our culture." I typed her words on the computer as she spoke.

After Reza committed suicide, I was forced into an arranged marriage, which I escaped before its consummation. It shows not only the pressure I was under but what pressure did to my parents. They had to marry me off to save the family reputation. Also perhaps my father had been convinced by all my grandmother and all my aunts and uncles that my "head was held too high." The process I went through for this arranged marriage—the shame, the guilt—was all unprecedented in my family tradition. I had to get married to save their honor.

And so it was that when this man came as a suitor—much older than me, well-off, from a well-known bazaari family, with a house, money, and ready for a wife—my grandmother said to me that I was very lucky to marry a man with such a fine reputation. And we went through the ceremonies of proposal. I was sixteen years old. I had to carry tea to the man when he came to call. I hated him. I saw him as an enemy from the moment I set eyes on him. But the family bombarded me with reasons. They said I didn't understand. They said that once I got engaged, then I could finish my high school diploma. They arranged the formal wedding [*aqd*] and agreed to wait until my graduation for the final ceremony, the *nikah,* and the consummation of the marriage.

I have a hard time explaining those days. Whenever they would ask me to go shopping, I would say, "It makes no difference to me." I was numb. I was in grief. It was so cruel. My mother's mother was the dominant one who would warn my mother: "Don't be weak, don't give in, or else she will go astray again." A few nights before the wedding itself, my cousin and his wife understood that something awful was happening to me. They saw that I still wore black in mourning. I was not allowed to be in full mourning, but I secretly wore something black for the boy I had loved. My cousin kept asking me whether I was really willing to go through with this marriage. "No," I said, "I hate him." "Why don't you protest?" they asked. "Why don't you say so? Tell them, say something." Again, I was numb because I was in a deep depression.

Even on the day of our wedding reception I still thought that this was not really happening. I was strangely detached. But then I was taken to the hairdresser's and made up and dressed in a wedding gown and saw that this really was happening to me. The night before the wedding I wrote a letter in the form of a diary that my mother found. In it, I threatened to kill myself if I were forced to get married. I saw this act as my way of retaliation, the only way to show some aggression, to take charge of my body. That experience makes me understand why so many women kill themselves. That is the only power they have over their own bodies and their own lives.

I thought, I can ruin it all. I knew that it was still up to me to prevent the whole thing. I decided to say "no" during the *aqd* and the *nikah* [the religious and legal ceremonies]. Later I realized that my parents suspected my plan. And they tricked me.

My father came before the public ceremony and asked, "Daughter, may I be your *vakil* [legal representative]?" I said, "Yes, of course," thinking he meant this metaphorically as "Will you trust me?" I didn't get suspicious. But I kept waiting and waiting for the *aqd* ceremony. Two mullahs performed the ceremony—one was my grandfather, the other was a sheikh. I remembered seeing other wedding ceremonies at which the bride was given three chances to say yes. I knew I would say no. I was waiting to say no at the first question rather than wait the traditional three questions. And then suddenly I heard everyone clapping, someone reciting the Qur'an, and everyone pouring sweets and *nabat* around and wanting to put honey on my tongue.

I asked, "When is the *aqd*?" I asked, "Where is the question?" They said, "Your father is your *vakil* and he has given his consent to your marriage. It is done." I started crying. I couldn't stop crying. The groom tried to comfort me. But he couldn't understand. He wanted to touch me. I said, "I will scream if you touch me." I begged my cousin's wife to get me out of the room. By then, everyone understood that something terrible had happened. The same night my mother came in to say, "*Abroo moon raft* [Our honor is gone]." They thought I was sick, crazy. My cousin and his wife and another cousin and my younger sister took me to the lobby of the Hotel Hilton where they brought me ice cream. And then I started to smile because I was free. Or so I thought. But now it was a scandal. The man and his family were embarrassed; they thought that perhaps they were tricked into a marriage with a crazy woman. They went to talk to my grandfather, the mullah.

Now here is the most important turn: my grandfather said that this marriage was *haram* [impure/unlawful]. He said, "It must be nullified." He realized I had been tricked. On religious grounds alone, he saw what was wrong. His reputation as a mullah was as a purist for truth. It was known, for instance, that when he read an *aqd*, he would do so three times to make sure he did everything right. So it was taken seriously when he announced that this marriage was nullified because I had not knowingly given *vikalat* [legal rights] to my father. If the marriage was to be *mahram* [lawful], we must go through the entire ceremony again. And he talked to me. And I said that I didn't know, that I was waiting to say "no" but that my father tricked me. And my grandfather who now understood talked to my parents. By now, my parents didn't blame me; they were afraid I was seriously losing my mind, and they simply said that we must reimburse the groom's family for the wedding and return their gifts.

After this event, they stopped bothering me any more with marriage. They probably thought I was mentally sick. So they left me alone. That was when they became more lax and let a cousin, Karim Aga, take me to movies and restaurants and they let me go to school. I started to trust my kind, nice cousin, who was modern (*motajadad*) and blamed the old culture, not me; who took me to movies; who taught me how to dance; who talked about the United States; and who said, "When I marry I want to take my wife to America. I want to resign from the army." We soon got engaged. After our engagement, he went to the United States and messed around with many women, but wanted to marry me—a young, naive, innocent girl, the kind he could control.

I was in the tenth grade and liked getting his very nice letters and gifts. I felt engaged and happy and well. And my parents were happy because their reputation had been saved.

But then, two years later, I passed the *Conkur*—the entrance exam into the university. I was second in the entire national entrance exam class—*Shagerd Dovom*—my name was printed in the newspapers. So once again, my father became excited about my education and started again to believe in me. But once again he faced family pressures because this was the first time in the history of my extended family that a woman was going to a university.

I remember all the phone calls after my name appeared in the newspapers, especially as the second-best student in my field. My father had to fight with so many relatives. One day my aunt's husband called him and said, "Congratulations, your daughter has been accepted in the institute of prostitution." And this upset my father very much.

The first year in university was great, a new world for me. It was like a new birth. I felt freedom. I felt empowered. I felt less dependent on my parents, especially because financially I didn't have to rely on my father anymore. I had a scholarship—all I received was two hundred tomans [about $30]—still, it was a lot. I had my own money for the first time in my life. [*I hear a laugh in Tahereh's voice for the first time, too.*] And this was a totally liberating experience.

Also I was getting politicized. This was the time that I started making political friends, activists, and I was reading different books, although my political thinking started during high school when I started reading books like Al-e-Ahmad's *Gharbzadegi.* And I also became anti- religion and godless when, even in the sixth grade (the twelfth year of school), I read Mehdi Bazargan's *The Evolution of the Qur'an* [*Soure Tahawwul-e Qur'an*]; I read *Rahe Teyshodeh* [*The Worn Path*] because I was struggling to understand arguments over the existence of God.

But suddenly I questioned my engagement to this man and realized it was a mistake. But when my cousin/fiancé realized that I was changing and maturing, he rushed back to Iran and said that we should get married instantly. He promised to take me to New York where I could continue my studies at Columbia University. So I agreed, and we got married in the middle of a summer after which he took me to the States in 1969. I was almost nineteen years old.

I imagined that in New York I would attend Columbia University. But, once there I realized gradually that this was not the person I imagined he was. He had written me that he was studying. I found out that he wasn't, that his only interest was business, and that he wasn't going to let me continue my education. With only a high school diploma himself, he was threatened by my university education and he had no intention of allowing me to attend Columbia. So I was in New York for four and a half months, crying every night saying that I wanted to go back to Iran and study. I made life miserable for him and miserable for myself. So he agreed, saying that of course I was homesick, and we returned to Iran—where we fought, he refused a divorce, and I couldn't study.

But I had a professor, Dr. Mohtadi, a professor of psychology, to whom I confessed my anxieties and fear of getting pregnant. She encouraged me to file for a divorce, and to my surprise, my parents agreed. My husband divorced me in 1972 claiming that the *Tudeh* [Communist] Party had rotted my brain. The truth was that I had no connection to the Tudeh Party, that I belonged to a younger generation of the independent Left—most of whom were highly critical of the Tudeh Party. I stayed at Tehran University till 1974. I got my B.S. and started my M.A., worked on that for just one semester while working on my scholarship to get here. I always won scholarships, all three times. That's why I feel so proud, because whatever I accomplished, I did on my own initiative. I had to have the highest grade-point average to get that scholarship and earn an admission from a good university, which I got from the University of Illinois. This was the second biggest event in my life, an emancipating event—and yes, it was my own triumph that took away some of the pain of things like divorce.

Homa Sarshar

Pari and I interviewed Homa Sarshar in her home in Los Angeles in 1990. Born in Shiraz in 1946, educated in Tehran, and generally known as the Barbara Walters of the Iranian community in California, Sarshar is a journalist who writes and hosts Persian radio programs, some specifically on the subject of life in exile. In 1995 she formed The Center for Iranian Jewish Oral History whose archives of interviews, pictures, and documents are available to the public, and whose aims are to promote the cultural heritage and contemporary history of Iranian Jews. She is currently at work on Esther's Children: A Portrait of Iranian Jews, *an illustrated survey of the history of Iranian Jews from the nineteenth to the twentieth century. She spoke of her childhood, her education, and the effect of the Islamic Revolution on her work as a Jewish journalist. I pick up her narrative at the point where she speaks of returning to school, of her work at the leading women's magazine in Iran, and of her unusual coverage of the spectacle of 1971—the celebration of 2,500 years of Iranian monarchy.*

I was born in Shiraz into an Iranian Jewish family. I am the second child and the first daughter. When I was a year old, the whole family moved to Tehran. My father was a businessman—in export and import. When I was five years old I went to the French school, Institute Maryam, a branch of the Jeanne d'Arc school run by French nuns. I got my diploma in French in the ninth grade; for the tenth, eleventh, and twelfth grades I went to Rassi in South Tehran.

I got married when I was nineteen. When I graduated from high school, I passed a *Conkur,* the entrance exam for Tehran University. I had been planning to become an architect, but as you know, this Tehran University test allowed you no choice. The results determined your fate. So my name was drawn out for economics, and because it was a big deal to be accepted at Tehran University, and because I had been accepted, I went and entered the department of economics, which I did not like at all. I felt that they might as well have been speaking Chinese. I stayed there for only six months.

This was also when I met my husband. My husband and I just went out a few times. It was, like so many marriages twenty-five years ago, an arranged marriage. Some of our friends introduced us to each other, we went out a few times, he came to our house, he proposed formally—as was common at that time and he was a nice man. He was an engineer working in the department of water and power, he was nice looking, and he was Jewish. We got engaged while I was still studying economics at Tehran University. When we got married I planned to take another entrance exam during the upcoming summer to switch fields because I didn't like economics. But I got pregnant very soon, a month after I got married, with my first son and the pregnancy was a final blow to my studies because I felt continually sick.

While I was in school I had become friends with a journalist who advised me to become a journalist—a field that I hadn't given thought to at all, not for a minute. But he was very certain of my abilities. He said that they were starting a new magazine called *Zan-e-Rooz* [Today's Woman], that he knew that I spoke French. That's all I could do, I said, speak French and translate. But he was certain I could do well. He said, "We are planning to start publication with a few friends and we need a few women. We know that we don't have a lot of women in journalism and therefore we want to train young women and young girls who are interested."

This was in 1965 when I was nineteen years old. The editors of the magazine invited me to a meeting where they offered to train me. I started working for three hundred tomans a month as a student. I was young and I was very happy, and as soon as I started the work I became very, very interested in journalism. It took me less than a month to find out that this was what I really liked to do. I started by translating news, entertainment news at that time from France, different French magazines. And while I was doing that, I was going to school. But now I knew I wanted to change: I no longer wanted architecture. I wanted either journalism or literature.

When I got pregnant I stopped going to school but I didn't stop working. But a year and a half after I had my first son, I got pregnant again—a year and three months after the first. And this was also another unplanned pregnancy that prevented me from studying. When my second son was three years old I registered his name in a preschool and realized that now this was the time to go back to study. So I returned to Tehran University. Once again I took the entrance exam, and this time I was accepted in the branch that I wanted— literature. I got my B.A. in French and Persian literature. Now at that time I was also working, I had my two children, and I was studying. It was a very, very tough three years for me. And I had my house to look after. I didn't have a housekeeper. And I had my salary—now something around twelve hundred tomans a month—and my husband earned five or six thousand tomans. So we helped each other very much. My husband took care of the children during the evening while I went to classes. In the daytime I worked at home because my work mostly involved writing and translating. So we managed. And little by little, I became known as a journalist at *Zan-e-Rooz* (the leading woman's journal) where I worked for many years.

Then it was 1971, the year of the big celebration [of 2,500 years of the monarchy], [a] time I felt I was growing intellectually mature and independent. I didn't like the images of women projected in our magazines.

As a journalist with a different point of view, my coverage of the celebration and my angle on the stories were different and exclusive. I decided to cover the subject of waste. I went into the kitchens, and I went to the beauty parlors and to places others ignored and did not think worth covering. There I saw that the celebrators of Persian monarchy were not even drinking the water from our country. They were drinking Perrier and Evian. My very smart editor who recognized mine as an unusual, exclusive report included it in the magazine. It turned out to be important enough to cause quite a controversy in the country.

At that time I also started to tell the magazine that I felt that I could not work anymore with them if they were not going to represent a more real and responsible image of women. But my editor did not like my disapproval; we argued and challenged each other's positions. So I finally left *Zan-e-Rooz* a few months after the celebration of 1971. And I joined the staff of the newspaper *Keyhan*, which was still part of the company that ran *Zan-e-Rooz*. I stayed there because Dr. Mesbahzadeh, the owner of the company, didn't want me to leave. He said, "Even if you don't agree with Davami"—the editor-in-chief for *Zan-e-Rooz*—"we want you to stay. You come and work in the daily newspaper *Keyhan* (Farsi)."

I worked as family editor and as general reporter for the paper until I left Iran. And meanwhile I had a few proposals and suggestions to start other projects. One of them was a proposal from IRTV, Iranian Radio and Television, who wanted me to have a family program on television. So I said, "Okay, I'll come," and I started and I had a program twice a week called *Chahar Divari* [Four Walls]—every Monday and Thursdays from 7:30 to 8:00 p.m.

And now, at this time when I began to feel that after a year of working on TV—this was 1977—I had just begun to get a grasp of the medium, I had just begun a new project that I had written myself. I was ready to create new programs, and suddenly everything was destroyed.

Mandana

When Pari and I interviewed Mandana (pseud.) in her home in 1992, she was working in a theater in a large Western city. Born in Tehran in 1963, she talked in Persian for two hours in a ostensibly seamless narrative about growing up, about rebellion against gender roles, and about the effect of the revolution and diaspora on Iranian marriage. The moments I select below illuminate with poignancy how her story—like the stories of Pari, Tahereh, and Mohamad Tavakoli—illustrates the ways family dynamics duplicate the dynamic of the repressive state apparatus.

In Iran at the age of fourteen, in 1976, I was introduced to political and social issues. I am now twenty-seven years old. We were a family of nine children and I was the favorite daughter in the family. I was never satisfied with the ordinary, which included the usual housewifely roles for girls in our society. Although my father was moderate, open-minded, and democratic, my brothers were not. My father was a landlord with orchards and estates; he was also a *Haji* [one who makes the pilgrimage to Mecca]. But he never made us wear the *chador*. One of my brothers, however, was very conservative and held traditional values—not, of course, for himself but for his sisters. The law in our house was that a brother's word was higher than that of the father. Since the age of fourteen, I worked and I read. But my brother disapproved of my reading books that he had not read. He would say, "If you have to read, read novels. Why are you reading philosophy?"

When I was sixteen I was involved in high school speech and theater activities and was very successful. I was also very interested in anything that had to do with electricity, but my family said that electrical engineering was not a suitable profession for a woman. But I was good in performance: in speech, I won first place in school and in the provinces. I played small parts on the radio and television in their children's programs. But my brother said that women who go into radio and TV were corrupt.

I worked in different communities, especially with women. I worked for three years in factories with about two hundred lower-middle- to lower-class women. I worked, during summers, mostly in pharmaceutical factories to find out the problems of working women. My brother was opposed to this and said, "What are they going to pay you? I'll double the money; stay home." But this motivated me even more. Later, when I was about to get married, I told my husband that I wanted to work, no matter how much money he earned. I was eventually fired from the factory where I'd studied the syndicate's books to see what rights women had in order to try to familiarize them with their rights. But my main accomplishment in the factory was to get a supervisor who harassed women fired. I was fired then also, but he was permanently removed from his position and the women were overjoyed when this happened. They knew the kind of man he was and were familiar with the propositions he had made to me. They even held a demonstration when I left.

Women are progressing, changing, evolving. Not all changes are progress, but the changes are good. One of the problems among Iranians in the United States is the increasing divorce rate. Why, people ask, do Iranian women ask for a divorce as soon as they leave Iran? The explanations are those produced by patriarchal thinking—that women in the United States have freedom and only want to have fun, so they forget their vows. That's not how I see things. An important change takes place in women when they come to the United States. In Iran women suffer so much from ignorant repressions—women of all classes—that when they arrive at a place that offers any opportunity, they break away from all restrictions. Also, however, Iranian women who have come into this society have proven themselves superior in meeting new challenges. But in contrast, men stay the same. They have had their opportunities and there is no more water for them to swim in. In 90 percent of the Iranian families who have come to the United States after the revolution, women have more responsibility than men. Women are the ones who run the family, who work, who cook. But it's very hard because they have to fight against so much that they have grown up knowing about themselves. The consequence is often severe depression.

Roqeyeh Arbat Kazemi

I talked to Roqeyeh Arbat Kazemi in her home in November 1994. She and her husband are both Azari. Arbat is the name of her village, some three miles from Tabriz, in which she and six earlier generations of her family were born. She was born in the mid-1930s. Her family owned and cultivated two villages—Arbat Olya (Arbat One) and Arbat Sogla (Arbat Two). They experienced the ravages of both the Russian occupation of Azarbaijan and the Shah's White Revolution of 1963. She lives with her husband, Abbas, and three children in Champaign-Urbana. In an earlier conversation, her husband explained that the Shah's land reforms, the White Revolution, had been a disaster for the country. By destroying the landowners, the Shah had also destroyed the delicate network of relations that sustained rural life and agricultural economy. Like many of the other Iranian women who live in Urbana-Champaign and work for local businesses, Mrs. Kazemi works in a large department store. Her narrative reveals not only the politics of Russian imperialism in northern Iran around the 1930s, but also power differentials in three generations of strong Azari women within Iranian-Azari culture— differences not recognized either outside or inside metropolitan, Persian, or non-Azari Iran. She spoke in both Persian and English.

I was born in the village of Arbat in 1935. The most important figure in my early childhood was my grandmother. My grandfather died when I was very young, and my grandmother was really a great woman, a strong woman, an amazing lady. I can never understand Americans who think that women in Iran have no power. Not the women in the villages that I knew. In all my years there, I never saw a woman take orders from her husband. In fact, I saw women work together with men. My grandmother had five sons, all of whom respected her totally. When my grandmother came home, all her sons stood up to greet her—every time she entered the room, no matter how many times she entered the room.

She had a mission. It was she who gave the orders and controlled the land: "You go to the city to buy wheat, you to buy barley, you to plant the trees."

My father, for instance, was her second son. His job was to be the traveler going from village to village; he would then tell villagers where and when to plant. My third uncle's job was to be in charge of planting trees; anywhere he saw water, he would hire people to plant trees. All our villages had beautiful trees. They also owned or rented some seven other villages. My father would rent villages from other relatives. So Abbas's father owned the village next to ours. His father and my father were first cousins. His grandmother was also very strong.

My grandmother's name was Kulsum Khanum. We called her Khan Naneh. Others called her Khanum. My mother was like her. She equaled my father in every way. I never heard my parents argue about anything. They were so open-minded and respected each other so much. I have not seen city men respect their women in the same way. Maybe it's because in the village, they worked together. My mother traveled to Tehran and to other places to do her buying and selling.

How did your grandmother organize her day?

My grandmother would wake up at dawn and first say her *namaz* [prayers]. Then she would wake us up in the morning and take care of us; she would encourage us to say *namaz*; she would give us chores to do. We children would all eat breakfast with her. Her daughters-in-law woke up late because they probably played cards till late at night. So we children were up early with her. All the families of the four sons lived in the same house as our grandmother. Except for my youngest uncle, the fifth son; he lived in Tabriz with his Tabrizi wife. Each of us had our own separate quarters in the house. And the house had a *birun* [outer quarters] and *andarun* [inner quarters]. Every night our mother would go downstairs and the six of us brothers and sisters would sleep around the fireplace. Our *naneh* was there with us. Grandmother would then sit on her *takht* [raised platform or bed] and give all the orders for the day: she would check on the condition of the goats, lambs, and camels. She would talk to each shepherd who would be lined up for the day's work; she would supervise the lunches for all the workers. There were at least a hundred workers who would take their orders from my grandmother each day. She would then get on horseback and check on everything in the village.

Our villages were between two little rivers—Arjirloo and Hashtrood. We had medical supplies in our house. Anyone who got hurt would come to our house and get any medicine they needed. If a man and wife fought, they would come to our house and my grandmother would settle the dispute after hearing both sides. Sometimes she would punish both parties. Now it's all gone. No one cared for them the way we did. They worked hard for us and they benefited from that work. They had food to eat all winter.

My grandmother used to tell us about Iba the bandit who would come with his army, surround the villages, and threaten to take the animals if he was not paid enough. Each household had its own animals in addition to the stock the village owned in common. When the village head, the Khan, was weak, the bandits would take advantage of all the villagers.

When the Russians invaded in 1940, my family was forced into political action: my uncle opposed the rule of Pishavari, the Russian-backed ruler placed in charge of us. He was a Communist who wished to separate Azarbaijan from Iran. They wished to make all the schools give up Persian and only study Turkish. Of course we all spoke Turkish at home. But we learned Persian, as if it were a foreign language, at school. I didn't like it then, but maybe that early learning of another language has made it easy for me to learn other languages. But there was no school in our village, so we children had to live in Tabriz to go to school during the year. Until I was twelve years old, I hated Tabriz because it kept me away from our village, my horse, my animals. We were dragged to school. Our parents brought us to our house in Tabriz. There we had a *naneh* and a *baba* [two old people] who took care of us. Our parents joined us once the first snows came. Otherwise they had to take care of their lambs. My mother would sell oil and cheese and dairy goods in the fall. In her house she started making Persian rugs. She designed rugs, hired weavers, and chose the colors.

Each villager rented a piece of land for which he was responsible; the more sons a villager had, the more land he was given. He kept three-quarters of the produce and gave one-quarter to my grandmother or to my father when he took over. Our family was so proud of village life. When my mother was pregnant with her youngest child, she was in the big city Tabriz; yet she insisted she be driven back to Arbat to give birth. She trusted in her midwife whose name was Kachal [the name means bald] Naneh. Really she had long and beautiful hair, so we called her Kachal Naneh. The birth was a complicated breech birth—the child was turned upside down. So Kachal Naneh took my mother and shook her by her feet and the child turned himself around and was born headfirst.

My grandmother died when the Russians took over Azarbaijan. During the two or three years in the early 1940s when the Russians controlled our lands, one of my uncles, Yadollah Kazemi, became a guerrilla fighter in the mountains. He was my fourth uncle. He was brave, but caused trouble for the rest of the family. He went to the Shah's palace and asked him to help. He too had his own story of meeting the Shah. He and a group of other Azarbaijani Khans camped in the palace for some seven nights, were fed well and with courtesy. But finally my uncle said enough of food, we have come to see the Shah. When Reza Shah didn't come, he stopped eating and went on a fast. Eventually the Shah came. My uncle said that his families were all in danger. And we were. When my uncle left, the Russians came and took my father and other three uncles to jail and kept them there for the two years we were occupied.

On the day that the Shah liberated Azarbaijan, the day that my grandmother heard that her sons were safe and released from jail, she had a heart attack and died. I was probably about seven years old. I remember all this vividly. They took us to Tabriz and then to another village to hide us. I remember the day the Russian army came to our village, my *naneh* took us out of the house. My father and uncles were ready to fight, and were dressed with their guns on. But Abbas's grandfather said, "Let these Russians go through peacefully—this too will pass—and don't fight with them." So they all had dinner together—all of them, the Russians and all of us and the Azarbaijanis who were ready with guns. The next day, I remember that they took my father and uncles down the road on their horses and halfway down the road, they made them dismount and took them prisoner. When the Russian army invaded, my *naneh* took the gun my father kept over his safe and brought it to my bed and hid it under my covers and told me to say nothing. The Russians took everything from our house—our rugs, the safe, my father's clothes, and our horses, everything— but they never disturbed my bed or removed my covers. Later, she dug a hole in the garden and buried the gun. We recovered that gun after the Russians left and Azarbaijan was liberated. We raised beautiful Arabian horses; each was dear to us, each had a name, but they took them all. They were going to kill my father and his brothers too, but my younger uncle's father-in-law, Mr. Sadiqian, bribed the Russians and saved their lives.

When they constructed a train service between Tehran and Tabriz, the Shah took the first ride and stopped in our village. My cousin gave him flowers. My uncle reminded him of the medal he had won for fighting the Russians and of his visit to the palace. But yet, when the White Revolution took place, the Shah pinned something on this same uncle and put him in jail. They probably knew my uncle would never stand for the *Takhseem Arazi*—the redistribution of villages to the villagers.

I was seventeen when this White Revolution happened and very happy, but my parents were sad. We thought it might be good. The villagers got what they thought was freedom, but they were like schoolchildren with sudden freedom. They didn't do the chores they had to do to keep the village and land going. So then they sold their lands and moved to Tehran. They had never been in a big city and were lost.

Last year in 1993 I returned to Arbat. Nothing was there. My people were all gone. After the White Revolution, some of my family left. After the Islamic Revolution, the villagers burned our house down. A beautiful house. They could have made a hospital or a school out of our house. Why burn it down? I had hoped they would save their lands and plant the fields.

In those days when we lived there, our villagers were rich. They had every-thing they needed. All my ancestors were born and lived in that village. Our villages had grain and fruit trees. We took care of all the needs of the villagers. The Shah's White Revolution destroyed the economy. People got lost. They were like schoolchildren left without a teacher to tell them what to do. When the land was given to them, they sold the land and went to the cities to clean streets and work in menial jobs. I saw them do this. I asked them, "Do you really prefer to clean floors rather than own and work your own land?"

At the start of the revolution, the villagers threatened to destroy the land-owner. My mother moved to the city with her sons. The burning of our house took place before Khomeini arrived. Later the villagers came to visit mother in Tabriz and said they were sorry, and that they loved her, and that they wished to have her return. Then for a short while, they took my older brother to jail because the Shah had given him a title. Those were such critical crazy days. There would be an announcement in the newspapers saying, "Anyone who has any complaint against this man should come forward." So if anyone came forward and said that he had raped a wife, or robbed a peasant, then he would be shot. But our villagers came and stood in line and said that they loved my brother, that he had been good to all of them. So after forty-five days in jail, the revolutionary guards let my brother free. So we were lucky. My parents' good deeds paid off in this debt the villagers paid to my brother.

My brothers who got degrees from the United States returned to Tabriz or to our village. But when the Iraq-Iran war started and the bombing of Tabriz scared his kids, my older brother grabbed them and fled to Canada. He is not happy in Canada, either. He was happy only in Iran surrounded with relatives.

I went back home a year after the revolution. My mother said, "Iran is going to still be Iran. Arbat is yours. You must come back and rebuild our villages." My mother said to us, "Don't go to America. Stay. This can't last. We have been through so many awful things. This too will pass." Of course that never happened.

Although we were given back our lands, there is no village life left. We once had a lot of everything—beautiful almond trees, apricot trees, plum trees. Now Iran has to import all this from Turkey. Villagers have gone to the city. They tell my brother that they don't know how to live in a city. One young man simply walked through a city street expecting the cars to stop for him. Instead he was hit and died.

Fereydoun Safizadeh

I talked to Safizadeh in his home in San Francisco in 1992. Then a professor of anthropology at San Francisco State University, he had organized for the American Anthropological Association a panel, in which I participated, on exilic discourse. I follow Roqeyeh Kazemi's narrative with Fereydoun's because of the differences they reflect between the female village Azari and the male city Azari. Born in 1947, Fereydoun is a Muslim-Azari from Tabriz married to a Tehrani woman. Here he tells about his childhood in Tabriz, his school and street experiences, his gradual awareness of the politics of class and of ethnicity, and his return to Iran after his senior year at Harvard University.

I was born in 1947 in a family of physicians; both my grandfathers and my father were physicians. My paternal grandfather was trained in Moscow and was practicing in the region of Iravan/Nakhichevan when Muslim-Armenian conflict in the area drove him, his brother, and their families into Maku, Khoy, Salmas, and Urmieh. My mother's side of the family is from Tabriz, and as World War II ended my mother's parents moved back to Tabriz. My parents, who were temporarily in Tehran because of the Soviet occupation of northern Iran, also moved back to Tabriz.

In Tabriz we were part of an extended family that centered around my maternal great-grandparents. After my great-grandfather's death, my great-grandmother and her three sons and their wives and kids lived in the same compound. There were always many kids for us to play with. Our house had been the house of my great-grandmother's brother. It got subdivided into three separate houses with their walled yards. My parents bought the main subdivision. Some of these old houses had their own *birun* and *andarun*. My great-grandmother's house was the place of congregation for the family and the relatives until the time she died in the mid-1960s. She came from an old Tabrizi family.

As to who was most responsible for my socialization, who I got my values from, how I learned to act and behave on the street and at home, and what I did all day as a child? I lived in my great-grandmother's house three or four nights a week. Why? Because her husband had died, she was alone, I was her first great-grandchild, and I was old enough to stay with her without too much trouble. I liked being there. I liked the orderliness of her house. For instance, she always had lunch at twelve noon. In our house lunch time was unclear. It always depended on my father's return from the clinic and his patients. We had a two-hour lunch break during the school day. I would walk from school to my great-grandmother's house, have lunch, and return to school immediately so I could play soccer for an hour or so in the school yard. My great-grandmother's schedule was more dependable. Then, at four o'clock after school I would return to my own house, check around, eat some bread and cheese and then go off to my great-grandmother's house again. This continued until I was in fifth grade. In this period stability and centrality was at my great-grandmother's.

I went to the *Dabestan-e Nemooneh-ye Tabriz*, a school started with help of the American Point Four program in Iran after World War II. There was a fair amount of American military presence in Tabriz as I was growing up; this was because of Azarbaijan's proximity to the Soviet Union.

I was socialized to behave well in public, to be considerate of the needs of others. However, some aspects of an elite life—for example, the ritual of being picked up from school by a chaperon as protection against the elements in the city—were a real problem for me. I refused it most of the time, and by refusing it I opened myself to the rough streets of Tabriz. Struggle with the bullies was a major concern and preoccupation. Too much pride was at stake to enlist parental involvement in the engagements. Nevertheless, the struggle against the bullies left its mark in the anxiety of feeling unsafe in public spaces. Although I did not directly experience it, friends were harassed and blackmailed by hoodlums in the schools. Often the sister/s of the blackmailed kids played a role in harassment. The tough kids would steal a photo of an individual's older sister and pass it around the school, and as a result the boy's reputation and honor would be compromised. We got into many fights on the streets, and fortunately I did not have an older sister who could be the object of harassment and unwanted attention.

I came to the United Sates in 1960 when I was twelve years old and lived with my parents for two years before they went back to Tabriz. My father was a Fulbright scholar at the University of Vermont Medical School. After his return, I went to a boarding school—Woodstock Country School.

Although I had been back to Iran numerous times between 1960 and 1971, I was finally free to go back to Iran after graduation from Harvard in June of 1971. During the sixteen months I was there I did fieldwork in a village outside of Tabriz on the relationship between subsistence farming and commercial dairy production, and made a film focusing on everyday life, the wheat harvest, and agricultural technology. I returned to the United States in 1972 for graduate work in social and cultural anthropology.

How did you understand conflicts in Iran as a child?

After the CIA coup d'etat of 1953 in Iran, the air of illegitimacy hung around Mohammad Reza Shah Pahlavi. Even as a child, one knew something was not quite right. One of my earliest memories was of military officers who were brought from Tehran to Tabriz in the middle of the night by airplane to be executed in the early hours of the morning. I recall my great-grandmother going to a neighbor's house to console the family of the executed man. So, I was never innocent of politics.

Outside Iran, it was on the Berkeley campus that for the first time I saw active student opposition to the Pahlavi rule in Iran in the summer of 1970. I saw students fund-raising to get fellow students out of a San Francisco prison for attacking the Iranian consulate. This was also when students in the United States became more fully aware of the activities of the Iranian secret service, SAVAK, both inside and outside Iran.

Rebwar Kurdi

The Kurds are a stateless nation of about twenty-two million whose moun-
tainous homeland is currently split between eastern Turkey, northeast Iraq,
northwest Iran, northeast Syria, and Soviet Armenia. Each of these countries
has criminalized Kurdish ethnic identity as a threat to the unity of the state.
Harold Pinter's **Mountain Language** is a recent play about the ban placed by
the Turkish government on the Kurdish language. After the disintegration
of the Islamic caliphate in the thirteenth century, Kurdistan was ruled by a
mosaic of Kurdish principalities and ministates. Pursuing expansionist and
centralizing policies, the two rival Ottoman and Iranian states turned Kurdistan into a battlefield between the sixteenth and nineteenth centuries. The two
empires were able to overthrow the Kurdish system of self-rule in the mid-
nineteenth century. The Kurds speak their own language, which is related
to northern Iranian languages, and are, for the most part, Sunni Muslims.
Although the Kurds established an autonomous government during World
War II in parts of Iranian Kurdistan, the Pahlavi regime soon took over the
state, executing and imprisoning many Kurdish nationalists and reimposing
a centralized language and system of government. The Islamic Republic
crushed the autonomist movement in Kurdistan with bombs, massacres, and
more imprisonments.

Rebwar Kurdi (pseud.), born in 1943, is a Kurd who escaped with his family
from Iran in the 1980s. I had long admired Rebwar's commitments and
invited him for a conversation and interview in my office during his visit
to the University of Illinois in 1992. When he revised and edited the original
transcript of our conversation in the summer of 1994, he asked me to omit
references to specific towns in which he lived. His narrative provides not
only another chapter to the story of Iranians in exile through the story of
the Kurds, but is an example of the articulation of ethnic neoracism with
nationalism, a racism that relies on the prejudice of cultural rather than
biological difference.[7]

I asked Rebwar, as I asked all others, to start with memory and identity
("Who made you? What are your earliest images of yourself?") and then to tell
of his early awakenings to Kurdish culture, to nationalism, and to politics;

of his memory of Mossadeq and the Kurds; and, more specifically, of his brother's arrest after the return of the Shah in 1953 after the CIA coup.

The earliest memory and the first image I have of myself is of a classroom and a school—1949, the first school I attended at the age of six. It was an overcrowded school and I remember the first day, a big class of about eighty students and a teacher who had to teach us Persian. But now I remember that he could barely speak the language. He was a Kurd, someone who had learned some knowledge of Persian and Arabic in traditional schools. This was a school in ————, the town where I was born and lived for the first seventeen years of my life.

The adult conversations I remember from my childhood were mostly about the experience of life under the Kurdish Republic of 1946. Two autonomous republics were set up in Iran by the Turks and the Kurds—the Azarbaijan Democratic Republic and the Kurdistan Democratic Republic. Later, I remember that in late summer afternoons when women in the neighborhood took a break, sat down in a corner in the alley and chatted, one of the themes was their memories of the Kurdish Republic. The same thing was done during long and cold winter nights. These are the images that are still with me: schools were all in Kurdish; students studied Kurdish books; there was a Kurdish flag, a Kurdish president, and a Kurdish radio station; students would march in colorful Kurdish dress and sing Kurdish songs, including the national anthem and a nationalist song, *Nishtmanman rangina, bahashti sar zamine* [Our homeland is colorful, it is paradise on earth]. It was illegal to sing these songs after the fall of the republic, but I learned them from the elders. Prominent Kurdish poets composed poetry [passed along by] word of mouth; Kurdish magazines and a newspaper were published. It was the difference between this wonderland they talked about and what I was experiencing (schools where my native tongue and national costume were forbidden) that forms one of my earliest memories.

I remember I did not feel secure. Not only had we lost our own school, we students had to celebrate the downfall of the Azarbaijan and Kurdistan republics every year on *Bist-o-yekome Azar* (December 12). The Shah's regime had declared the day a national holiday—all government offices were decorated, shops and public places had to decorate for the occasion, and the army and school students had to march in front of a huge portrait of the Shah surrounded by army generals and heads of government offices.

We didn't know any Persian. The only source for knowing Persian or contact with Persian was the radio. And at that time few families had any radios. Only the rich families. I know that we didn't have a radio until the early 1950s. The other source of contact between Persians and Kurds would be government officials or those in the army, a military garrison, because most towns in Kurdistan had a military garrison.

But I became especially conscious of my Kurdish identity when I was about fifteen years old. This was 1958. I was in the third year of high school. The Ministry of Education had just started the practice of student camping, which they borrowed from American or European traditions. Summer camps. And I took part in the first summer camp. The camp was dominated by non-Kurdish students and teachers, and we were given the worst part of the camp with one tent and very few supplies for activities. Experiencing discrimination for two weeks made me more aware of my Kurdish identity. As a child, I soon learned that there were two kinds of people—the Kurds and the *Ajams*. Ajam was the name we called both Persians and Turks.

How did you understand the class to which you belonged?
I would consider my family in my home town to have been middle class, or probably between middle and upper class. This really doesn't mean that we were rich, but we quite clearly were much better off than many other families in the city. We had some real estate. Because of my father's profession [he had a shop in the bazaar], I had regular contact with villagers who would come to the city to sell their produce and buy what they needed for the year—clothing, tea, sugar, and whatever they couldn't themselves produce. I also traveled to villages in the summer.

I remember after school we came home and played in the streets with friends. But we had restrictions. In the summer, for instance, my parents would not let us go to the river and swim because they said it was not safe. But we would usually go anyway and sometimes we would be punished for disobedience. The town didn't have any facilities for kids. No libraries, no playgrounds. Later, when I was about fourteen and got interested in studying, I always felt the lack of a library.

In my home, however, we had many books because my mother and one of my brothers had collected books before the 1953 coup while there was still some freedom of publishing. He collected literature, mostly translations of poetry and novels from Soviet literature, and progressive and radical authors that were published in the 1940s and until the 1953 coup. Of course, the press of the period was politically polarized into those supporting the Pahlavi regime and those struggling for a democratic and independent political system.

My most bitter early memory is of my brother's arrest in the fall of 1953 in the aftermath of the CIA coup that brought the Shah back to power. After my father found out about the location of the prison in the hands of the army, it was all bad news. That year was a particularly cold autumn. My brother was kept in an unheated room filled with water, and was tortured just because he had sold an undesirable publication. He got so ill that he never recovered from it, leading to his death later in his life. This is the worst memory of the first twenty years of my life and also my first, my earliest awareness of what the government did.

Let me tell you about another memory, a radio memory of nationalism. This was Radio Cairo. For the first time after the Republic, there was a radio station that aired the Kurdish national anthem, Kurdish revolutionary songs, and Kurdish literature and poetry—all of which had been illegal. It began in 1957 with a daily half-hour program in Kurdish—so important in the life of us Kurds. Everyone went home to listen to this program. Nasser, who was in power at that time, was much against all pro-Western monarchies—the Iranian, Iraqi, and the Jordanian. And this was one way of showing it.

When I returned to school after summer camp and was in the fourth year of high school, we were asked to write an essay on how we spent our summer. My story was about swimming in a river, after which, when I return to put on my clothes, I find a letter in my pocket. The letter contained a message saying, "We are free now and you should try to be free, too," as if it were a message from Iraqi Kurds inviting us to do the same. After I read my composition to the class my teacher told me that I should be careful: "You never know who might be [spying] in the class."

This is what I mean by my youthful nationalism—it made me opposed to the Persians and the Turks and the Arabs. Really, I would say I hated them, just as I did Iranian history and all Iranian kings. I was looking for some Kurdish history.

I wonder how your experience as a Kurdish child shaped your response to the Shah and to the Shahnameh, the Book of Kings.
In school at the beginning of every day we had to sing a song of praise to the Shah. It was either the Iranian national anthem or another song known as *Ey Iran* [O Iran!]. We had to line up every day before going to class and sing one of the songs. But we always changed some of its lines so that it was against the government, and against Iran and everything related to this regime. We were very conscious that we were not Iranians, and so we modified the verses to turn them against the Iranian government. For instance, I remember we changed the first line in the national anthem *Shahanshahe ma zendeh bada* ["Long live our king of kings"] into "Death to our king of kings!" by chanting *mordeh* [death] instead of *zendeh* [live]. Or the last line of *Ey Iran* [O Iran!] was *Dar rah-e to key arzeshi darad in jan-e ma, Payandeh bad khak-e Iran-e ma* [Our life is not worth sacrificing for your sake; may our land of Iran last long!]. We, especially students standing in the last rows, would replace *Iran* with *Kurdan* so that it said "may our land of the Kurds last long!"

The other point about *Shahnameh* is more complex. My mother, for instance, had read *Shahnameh*, although she came from a village at a time when no schools were available in rural areas. One of her brothers, a very enlightened man, worked as a scribe for the landlords. He taught his sisters, including my mother, to read and write. But another brother was not as enlightened, and he strongly opposed allowing his sisters to reach this scale of literacy. Eventually they made a compromise. The girls were allowed to read but not taught to write. So my mother knew most of *Shahnameh* by heart. She would always quote to us lines from the poetry of Ferdowsi, Saadi, and Hafez on different occasions.

She would use lines of poetry to prove her points. For instance, my father and mother are both religious. My father always expected us to do our daily prayers and fast in Ramadan. Sometimes we fasted, but mostly as a social event. And I didn't like to pray. When this caused conflict between us, my mother would recite from Saadi: *"Ibadat be joz khedmat-e khalq nist / Be tasbih o sajjadeh o dalq nist"* [True worshiping is service to people. / It is not prayer beads and genuflection]. Although she was more religious and more devoted to Islam than my father, she would defend us by using Saadi, who had said that serving the people was more important than the formalities of ritual prayer. She always argued that if the people in the town were happy with her children, God also would be.

I remember my mother's books. She had *Shahnameh,* the poetry of Sheikh Attar the great Sufi,[8] Saadi, and others. Most of these books were printed in India. I remember that the paper was yellow and the print was different from those published in Iran.

Did your mother ever learn to write?
By the time I had left Bardashan to go to college in Tehran, she knew she needed this skill and was really troubled because she couldn't write to us. So she had to find someone in the family to write her letters and in spite of the time required for her household work, she started to practice writing. It's still easier for her to say what she wants to say and to have someone else write it for her. But she's a very good reader.

On stories in the *Shahnameh* I remember most clearly, when I was a child what interested me was the fight between the *divs* [demons] and the *pahlavans* [champions, heroes] like Rustam. I couldn't understand more than this. I didn't like the story of Rustam and Sohrab—father killing son; it was a sad story. My mother would quote lines from the book as proverbs and as maxims. I remember her saying, *"Har an kas ke Shahnameh khani konad / Agar zan buwad pahlavani konad"* ["Whoever reads *Shahnameh* / Would be heroic even if the reader is a woman"]. We know now that this is a male chauvinistic statement, but in the absence of an advanced feminist consciousness, it made a point about how women could be empowered through this national epic.

However, in a later stage of my life, my attitude toward the *Shahnameh* changed. Last year, my mother sent me a tape in which she recorded all the advice she had given us; she said it was her will to her children. It included many maxims from Saadi's *Gulistan,* and a long poem by the Kurdish poet Sheikh Raza Talabani. Her advice was to remember God, to observe Islam as our religion, and to be good to people. For the first time, she said something that was critical of Saadi, although in a very respectful manner. She said that following Saadi's advice about seeking education everywhere under any conditions, she had encouraged her children to pursue studying; the result, however, was that they were so dispersed that, in her last years of life, she found herself alone and away from all her children.

Could you relate the stages in which you recall developing Kurdish national and cultural identity?
By the sixth year of high school, when I was in Tehran, I grew even more intensely nationalistic. Although I wasn't able to speak the Tehran variety of Persian, I was in the center of power. But, Tehran offered new opportunities for political and intellectual development.

In Kurdistan, for instance, we had no resources to study about Kurdish history. Before I moved to Tehran, the only source I had access to on the history of Kurdish literature was published in 1952 in Baghdad. This type of book was illegal in Iran, but one of my relatives had the book. Yet I couldn't find *Sharafnameh*, the history of the Kurds. I looked for it everywhere. I knew that two persons had the book, but they were really scared of being found out and wouldn't give the book to anyone, even though this was a sixteenth-century history of Kurdistan written in Persian, translated into Russian, Arabic, Turkish, and French, but not English. Later, of course, in 1964, this was published in Tehran. But anyway, at that time I remember when I came to Tehran, I looked for libraries; I had heard about *Encyclopedia Britannica* and the *Encyclopedia of Islam*. I was in the sixth year of high school and seventeen years old.

Through one of my classmates I found out that I could get access to the library of *Majlis Shoraaii Melli* [the National Assembly], the Parliament of Iran. They said if I got a letter from the high school and applied for a membership card I would have access to this library. I did this and I got a membership card. I remember the experience of going for the first time into the library. I found the cards. They had books in English, French, Persian, Arabic, and other languages. I soon found that they had the *Encyclopedia Britannica*. I remember my excitement. I still remember that I asked for the volume J to K, which was volume 13. And when I opened it, I still remember the feeling of being overjoyed with seeing an article in English about the Kurds, their history and geography. I saw there were other sources cited at the end of the article. I took notes and looked for more books in the library. They had some of the items on the bibliography. From that moment on, this library was my place. After school I would run to the library and read these books.

Meanwhile, many other changes, other events. In Iraq the situation changed. The government began to suppress the freedoms that the people had enjoyed since 1958. Kurdish nationalism and revolutionary songs were no longer aired on the radio. And so in 1961, the Iraqi government attacked Kurdistan and the

Kurds engaged in a resistance war. I was overjoyed with the idea of Kurdish patriotism, and my dream was to join the *peshmargas*—the advance guard, those first to die—in the mountains that I loved so much. The war of resistance was very successful in the beginning, and it became the main preoccupation of my entire life.

So, during my first year at Tehran University, I was not interested in my classes. But I engaged in political and cultural activism once I found out that the Kurdish students were organized and politically active. We were able to get mimeographed publications of the Kurdish autonomous movement in Iraq.

Now I had access to so many libraries—Tehran University libraries, the National Library, the library of the British Council, etc. They had several books on Kurds, Kurdish grammar, and travel accounts of Kurdistan. In fact, I spent most of my time in libraries and bookstores. I remember one of the books I asked for was Oskar Mann's *Die Mundart der Mukri Kurden* (published in 1906), which included the texts of some sixteen Kurdish popular ballads. Some Kurdish students did not share the general nationalist thinking; they were leftists interested in Marxism and the Cuban revolution. One of them, Esma'il Sharifzadeh who became well known later and lost his life in fighting the Iranian government, once asked me (in 1963) if he could come to the National Assembly's library with me so that I could borrow a book for him. The book he wanted was the Persian *The Communist Manifesto*, which was illegal to own or to read. In spite of the risk involved, I asked for the book together with two other titles for myself. And I got it.

Jahan Kurd

Pari and I interviewed Jahan (pseud.), a young man in his thirties, in Los Angeles in 1990. Unlike Rebwar, his memory is that of a city Kurd, one who moved to Tehran as a child and then continued occasional visits to Kurdistan. I include only one of his many anecdotes because it records a moment when the city Kurd becomes aware of a different cultural past, one that will become a part of his constructed ethnic identity.

Ever since I was a child, whenever somebody would ask me, "What's your last name?" I would say "————." And they would say, "Oh, you're a Kurd." So I knew that I was a Kurd. And we would go to Kurdistan, and I could speak Kurdish.

I had been raised and brought up with Tehrani values. Yet I understand and can relate to a lot of Kurdish values and ways of life. When I was about nine or ten years old, in Kurdistan, I had long hair and a BB gun, and in one of the tiny villages up in the mountains one day, a lot of the local boys gathered around me chanting, "Are you a boy or a girl?" They said that an old man with long hair is a dervish. But a young boy with long hair must be a girl.

Their numbers increased and at one point I had about twenty little kids around me screaming, *"Khor i ya kech i?"* ("Are you a boy or a girl?") And then I turned around with the BB gun I was carrying and pointed at one of them, who was the biggest one, and I said, "Okay, I'll kill you right here. That's enough." And he came and grabbed my wrist and actually sort of dragged me to his home and I couldn't do anything. He was much stronger than I. And I didn't know what he was doing. He wasn't hostile toward me. He just said, "Follow me, come with me." And he took me to his home and I saw that his mother was making *doogh* [a yogurt drink]. He told his mother, "The son of so-and-so wants to kill me." And the mother looked at me and said, "Could you go to that room?" Of course I didn't know what to do. I just went into the room in the basement. She brought me some ice cream and some bread and some salt. She put it in front of me and she ordered me to have some. I just took a piece of bread, put some salt on it, and chewed a piece. And she said,

"*Halla ke noon o namak e madaresh ra khordee*" ("Well, now that you've had the bread and salt of his mother"), "you cannot kill my son." And when I left there, for a few days I was in a daze. What did I do? What's going on? Which am I? Am I a Kurd who is part of these clear values or am I a Tehrani who casually threatens to kill one of his mates? But the Kurd lives on another planet.

Daryoosh

Daryoosh is a Zoroastrian married to my cousin (dokhtar khaleh) Soosan. Born in Tehran in 1949, he left Iran to study in the United States in 1969, returned to Iran in 1976, and left after the revolution in 1979. He currently works as a computer programmer in Los Angeles. I use his narrative as a way to introduce Zoroastrianism, yet another religious formation constituting and contradicting the unitary nation and its diaspora. One of the oldest monotheistic religions was founded in northern Iran by the prophet Zoroaster sometime between 628 and 551 B.C. Its supreme deity, the Ahura Mazda (or highest knowledge), is represented through such qualities as good thoughts, good deeds, and good action, and through such symbolically celebrated elements as fire, water, and earth, which are to be protected from pollution. Its central scripture, the Avesta, contains laws, hymns, songs of praise, and codes of ritual purification. It was the state religion of Iran for several centuries during the Achemenid and Sassanian dynasties, but became a minority religion after the Arabs conquered Iran with Islam. In the tenth century, a large group of Zoroastrians, fleeing religious persecution in Iran, settled in India and called themselves Parsis. The most recent count of Zoroastrians[9] records about thirty thousand in Iran, eighty thousand in India, and over three thousand in the United States.

One day, when I was about five [1954], living in Tehran in an old house with a garden full of jasmine, honeysuckle, and a pond, my grandmother, who lived with us, decided she was nearing death. She therefore insisted on returning to Yazd, her birthplace, to die. So we all packed up and, in my father's 1949 Ford, we moved to Yazd, our belongings on the roof of the car.

In Yazd we stayed in this old, old house with *baad gir* [medieval cooling towers]; he points to a picture in a large illustrated book, *Our Homeland Iran*, and says, "This was our house." It was huge. It was made out of *kahgel* (hay mixed with mud) with brick walls. In the summer we slept on the roof. We had a garden that we called *Naarenjestoon* (abode of oranges) because it had trees growing at least ten meters below the surface of the ground. This [*Daryoosh points again to the picture*] is Maidan Meecharma, which is still there in the center of town. As a kid I used to accompany my dad on his rounds. I couldn't wander around by myself, not only because I was young, but because I was Zoroastrian. So we had this area of town that had only Zoroastrians living in it. In this same area was a school I attended—first to third grade—the pictures show how segregated we were; the Zardoshtis [Zoroastrians] and Muslims didn't mix.

When did you first become aware of cultural and religious difference?
I remember one particularly revealing story: I and my father went to a place that sold vegetables, fruit, and yogurt. Father decided he wanted to taste the *mast* [yogurt] before buying it. He put his hand in the huge bowl and licked his finger to see if it had turned sour. Suddenly the shopkeeper shouted: "Ah, *gor, gor,* you have touched the *mast!*" Father said he would pay for the entire bowl of yogurt, and asked how much. The man said, "You have also made the bowl unclean." "All right, how much for the entire thing?" My father had to pay about five tomans for the whole thing—that is probably equivalent to fifteen dollars in current terms—which was a lot for yogurt, but my father paid for it. Then when we came out, my father said what a strange man, when you find *ta'asob* [intolerance or prejudice] something strange happens that makes you lose touch with reality. This man doesn't realize the worth of the bowl he has just given me with the *mast.* In fact my father still has that bowl—a beautiful antique ceramic piece.

This was Yazd where Muslims were rigid believers. Our world was divided between the inside where everyone was a friend, but as we left our quarters we had to watch out. Out there was a different world where we were *najis* [unclean]. It was as if we entered another world in which we had to translate ourselves. For instance, we couldn't laugh or run or touch things because it was the environment of strangers.

In our quarters, I remember the making of *halwa ardeh*—sesame sweet. I remember the sesame ground in huge wheels. I remember a Haji's sweet shop. He was a very kind man who would *ta'arof* [politely offer] his sweets to me. I found it strange that a Haji would be so kind and offer sweets where other Muslim shopkeepers didn't want me to touch their stuff.

How would they know you were a Zardoshti? And how did you understand your own difference?
Perhaps because of the way we clothed ourselves. I remember Muslims wore dark clothes while we always wore bright clothing. I still don't like seeing black. Unlike Muslims, Zoroastrians needed only a few basic rules about cleanliness and truthfulness, and a few observances. Our ideas of cleanliness were different from what we saw around us. One of our signs of cleanliness was our [required] thin muslin underwear, which was always white as were

our caps. That is what I understood by cleanliness—you had to wear white, which showed dirt and therefore indicated when it needed to be washed. Our religion was very peaceful. Islam was not. I once saw a Moharrum procession in Karaj with the mourners beating themselves until they bled. I was shocked. During the Shah's time such *dastehs* [processions] were illegal. In spite of all the differences I've listed, my closest friends as I was growing up were either Muslims or Jews. Our school was exclusively for Zoroastrians; so was our gym. We had *poorsa* [open house] and *rooza* [fasting]. The open house would admit and accept anyone. For instance, such a day might be the anniversary of my grandfather's death; I remember the feast—the bread and meat and greens. We'd have roast meat with greens of every sort around it.

Another story I remember about Yazd and its Muslims is that one of the men who had worked for my father was going blind. He had cataracts. My father said that he should come to Tehran, stay with him, that he would take care of his eyes and his surgery and would then return him to Yazd. This old man couldn't see; he stayed for three days in the hospital, but when he came to our house, he wouldn't touch anything because he feared it was *najis*. He sat in the corner of a room on a piece of cloth in which he had packed his clothing, and he would sit only on this cloth. Once my father went out and got him a primus stove and his own set of dishes that he would wash in our pond. He refused to eat our food, but he didn't mind accepting our hospitality and my father's money.

I found it very interesting—learning to translate always. In America too I feel the same—almost. I still have to translate myself for others.

In high school, we had to attend classes in Islamic religious studies. There was much in Islam I couldn't understand. Zoroastrians are a peaceful people, and our religion never speaks about war. When they spoke of Imam Husain in battle at Karbala, it didn't make sense to me. The rules of five prayers also made no sense to me. One of the things we were taught was *wozoo*—the ritual cleansing before Muslim prayer. I never got this—the source of the water had to be over three-feet deep—I remember that in Yazd, Muslims would go to these filthy ponds, but it was the right depth. Well, the religion, we were told, only specified the depth and source of the water, not its purity, so whatever was was right.

Our rituals were different. I remember ritual journeys to Pirsabz—a beautiful place with waterfalls and greenery. The Zoroastrians go there once a year. Why? The legend is that the daughter of Yazdgird, as they were fleeing from the invading Arabs, shed tears in the caves and her tears produced the greenery. The area was full of caves. We would light fires and candles, and there right in the middle of the desert would open up a heaven—these caves. We set up tents in any flat area and there were lights. It was cool and green and everybody laughed and sang and danced till 2:00 a.m. We would go in family groups every year from the time I was six till I was about ten. And that's my fondest memory of Yazd.

My experience of religion in my own house for many years centered around *Norooz* [the Persian new year] and preparations before, during, and after the new year. We had to, at *Tahvil* [the moment of the equinox], go to Shah Bahram's site in downtown Tehran. We went to our temple, *Dar Mehr*, "door of love" literally, and said prayers to do, say, and think the right thing. Then we lit incense, which I loved. To help the needy we bought oil—mustard oil, I think—for the oil-burning lamps; we bought the oil from the needy. Then everyone would come in and we would wish them a happy new year and kiss and hug and then we would eat roast beef and *noon, panir, sabzi* [bread, cheese, herbs], and *gipah*. This was rice mixed with beans and meat all stuffed into the stomach lining of a sheep, which would get sewn up like a coconut and would then be simmered in a soup. Once it was cooked, the inside of the lining was not wet. Then we ate a special delicious bread called *seerog*; the dough would be made by elders in the family, a soft dough, flat, sticky, twirled like pizza, and when dropped in a frying pan would turn light red and bubble, onto which they'd sprinkle sugar and *advieh* [cinnamon, cardamom, cloves] and almonds and pistachios.

Each time a different family would be responsible for the table—this was called *porsa*. At home we gave gifts to each other. Father always gave us our gifts wrapped in a green handkerchief and a white handkerchief. Inside the handkerchief was oregano, marjoram, *seenged* [jujube berry], candy, and our money—always a multiple of seven, which was a mystic number. The younger you were, the less you would get. After returning from the temple, we would visit the oldest relative in the family—our grandfather. He would have a gold coin for us. He would sit in his chair and we would line up and have a piece of *sarv* [evergreen] in our hand for him. First the youngest would take the smallest gold coin—the *rob-Pahlavi*, the quarter Pahlavi coin. Grandfather would have a piece of evergreen too and would say, *"Eid shoma mobarak"* ["happy new year"], and we would say the same and he would hug us. We also would say *"chesm-o-dil-tun-sabz-bashe,"* or "may your eyes and heart remain green forever." Then he would give us our coin. The kids would try to trick Grandfather by standing in line again.

We were about nine kids, followed by my parents who would be given full Pahlavis. Even now my mother carries *sarv* [evergreen] with her to weddings along with the traditional candy. My father always said that religion was our choice, that to be a Zoroastrian you have to make a *Sedreh Koshti*—*Sedreh* is the white undergarment that Zoroastrians wear; *Koshti* is a white cord. Every morning during prayers, you make a commitment by tying a knot in the white string. As you fulfill each task, you untie a knot.

Here in L.A. my son attends a class every two weeks with priests who help educate young Zoroastrian children in the Avesta. One of the requirements for becoming a Zoroastrian is to do the *Sedreh Koshti.* Prior to that you are required to study other religions so that you become a Zoroastrian by choice rather than by parental decree.

Kambys Shirazi

Born in Mashhad in 1953, Kambys (pseud.) grew up in Nishapur and moved to Tehran to attend college in 1972. He is an economist who works on developmental problems in third-world countries. Because he was one of the few interviewees to have attended the most politicized and active of the colleges at Tehran University—the college of engineering—I asked him to talk of his understanding of class, gender, and politics while he was a college student. I found the narrative of this small-town country boy, and of his brothers' and sister's migratory movement from country to city and then to the United States, a revealing tale of individual enterprise and of the political conditions that encouraged flight. Like Rebwar Kurdi and Roqeyeh Kazemi, he is from the country rather than the city, from an outlying province rather than Tehran. I retain here only the parts of his narrative where he speaks of class, of gender politics at the university, of the political culture of the college of engineering, and of his reasons for leaving Iran. I asked him how he acquired the irony, humor, and distance I observed in his responses to Iran and to the revolution.

Who am I. Perhaps part of the answer lies somewhere in my divided background. My parents came from two very different families. My father's grandparents were very religious, very strict; my mother's family, very relaxed, very open to any kind of discussion.

My mother came from a small town [we'll call it Kuchek] of about ten thousand in northern Iran. My grandfather was the doctor in the town. He was not a formally trained doctor. He was trained at a religious school as a doctor—*Tebb-e Qadim* [traditional medicine]. He had a lot of books around the house. Although he died when I was twelve, his education and vision generally influenced the environment of the house—an environment that was upper-middle class or upper class.

The culture of the entire town was relaxed. People felt entitled to their fixed positions in that town and settled into them. As a result, people seemed to be rather relaxed about life. Everyone had something to do. Your earnings, your respect, etc., did not come from your merits. It came from where you were born. We went to Kuchek almost every summer until I was about ten or eleven. When my grandfather got sick, we went and stayed for about two months. We stayed with my grandfather. He had a big garden, with lots of trees and fruit where we were free to do whatever we liked. Kuchek was a rural town. Just at the edge of the garden there were fields. It was a treat to go wherever we wanted. It was such a safe place where everyone was friendly. The adults never cared where we went. When I was as little as six, I could walk for a mile or two away from home exploring by myself. I loved it. Farmers, for example, when they were threshing wheat, would let you ride on their *bardoo*—their threshers.

Kuchek and my mother's family contrasted with my grandmother's house from my father's side in Mashhad. She was very religious and never hesitated to wake me at 5:00 in the morning to say my prayers. Mashhad was perhaps my earliest firsthand experience with fanaticism, though my father was skeptical about faith—doubted and questioned conventional wisdom.

Also, this was a time when the general culture in Iran moved toward Westernization. My father admired my grandfather from my mother's side long before he became related to them. They lived in a very small town near Kuchek. My father ran the post office. My grandfather ran the hospital, a kind of clinic. They met when my father was about twenty-four and belonged to the same Sufi sect.

Understanding that class means something different in city and county, how did you experience and then understand class difference?
My mother's attitude about class probably should be acknowledged first. Kuchek was a totally structured society, in the sense that it was clear who belonged to which class, who was landed and who wasn't, and so on. When we visited Kuchek, one thing was very clear: who we could and could not associate with. We were not encouraged to associate with lower classes; my mother had fixed ideas about how we should talk to them if we did. Also, we were expected to be deferential to the upper class. I think in that village we were right in the middle but tending toward the upper class because of my mother's side of the family. My father came from a very middle-class family quite different from my mother's. He followed the rules, but he never tried to teach us how to talk to other people in terms of class. Outside his bureaucratic position, he treated all classes the same way. His behavior influenced me a lot. I didn't like the way my mother handled class.

Actually, the geography of Kuchek, the way the town was set up, repeated these class differences. There was the upper side of the town, where the upper class lived, with cars, and then, as you moved toward the middle of town, houses became smaller. And there were no more cars. Downtown consisted of government offices and its employees. Then, toward the lower part of town, there were the lower classes. The land was graded, not north and south, but rather from west to east; so I think it was the western part of the town that was the highest plane.

In other words, the land sloped from where the upper classes lived toward where the lower classes lived, and I think the flow of water determined this. Water flowed first to the upper-class houses and then to the others. The place was irrigated by two streams of water. One came from a very long distance away, and it was sweet water. The other one was salty water, and it was used for irrigation. Both of them came from the same route though their sources were different. There was a very extensive irrigation network that routed these two streams. All the upper classes had these streams going through their houses. Also, it flowed through my grandfather's house. I remember especially that the salty water sparkled. They muddied the sweet water because it had to flow great distances and they wanted to make sure the stream bed was covered with a little mud so the water didn't sink in. People were employed upstream to add clay to the water. It was not fun to jump into that water. You weren't supposed to, because it was drinking water. The other salty one, for irrigation, you could jump in.

Once when my older brother returned from England in the summer of 1968 full of Marxist ideas, I witnessed a revolt inside the house, all of us against my mother on the issue of class, on the excessive respect she showed to the upper classes who dominated society. I was in high school, fourteen years old, and had no idea who Marx was. My brother would make fun of my mother. Sometimes she got angry—"What has my family done to you, or my relations on the upper side of the town, that you are talking about them like this?"

We lived a middle-class or lower-middle-class life. What defines class for me? Well, we didn't have a car. We didn't have many appliances. My father had a good position as chief of the post office. But his income was not much. We couldn't afford our own house. Rather, we lived in a house rented by the post office for my father.

One incident that made me very aware of where I stood economically happened when I went to Tehran University in 1972. I thought that I would go to a dormitory because it was cheap. You paid two hundred tomans [about $25] for two months and you could stay for a year as opposed to renting a room, which was at least two hundred to three hundred tomans a month. I was interviewed by a professor in charge of allocating students to dormitories. They told us to bring documents proving our father's income. When I produced the document from the finance ministry showing that his monthly income was fifteen hundred tomans [about $180], the professor in charge accused me of bringing him a forged document. He couldn't believe that anyone could live on so little. It was then that I understood that I was not yet middle class, because middle class meant that you could afford to rent a room. And I couldn't. So I understood class only when I moved to Tehran.

Could you talk about gender politics at the university?
I have thought about this issue quite a bit, because this was an everyday problem when I was at Tehran University. The setting was like this. The engineering school consisted of mostly men. There were a few women, most of whom came from lower-middle-class and middle-class families. The upper classes usually sent their kids abroad. I would say most of the men who were in my classes had never spoken to a woman in their lives, except to mothers and sisters. They are brought up in such a segregated society that when they actually want to talk to a woman, they don't know who these creatures are. Women, I believe, have similar stories on the other side. Their languages were different, the words we used were different, and there was very little contact even on the university level.

There was also the geography and politics of seating in university classrooms. There was a woman in our class in engineering school who complained that no one would speak to her because she was female—or sit next to her. Whenever she came into class, even if there was an empty seat between her and some guy, the guy would simply get up and move to the other seat farther away. My understanding was that men felt uncomfortable simply because they thought that being next to a woman was a distraction. She talked to me once in a while because nobody else would talk to her.

There was always this sense that if you get close to a woman, the intention must be sexual. Therefore, parents protected their daughters' reputations from men, assuming that all contacts were necessarily sexual. The scrutiny of female behavior was so intense that if ever a woman broke that code of behavior, she was branded an outlaw or an eccentric—the sort you don't marry. All this led to a lot of sexual frustration, whose effects I saw in the harshness and constant fights between Iranians.

Let me give you an example that I think shows the root of the gender problem at this university. Women at the university had the worst dormitory. The rooms were all too small and cramped. So the university decided to take over one of the buildings in the main dormitory area, the northern part of the area where there were men's dormitories, and give it to the women. But this event, which became the source of agitation, was read as a sign that the university intended to bring women and men sexually closer, to engage them in illicit deeds in order to prevent them from being good revolutionaries. The reaction was very harsh. Women were beaten, their buses were burned, and they were kicked out of restaurants. They were called whores. This was not just fundamentalist Muslims. The so-called Marxists had exactly the same fury. Socially, Marxists behaved exactly like religious Muslim fanatics. There was no difference. The difference was a scarf. That was it. Leftist women didn't wear a scarf. Muslims did.

Could you talk about the political culture in the college of engineering?
The engineering school's culture is an old one. It was known to be the best school for the smartest, most select, most ambitious students who had made the highest scores on the entrance exams. The engineering school therefore experienced its share of repression from the regime. There was a history of activism in this school going back to the time of Mossadeq in the '50s when it had been most visibly active in his support. Four students had been killed on campus while protesting the coup after Mossadeq's fall, a protest incited by Nixon's visit to Iran shortly after the coup. When, during campus demonstrations, the police arrested some engineering students, that day became known as Student's Day—the sixteenth of Azar.

By the early 1970s a legacy of political culture and protest was built around that engineering school. You didn't have to look very far to see that income distribution was intolerably bad. When the Tudeh Party started in the '50s, strong Left-leaning students joined because that was also a time of great social injustice. The organizational skills of the engineering college were tremendous. There were networks where students would signal indirectly to each other so an outsider would not be able to understand. Sometimes, the whole college would shut down in protest. The guerrilla movements had their own network.

So there were several networks—the Fadayaan network, the Mojahedin network, the Tudeh network, and other religious groups who sympathized with Mojahedin, but kept their distance. Essentially, the school split into two groupings, the secular Left and the religious groups, and each one had its own library. The students had managed to gain control of almost every activity in the college. We had a system of representation; each class would select one student as its representative. We had about thirty representatives who made the schedule of exams. Imagine the complexity—the exams were two months long. I was a representative for three years and spent hours begging students to let me schedule the exams so they would be done in two or three days. Sometimes in the middle of the semester the entire schedule would fall apart and protests would close down the university, and we would all come back two months later.

So we controlled the scheduling of classes, we controlled the copying or xeroxing, and we therefore controlled the networks. We could shut down any activity at critical points (for example, to stop an exam). The SAVAK and the university officers also interacted with the system by hiring spies. When people got captured, you suspected that insiders had provided the information.

After the revolution we learned a lot about that. People came to my house who were friends who I never thought could be SAVAK, yet they turned out to be SAVAK. One of them was someone who helped me find a house; he was always there. When I started thinking back on this, he had the signs of SAVAK, but I just didn't see it. Once he came with a transmitter that was the size of my finger and could stick to any metal. And when I asked him where he got it he said his uncle had gotten it from Mecca. It didn't occur to me to doubt him; I had known him so long. I was in political trouble myself. He could have gotten me into much more trouble but didn't. He wanted me to help him with his exams; he was always failing and obviously was not the same caliber as the rest of us.

The story of my near arrest is this: SAVAK did not have my address once when they were looking for me, so they went to my uncle's house. I had advance notice about that, so I ran off to Nishapur. When they arrived at my uncle's house the second time, he turned to them and said, "My nephew would never get in trouble with SAVAK, impossible. Right now he's at home with his parents studying"—not knowing that was where I was hiding. You can imagine the rest. I thought I had gone to Nishapur to hide from this trouble.

It was my birthday, and I had taken the car that morning to be fixed. When I brought the car back home, my father went inside and I stayed outside to check something on the car. My father came back out and said SAVAK was here looking for me. I jumped into the frozen canal next to the house and ran away. My uncle was supposed to come to my birthday. I went to his house and spent the night there. The next morning I caught a bus and went to Mashhad. I stayed in my own room at the university for a couple of weeks until the university opened. This is 1976. I went to the dean of the college of engineering and told him what had happened. He didn't believe in this kind of student activity. He made me see the vice chancellor. I took my uncle with me. The vice chancellor called SAVAK, who, because I had come forward by myself, promised to let me go after twenty-four hours. That day I was taken in for questioning; I was released about noon, but I had to come back the next morning. When I went home I discovered SAVAK had come and taken everything from my room. That was my fault for giving the address. It turned out that I had been present at a demonstration where someone had been arrested. He had been pressured to tell, so he gave my name. He actually came that very day and told me this and asked me to tell them I wasn't there. They didn't believe me, so my travel outside Iran was held up for six months.

My trouble with SAVAK convinced me to leave for the United States.

Keyvan

This and the next two narratives are from young men who were compelled to leave Iran as teenagers to avoid the consequences of war and revolution. Keyvan was twenty-three and an undergraduate at the University of Illinois when I spoke to him in 1990. Born in 1968, he was in high school in Iran during most of the revolution and will discuss that experience more specifically in Part Two. His sense of national identity and religion is produced out of the nexus of a particular family, class, and time that he describes below.

My adolescence was that of the revolution. My family was typical in many ways. What was not typical was that we were more educated—both my parents were doctors. We had a different kind of life from the other families we knew. My parents resisted the easy way to get money, refused to get involved with politics, and also refused to do abortions. After my mother went to Mecca in '72, she decided not to drink or swim or take pleasure in what she had before.

My sense of religion is therefore filled with conflict, and the source was my family. My mother is very religious and says her prayers five times a day. She would like to fast but doesn't. It was her practice that turned me against religion. I saw it as a trap and as a chain that she had put on herself. And when the Islamic Revolution took place, even though I was a child, I distrusted it. Religion also was a source of conflict between my mother and father. I felt one didn't need religion to be morally correct. I respected my father, who was morally upright without religion.

I got my sense of being Iranian and my sense of politics in school very young. We had to recite such verses as:

> Ma Golhaaii Khandaan eem
> Ma Farzandan i Iraneem
> Iran ra doost dareem
> Ma keshwar khod ra dooost medareem
>
> [We are flowers of laughter
> We are sons of Iran

We love Iran
We love our own country]

So from kindergarten and early recitations of such rhymes, we were given a sense of the grandeur of Iran stretching from China to Egypt. We found a sense of identity through our history courses. We were made proud of the past, but we saw how the country had now shrunk as a result of the USSR taking one part, the British another, and so on. We learned of the destruction of the Moghuls, the Arabs, the Greeks. Our xenophobia began in the Shah's time when we were taught a distrust of foreigners as the sources of fragmentation of the Persian empire.

I still love my country but can't do anything about it.

The image of war we received as I was growing up was all about its glory. When we were in school, volunteers would come and ask us to join; they would bring in coffins of dead schoolmates for whom we were to pray, and we would cancel classes in their honor. The book that helped me get past this phase and see through the war and begin to understand was *All Quiet on the Western Front*. I gave that book to a teacher who wanted to join the war. Stupid of me, because the teacher could have turned me in.

Before the revolution, one thing that bothered me was the rich kids with fancy jackets in school. The richest were the Communists—they would throw out fancy words I didn't understand, their fathers were driving BMWs, and they were talking proletariat. I saw the transformation of our teachers who became brown-nosers of the government. Eighty percent of the students I knew felt a sort of bonding with each other. The revolution made us even closer because we could talk about our confusion. We started our own networks, started a chemistry lab in the basement of my house. My friend and I really got involved in chemistry because both of us wanted so badly to blow up someone. But that early passion contributed toward both of us later becoming interested in chemistry in college, where I became a chemical engineer.

My identity was born out of learning self-defense against the unexpected. Often we had no lights, no power; the war brought a constant shortage of electricity. I feared the loss of my father.

I learned about sexuality and gender difference in typical ways, too. My parents don't know this, but I would read their books on sexuality. But those books probably taught me more about sexual diseases than about sexual intercourse. The mixed messages I was getting were many. Sometimes I would walk back from school with students. If a girl would look at us, that would make our day. If a button was open on her dress, we would be ecstatic. There was a girls' high school next to ours. To avoid the accidental mixing or encounter between boys and girls, the Islamic government changed the times that the schools would start and end. So we would wait to take a bus, hoping we could sit behind a girl, praying that one would sit by us, hoping we could steal a look.

Soheyl

I interviewed Soheyl (pseud.) in the summer of 1990 at my home. My friend Evelyne Accad called me one day in the summer of 1990 and asked if I would pick up a young man flying in from France. His father had been a student of her friend Paul Vieille, the French sociologist who had lived and worked in Iran. Born in 1962, Soheyl lived in Iran until his parents compelled him to leave to avoid being drafted into the Iran-Iraq war. I taped his stories during the few days he stayed with us in 1991 while his dormitory was closed. His story is relevant to understanding the immigrant experience of young men of his age group who left Iran as teenagers. He was a strangely melancholic youth, articulate and passionate in his opinions on social issues. He spoke in Persian.

I was born in a small village in central Iran in 1962. My father worked as a high school teacher but also studied for advanced degrees in Tehran, and also studied foreign languages. He married my mother, who had been one of his high school students. She was seventeen years old and very beautiful, but, my father said, a very weak student. When she got married, she quit high school and got pregnant at the age of eighteen with the first of four children. I am the oldest. We moved from house to house and city to city some twenty times.

I suppose the most important force that formed me was the relation between my mother and father. Their differences were projected onto me. I saw my father as an emotionally unreliable man—a lack that revealed itself in his relations toward me, my mother, and my sister and brothers. I saw a lack of respect in my father toward my mother and a lack of connection between my parents. But that was not the end. We eventually discussed this problem with him and he has changed. We made him understand that he *had* to change his behavior toward us and his wife. And he did.

But what you need to understand is that we grew up not only in a nuclear family, not only in an extended family, but also as part of a street family. We spent at least four or five hours a day playing outside with all the kids in our neighborhood. And that was important in my formation.

But I was also formed by a traditional family. When I say traditional family, I mean the extended family: the father, the mother, the children, the aunts, the uncles, etcetera—something like a tribe. When a tribe is dissolved, the family is dissolved and the individual feels isolated.

My family is both modern and traditional. My father was born in a village in northern Iran in a house so primitive that I couldn't believe my own eyes when I saw it. It was built with a few stones on top of one another. My grandfather supported a family of five collecting and selling wood for fireplaces. The village clergyman served also as the schoolteacher and the village doctor. This is where my father came from. He told me that whenever he saved a few pennies he would go to Tabriz (the nearest large town) and buy a book. He taught himself German, and later on he came to Tehran and became a teacher. And at the time of the Shah's rule he got a scholarship to study in Europe and became what he is today—a sociologist and writer.

In Europe, he witnessed the events of May 1968, the revolution of a class of young semicommunists, semianarchists against the ruling class, and this event had a grave impact on him. He stayed there, studied, and received his doctorate degree in social research, returned to Iran, became a university professor, and joined the Iranian intelligentsia, and if the revolution hadn't occurred, he would've probably accomplished even more.

But, in spite of all that education, this man, in the context of his own family, acted like his own father had acted in that northern village; all the events of May 1968 and all the schooling he had in Europe did not change him from the patriarch he was. The books he wrote reflected a modern liberal totally different from the traditional authoritarian he was in his own home. Of course Europe had changed him some; he had become more refined and polished, and less of an extremist, but his essence hadn't changed. My father is an example of a type of Iranian intellectual who succeeded in public but not in the private sphere, who was totally lost when it came to the way he treated his children.

And therefore, what bothers me most about Iran is the patriarchal family system. I really can't stand it. I have never had an Iranian girlfriend because family customs compel a girl to be totally dependent on her family. A man and a woman have totally different perceptions about their roles in their parents' home. I know about myself, for example, that when I was growing up and later after puberty, I always had a sense of rebelliousness toward my family. I always saw in Khomeini certain characteristics I saw in my own father. And in my uncle and my male cousins. I know them and I know how they behave in their homes. Khomeini didn't fall from the skies. Khomeini is a figure who represents the Iranian man. He is like my own father who insisted that I must study mathematics and biology, not caring what I preferred. In spite of all his theoretical knowledge of freedom, in spite of his living through Paris in May 1968, in spite of all his books and articles about freedom, in the context of his family, he was a dictator.

Ali Behdad

Ali, born in Sabzevar in 1961, was compelled to leave Iran as a teenager in 1979. He teaches in the English and Comparative Literature departments at UCLA and has published widely in colonial and postcolonial literature and theory. I visited Ali with my tape recorder in May 1994, when he talked with characteristic thoughtfulness about his ambivalence toward his past and present, about what Iran represents for him, and about his current understanding of his specific exilic melancholia.

Some of the current contradictions I experience have their genesis elsewhere, in my childhood and in my relationship with my parents.

My mother married my father when she was fourteen and he was nineteen. We lived in Sabzevar, a town in northeastern Iran near the holy town of Mashhad. My mother was from one of the best-known families in Sabzevar—the Oskoowi family. And in fact that's what my wife refers to as my Oskoowi complex, because in it lies the source of some of my attitudes. They were merchants originally from Oskoo in Azarbaijan who settled in Sabzevar; they had the monopoly over cotton and cumin in the town. My father was from a landlord family turned merchant—one who failed, obviously inadequate in relation to the Oskoowi. He later became an accountant in the National Bank. Their relationship was one of inadequacy; they are a very unhappy couple.

What aspects of your personal and cultural identity can you trace back to Sabzevar?
I now crave the kind of intimacy I experienced there. This I associate with *Irani boodan*, with being Iranian. We had a big family and always socialized at least once a week in family *dowrehs* [gatherings]. In the summer we would go to our *baghs* [gardens] in villages in Abari or Kasqan—and these are among my more pleasant memories. Many childhood memories in Sabzevar are connected with my later intellectual engagement. For instance, when I was about twelve, I was friends with a couple of boys who were reading Ali Shariati. So I started reading Shariati. Ali Shariati in fact is from Sabzevar, and I remember once passing

his car as a child and my friend Kaffash pointing him out to me and saying that Shariati wasn't "that kind" of Muslim, that he liked Western music. And Kaffash, the friend who introduced me to Ali Shariati, is now the president of some university in Sabzevar. Shariati, of course, talked of Patrice Lumumba, so that led me to read Patrice Lumumba and Martin Luther King.

Sabzevar was also where I became religious—a revolutionary religious—because at this time the mullahs were really working toward the revolution. This is one of the details that leftists in Iran don't talk about. But mullahs came from Qum to teach the Qur'an and revolutionary Islam. And one summer I did that. I went and learned to read the Qur'an with *qaraat* [the proper rhythms]. But in weekly evening meetings, these same mullahs would talk about revolution in the disguise of religion. And this is the network that finally made the Iranian revolution. That's why the leftists lost—because they never understood the power of the mullahs' access to the smallest towns and villages. These memories gain in importance with time. We moved from Sabzevar to Tehran when I was thirteen.

Isfahan, the capital of Iran in the sixteenth and seventeenth centuries. The photo is from a postcard showing the main square, known as Maidan Imam (formerly Maidan Shah), built under Shah Abbas (1587–1629). Photographer unknown.

Bombast Najmabadi (Najmabadi Blind Alley), in Afsaneh Najmabadi's neighborhood. Photo by Zohreh Sullivan.

Mohamad Tavakoli's neighborhood in South Tehran. Photo courtesy of Mohamad Tavakoli.

The mosque in Mohamad Tavakoli's neighborhood in South Tehran. Photo courtesy of Mohamad Tavakoli.

Zia Ashraf Nasr. A framing voice in the book, her life spans the century and two revolutions. Photo courtesy of Mrs. Nasr.

Maidan Azadi (Freedom Square), earlier called Shahyad Square. This was the arrival point of many revolutionary marches. Photo courtesy of Taimur Sullivan.

A bazaar passage surrounding the central square in Isfahan. Photo by Zohreh Sullivan.

Left: A home in the village of Zabol. The structure, made of *kaghel* (straw and mud), shows that no matter how poor, homes are enclosed with walls whose interior shows a *birun* (outside) and an *andaran* (inside). Photo courtesy of Zahra Dowlatabadi.

Below: A common street scene all over Iran—a boy carrying his daily bread surrounded by vegetables. Photo couresy of Zahra Dowlatabadi.

A less common scene—a chic fruit, nut, and sweet store in Tehran. Photo courtesy of Zahra Dowlatabadi.

Above: A Tehran street scene with murals of the Ayatollahs Khomeini and Khamenei on the right and the martyrs of the war on the left. Photo courtesy of Taimur Sullivan.

Left: With skulls as stars and bombs as stripes, this is one of the few remaining "Down with the USA" signs left in Tehran in 1999. Photo courtesy of Taimur Sullivan.

Hoseinieh Ershad, in Tehran, where Ali Shariati delivered his revolutionary lectures. Photo courtesy of Zohreh Sullivan.

CHAPTER 3

Revolution: Narrating Upheaval

> Bliss was it in that dawn to be alive,
> But to be young, was very heaven.
> —Wordsworth, *The Prelude*,
> on the French Revolution

The Eye of the Hurricane

Although Mohamad Tavakoli and Tahereh were children in 1963, because they lived in South Tehran they remembered the 1963 anti-Shah, pro-Khomeini demonstrations in the bazaars. The symbolic, strategic, and social center of conservative political activity in major cities has historically been the bazaar. Analogous to a medieval Wall Street with control over guilds and craftsmen, it is made up of a concentrated cluster of shops in alleys where artisans produce and merchants sell such goods as copperware, rugs, fabric, and other small-village crafts. The *bazaaris* played important roles in undermining the Constitutional Revolution of 1905–1911, in the anti-British agitation that led to nationalization in the 1950s, and in supporting the 1979 revolution. Traditionally conservative, they unified in opposition to the government, first in 1977 when price-control campaigns were imposed upon them, and then after the student killings in Qum and Tabriz. Of Khomeini's promises to the *bazaaris*, the most seductive was his anti- imperialism that translated into a support of Iranian production of Iranian goods.

Agitprop and the Political Drama of Protest

If the causes of the revolution were complex and multiple, its dramatic form was simple, unified, and modeled on religious protest.[1] The *bazaaris* and the clerical leadership (*Ulama*) made use of each Moharrum from 1977 to 1979 to agitate large masses in replaying the drama of Khomeini as the martyred Husain with the Shah as the arch villain Yazid. Several of my interviewees repeated the chants to me. Here is one of the most popular, quoted by Michael Fischer:

> CHEERLEADER: Naft ki burd? [*Who took our oil?*]
> CROWD: Amrika! [*America!*]
> CHEERLEADER: Gaz ki burd? [*Who took our gas?*]
> CROWD: Shuravi! [*Russia!*]
> CHEERLEADER: Pul ki bord? [*Who took our money?*]
> CROWD: Pahlavi! [*Pahlavi!*]
> REFRAIN: Marg bar in Silsila-yi Pahlavi! [*Death to this Pahlavi dynasty!*] (1980b, 190)

By the summer of 1978, enough blood had sanctified the protests to draw in slum dwellers and suburbanites, students and poets, intellectuals and *bazaaris*. Even political prisoners in a Tehran prison went on a hunger strike. There were demonstrations in several towns through the month of Ramazan, which began on August 5. But the major tragedy of Ramazan 1978 was the Cinema Rex fire that killed some four hundred people and was instantly blamed on SAVAK (though this judgment was later reversed). Immediately after Ramazan, on the day known as Black Friday, September 8, thousands gathered in Jaleh Square in Tehran. When students and ordinary citizens sat down in response to a command, they were fired on by troops. Stories about this event differ, but the body count was high enough to provoke a storming of government institutions by the crowd. Eight days later a catastrophic earthquake in Tabas killed over twenty-six thousand people.

Khomeini's expulsion from Iraq was followed by a series of strikes by workers ranging from taxi drivers to postal workers, teachers, and bankers. When the oil workers went on strike on October 18, the government started to panic. Queen Farah went on pilgrimage to Najaf to ask the Ayatollah Khoi for help in negotiating with the opposition. But it was too late. Strike leaders were arrested; oil company helicopters were stoned; Prime Minister Sharif Emami resigned; and Karim Sanjabi, the leader of the National Front, was arrested.

A second Moharrum of the revolution began with banners, new slogans, and more theatrics. Men in white *kafans* (death shrouds) marched in the streets in defiance of antidemonstration laws, and balconies were ablaze with the sounds of "*Allah-o-Akbar*" ("God is Great").

January 1979 began with a new prime minister, Shahpur Bakhtiar, who tried to calm the nation by supporting the Days of Mourning desired by Khomeini in Paris, by lifting martial law in Shiraz, and by making peace with as many ayatollahs as he could. All the networks in the United States carried shots of jubilant crowds putting carnations into the gun barrels of soldiers. On January 16, 1979, the Shah left Iran.

1978–1979: Objective Impact, Subjective Responses

"A great, great time in the history of Iran," said Yahya, echoing so many of the younger Iranians who had experienced the short-lived *Bahar-i-Azadi,* or Spring of Freedom. Others spoke of the ecstasy of open discussions, books, new publications of forbidden books, open debates on TV between Marxists and Islamicists, and the headiness of sheer liberation. For the historian Mohamad Tavakoli, the revolution of 1978–1979 fulfilled the promise of what was begun in the first Constitutional Revolution of 1906.

The differences made by the revolution in the lives of the people I talked to depended on specific intersections of age, class, religion, ethnicity, politics, and gender. Those who could afford to, or who had family abroad, or who were desperate enough, fled the country. Some groups, like Baha'is, were chosen objects of extermination. So were many Kurds and leftists. Accepted "people of the Book" such as Jews, Zoroastrians, and Christians were not officially persecuted, and the Constitution recognized the legitimacy of their claims to religious rights. But the discrepancies between official history and lived experience tell much about the monolithic reconfiguration of the land. Such diasporic communities as the Armenians, for instance, needed to renegotiate community and identity during the Khomeini era.[2] The major advocates of minority rights after the revolution, Ayatollah Montazeri and Ayatollah Beheshti, were both silenced—the former through forced resignation, the latter in a bomb blast in June 1981. Most Armenian school principals were replaced by Muslims; teaching the Bible and the Armenian language were both discouraged, and *kalbas* (bologna, ham, salami) factories were closed down. But ironically, according to Eliz Sanasarian, most Armenians prefer to stay in Iran rather than move to the West because they prefer "the close-knit, isolationist, and nonassimilationist setting provided by this regime" (1995, 261).

Many of the older men and women, particularly those who had been students abroad, were stunned to find themselves marginalized, imprisoned, and finally exiled by the event they helped create. Beguiled by the ideal of revolutionary unity, even an educator and activist as sophisticated as Afsaneh Najmabadi was surprised by the multiple fragmentations, the resentment and anger between women of different classes. The old categories and master narratives of reading women as sisters, or of revolution as liberation, were insufficient to explain this new order, this new rage. Najmabadi and Tavakoli both said that without such precursors as Ali Shariati and other intellectuals whose idea of the secular nation rested on the bedrock of Islamic foundations,

Khomeini would not have become such an overdetermined symbol. The paradox, as pointed out by these two scholars, is that the contradiction had been foreseen and "resolved" in the precursors of Khomeini in the very terms that had allowed the latter to emerge as symbol of revolutionary fervor. I therefore offer a brief reading of one figure appropriately called by the historian Abrahamian the leading intellectual, "the Fanon" of the revolution—Ali Shariati.[3]

An Antecedent of Hope and the Road Not Traveled

Returning to Shariati will show the squandering of an opportunity to transform Iran on the basis of a secular idealism that keeps faith with Islamic traditions even as it activates those traditions as agents of a partnership with the humanistic imperatives of a liberal modernity. Diversity and not unity characterized the outside energizers of the revolution of 1979, intellectually motivated by (among others) young Marxists, Maoists, Trotskyites, and Mojahedin. Inside Iran those long disillusioned with the failures of the Iran Novin, the National Front, and the Tudeh rallied around a new unifying center—the radical philosopher Ali Shariati, whose lectures drew crowds of dissidents and intellectuals desperate for new leadership. After five years at the University of Paris during years that coincided with the Algerian Revolution, he returned to Iran in 1964 to teach and to be repeatedly arrested. Freed under international pressure, he lectured at several universities on the history and the sociology of Islam. His fiery lectures provided alternate models of cultural identity for those who felt betrayed and exiled within Pahlavi Iran. His death in 1977 made him one of the early martyrs around whom the revolutionary cause rallied.

In the great blurring between revolutionary ideologues, many of my young interviewees, Yahya for instance, believed that Khomeini continued Shariati's ideals: "I thought that both Islams were the same—Shariati's and Khomeini's." He was bitterly disappointed to find out otherwise. The rallying points in Shariati's philosophy combined radical Marxist, existentialist, and socialist challenges to the status quo, showing them to be already part of Shiia Islam.

The great challenge, said Shariati, was to learn to be human in an age that stifled morality and independence of thought. In a vocabulary that popularized, modernized, and globalized Islam, he asked for a daily *jihad* (war) against instrumental thought and a return to a critical Islamic "Self," to *tauhid*—a Oneness that informs and links the ordinary to the divine.

In Paris, Shariati edited *Iran-e-Azad* (Free Iran), translated works of Che Guevara and Frantz Fanon, argued with Fanon about using Islamic unity as a weapon against neocolonialism, and studied with famous scholars at the Sorbonne. In his series of influential lectures entitled *Return to the Self,* Shariati called for resistance to Western cultural imperialism through a cultural revival, a return to the self embedded in the social and material practice of everyday life—"not to the self of a distant past, but a past that is present in the daily life of the people."[4] Shariati's call for the recuperation of a new Islamic identity as weapon against global capital is not an example of strategic essentialism in the service of a naive but necessary fiction of the self; this is a more popular, culturally constructed notion of self as a productive force in the service of nationalism deployed against the deterritorializing imperatives of Western global capital.

But that newly realized Islamic self was necessarily gender-inflected. Woman, for Shariati, is at once the revolution's greatest hope and greatest threat. Woman, he argued, was the easiest path to the loss of cultural integrity. "The West falls upon the soul of the Easterners like termites . . . they empty out the contents . . . destroy all of the forces of resistance." So, too, women have been emptied of power and selfhood: "They are not able to explore and nourish the spirit and their thoughts. Even the rights and possibilities which Islam itself has given to women, have been taken away from them in the name of Islam. They have placed her in the same category as a washing machine. Her human values have been lowered to 'mother of the child'. . . . This is exactly like paralyzing her and then saying that because she is paralyzed, she is deprived of everything."[5] Shariati's much celebrated *Fatima Is Fatima* used the figure of Muhammad's daughter not only as a model of revolutionary resistance to the monarchy in the 1970s, but also as a figure who could resolve the problem of how women could enter modernity and remake themselves as neither Western nor traditional.[6] Its vocabulary and arguments inform almost all manifestoes by women after the revolution. By authenticating a new concept of Islamic womanhood as an alternative to the Pahlavi "Westoxificated" images of woman, it is also a text that once again uses the body of the woman as the site on which to compose national and ethical values.

Shariati criticized the "web" of conservatism, patriarchy, and ignorance that, by confining woman within the home, excludes her participation in the public sphere (1980a, 109–10). In valorizing the figure of Fatima, not as daughter of Muhammad, wife of Ali, or mother of Hassan, Husain, and Zainab, but as "herself" (hence the title of the book), Shariati reminds his audience of the denigration to which Islamic culture (not Islam) has subjected the image of women. He contrasts the endemic misogyny in Persian and Arab poets ("It is better to bury women and dragons in the earth, / The world will be better off if cleansed of their existence" [1980a, 124]) against the civility of Qur'anic respect for women.

In opposition to the ubiquitous image of the traditional royal family whose patriarch claimed to respect only women who, as "natural" wives and mothers, were also "beautiful, feminine, and moderately clever,"[7] Shariati posited another way of seeing. He exposed the scandal of the traditional and unacknowledged traffic in women bartered in a form of unexamined homosocial exchange against which Fatima, as ideal mother, wife, daughter, and warrior, can become the emblem of new revolutionary values.[8] Such values are needed, Shariati claimed in *One Followed by an Eternity of Zeros*, to defend the Muslim against neoimperialism that comes to Iran disguised as modernization. "Foreigners," named as "the instruments by which we have been destroyed," have "seduced us into playing in sandboxes, playing with blood" (1979b, 2). Their effects on Muslims are those of the colonizer on the colonized because we resort to ambivalence (fragmentation of selves and identity), to mimicry (of Western desires), to disavowal (denial of Islam through identification with the oppressor). His lectures are a powerful example of how cultural nationalism developed in Iran, as it did in other countries, against real and imagined alterities in cultural imperialism.

Shariati, nevertheless, articulated a dynamic new model for Iranian identity, one that embraced parts of the pre-Islamic past condemned by the traditional clergy, and that revised the structure of Islamic Iran as a model in opposition to the alienation and inauthenticity encouraged by the consumer-ridden neoimperial machine. Historically, whether in Algeria, Vietnam, or Iran, nationalism has provided the crucial mechanism for opposing colonialism and imperialism. For Shariati, national authenticity was an antidote to the designs of the multinational markets on individual desire, and authenticity could be found in his philosophically eclectic and religiously armored construction of cultural identity.

When Shariati died in 1977, his mantle was divided between unlikely inheritors, each of whom had different notions of "authenticity," revolution, and nation. Together, they constituted part of the coalition that constructed the siren call of salvation for the *paberehneha* (the barefooted) and the *moztazafin* (the downtrodden). That call was represented by revolutionary slogans presumably generated by spontaneous passion for the construction of yet another, more essential, yet alternate and oppositional national identity—once again relying, as revolutionary movements always have, on the *imagined* masses and *imagined* authorities to construct a social reality.

Was There a Revolution for Women?

Zia Ashraf Nasr, the oldest of my interviewees, believes not: "Now the veil enslaves woman. . . . When you see the Iranian *Majlis* [Parliament] on TV, you see something black in the corner and you don't know what or who this is. Is it a human being or a black bundle? It shouldn't be like this."

The women who marched for the revolution were a heterogenous group who represented social and political organizations as different as the conservative Women's Society of Islamic Revolution, and as radical as the Revolutionary Union of Militant Women whose parent organization was the Maoist Communist Party of Workers and Peasants.[9] Gradually, as evidenced by the writings of Khomeini and Motahari and the resurrection of Shariati's *Fatima Is Fatima*, all differences withered into a single truth: the only acceptable woman in the Islamic state was the Muslim woman who was the "pillar of the family," and who abided by all the laws laid down in the *Shari'a*.

Newly-hardened positions were articulated most publicly by Mrs. Gurji, the woman representative responsible for drafting the new Constitution of the Islamic Republic: "I feel ashamed to talk about 'women's rights.' Have any of our brothers in this assembly mentioned 'men's rights'?" (Azar and Yeganeh 1982, 55).

Some of my younger interviewees discovered the beginnings of cultural revolution when they returned to school to find themselves faced with a new world of rules, dress codes, and disciplines. Mandana remembered the discomfort of gym classes in *hejab* (official state modest covering: loose covering and headscarves); she recalled her first punishment when she violated the rule for dark colors by wearing red socks to school. Because private schools were permanently closed, children were moved to new schools where old class affiliations no longer existed, and where they had suddenly become the outsiders.

Mahnaz recalls attending classes in neighborhood schools with tribal girls, and with the poorer children of neighborhood gardeners and servants. She remembers the mockery and taunts of the *mostazafin* (the downtrodden, or the oppressed) who, the children reminded her, were now in charge. After a few months, she said, these divisions broke down and the children learned to trust one another. But Mahnaz soon saw that the apparent power of the oppressed didn't extend to the daughters of the oppressed. Something, she figured, was missing in this revolution. Her most poignant memory is of her closest friend Safieh, one of the *mostazafin*, who was the best and brightest in the class and whose gendered restrictions as a female remained unaffected by the revolution. Still subjected to a patriarchal bondage that was centuries old, she was taken out of school at the age of twelve because, her father thought, it was time for her to be married. And too much education ruined a girl for marriage. Although several narrators observed that the role of women rigidified after the revolution, others said the reverse.

Child marriage was, once again, encouraged. Whereas women's groups and the Family Protection Act of 1967 had raised the age of consent for women from nine to sixteen, Khomeini reversed that and advised all fathers to marry off their daughters as soon as possible, even at birth, even without the consent of the children, provided the consent might be obtained later.[10]

The historian Mohamad Tavakoli, however, told me a different story of revolutionary liberation: his sister, he said, would have remained part of the *mostazafin* had it not been for the new possibilities the revolution opened up for her class.

The story told to me by Mohamad Tavakoli about his sister's rise and resistance to patriarchy is also a story about the incommensurability between ideology as it does its cultural work and ideology as it gets absorbed into personal life. Mohamad, born as we heard earlier in Chaleh Meidun into a family of eight sons and one daughter, saw the little sister as the repository of family honor; therefore, from the age of seven on, she was the object of brotherly concern, protection, and wrath if, for instance, she appeared improperly exposed or if her *chador* slipped. Like other girls in her conservative neighborhood, her movements in public were limited to trips to buy bread or go to school.

When the revolution started in 1978 Mohamad's sister disappeared from her home for three days with no explanation. She was then sixteen years old. When she returned home her angry father and brothers discovered that she had been making Molotov cocktails near Jaleh Square during one of the decisive battles between the army and the people. During the ensuing family fight, she wrestled with her father, knocked him to the ground, and kicked him. The father, who ironically had been the most conservative and religious member of the family, found that the revolution had become his daughter's excuse for revolting against him. He left his home and went to his village of origin, promising never to return until his daughter left the house.

Her rejection of paternal power, however, did not preclude subsequent attachments to other centers of male power. In the early 1980s, Mohamad's sister flirted with the possibility of joining various leftist Islamic groups and temporarily even abandoned the *chador*. During the elections for the Assembly of Experts she came into contact with the Party of the Islamic Republic, liked their simplicity and clothing (the men, for instance, wore no ties), and became active in their cause. When she completed this trajectory by marrying a member of the Revolutionary Guard, she continued her education, became principal of a high school, and established an educational collective. Mohamad says that all the brothers are now afraid of her and warn him to be careful of what he writes in letters home. She has recently considered running for Parliament.

The strictures against women therefore contained and nourished their contrary—an inversion of power, and an alternative modernity. The collapse of old certainties led to the invention of new spaces for rethinking women's issues and the male-engendered narratives of Islamic laws.

Great Expectations and After

Everyone I interviewed had generally similar stories about their expectations of the revolution: they assumed that the clergy were only the symbolic leaders of the revolution; that after the Shah was deposed their lives would not change in any essential way except for the better; and that Khomeini would return to prayers and fasting in Qum, leaving the country in the hands of the secular leaders of the revolution.

A student who fled Iran in the early 1980s to avoid fighting the Iran-Iraq war tells of a meeting between Khomeini and some leading Iranian leftist academicians, including his father. When Khomeini warned them that if they did not follow his orders and didn't use their pens for the benefit of Islam, he would break their pens, that was it, the student said. Khomeini's message was loud and clear. "My father came home that day looking as if he'd lost all his ships at sea. He knew that his revolution had been lost."

The revolution, according to the ayatollahs, gradually won the contested space opened up by the fall of the monarchy in part because of the naiveté of the Marxists, the Fadayaan, the leftists, and the intellectuals whose theories of modernization, industrialization, progress, opposition, and liberation, simply put, failed. Western writers on Iran frequently misread the signs of prosperity: the White Revolution, much publicized as the Shah's effort to end the power of landowners, in fact resulted in increased rural poverty, displacement, and unemployment of peasants who fled the countryside and created massive slums around urban areas.

None of those theorists had considered the theatrical power of *Allah-o Akbar* echoing through Iranian nights and rooftops, nor of the poetry, prayer, and prophecy that provided haloed orchestration for revolutionary fever.[11] There were rumors and fictions of the supernatural. A woman in Qum claimed to have found a hair from the Prophet's beard in the Qur'an and received a revelation that the Ayatollah's face would be seen in the moon that night. My cousins in Tehran tell me that every balcony in the capital was filled with people staring at the moon and (so my cousins swear) seeing in it the face of the bearded Ayatollah. (This sighting might have been the precedent for the Jordanians claiming in December of 1990 to have seen a framed portrait of Saddam Hussein in military regalia embedded in the moon.) The following poem appeared in a local Iranian magazine (*Jonbesh*) in January 1979:

> The day the Imam returns
> no one will tell lies any more
> no one will lock the door of his house;
> people will become brothers
> sharing the bread of their joys together
> in justice and in sincerity
> There will no longer be any queues:
> queues of bread and meat,
> queues of kerosene and petrol,
> queues of cinemas and buses
> queues of tax-payments,
> queues of snake poison
> shall all disappear.

And the dawn of awakening
and the spring of freedom
shall smile upon us.

Imam must return . . .
so that Right can sit on its throne
so that evil, treachery and hatred
are eliminated from the face of time.
When the Imam returns,
Iran—this broken, wounded mother—
will for ever be liberated
from the shackles of tyranny and ignorance
and the chains of plunder, torture and prison.[12]

This poem was not written by an Iranian exiled from her country. Yet the nostalgia, the idealism, the anxiety suggests the self-alienation that the writer experienced while living in her homeland during the reign of the Pahlavis. The poet herself (to paraphrase Levi-Strauss) is the place where something happens.

The voices that follow in this section record individual experiences of the crisis in understanding a revolution that changed shape even as people celebrated it with songs, slogans, and banners. Each narrator remembers a slightly different moment that tolled the death knell of her or his particular notion of revolutionary possibility and its narrative of universal freedom. Months before the taking of the hostages and the occupation of the American embassy (which for many was the last straw), there were other signs and portents. For some women, the moment was July 12, 1979, the day on which four women charged with prostitution were executed. The crisis was heightened by their realization that their particular leftist organizations had no category within which such an occurrence could be privileged. Instead, the Left seemed to be reenforcing the patriarchal values of the Islamic regime, failing to see the relevance or urgency of women's protests. For some, it was the naming of new and imagined "enemies," followed by the attacks on Kurdistan. For many it was the day the government closed the offices of the leading liberal newspaper, *Ayandegan*. For one woman, it was the day on which women bathers in the sea were flogged. For another, it was the day on which coeducation, even in elementary schools, was banned (summer 1979); for Lily, it was the day she saw "Zahra Khanum" who cursed her and all women like her. For Afsaneh, it was first the killing of prostitutes, then the women's march on March 8, 1979, then the hostage crisis, and finally the Iran-Iraq war. The women's march in 1979 was a day for which all her education, politicization, and theoretical knowledge of "masses" had left her totally unprepared. Practice finally defeated theory.

I start with the narratives of ten women.

Faranak

I interviewed Faranak in her home in November 1999. Born in Tehran in 1958 to what she described as a middle-class nonpracticing Muslim family, she grew up into politics through a family culture whose conversations revolved around "the bastard Shah," the waste of oil money, and poverty. She attended Valiullah Nasr and Kharazmi high schools in Tehran, studied architecture at Tehran University, lived through the revolution, and later, after her flight from Iran, did field work in Chile and Mexico before completing her Ph.D. at the University of California in Berkeley. Her experience represents that of young Iranians whose political sensitivity to injustice under the Shah translated into resistance to the evolving brutality of the new Islamic regime. Her narrative, which I keep intact in this chapter, documents the work she and her sister engaged in when, in the late 1970s, they joined underground political organizations. Her sister Farshad was arrested and executed in 1982, after which Faranak fled Iran. I asked about the kind of background that formed her later political consciousness, about her experience of the revolution and exile, and about her current postexilic state.

I grew up into social consciousness through my father, a fervent supporter of Mossadeq, and a member of *Jebhe Melli* [the National Front] whose sadness over the loss of our one chance for democracy was so deep that even when he was dying two weeks ago, he asked to be buried with a copy of Mossadeq's book. His political sensibility combined with our mother's social responsibility is what made us political. We also grew up with a generation of activists who were influenced by Samad Behrangi's allegories of resistance and middle class selfishness—*Little Black Fish* and *Mr. Goodfortune* (*Aga ye Choqbakhtiar*). In the seventh grade we started reading these and other social critiques and underground books. Books by Ali Shariati, Islamic Marxist tracts. We didn't care if the books were Left or Right so long as they were forbidden. My entrance into the organized student movements occurred through the usual channels. We went for walks in the mountains where we sang revolutionary songs, talked, and got recruited.

I remember the first major demonstration in 1978—a march from the north all the way to the south of Tehran that accumulated masses of people along the way. My father had gone to this demonstration without telling us. But as they marched past our house, I and my older sister, without telling our mother, joined them. I was twenty and my sister was twenty-five. That was a time when I didn't even know who Khomeini was.

Among the many anti-Shah movements, we joined the Marxist groups, and perhaps because it contained my friends, a small unit called *Vahdat Enghelabi e Iran* (the Revolutionary Union of Iran). My sister joined *Paykar* (struggle). The two events responsible for turning our family against the revolution were the violence against the demonstrators of International Women's Day when thugs called women "prostitutes" and beat us up, and then the closing of the newspaper *Ayandegan.* My sister and I were part of this demonstration and ran through the streets to escape the violence.

Our postrevolutionary organizations identified with *Khat i Se* [third line]— that is, an alternative to Russia or China. We sought a third alternative Marxist-Leninist path for an independent Iran. After I entered this unit, no longer part of a mere student organization, I joined a division to educate and raise the consciousness of workers. Under the umbrella of the national campaign for literacy in factories we actually taught union rights and the rights of workers. For ten months in 1979 we went to workers' houses and stayed overnight until the factory figured out we were in disguise teaching more than reading and writing. We were called to the Komite, interrogated, and fired from the factory. This was scary. But I needed another avenue to feel useful and joined a division of our organization that was proletariat. We could choose to belong to outreach, public relation, or student groups. I wanted to work with the proletariat I had read about and idealized.

This was also the time that universities were closed because they were known to be the main bases of opposition to the new hardline regime. We had an all-night sit-in. And I and my sister and 120 others slept on the street outside the university for two nights. About 3:00 a.m. [the second night], the guards attacked and shot several students. I remember the screams, the shooting, the blood, the fear as we ran that if the guns didn't get us, some other form of male sexual violence would. My sister and I got home by morning to a mother who was devastated. We had of course lied to her about where we were going and said we were spending the night with friends. That event turned me into a full-time activist. I got a factory job under the pretense that I had only six years of education, that my father had died, and that I therefore needed a job. Our mission was recruitment of workers to challenge the status quo—difficult because half the workers were unsuitable candidates and the other half already recruited.

When I didn't find the ideal proletariat in the first shoe factory (*Kafsh Jam*) I moved to heavy industry, Arj, where I expected to find a history of work. It was again a disappointing search for recruits. In the locker room I would find women who prostituted themselves after work or were drug addicts or subjects of domestic violence—all so common and so justified. Remember I was only twenty-two; idealized the workers; hated the middle class, my home address on Pahlavi Avenue, our comfort and our food. But the working class didn't give me what I expected either. I learned about how class produces invisibility at another factory where as a servant in a scarf running errands and serving tea I was invisible to administrators and their off-color, anti-woman jokes.

After a year I was leader of a "nucleus" reading group with newly recruited workers. We'd read Marxist-Leninist texts every week and meet in the homes of workers with sympathetic parents. They recruited workers to distribute flyers and serve the resistance. I was responsible for this group and gave dates for our demonstrations, for distributing flyers, and other ways of serving the resistance. We went out in groups of three at 2:00 or 3:00 a.m. with flyers that proclaimed against the regime and its specific infractions of democracy. One would be in charge of storage, another would guard the head of the alley, and a third would distribute small amounts of flyers at a time so that they could be easily disposed of if caught. This was our activity up to the time that Bani-Sadr fled, when times got really bad and the hardliners came to power. Now they arrested anyone against them—Islamic or non-Islamic— and somehow had abundant information with which to target the suspects. Although we thought we were an underground movement, everyone knew if you were a Marxist or an Islamic Mojahid. Once the mass arrests started, they found everyone and destroyed entire organizations. The new spies weren't like SAVAK. They weren't paid. They were true believers who informed the Komite. We were unprepared.

My sister's arrest has a background. Our organization's protocol was that if anyone got arrested we had to be prepared for a month to make sure they hadn't talked and given away identities. We could not go home; we had to remain underground in hiding. If after a month there was no sign of leakage, then it was safe to come out. So when one of our close female friends got arrested, we followed the rules and left home. But we went to work—I in an engineering firm, my sister in an English language institute. We didn't think that those arrested knew of where we worked, but someone must have. My sister was arrested at work, kept in prison for twenty days, after which they called my parents to say she had been executed together with fifty other women—all in one night.

My sister wrote a letter the night before she was executed. [*She shows me a copy of that letter.*] The guards allowed this *vasseyat nameh*—last will and testament—in which she said goodbye, expressed her love for the family, asked her parents and family not to mourn or wear black, asked them to stick together, enjoy life, and make each other happy, and reminded them that she had had a good life, though short. I can't imagine such bravery, how knowing that she was to die the next day she could write such a letter. A very beautiful person. I never figured out why they arrested her and not me. I wished they had taken me. I lived with survivor's guilt a long time. There had been no court, no prosecution. This was the time when Khalkhali [the hanging judge] had ordered: "Kill them. If they are guilty we've done good, if innocent, they'll go to heaven. We win either way."

The order for my arrest was out. They would call my parents from the prison and ask for me; my parents would say they didn't know where I was. I left my place of hiding twice only to get arrested. I had gone to meet a worker in whose house we used to have meetings. I went to say goodbye. I suppose we looked strange—she wearing *chador*, I in my intellectual's loose clothes and scarf. So we got arrested and interrogated in two separate cars. The co-driver had a machine gun. A woman Hezbollahi sat beside me in the back. I saw the end of my life pass before my eyes. We were arrested close to my home and as we drove past my house I asked them to stop and check with my parents who'd confirm my innocence. They did. En route they asked me questions, whether I knew names of political persons. I gave them a few names that thrilled them. When she asked "which organization?" I replied the organization of the Islamic Republic of Iran. She got angry and repeated the words "political organization." I said, yes, they were really political and committed to the Islamic Party. She gave up and thought I was too stupid to know what they meant.

But through luck, they let me go. Then I fled with a small group smuggled on horseback from Azarbaijan, five adults and three children—through Kurdestan to Turkey, where I went to the Norwegian embassy. I had asylum before leaving Iran through contacts with the Norwegian charge d'affairs who had heard of our condition, set up a secret meeting with me, got information and passed it on to the human rights commission who said they'd take responsibility for me once I left the country.

How do I feel about Iran after all that happened? I have so much love for the generosity and sweetness of the people and for the place; we traveled so extensively through Iran, through villages—Yazd, Kerman, Kashan, Isfahan. I feel lucky not to be bitter and not to confuse the beauty of the people I saw with the ugliness of the time.

America? I don't know how I feel about this country. I feel no passion for it though I'm comfortable here. I do know how I feel about Norway that first received me as a fragile, fearful, suspicious, broken-down little girl who felt like an old woman. I want to talk about the happy part of my exile—Norway. I was the first Iranian political refugee who arrived with official political asylum. Norwegian society offered me a vision of possibility—I saw emotional fairness, justice, political correctness, and social equalities. From a place of hardline brutality to arrive to a place so peaceful and so calm was needed therapy. I couldn't live in the present or for the future, and Norway gave me the time and space to deal with the baggage of my past. The first thing I did when I arrived in Oslo was to call a journalist at Oslo's largest newspaper, to buy a pack of cigarettes, and to smoke walking through the streets with the breeze blowing through my hair. Hard to believe this delicious freedom after my seven months in hiding between the execution of my sister and my flight. When the journalist called me back, I told him I'd arrived that very day from Iran and that I had a story to tell. And the stories I gave him were the debt I felt I owed to my comrades. The next week saw three series of front-page stories on Iran.

I lived in a remote refugee house with thirty Vietnamese boat people and remember a touching moment. We had a Vietnamese cook who fed the group Vietnamese food. Iranians only eat Iranian food—we don't eat foreign foods—and I found it hard to stomach this new and different taste and smell. So after a few days when I saw I couldn't eat I decided to stay in my room during mealtime. One day I heard a knock on my door and saw the outstretched hand of the old white-haired Vietnamese cook with a gift of a huge red apple. He had noticed me not eating or coming for meals and had chosen to bring me something he thought I might eat. We had no words for each other, but he could see the gratitude on my face. Through experiences like that I gradually figured something else about humanity—that its goodness could exceed cultural difference. These refugees from South Vietnam were on the side of the United States and proud of killing communists—their ideologies were antithetical to my orthodox Marxist background. They were the enemy. But I got attached to them on a level other than the political and gradually began to see life in terms other than the black-and-white absolutes taught to me in my organizations.

There are places I've lived in since my exile I'm passionate about—South Africa, South America for instance where my attachment is to a cause, a way of living, a culture, the celebration of life, the energy of feeling. The year I lived in Chile (1984) I studied urban movements around issues of housing. In 1986 I came to Berkeley where my dissertation on the problem of single mothers as heads of households and housing in low-income groups took me to Mexico from 1992–93. Although I studied urbanization and development problems in developing countries similar to Iran, I knew I couldn't return to Iran. So I studied Spanish and made Latin America the center of my work.

To your final question, do I think of myself as an exile? Yes. I think of myself as an exile because that part of my history is my origin, but it no longer determines my everyday decisions. Once every move I made was determined by my certainty of return—in an imagined "six months." But I gradually realized that return was a fantasy, that I had to live my life here, that I should begin to feel an immigrant. Yet, exile is my point of origin.

Pari

Pari has already described her childhood, her education, her politicization, and her early careers. Although she was in the United States when the Shah left and Khomeini arrived, she was in Iran for some of the crucial events preceding the revolution and felt its impact on the villagers with whom she worked.

I was in Tehran in 1978 when the Cinema Rex in Abadan was set on fire. That was a turning point for the revolution. Because we saw the Shah then as a symbol of evil, we fell easily into thinking that he wanted to ruthlessly exterminate any opposition. So we thought that he destroyed the cinema to get at the Fedayeen or Mojahedin collected in the cinema. But now we know that the burning of Cinema Rex was done by the opposition. I say the opposition rather than Khomeini, because it's no use blaming only Khomeini. That's playing into the hands of many people who to this day believe that Iran can be saved only by a dictator, by one man, because they believe we as a nation are immature and that someone else has to decide for us. In other words, we prefer to see ourselves in the role of children taken care of by an all-knowing father, children who can then complain about the "lack of freedom."

In those days something was happening, though we didn't know what. At the time I was working with Iranian women in villages. Just before the revolution, early 1978, I was in a village near Shiraz. We were to hold a workshop, but the group of students who were supposed to help had disappeared. When I got back to Tehran I saw that soldiers and cannons were all over the streets. I asked the taxi driver what was up. He said, "Haven't you been in Iran?" and explained the trouble between the government and the opposition. Later I understood about the disappearance in the village. The young women in the village would all run off to hear the BBC and knew what was happening.[13]

Why didn't they tell me? Simple. They didn't trust me. I was, in spite of their affection for me, an agent from the government, sent by a ministry of government to run a government program in the village.

I remember the time around Black Friday, September 1978, the time of the massacre in Jaleh Square. The villages grew agitated. It was dangerous for me to keep going there. I left Iran to attend an International Children's Congress in Germany in May of 1979, taking a leave of absence from my work. I also needed to attend to my daughter's problems with her boarding school. But after six months, things got worse in Iran, and eight months after I left Iran, the revolution happened. I was told that my life was in danger. I was told that women who had promoted the status of women or who had worked for women's progress had committed a "sin." I could not return.

When I returned to Iran in 1980, I wanted to visit the villages in which I had worked. My former assistant told me not to. He thought they might kill me if I did. Why? Well, most of these girls had said, "Khanum Pari has said that we should not be beaten; Khanum Pari has said that men and women are equal." Now, after the revolution, those men who feel I "spoiled" their women and who have renewed power to return to the old hierarchy might vent their anger on me. Now all these projects I helped to build have been dismantled; all the women I hired were discharged. And all this has remained on my conscience for these ten years. How hard we tried to help and instead what harm we unknowingly did. How we raised hopes that were dashed. How many hopes for independence I created, and how, with the return of fundamentalism, most of those girls were probably ashamed even to admit they were literate—let alone independent. It was now shameful to be literate, because in the villages, and even in towns, it was not uncommon to believe that an illiterate woman makes a better wife and mother than a literate one. She would, after all, be more submissive and obedient.

This is, after all, a totally male-ruled society. And one of the effects of this revolution on female behavior—say, in the courts, and I have spent months going from one to the other—is that if you are a woman, the best you can do is to be silent. They don't expect you to speak to a man who is *namahram* [unlawful] to you. They will speak past you to a male in whose company you are, and expect you to overhear.

I had, for instance, to go to court to settle my father's inheritance. Unacceptable by myself, I had to go with a man to whom the mullah would speak. With no husband or father, I am at the mercy of a brother who contests that inheritance. One day, sick and tired of waiting to see the head mullah of the court, I went to an office and asked to see the mullah. The man at the desk said that I had to make an appointment and return. I said, "Now is the time I have come to make that appointment, and I will wait until he can see me. I will sit in that chair and wait for ten hours or overnight but I will not move out of this chair." After two hours I was told me to go in but warned not to sit in front of the mullah and not to cross my legs.

When I entered, the mullah who headed the court wouldn't look at me. He was a powerful man because, as *haakim* [ruler], all decisions were finally his. I told him about my situation: "Look, I can't rent a place because I am a woman and don't have the money to pay for it, and as a single woman no one would rent any place to me anyhow; I don't have a job so I have no income; I had a rich father, and yet I can't sell any of his property because I am a woman and am forbidden from dealing in real estate." Why was I forbidden? Because my brother had been in prison and therefore that had cast its shadow over me. Then finally I broke down and said, "I don't know what to do. I am too proud to go into the streets and beg but I need some place to live and have exhausted all my resources."

Finally he said, "You have moved me. I promise you I will reach a decision soon. Let's call your brother in." When my stepbrother came, the mullah asked, "Why don't you support your sister?" He replied, "Why do you expect me to support a woman ten years older and more educated than me, who could get a job at your universities? Why don't you give her a job instead of asking me to support her?"

Lily

Educator and writer, Lily earlier talked of her life in Iran as a child, a student, and a worker for the literacy campaign. She now tells her story of the revolution and her departure into exile.

We left Iran in 1979. I experienced the Spring of Freedom. It was a very strange feeling. I was not young enough to share that ecstasy with the youth. I could see what was happening and I was not happy. But I was not old enough to lose my faith in the people and say that all our lives depend on the king and that we would be lost without him. I had grown angry with the Shah toward the end and was very much in favor of some sort of radical change.

And that spring, it really was the Spring of Freedom. It was magnificent to walk on Shah Reza Avenue and see all sorts of people standing around discussing all sorts of subjects they were not earlier allowed to discuss— forbidden books, politics, arts, everything. You could feel the solidarity of people toward each other. But this "spring" ended.

There was a shadow that I felt on one particular day. That was the day I saw Zahra Khanum. [*She means a type of traditional woman, hence the name "Zahra."*] Zahra Khanum was a woman from the south of Tehran. She had a *chador*, but not casually worn. She was shrouded in it. That day, I was walking from Shah Reza Avenue up Vesall i Shirazi and suddenly I heard her say, "*Pedar i Shoma ra dar avordeem*" [a familiar curse that implies the exorcising of fathers, or, we will damn you]. I asked, "*Pedar i Kee ra Daravordi?*" ["Whose fathers do you refer to?"] "*Een zanaye patyare—jam shodan—meegan ma chador nemkhaeem, ma azadi meekhaeem, ma ketaab mekhaeem.*" ["You women who organize demonstrations and say that you don't wish to be veiled, that you wish for freedom and for books."]

That was the first time I felt the shadow. Then the book burning started. One day I came to the office and I said to my coworkers, "What's going on in Shah Reza Avenue? They're burning books." And then a coworker, a young girl, a Zoroastrian, said, "Hah, we experienced that one thousand, four-hundred years ago. Now, you are going to feel it too."

Now that I look back, the warning signs were there, only we couldn't always read them. When I first read Khomeini's book, I went to a friend at work who was also an educator and a revolutionary and very much against the Shah. I asked him if he had read Khomeini's book. It was 5:30 in the morning; you know we used to come early to the office to be able to speak openly, not during office hours. He said, "Yes." "And you still believe in this man as a leader of the revolution?" He said, "Yes, but he wrote this book fifteen years ago." I said, "Is there anything in this book that he has since denied?" He says, "No, but this was fifteen years ago." I said, "But what if he still believes in this rubbish. A person who has written this is a second Hitler to me. Thank you, I don't want him as a leader." And this is another problem. I don't know how many of those who hailed him, the young intellectuals, had really read the book. I knew that if he would succeed, something awful would happen.

Would you tell us about the persecution of Baha'is?
About three years before the revolution, I became a Baha'i. It took me twenty-five years to make such a decision. I had somehow picked up so many prejudices against Baha'is in that culture that I feared they were heretics—or worse, traitors to Iran. But I gradually learned the falsity of that. Baha'is suffered so much persecution through their history. Falsafe destroyed the Hazirat (Baha'i Center) during the Shah's time. Reza Shah closed Baha'i schools. Thousands of people were killed for their faith. I had seen many Baha'is lose their jobs. I was very close to my husband's family and to many other Baha'is. Gradually I became really interested in the philosophy of this faith. Finally, I registered as a Baha'i. I did that being completely aware of the consequences. Fortunately, Baha'ism is such a liberal religion, nobody questions you on your behavior. But my becoming a Baha'i meant that I needed to remain apolitical. Very few in Iran knew that I was a Baha'i at that time because I came from a Muslim family.

A few months after the revolution, Iraj and I decided to go and see our children. Just before leaving, I had a telephone call from the Prime Minister's office saying, "Your husband can leave but you cannot." I asked, "Why?" They said, "Oh, nothing, it's nothing important. You just have to bring another paper from your office and then you can go. Tell your husband to go and wait for you in Europe and then you can join him and go to see the children." I said, "Okay." Iraj said, "I am not going." I said, "Yes, you are going. The children need to see you and the man himself says that in two days I will be out." These two days went on for seven months. And then in the middle I was told, "Forget it. We are not going to let you leave." I was never told why. But I left. Three months after our arrival in the United States the real persecution of Baha'is started. We were told to stay out and not go back.

But the persecution of Baha'is had really started while we were still there. For example, the old house of the Bab, a beautiful work of art, was an old nineteenth-century Qajar house in a back alley in Shiraz. That was destroyed.

People like Dr. Davoodi, who was professor of philosophy at Tehran University, disappeared and was never found. Before Iraj left he was arrested and questioned for many hours and then released. In 1980, the real persecution of all groups against the regime started. They arrested people; they tortured leftists; they tortured and killed others, and the Baha'is specifically. Certainly they never said that they were arresting Baha'is because of their religious beliefs. But entire assemblies—many professors of the university, the most educated of our people, many artists—were executed. The only woman meteorologist of Iran was executed. A whole group of twelve eminent Baha'is disappeared and we still don't know where. They were all abducted. Sixteen people in Shiraz, among them sixteen- and fifteen-year-old girls, were executed. Altogether, over two hundred Baha'is were officially eliminated under false pretexts.

In those days, we believed in literacy for women; we believed that literacy would create better mothers; we believed that our work in literacy would make better housewives, better workers in the factories, and better citizens. The people we reached were willing to send their daughters and wives to literacy classes. But then, after the revolution, these people were told that they should not send their women to classes where men were teaching.

Now, what have we learned from all those years? I don't know whether there is a literacy campaign now in Iran. But if one day someone wishes to start a literacy program in Iran, we should remember the things that we learned from the past. We should give first priority to girls and women because this is where the statistics show our main failure. We should use literacy and education as a source of empowerment of people, of liberating people from prejudice, from materialism, and from self-centeredness. We should not ever again let literacy and educational programs be used as political means for politicians.

Homa Sarshar

The story of Homa Sarshar's "cleansing" from her position as translator and writer for the major daily newspaper, Keyhan, *is an event that reveals the process of homogenization in state and social organizations in preparation for the new nation. She has narrated a version of this story on the Iranian radio station in Los Angeles.*

I remember the day martial law was declared. It was the start of the revolution. At that time Sharif Emami was Prime Minister. And I remember that he ordered the people to close the cabarets and the casinos. But at that time there was also a hidden order people didn't know about, that I didn't know about myself, but that we found out about later: they wanted all women and minorities out of television and radio. Although I didn't know that, they called me from the television station and said that my program would not be aired for a few weeks and I didn't need to record any new programs now. "We'll wait and see what happens," they said. I thought maybe this was something personal, maybe my program was not good enough or maybe there was some problem with the program. I was confused.

And this was exactly the time I was fired from *Keyhan*. Maybe two or three weeks after the call from the television station, my editor in *Keyhan* called me one day. At that time as chief editor for the family page, I helped them translate the news from the France Press. And when Khomeini went from Iraq to France there was constant news about what he was doing in Neufchâtel. The first, second, and third days he was in France, I went to the wire room and I asked for the wire from France Press and they said there was no wire. On the first day I didn't say anything—maybe, I thought, there really is no wire. Maybe there is some censorship going on. But on the second day when I read *Keyhan* and saw a translation of the France Press news about Khomeini I went to my newspaper office and asked, "What happened? You said you didn't have any wires to translate." And the man said, "Well, the wire arrived in the afternoon when you were not here." So I said, "Okay. Do you have any wire today?" and he said, "No, not yet. I will let you know." And I waited at *Keyhan* until 1:00

p.m. And I asked again, "Any wires?" and he said, "No." So I left. And again the next night and afternoon I saw that other news had once again been translated in *Keyhan* from the French. The third day I went to my news editor and asked, "What's going on?" He started to laugh and said, "Don't get involved with this. Go on, do your work. Go out, read something, or just occupy yourself." I said, "I'm not here to read or to entertain myself. I want to work." He then said to me, and these are his exact words, he said, "*Bekhodi to karhaye bozorgtara dekhalat mekoni dokhtar joon*" ["You interfere pointlessly in the work of your elders, dear girl"]. I said, "I am not your *dokhtar joon* [dear girl]; I am a grown woman, and I work here and I want to know what's going on." And he said, "You know, you must be crazy to think that anyone would give Ayatollah Khomeini's news to a Jewish woman to translate. This news will become *najis* [unclean]." And that was my last day at *Keyhan*. I said, "Okay, I understand." I took my purse and belongings; I emptied my drawer; I took my files and left and never went back. I had known that man for five years. I had worked with him closely at one table, around one table for five years, and I had known him for seventeen years since the day I joined the larger *Keyhan* company.

Did you grow up sensing prejudice against Jews?
No. But I heard from my family that in Shiraz it had been very tough for the Jewish people to live during Reza Shah's reign, but not during the Shah's reign. Personally, I never felt any racism or prejudice against me as a Jew until that day at *Keyhan*, that day before the revolution.

I was naive about this. Whenever we talked between ourselves—Jewish friends and family—they were always troubled and cynical or pessimistic about the way that the Islamic government might react to the Jews. And I was always the one who would protest and say, "Look, look, look at me. I'm a good journalist here. I'm a well-known woman. I'm working on Iranian TV. I'm working in *Keyhan* and nobody bothers me—so what are you all the time complaining about?" But that day when I got fired, that changed it all; now what they had said suddenly made sense. They had said, "You never know. It will happen some day." But I didn't believe it at that time.

So with the revolution I was out of two jobs—*Keyhan* and television. They fired my husband after the revolution, but me, I was fired before the revolution.

My friends at the journalists' syndicate said I should not resign. "Don't worry, we will eventually overrule all these crazy people once the revolution comes." And I said, "I'm not very optimistic about the revolution because I see my colleagues' behavior." Eighty percent of the people in *Keyhan* were either leftists or Mojahid or Tudehi [communists] and everybody else knew about it. Yet at the time of the demonstration, all the women from *Keyhan* went out with *chadors*—and I said [to them], "What are you giving me? What future are you showing me? You say that this playboy I know who always drinks and plays cards is now a revolutionary? What else can I expect? Do I need to see all the women with whom I used to work declare that they are Muslims and are now under *chador*? What can I expect from this revolution?"

My mother called one day from the United States and said, "Here on television they say that there will be a revolution in Iran. Come out, come out of the country. Don't stay there." I said, "Nothing is going on. Everything is normal." And she said, "No, it's not normal. You should come out." My father at that time was working in Rasht outside Tehran. He was a partner in a big liquor manufacturing company making vodka. Of course he closed his office and his factory for fear of them being burned. My father was afraid. He came to Tehran to my house. And we left the country, all six of us. My family, my father, and my sister. I couldn't believe what I had done, because I left Iran without even saying goodbye to the country. I was planning to come back. I just shut the door to my apartment and I came here.

Mandana

Earlier Mandana spoke of her family and her brothers' policing over the lives of their sisters in her family of nine siblings. Her story about her life during the revolution is inseparable from gender-specific problems of authority, choice, and disempowerment. In the sections I have omitted, Mandana talked about how her brothers, always rigid, grew more so at the time of the revolution. They discouraged her from electrical engineering because it was an "unsuitable" profession for women. Her brothers also found her other interests in radio, theater, and television to be "corrupt." She tells of her resistance against the patriarchal strictures of both family and state.

The last play I was in was to run for two weeks—this was after the revolution. One day my parents came to see the play. Though the theme of the play was political, we had permission to put it on. The playwright was Mehrdad Jamak. The producer and director was an Armenian. Because the play was about events resulting from the Shah's departure, it had the Islamic regime's approval; it followed that I would also have my brother's approval since he was an ardent supporter of the regime. But that was not to be.

My part required that, in a nice suit and makeup, I'd walk on stage and my first line was *Salaam* [greetings; literally "peace"]. Apparently a Hezbollahi woman came and sat by my mother and when I said *Salaam*, this woman said *Salaam o zahre-mar* [greetings with snake poison]. My mother was caught in a bind. On the one hand she thought that, yes, my daughter should not be without a *chador* in this regime; on the other, she didn't like to see her daughter being criticized. So she changed her seat.

But before the regime could stop us, my brother became my first censor. My brother, who had read the reviews but not seen the play, said one day, "I won't let you go on stage anymore." I said that I had rehearsed the role, that I was there with the permission of my school and the regime and my parents, that they had sold tickets for my performances. My parents had seen the play and liked it, but assuming that my brother was acting out of brotherly "honor" (*ghayrat*), they finally agreed to undermine and suffocate me. I was upset and told them that if they tried to stop me I would simply leave home and continue with the play. Later I was in another play, but by then things had changed. An Islamic form of theater was introduced. They tried to keep women from acting on stage; they'd say that brothers should not look at sisters. They even wanted men and women to rehearse in separate rooms. This of course was impossible.

I was arrested three times. Once, I was working with a tailor's syndicate that was first infiltrated by the Tudeh Party but was then infiltrated by the regime. So I took part in the syndicate's meetings and saw what was going on. I was arrested while in that syndicate. Of course three hundred other people were also arrested, so they had to free us. The other two times also had to do with this syndicate. Once a woman had reported us, saying that we were having clandestine meetings. So they arrested us. This was before Beheshti's assassination; fortunately, the system hadn't hardened yet, and I was freed easily. If these arrests had happened a year later, I would not have escaped with my life. After my second arrest, I changed my name so that when they came to arrest me again I said, "You've made a mistake! I'm not the person you are looking for."

I saw opposition and resistance differently from some of my colleagues, who thought resistance meant going and cursing the regime and then being executed for it. Resistance wasn't what Kianoori[14] did either—to go on television and apologize for what he had done. Resistance is that which most effectively brings about change over a long period of time. I must add that during one of my arrests, the political group to which I belonged criticized me and my actions. They wanted the heroics of arrest and torture, but I didn't. I was, however, able to effect getting another woman out of jail.

Afsaneh Najmabadi

Like Kambys, Tahereh, and hundreds of other activists, Afsaneh returned to participate in the revolution only to watch it become something quite other than what she had expected. Here she charts the four moments that registered her growing awareness of forces within the revolution for which her idealistic and intellectualized leftist preconceptions had left her unprepared. She eventually left Iran in the summer of 1980.

Because of my involvement in radical politics, I had not returned to Iran since 1970. My father had warned me against returning because he had found out that SAVAK had files on me. But once the demonstrations started in the summer of '78, all I said was, "I'm going." I arrived the day after Black Friday, September 1978. When I went back again in 1979, the Shah had just left. And I went there to make my revolution. [*She laughs.*] What else can I say? There were thousands and tens of thousands of us who came back. It was wonderful, remarkable—an illusion of total freedom. You could say anything. You could write anything. You could give a speech on a street corner and instantly collect an eager audience of two hundred. Because the old state had collapsed and the new state hadn't emerged, there was nothing in between but complete freedom.

So many of our illusions were the result of taking for granted our sense of a linear history, of the progress of secularization as an inevitable fact of history—so that religious movements and Islamic movements were, we thought, anachronisms. I, like other Iranians, chose to imagine that the revolution's religious coloring was only a temporary phenomenon that would disappear with the necessary second, radical revolution. We were certain that after six months Khomeini would go to Qum and it would be secular politics as usual. People would say, "Six months, just wait six months." And it's true. After six months, very important exclusions and eliminations happened, but it went the other way around: all secular politics got butchered and eliminated.

I read the revolution in terms of a paradigmatic shift of politics between the Constitutional Revolution and the Islamic Revolution. This didn't happen overnight. It evolved over seventy years, but accelerated in 1953—the aftermath of the overthrow of Mossadeq. The Constitutional Revolution came out of nineteenth-century Iranian fascination with the West. That fascination read Iran's central and social problems in terms of backwardness compared to Europe, and the central drive of the 1906 Constitutional Movement was to overcome backwardness. There were nationalists and bureaucrats and constitutionalists all attempting in different ways to address the same problem. Even a figure like Jamal-ud-Din Afghani,[15] with his pan-Islamism, could be read as an answer within the same paradigm, because he felt that through a pan-Islamic resurgence Islam could enter modernity.

But now if you shift to the core of the Islamic Revolution, its paradigm is no longer a reaction to backwardness, but rather to the loss of an essential soul. The new problem and paradigm is how to recover that soul. And this, again, I would say is not an exclusively Islamic concern. Even the Left flirted with *Gharbzadegi,* or the problem of Westoxification. So those are the paradigms by which I order the disorder of politics in Iran. And it required significant disillusionment with the first paradigm for the second to become hegemonic. The current Islamic paradigm was nurtured by other currents that came from secular politics. We need to attend to the linkages and chains of intellectuals who served as intermediary figures that made it possible for Khomeini to become Khomeini.

Can you recall the stages of your disillusion with organized politics and with the revolution?
I spent the years between 1980 and 1988 in a state of mourning—mourning for the revolution that went sour. I didn't have any illusions about Khomeini, and I gradually lost my illusions about the Left. A gradual disillusionment with organized politics, both in the United States and in Iran, led to my resignation from membership in organized groups. My initial activities were centered around organizing a leftist coalition against conservative strains in the revolution. But the Left lost to Islamic discourse, which became the dominant hegemonic discourse. I started becoming disillusioned with the Iranian Trotskyites and generally with Iranian politics in '79. But there was a particular incident that really ruptured something inside me, that alienated me from the revolution, from group politics, and made me resign from all parties. The incident that began my break concerned their reaction to the killing of four prostitutes in Iran. My primary involvement in politics was publications. I was editing an Iranian Troskyite journal in England when we moved to Iran to be part of the revolution and there, too, I was part of the publications office. One morning in July 1979 I saw huge headlines about the execution of four prostitutes. I went to the office of the administrator of the organization and said, "I'm going to have to write something on this." Because I felt that this killing meant something important. There was no way I could

theorize it, politicize it or anything, but somehow I had this gut feeling that when you start executing prostitutes, something significant and terrible is happening. Yet I couldn't convey my horror to anybody. Nobody could figure out why I was so upset about four goddamned prostitutes being executed. They felt the revolution was more important. The opposition press was being shut down, other freedoms abolished, the Constitutional Assembly was being scrapped and being replaced by this Assembly of Experts—*Majlis Khubregan.* And I walked on the street and cried for hours because I couldn't communicate in any way why I thought this was crucial enough to run an article in our press. I couldn't write an essay. But I knew. There was something inside me that just went crunch. If I couldn't communicate with this small group of my cothinkers, how on earth could I communicate with anybody?

Then there had been March 8, 1979, on which many women's committees organized activities to celebrate International Women's Day. We had been used to breaking our backs to organize any meeting to which nobody came. But now, all you had to do was to put a small advertisement in *Ayandegan,* which had by now become a sort of nongovernmental voice in Iran, and it would result in hundreds showing up. We had over 250 people showing up for a planning meeting.

On the seventh of March Khomeini held an audience with some groups of women, in the course of which he had uttered one of his famous one-liners. He said, "Women can go to offices, *but* they must go veiled." This was on the day before International Women's Day. So for the next few days there was this spontaneous outpouring of women on the streets demonstrating against Khomeini's statement going to the Minister of Justice, to Iranian television, to Tehran University.

Now it is March 8, 1979. And one of the beautiful slogans invented for that day was *Azadi bayad nabayad nadare* [Freedom has no musts]. In other words, it was a direct response to Khomeini's decree, "Women can go to offices, *but* they *must* be veiled." They protested his use of the word "must." The demonstration, now mostly directed against compulsory veiling, set off debates among the Left. The Left accused women of falling into the trap of taking these trivial issues seriously—instead of, for instance, worrying about an imperialist invasion or a coup d'etat. So most organized leftist groups didn't participate in demonstrations against the compulsory veiling, but a few did. And the ones who did were hoping to turn it into some sort of anti-imperialist occasion.

Suddenly there were all sorts of exclusions and new legal restrictions on women. Women who had graduated and finished their courses in legal studies were told they were excluded from *tahleef*—the oath required to become judges. There are no women judges now in Iran. And this because during the Shah's reign women had been allowed to become judges. It was against such happenings that we decided we needed a rally at the huge stadium in

Tehran University that attracted all groups and that integrated many issues. Each group would have their representative on the platform to say what they wanted. I had been selected by the Trotsky group to which I belonged to speak on the platform. It was called the Socialist Workers Party (*hizb-i kargaran-i susialist*), but it affiliated itself, in the tradition of leftist opposition of the 1920s and Trotsky, with an alternative International Communist tendency.

The regime paved a huge football field in the center of Tehran University for Friday prayers with a raised platform that became the speaker's platform at rallies. Once on that platform, the speakers looked down on the crowd and saw a mass of black heads moving—like a wave of blackness. The heads of black-haired Iranian women. I had never talked to a crowd that big in my life—nor ever since.

I gave a very emotional talk, telling people that we don't like others telling us what to wear. Yet we knew people were sensitive about distinguishing themselves from pro-monarchy people. So when we raised this issue, we said we were as opposed to compulsory unveiling as to compulsory veiling. We tried to emphasize choice. We also didn't want people who had opted to wear a veil to feel we were against them.

So there I was talking, my talk interrupted by the crowd agreeing and cheering, and behind me I heard this woman from another committee—the Society for Women's Awakening—who was against the march on the street. I heard her telling her comrade in a voice I'll never forget, "Look at these painted faces. I will never go on the street on a march with these women." And she said it with such hatred, "these women, these painted dolls—the filth of the Pahlavi regime."

And something happened; I almost fell off the platform. I suddenly went dizzy. I almost fainted. All I wanted to do was turn around and say, "I don't care what they look like. I want to go out on the streets." I was angry at this sort of compulsory writing of a particular meaning on a woman's body because of her appearance: it was irrelevant, because it didn't matter if they had twenty shades of makeup on their faces. But it also suddenly shook me up, because I realized she was saying the politically right thing.

I was the one transgressing across all kinds of political and cultural class lines. I was moving toward people I should in principle have opposed. We finally did march on the street and demonstrate. But the march became dangerous. By the time we got to Maidan Azadi, everybody's concern was how to disperse and not get killed by thugs attacking women. And how to do it in an organized way so people would not be isolated in small alleyways and get stabbed.

The hostage crisis became my final break with political organizations. The first was the killing of the prostitutes, the second was the women's issues, the third the hostage-taking, and finally, the last straw was the Iran-Iraq war. All these were even more intensely disillusioning in the context of knowing that the Left supported Khomeini, the hostage crisis, and the Islamic Revolution.

After I left Iran in 1980, I wrote my dissertation, had a baby, and came to the United States. I call it a depression baby—a reaction against the failure of the revolution. Many Iranians reacted against the revolution by having babies.

Tahereh

Like the previous three narrators, Tahereh returned believing in the power of people like herself to effect a cultural and political revolution. She reflects a deep cynicism toward her "arrogance," and her once-naive faith in the power of intellectuals. Like Afsaneh, she too expected a linear progression to history and to life.

Maybe in our politics we all grew too optimistic in relying on ourselves and our power. If I could overrule my grandfather, my uncle, and everybody else who was against me—and they represented the older generation, the old-fashioned, fanatical ones—it stood to reason that we as the leftist, as the young generation, as the alternative politics, could also overrule, dominate, and eliminate the power of the old, the Khomeinis, and the mullahs. We relied too much on new ideas, on self-reliance, and on the power of the intelligentsia, which itself became manipulated.

My life was evidence of the dangers of this myth of optimism. We became so *porroo* [literally, full of spirit; the term implies arrogance] that we thought we were capable of saving, changing, and rescuing our people. Especially since the "people" didn't want us or our rescue. We didn't understand that the people didn't want us.

Tell about your involvement with women's demonstrations and protests.
I was part of those marches. I went to Iran after Khomeini came to power for the women's demonstrations of March 8. From the beginnings of the revolution, as long as I was in Iran, I was a part of the opposition to what I saw as a small faction of the clergy imposing rules on women. I thought that by opposing this small faction we could eliminate it and then make the other factions—the Left, the democrats—more powerful. But of course this didn't happen.

Did you identify with the chadori *sisters?*
No, I was even criticized by the leftist organization I worked with for not wearing the *roosari* [headscarf]. When I led study groups in women's and

student organizations affiliated with the Fadayaan, they would send women comrades to criticize me: "You sound like these feminists." And "feminist" was a *fohsh*—a curse, a bad word. They accused me of talking too much about women. "Don't make any differentiation," they said, "between men and women, and also try to be like other people—we have to wear scarves." And I said, "If I wear that headscarf, it will contradict my own belief in equality between men and women. What's the sense in women and not men covering their heads?"

I remember that in one of these marches many of us who were more Left-oriented led the march toward the Fadayaan headquarters and many others went to the headquarters of the Mojahedin. Although we marched to their headquarters, the leaders did not meet us. There were two reasons for their neglect. One was ideological—they were insensitive to women's issues; and the other was political—they were intimidated by the possible accusation that they were complicit with these bourgeois women who, in the middle of this fight against imperialism and injustice, were arguing over a minor issue like the veil.

More discouraging things happened, not only when the government and clergy became more powerful, but when the Left split, the Fadayaan split, and the fragmentation led to our feeling disillusioned, confused, powerless, betrayed by the leadership of the Left.

In my personal life, disillusion coincided with the arrest of my family members—first my youngest sister who was a Mojahedin and much younger than me. I felt always as if she were my daughter. She was arrested in 1982 when she was only eighteen. She was in prison over four and a half years. She was so young and naive. My sister's story is powerful and horrifying. They executed her [political] husband. After the Mojahedin were declared illegal and went underground, their system required its members to get married so as to live in a team, in a sort of family configuration. A few months after she got arrested, my brother got arrested. Following his arrest, another brother got arrested. Finally the youngest one, who was only fifteen, got arrested. And then, because of all these pressures, my father became very ill and died.

All this is what I lost in the revolution.

Mrs. Ghandsaz

I interviewed Mrs. Ghandsaz (pseud.) over a two-day period in her apartment in Los Angeles in 1992. She had somehow heard of the interviews I was conducting, telephoned, and asked me to visit her. I apologized, saying I had no time and was leaving in two days. She called again insisting that I record her story, which she was certain would be unlike any other. It was. Once I started the machine, I felt in the presence of a one-woman play by Samuel Beckett—perhaps Not I. *At the end of the first three hours, which focused entirely on her own sorrow, she hadn't yet reached the death of her husband. She claimed that her suffering had been greater than that of any other human—comparable, she said, to the Holocaust. This is a highly condensed version of her six-hour monologue over two days; she resisted any effort to turn the meeting into an interview and ignored most of my questions. I decided not to split her narrative into other parts of this book, to keep it intact and centered on her obsessive reading of the life and death of her husband. She spoke in Persian.*

At the age of twelve I was married to my cousin through an arranged marriage. My husband had lost his father when he was twelve years old and was forced to become the head of the family. My father, a well-respected merchant in the bazaar, took my future husband with him to his chamber in the bazaar and introduced him to other merchants. We started our married life in a two-bedroom house, where, when I was fifteen, my first son was born. My husband was honest and gentle—everybody liked him; he saved factories from bankruptcy and workers from joblessness. He also set up a factory about thirty kilometers from Isfahan that produced 180,000 meters of cloth a day, and ninety-two types of fabric including a worsted wool that competed with the best from England. But I lost everything in this revolution. During the twenty-seven years I was married to my husband, only twice did he travel abroad with me. His whole love was his work. Everyone worshiped him like an idol because of his modesty and reserve.

After the Shah left the country, the harassment started gradually. I have two beautiful daughters. We started receiving telephone calls from men who claimed they were my son's classmates. One would say, "Now it's your turn to be on foot and our turn to ride. Your daughter is mine. At which registrar's office shall we be married?"

Then arrests and lootings and imprisonments started. The banks were set on fire. My husband rationalized all the other killings by saying the victims had done something wrong. This went on until we heard Elghanian was executed. Elghanian was another rich Jewish businessman, not much below my husband in rank. They accused him—like they did my husband—of Zionism. One day, three men with machine guns burst into my husband's office and told him that the governor wanted to see him. My husband was stunned. They pushed him into a jeep and drove away.

This was in September 1980. The workmen, who had always been very friendly, told my son about his father's arrest and offered to help him escape. But while my son was getting out of his work attire, gunmen arrived and grabbed him by the neck and took him away, too. We were completely unaware of all this until a worker at my husband's factory called to inform us. I called several friends who said, "Mr. Ghandsaz is liked by everybody. They probably want to ask some questions. No problem. He'll be back." I got in the car and drove to Najafabad, about thirty miles away. I went to the court with some factory workers I had picked up on the way. Whenever I asked where my husband was, the guards would tell me, smirking, "We didn't take your husband. He is at his office."

I threw myself in the middle of the street, beating myself, and calling to God and the prophet, saying, "I want to see my husband. No matter what he has done you have to let me see him and find out on what charge you have arrested him." For fifteen days, I did not know where my husband and my son were. I ran from one clergyman's house to another, so much that the soles of my feet were full of blisters and infection. Despite that, God seemed to give me a strength that kept me going. I went to the clergyman we all respected—Mr. Khodemi. I said, "During the Shah's time my husband always sent the portion of his income required by Islam as *Zakat* to you to distribute to the needy. Haji Aga, I want my husband. I don't know where he is. I haven't seen him for fifteen days." He was hard of hearing. One of the other clergy shouted in his ears, repeating what I had said. He gave me a letter to take to the court in Najafabad. I went there with our friends and showed the letter.

The *pasdar* [revolutionary guard] who took the letter was rude and nasty. He was a vile, wretched, drunken, lice-ridden, dirty, indigent fanatic of a *pasdar* who was disrespectful toward the holy man who had written the letter and toward me. I lost my cool and said, "Do you have any brains? Do you know whose signature you are rubbing on your back side, stupid?" When I said this, he raised his gun and hit me on the mouth with its butt. You can see all of my front teeth are cracked. He said, "You shit-eating, impudent Jew, you have no right to talk like that." I said, "Eat shit yourself, drunken low-life." A shouting match and fistfight ensued. Several *pasdars* attacked me—one of them pulled my hair, another one my *chador*. They tried to take me away. I grabbed a railing nearby, hung onto it, and shouted for God's help.

Across the wall a man heard my voice. I couldn't see him, but he called out my name. I didn't recognize him. I asked his name. He said he was Hossein and that his brother worked at our factory. He whispered, "Aga ['sir,' 'mister', meaning 'your husband'] is here, Aga is here."

I had been there from 7:00 a.m. to 3:30 p.m. with my children and my old, bent-over mother-in-law who was wailing to see her son. I was screaming to visit my husband and my son. We cried, and my daughters, my sister-in-law, our Muslim friends who had come with us cried, too. We continued our vigil till the next day when we noticed a jeep full of *pasdars* drive up. All of a sudden I saw my husband, whose eyes were covered with a black kerchief. They led my husband toward and into a *jub* [open ditch]. My husband fell flat on his face, gave a cry of pain, and called on God. We all rushed over to help and I said to the *pasdar*, "You are devoid of any human dignity. Why did you do this?" My husband recognized my voice and said, "Be quiet. Otherwise they'll arrest you, too." I said, "Let them. You remember you used to tell me you had a goal and that I didn't. You see now what happened to your goal, how you are being rewarded and shown appreciation for your efforts?" They picked up my husband and took him into a room.

For about half an hour we stood there, crying and weeping with our friends. The passersby who knew my husband shouted that they were bringing disgrace on the people's revolution and dragging the name of Islam into the slime. "This man," they said, "is the person who brought prosperity to Najafabad. This building where you are holding him was donated by him and used as a woman's place during the Shah's regime." A crowd gathered.

They eventually took me in to a small window through which I saw them bring my husband into the room. He was still rubbing his eyes. When he saw me, he started crying. I said, "Do you now see how right I was? I told you that these people were not true practitioners of Islam, that this was not a true revolution, and that you were duped. I was a woman, but you had a little too much self-confidence and that's what let you be fooled."

His friends and all our family started writing petitions. I have the photocopies. For the next eighty days, I dashed from one court in Tehran to another, to Qum and Isfahan with petitions. They kept my husband in jail for eighty days.

She gave a detailed account of every office she went to and every lawyer and prosecutor she appealed to, and of her visit to the magistrate who told her

that complaints against her husband had come from a few factory workers.
One day her husband was temporarily released.

Then the door opened and the *pasdars* called us in. I saw my husband sitting
in a corner with his head bowed. We waited until 2:30 in the afternoon when
my husband was released and ordered to call on the senior judge of the court to
discuss repossession of his factory. In the meantime the workers came to our
house every day, encouraging my husband not to give up, assuring him they
wouldn't let these *akhoonds* take charge of the factory. He had been free for
about twelve days when he received a phone call asking him to go to the court.

But at 7:00 p.m. our driver called to say that my husband had been arrested
again and we had better leave. I, my mother-in-law, and my daughters went
to the house of a Muslim friend and told her about my husband's arrest and
tried to plan a strategy with her husband. The next morning we set out for
Qum. There were eight of us and we took a clergyman from Isfahan along
with us. We went to a hotel behind the shrine. At 11:00 a.m. we were taken to
one of the more prominent clergymen. I told him, "What you are doing now
is making people mistrust Islam. Muslims and Jews used to live side by side
with each other. My own brother is married to a Muslim girl and they have
a child. Any family tree indicates that my ancestors lived here in what was
known as *Dar-el-Yahoud* [Abode of the Jews] for many generations. Do not
allow the name of Islam to be dragged into the mud. If you want money for
religious purposes tell my husband so, and he'll be happy to give more than
what he has been giving in the past."

He said, "I will order the court to look at his file immediately. I have heard
a lot of good things about him—that he has served his country—and I'll write
of what you said and give it to the judge." I got a promise that my husband
would be free.

During all the time my husband was in jail, I saw him only twice. I spent
most of my time going from Isfahan to Qum to Tehran, going to the courts
and clergymen. When I went to Qum I told the seven-member committee
investigating his case how my husband had lost his father at the age of twelve
and begged them to have pity on his old mother. I told them that my husband
had served this country—that if he had not been a Jew, they would have made
him a prime minister.

I don't know whether to talk of the days or nights when I and my children
were at home alone while two hundred armed men were running in the streets,
confiscating our belongings, shattering glasses, breaking into the house, and
holding us at gunpoint. I fought with these people. They broke my teeth with
guns, broke my hand, broke my vertebrae, but I continued fighting them and
I am proud of doing so. I proved that I was a strong, defiant woman. One day
I heard that Radio Isfahan had announced that people had been executed, my
husband among them. I said, "That is impossible. It can't be." We called other
friends. Our clergyman friend said, "Don't do anything at all, we are on our

way!" We got into the car and drove to Qum. The driver stopped in front of the court and the clergyman got out. After two hours he came out with the prosecutor. I ran across the street, grabbed his cloak, and fell on my knees and said, "Haji Aga, I have come to the Shrine of Maassoumeh. Don't send me back in despair. I want my husband from you." He lifted me up and said, "Get up, sister. God's compassion is on you." I said, "Then my husband will not be executed?" He said, "No! There have been a number of accusations made against him, but when I looked at his file and studied it carefully, I realized they don't have any proof."

Maybe it's not nice to say this, but because your goal is to know what exactly went on I will add this: this clergyman did not protect us just like that. Our friends had promised him one million tomans as a bribe. He said, "In two weeks you should go to the court in Najafabad, 7:00 p.m., and make a scene there and ask why your husband's trial has not taken place. Tell them you want your husband. If you cry and scream, they'll be forced to put him on trial and since they don't have anything against him he'll have to be freed."

So I went back on the road between Qum and Tehran. Several of the *bazaaris* said to me that everything was in the hands of Montazeri's son. "Let us go and see him." They asked me not to display my temper no matter what was said. Their official reason for visiting Montazeri was to congratulate him on the birth of a child. His wife's father was from Najafabad and their family knew my husband. So we went and my friends sat with Montazeri and started whispering, trying to strike up a bargain with him for my husband's life. Once or twice he pointed his fingers at them, saying, "Forty million, give me forty million and I'll have her husband behind his desk in the morning."

She relates how she explained that all her husband's money was in the bank and that his accounts were frozen. The next day a pasdar *called, changing the figure to ten million. They arranged for a meeting place to exchange money and husband by* 1:00 a.m. *the following morning. If they did not receive the money by that time, her husband would be executed.*

I sent my brother and brother-in-law to Isfahan to knock at our friends' doors to raise money. The total we collected was a little over a million. Around 2:30 to 3:00 a.m., my brother and brother-in-law got into two cars to deliver the money. On the way, they noticed that the road to the factory was lined with *pasdars* with radars in their hands. My brother sensed a trap, but they could do nothing. Jeeps and cars appeared on the road—including Mr. "A," the warden at the jail who had come to our house in Najafabad two days before delivering a last will and testament written in jail by my husband. "A" asked my brother for the money. My brother said, "It's in the car behind us." As he was saying this he noticed about forty or fifty *pasdars* come out with their guns pointed from among the trees. My brother says, "Mr. A, you swore that you wanted to save Mr. Ghandsaz. Where is he? I don't see him." There was a cream-colored car among the sedans. Mr. "A" pointed to that car and said, "He is there." They aimed a flashlight at the car but nobody could be seen inside.

My brother said, "You swore on your honor. Where is he? We brought the money you asked for." Then my brother saw my husband alive on the floor.

She recounts how at this point her other relatives were arrested and driven away with her husband because they reneged on the money. Her sister hears the shot that killed Mr. Ghandsaz at 3:00 a.m.

My husband's execution ended my family's interrogation. We had to promise never to go beyond a certain area and never to enter Najafabad.

In the meantime, in Isfahan, our relatives had been kept under arrest and the *pasdars* were refusing to hand over the body of my husband. When Muslims and Jews went to the courthouse in protest, the Muslim elders brought straw with them and the Jewish elders the Torah. They converged on the courthouse and asked for my husband's body. The officials answered, "No, we are sending the body to the Valley of the Cursed!" Then the Muslim elders from the bazaar threw the straw over their heads [a sign of mourning] and beat their chests and said to the *pasdars*, "Don't cause any more shame and degradation for Islam. Give them the body!"

Our own rabbi said, "I will not leave here and will prevent you from leaving too, until you give us the body." This the *pasdars* eventually did. My Muslim friends accompanied me to the mosque saying they wanted to apologize to my husband. When I went in and lifted the shroud to look at him, I saw that his body was full of bullet holes. All the flesh had been removed from his body and nothing was left but a skin over bones. We had a ceremony for the dead and eulogies. Our door was kept open and friends, relatives, strangers, and workers from the factory called to console us.

Now I am here. I was told to ask the charity Jewish organizations for financial assistance, but my pride would not permit me. After we came here, Rabbi David and other Jewish community leaders interceded on our behalf and it was agreed that my brothers-in-law would take care of my daily expenses. I work four days a week in a clothing store that my son has opened downtown. The other three days of the week I spend in my friends' homes designing, planting, and pruning their gardens.

Zia Ashraf Nasr

The oldest of my interviewees was compelled to leave Iran in her seventies to follow her children to the United States. Her son Hossein was forced into exile because he had been part of the inner circles of the Pahlavi court. Because she considers herself one who believes in the values of Islamic philosophy and practice, it pained her, she said, to speak of her response to the Islamic Revolution.

This revolution is not Islamic. This "Islamic" idea of women you quote to me from Khomeini—his "Islam" has been contaminated with many things that didn't exist at the beginnings of Islam. One of them is the disparity between men and women. This should not be labeled "Islam." I believe, based on the life of the Prophet and the first leaders of Islam, that Muhammad himself did not discriminate against women. He considered his daughter Fatima superior to men. He made her the beginning; he made it so that all the Imam family histories originated from her. Why? The Prophet had sons from other wives. He had daughters and sons. But he didn't give any of them as much power as he gave this girl so that she would be the ancestor of all the Imams.[16] After Fatima, her daughter was privileged—Hazrat Zainab who supervised the caravans, who took care of the family in the desert of Karbala, who brought the family in its imprisonment from Karbala to Medina. There were other men after Imam Hosein's martyrdom—Imam Zeinul Abedin, for instance. But it was a woman, Hazrat Zainab, who supervised the family, who took charge. Even in Yazid's court, it was she who lectured at him, and what a sermon she delivered. She was a woman, yet she was at the head of Islam. Then why should a woman, later on, stay home and the man go out? They changed Islam. The Islam of today has been so badly interpreted that it has put young people to flight. Now the veil enslaves women. Now women have been packaged and bundled so that one has to guess from the shape that this is a woman. When you see the Iranian *Majlis* [Parliament] on TV, you see something black in the corner and you don't know what or who this is. Is it a human being or a black bundle? It shouldn't be like this.

Mehrnaz Saeed-Vafa

Earlier, Mehrnaz Saeed-Vafa talked of the part played by her particular family, her gender, and her Muslim culture in her early formation, and then of her awakening into film and television as a source of power, possibility, and creativity. I asked about her involvement in politics before and during the revolution.

Politics? No, I was never involved in politics. I took photographs all over Tehran and in other cities, but all the pictures were destroyed as was the archive of magazines and newspapers I had collected, and the films of demonstrations and the interviews. My character is not that of a joiner of groups—I may be sympathetic to a cause, but I don't join. I was working on a film in a village near Qum when the demonstrations started. Television was the first institution to be closed down after the revolution. We could not work. So, too, the university where I taught—that was closed down for the cultural or educational revolution. So for two years I didn't teach; I worked at translation, wrote some articles, taught small groups, but mainly I took many photographs and made many tapes.

For me the revolution began in my neighborhood. Our neighbors varied from the semireligious to the extremely religious. One was a doctor, head of Loqman Hospital; he had two Mercedes-Benzes and two wives, one living upstairs, the other downstairs. He really enjoyed the revolution—I supposed he thought he could now get a few more wives. Everyone looked for what they could personally gain from the revolution. The religious neighbors were distant and hostile toward me because I was both westernized and in film. The women in my neighborhood gathered and talked and gossiped and shopped together. But because I was never part of their group, I was an outsider. So they never socialized with me to begin with. But the revolution was a provocation for them to attack and criticize me—you aren't religious, you aren't one of us, you are Westernized. The doctor accused me of being antirevolution. But slowly things began to change. The first change occurred when one of our most religious neighbors had a son killed in the Iran-Iraq war. They instantly lost their faith in the revolution and felt only anger. Another neighbor had a husband laid off work and her son taken to prison. So year after year, as the neighbors began to feel real loss, they also began to lose their faith in the regime. So that's how the neighborhood became a site where I saw the revolution change.

When my mother returned to Iran three years ago, she said that the neighbors had changed again—that they were jealous and envious and angry at people who did not experience their hardships during the war. One did not need to study groups like the Hezbollahs or the Mojahids to understand the revolution. All I needed to do was to study my own neighborhood, multiply that by a few million, and I had the scenario. All the larger class tensions, personal tensions, religious tensions played themselves out in my own backyard. This was a predominantly Muslim neighborhood with one Armenian family and one Jewish family. The Armenian family stayed. So did the Jewish family though they sent their children to Israel, which they considered their homeland.

A good thing that came out of this revolution was ridding ourselves of one aspect of the commercialism surrounding womanhood, the commercialism that exploited women. It was good to see the government respect serious women filmmakers, serious women teachers, to see women as committed workers rather than those who merely flirted with their professions. All the years I was in Iran after the revolution, no one harassed me or bothered me. I was respected for the work I did. They needed some women in the field they could trust, who could serve as token representatives of women to counter the accusation that Iranian women had no opportunities in Iran.

Barbod

Born and raised in Iran, Barbod attended film school in England, after which he worked in the United Kingdom for two years as a photographer, a freelance news journalist, and a cameraman at a television studio. In 1969 he returned to Iran, where he worked in television and in film until the revolutionary censors made it necessary for him to leave in 1980. He currently lives and works in Los Angeles where Pari and I interviewed him in 1991 and 1992. I have chosen to omit his narrative about childhood and early politicization, focusing instead only on his work there and here. But because his work overlaps his involvement with the revolution, his story is as much about the effect of the revolution on film as it is the story of Barbod's awakening to the everyday realities of political power and the contradictions between theory and practice within the Islamic government's secret ties to the West, even during the hostage crisis. Asked to position himself for an introduction on tape, he began with the following words:

Who am I? I'm a filmmaker. After some four years in Europe, I returned to Iran in 1969. My first feature film was made in 1970, and by 1971 it had become a hit. I won a couple of international awards for my films. I worked till 1979 in Iran. I was a producer, a cameraman, and a director. Before the revolution started I considered myself generally pro-Left but not involved with any political group. I had sympathies for leftists who were actually fighting against the Shah and the system. I was pro- anything-against-Shah. When the revolution started I felt that something monumental was happening, and I joined the revolution immediately with my camera.

I photographed Khomeini from the moment of his arrival till I left. I was among the cameramen who were right there on the steps of the plane and who took his picture the moment he arrived and followed him all the way to Behesht Zahra [the national cemetery] and then to the school in back of the Parliament and on. Khomeini had the kind of dedication you see in committed political activists, those willing to die in front of the firing squad. He stood by what he said and believed he was implementing the word of God. All sacrifices such as death were therefore a necessary part of fulfilling the duties of an Islamic leader. What he did in Iran, I think, is a disaster. He threw Iran back by fourteen hundred years—a return to a past that didn't work—but he was a great power capable of creating mass hypnotism and mass hysteria.

Standing against him in those days was like a small tree against a heavy flood. He would break anything in his path. He didn't compromise. He didn't care about material wealth. He didn't care about respect. He didn't care about how many followers he would have. He didn't care about how many followers he would lose, who liked or disliked him. He only cared about his Islam. He believed in God's war, which is eternally true. He didn't care if you were in the twentieth century. You could see this through his face, through his eyes, through the way he treated people.

I saw him up close. He walked among those multitudes of people like a knife cutting through a cake. A man of no ordinary emotions. If, for instance, you told him that hundreds of people were killed on the war front, he would say, "God bless them, for they will go to heaven." And you could see no sign of emotion on his face. But if you said that "Imam Husein was killed in Karbala," that would start him weeping just like clicking a button. Khomeini is a tragedy that happened to our country. Someone with so much power should move people forward. He moved them backward.

What did you expect from the revolution?
I expected freedom from injustice and from poverty. When I went to Hamoon and Sistan shooting films of the people and land and saw the poverty, that was when I really became aware of what was wrong with the country. Like others, I thought that a man who claims to be a man of God thinks of the welfare of others more than worldly people do; we thought the clerics were not greedy and that at least a man of God cannot be a Shah. That's why I joined the revolution; but when I saw it turning against all those revolutionary principles we believed in, when I saw it becoming another terrible dictatorship, I had the honesty to say that I had made a mistake.

What do you think went wrong with the revolution?
I think it was like a mass hypnosis, a mass hysteria. I sensed rising anger and resentment in many levels of society who were not educated into that kind of modernization inappropriately tailored for our society. Also, those who joined the revolution wished for fantasies because there was no manifesto, and no document. The *bazaaris*, for instance, thought they would get rid of those few big companies who controlled prices outside the bazaar, because there were five or six major names—the Elghanians, the Sabetbazariks—who controlled all the import and export. The bazaar had lost its privileged position to these people, so the *bazaaris* joined the revolution in hope of getting rid of the major industrialists. Other groups had the same fantasies.

You told me earlier that your documentaries could be read as a record of the history of the revolution. Could you elaborate?

I worked to record what I saw. What I did was to capture events from the first day of demonstrations. I was there with my camera and covered the action right to the victory of the revolution on the twenty-second of Bahman. I captured forty hours of documents and thousands of pictures—more than two thousand negatives, slides from what happened, and forty hours of film. I made a documentary from the footage called *Soghoot Panjah-Haft*, or *Crash of '57*— made from day one of the uprising and shooting. It was generally considered a unique document in commercial Iranian film history because it led to a first showing of a documentary in the cinemas—in places that release feature films. But as the revolution settled, my enterprise and the film were taken over by the religious factions.

I believe the history of my film is one of many ways to demonstrate the history of the development of the revolution. As the years passed the religious censors started to edit, to cut pieces from the documentary. They tried to prove that certain people whom they preferred to edit from their memory and record of revolution were not actually recorded in my film, so they cut them out. They cut out undesirable political groups, and they cut out images of women without scarves.

The story of my film proves one aspect of the history of the revolution— its censorship of history and the process through which the revolution came into being. In the beginning censorship had no face. It seemed to be a matter of taste. But as the revolution settled, as the government became stronger, censorship took on a more unified face. So, they finally banned my film and what they wrote in the censorship papers is evidence of how the revolution began to define itself. They wrote: "In the history of nations there comes the moment that people need not know the truth; and since your film is a document, since this film is documentary, you are not allowed to show it."

Only with their particular version of the revolution could they say that women without scarves were antirevolutionary. But I had evidence to the contrary. They were in my film as part of the revolution. I had hours and hours of footage of women without scarves actually fighting against the veil. Those who had fought in the street for the revolution had not been clerics or religious people—they were the Fadayaan and Mojahedin and Tudehs and other groups. Those who took over the military bases were guerrillas trained by Mojahedin and by Fadayaan—not by the clerics. Those who took over the television stations were the branch of revolutionaries who were the Tudeh Party. But later, the Islamic groups chose to deny the existence of these people. The women who took over the American embassy in the first attempt had been Fadayaans, and I have footage of these women with guns and without *chadors* or veils or scarves or anything of the sort. But all these had to be eliminated from the film.

I refused. So the film was banned and that famous sentence was written on the censorship papers. I believe that any government that censors art and artists and writers, that limits the people's right to know the truth, is not one with which to work anymore. So that was the ground for my departing Iran. Till that final censorship I had thought there might still be a chance to hope, a chance to remain and work with the people.

Then when the Iran-Iraq war began I went to the front. In the very early days of the war I went to Khoramshahr, to Abadan, and to the Persian Gulf. I went six times to Iraqi soil. I filmed the explosion of Al Baqe Ommayed—this became famous footage shown all over the world of the exploding of those two main Iraqi oil bases. And I also made a ninety-minute documentary about the war shown in the first film festival in Iran organized by the Islamic government. A controversial film, it was in essence antiwar even though it was about the war.

Mainly it concentrated on the navy. Most of the film was shot with the navy on operations where I was present with them at the front. Later on the government found that some of those heroes after whom ports and ships were named were not necessarily Muslims. Some of these famous men belonged to leftist political parties, as Nakhoda Hemmati did. When he drowned, they named the complete fleet of ships after him. But when the new regime found out these facts, they changed the names of ports and ships and fleets. And more parts of my film were banned by the government.

Although while I was blacklisted as a filmmaker I was not allowed to make any films, the Iranian government needed somebody to dive in the Persian Gulf and film underwater the damage done to the oil rigs and platforms in the sea. They had nobody left to do that work but me and another friend. Here's the hypocrisy: because I was blacklisted, the government gave us ID cards under different names so I could do this government work under another name!

In 1980 I joined a company for underwater filming with my friend the diver. Together we worked for the Iranian offshore drilling company, and we got permission to go to war zones in the Persian Gulf. Our job was to dive for ships coming into the harbor. When they were ready to anchor, we had to dive down to check that the place of the anchorage was safe and not colliding with the oil pipes. One of the more intriguing things we discovered during that time was the precise cargo many ships carried into the harbor. They carried armaments from countries who claimed that they were *not* sending armaments to Iran. I can give examples: all the helicopters belonging to the navy were Italian. There were parts coming from France because all the battleships in Iran were French. I saw equipment from Germany, from Sweden, from Israel, and from the United States—all countries that pretended not to be sending armaments. They anchored in a special harbor away from other ships, and we had to dive under to check their anchorage. When we came up we would board the ship, talk to the captain, and would find out what they were carrying and who they were carrying it for. This was how Western countries violated their embargo against Iran.

My greatest discovery—this seems like a huge black joke—was of the involvement of the Islamic Revolution with the West. We became good friends with all the other divers from the Iranian Navy with whom we worked daily. One day we went to the club and we found a lot of people absent. We asked where these divers were and were told that they had all gone to England. I was shocked. How could this be? In the middle of the war how could they go to England? What for? We learned that they had been sent there for training. I said what training? They said they were going to put certain sorts of armament on the Iranian hover-craft. Now Iranian hover-craft, even during the Shah's time, were not mobilized. They didn't carry armament, only soldiers. But now they needed them to carry armament because of the Basra offensive, and the only way we could move on shallow water was on hover-crafts. Yet the British were publicly supporting an embargo officially condemning Iran; they had cut off all diplomatic relations and recalled their ambassador. Yet here they were training, not only our army, but also helping to arm the hover-craft they had earlier sold to the Shah's Iran.

To me that showed the contradiction between public and private policy in the West: high moral antiwar standards were for public appearance to the world, but they would help all they needed to if they could get secret financial benefits from this war—money and oil. Everybody was pouring in their arms and selling their junk to Iran and Iraq in order to make millions and billions of profit. I saw the stuff with my own eyes. I saw navy choppers, air-to-sea missiles, F-14s and F-16s—not the sort of item that you can buy in pieces or in supermarkets. Even Israelis cannot sell them without American approval. Neither could Pakistan. We witnessed many other tricks like the deals made between Iran and Iraq—enemies—so that certain ships would be blown up and not others for the benefit of collecting insurance.

It was not really the war of Islam against its enemies, or of Iran against Iraq, or of the Persians against Arabs. It was a war of economies. It was a war that would benefit the West, and it did, and now the West is benefiting from repairing what we have ruined during the war. Each country has ruined industries, cities, and roads, and for the next twenty years all the income from their oil will be spent on buying more help from others.

Still, before I left, the Islamic government wanted me to make a film for children about the revolution. But they wanted me to fill in everything they wanted about the revolution through fake drawings, not with the actual footage. And I refused. Then they asked me to make a film for children about the war—a film to persuade kids into believing in martyrdom, into wishing that their fathers would becomes martyrs (shahid) of war. There I stood firm and said I would not do it. And I was forced to go to court over this refusal. In court I said I could not say anything to the children of Iran that I would not say to my own children who I hoped would not wish for their father's death, to which they declared, "This is the Imam's war—and the Imam wants the people to wish for martyrdom."

And after that court appearance, the judge called me and said I had ten days to leave the country; otherwise I would die. They had lost all their arguments against me in that civil court. It would take, he said, ten days for the case to be taken to the revolutionary court. Within this period of ten days was my only chance of running away from Iran. If you can do it, he told me, you will save your life. Or else they will either force you to make the film or they will kill you.

So, I left the country. I think the main reason for leaving was because I was not able to make any more films in that country. If I had been willing, they were willing to compromise with me, to allow me to make ideologically correct films for them. But then there was the matter of my honor and what I believed. To give it away to them, to become their tool, that was against what I had worked for all my life.

I left the country and I became an exile.

Rebwar Kurdi

His early childhood idealization of Kurdish nationalism, the torture of his brother by the Shah's secret police, and his activism through the 1960s and 1970s combined to make Rebwar a strong supporter of revolutionary possibility. This part of his narrative records the change from celebration to mourning, particularly through the attack on Kurdistan that told him his revolution had been "hijacked."

I returned to Iran in March 1979 to join the revolution. The day that the monarchy fell was the happiest day of my life. Although I worried about the clerical leadership of the revolution, I was full of hope. I knew already that in Kurdistan, people were in control, not the central Iranian government. Yes, *Bahar-i Azadi*, the Spring of Freedom. Happy times. No trace of the monarchy. Nothing was more relaxing than seeing the hated statues of the Shah taken down. Now I could see all the revolutionary literature, everything previously censored printed here. And people were reading it. And the freedom on the campus! In the past, every time we went to campus, the police would check our IDs. Now there was no trace of it. Students were selling revolutionary literature and putting up wall newspapers. It was my dream realized. But not entirely.

I didn't stay in Tehran for more than a few days. I went back to Kurdistan, finding Bardashan had changed noticeably. The new Islamic regime was not in control. The Kurdish political parties and people were carrying their own rifles; they had not obeyed the government decree for disarming, issued soon after the surrender of the army on February 22. When I went home it was as if I had always been there.

It was clear that the revolution had made a difference in people's lives. The first difference was freedom. You had Kurdish newspapers around, posters on the walls, you saw Kurdish costumes, you saw students going to school in Kurdish dress and the local TV stations had Kurdish programs.

When did you first sense the problems of the revolution?
From the first day there were signs of resistance to oppression. One slogan on a banner in Bardashan read *Dar bahar azadi, jayi azadi khali* (In the spring of freedom, freedom is absent). By this time Islamic groups—those related to various factions of the government—had started suppressing revolutionary and non-Islamic literature outside Kurdistan. In Tehran and outside Kurdistan they suppressed any so-called non-Islamic slogans and demonstrations. Leftist groups had been attacked and their slogans torn down. Even before the Shah fell, it was only on the campus of Tehran University where the leftists had more power that non-Islamic slogans were tolerated. In Kurdistan, the leftist nationalist groups were dominant. So slogans were predominantly non-Islamic: "Freedom for Kurdistan," "Kurdistan—A federal state," and themes on the demands of workers and peasants. When Khomeini came to power, Kurdistan really was not under his rule. Only in Sanandaj, a nonclerical but religious Kurd, Ahmad Moftizadeh, supported the Islamic regime and sought an Islamic alternative to secular Kurdish nationalism. Although he was popular among certain people in the city, he had to pay for his alliance with the central government. He was branded a collaborator and had to leave the city in disgrace.

The Islamic Air Force dispatched its Phantoms and helicopters, bombing the people of Sanandaj, killing and wounding many hundreds, on the first new year [March 21] after the fall of the Shah. This was a major turning point. Now people argued that there was no difference between the two regimes, and many said the Islamic regime was worse. By the time of the referendum for the approval of the Islamic Republic[17] [April 1979], Kurdistan boycotted the referendum and no one voted for the Islamic government. However, the government falsely published figures claiming that the majority of the Kurds had voted in favor of the Islamic regime. I was there and saw no polling stations anywhere in the two neighboring cities that I visited. Fraud and deception were common under the Pahlavi monarchy, but no one had experienced any lies on this scale.

It takes a long time to even recall the numerous struggles that went on in Kurdistan. As the conflict escalated, the population of an entire town, Marivan, about twenty thousand people, in protest against the government's airlifting of *pasdars* [revolutionary guards], left town for the woods in protest. New forms of struggle emerged in Kurdistan centered around the demand for an autonomous Kurdistan as well as demands for land redistribution, employment, and freedom. The government eventually used force on the infamous day of August 19, also known as the 28th of Mordad [the anniversary of the CIA coup that returned the Shah to power]. And Ayatollah Khomeini chose this day on which to order the Iranian army to crush the autonomist Kurdish movement.

He ordered the army to attack Kurdistan. The news was announced at 2:00

p.m. on the main news program on the radio. I heard it while walking home with a friend. About two hours later Phantom jets broke the sound barrier over cities in Kurdistan. Soon military aircraft began landing troops and arms in the Sanandaj airport. The war began, and the capture of each city by the Islamic army was followed by immediate executions. Revenge and intimidation, as practiced in medieval times, was the policy of the army. Kurdish forces resisted in two towns. The war continued for about four months until November 16, when the government announced a cease-fire.

Like many political activists without party affiliation, I joined other friends and went to the countryside. There were fights on some of the roads and in some villages where the army and *pasdars* committed massacres, but there were no major battles like the next government offensive.

I had been drafted into the army after I was done with college. So I had basic skills, but I was not really involved in military operations. My friends and I did political work in the villages around the cities. Twice attacked by helicopters, we shot back at them, ineffectively of course. At one village, where I was stranded for about three weeks, I mobilized students and their parents to rebuild an abandoned school and began teaching the students in Kurdish.

I went to Tehran in early December 1979. I stayed for a few days, then returned to Kurdistan where I stayed with friends—and this period I remember as one of the best of my life. Hanaran was paradise. I felt the full freedom and saw Kurds in power in place of the despotic Islamic regime. Restrictions on women's clothing, on selling or reading revolutionary literature, on freedom of association and thought that had been imposed in Tehran and other places did not exist here. There was security and absence of crime, although people were carrying arms. I remember that one of the things people always recalled about the Kurdish republic of 1946 was the security and safety that everyone had enjoyed. Here shopkeepers would leave their shops unattended. Revolutionary organizations suppressed in Tehran and elsewhere in Iran had their offices running here in Hanaran.

The government's cease-fire was designed to buy time. By spring 1980, the army began the second offensive that continues to this day. The killings and massacres committed by Tehran's armed forces were unprecedented. Although the government was able to defeat the autonomist movement militarily, it was obvious that it had failed to sell its politics and ideology to the people of Kurdistan. When I had to leave the country, it was a bitter moment in my life. I did not want to leave. I felt that they, the new rulers, should get out, not me. They had hijacked a revolution.

Kambys Shirazi

In the prior part of his story, Kambys spoke of his childhood in small northern towns, his early understanding of class and politics, and his move to Tehran where he was politicized in the engineering school of Tehran University. He moved to the United States during the 1970s. Of his long and interesting narrative, I include only a small section on his reactions to the changes in his old friends in 1979, and to the closing of a major newspaper—Ayandegan—a sign of a dark turn in the revolution after the promising Spring of Freedom.

Many of my friends who had been anti-Tudeh in our college days were now part of the Tudeh Party. We spent many nights talking about this change in their affiliation: what had happened, and what was it that they saw in the Tudeh Party? They thought that among the many leftist groups, the Tudeh Party was now the most reasonable.

Other than the war against the Kurds, the major event that affected my feelings on the revolution was the demonstration against the closing of the major daily oppositional newspaper, *Ayandegan*. I wanted to go and see this demonstration and participate in it. Now the headquarters of opposition groups, especially student groups supporting these parties, was in the *Daneskadeh Fanni* [the engineering school of Tehran University].

The Tudeh Party happened to have a good backing in this engineering school. They had taken over one side of the main corridor and had posted pamphlets and news about their organization. They had, for instance, a long series of papers posted with questions and answers about the history and character of Tudeh Parties. People didn't trust them. People questioned some of the damaging things they had done in the past, and the Tudeh had posted an answer to every single query. This was a remarkable public act. Nobody else had this kind of literature ready to defend themselves. But, the position the Tudeh took was that we should cooperate with the present government of Khomeini. Maybe they thought they would later replace his government with socialism. The other political groups were more radical and thought in terms of overthrowing the government—a very difficult, uphill position. To me, in this early stage of the revolution, it didn't make sense to overthrow a government that had legitimacy in the population.

These groups were basically reading Iranian history in terms of Russian history, I thought, and saying that, "Well, in February was the first revolution, so in October there is going to be a second one." And I was there right in the middle of this fantasy during the summer of 1979, and I thought, "These guys don't know where they're going if they imagine revolutions come so easily in pairs."

But I wanted to go to the demonstrations against the closure of the newspaper. And of course, my Tudeh friends wanted to go with me, because they were curious to see the happenings. Because they thought I was doing a crazy thing by going, they felt they should protect me. I took my camera. There were some two or three thousand people at least in front of Tehran University. The situation was tense. The demonstrators shouted, "Down with fascism!" And they were surrounded by Hezbollahis.

My friends preferred to think that the newspaper was printing lies and that I should not participate in the march. I insisted on staying and taking pictures. Perhaps they were remodeling or maybe reconstructing the *Ayandegan* building, because there were boxes and piles of dirt and brick around. So I went on top of one of these piles to take pictures from the top. There was much chanting of protests around me. Suddenly there was an escalation of tension as people started running. Apparently there were groups attacking the demonstrators. What had made everyone run away was that a truck full of bricks had planted itself in the middle of the street. Somehow demonstrators instantly appeared, took these bricks, and simply threw them up in the air. Obviously, these bricks landed someplace. You saw these bricks going up and coming down and suddenly there was blood all over the place.

There was simply no place to run. You could only hold your hands over your head to protect yourself. Everybody who had a book or any protection held that over their heads. I left and returned an hour later with other students to see what had happened. The people had left, but bricks were all over the street. The street was closed, *pasdars* were guarding the area, and the area was full of Hezbollahis. Suddenly I saw three angry teenagers coming by us. Their shirts were open and their veins were throbbing, and one of them yelled, "Communists! Where are you? I want to kill you!" (*Komonist! Kojai? Mekoshameth!*). I'm sure the guy didn't know what the words meant, but he knew anger and violence.

Anything I knew about fascism in Spain, in Germany, in Italy—this sounded like it. In my mind, I likened fascism to a disease that you catch. And there must be good reason to catch fascism in this country, so let's think about the reasons. My Tudeh friends would say, "Fascism occurs only in advanced capitalist societies, not in a backward society." I thought, "This society is sick." I would say that this is fascism, and they would say, "No, this is simply a phase. The middle class is in control. It needs us to support the working class and the poor, and this will soon be a democratic society. Once we get rid of the mullahs, we will have true socialism." There was nothing I could do except return to the United States for my Ph.D. with a sense of helplessness.

Under the Shah there was a lot of repression. But among people there was a sense of possibility: you could, for instance, overthrow the Shah. It was with that sense that I went back, and I think that was the ecstasy of *Bahar-i Azadi*. But it was a very short spring, and by the middle of the summer it was over. Soon the winter would come.

Mehrdad Haghighi

After a childhood in Tehran and an apprenticeship in India, Mehrdad Haghighi, a contemporary of Pari born around 1936, returned to his hometown, Shiraz, where he lived until the revolution. Forced to flee Iran in 1979, Haghighi lives in Los Angeles where Pari and I interviewed him in his office in 1990. I use his narrative as a chance to reflect on Baha'ism—the religion targeted as an enemy of the new Islamic nation.

Ever since visitors began to record their impressions, Shiraz has been associated with gardens, poetry, beauty, and sainthood. In Shiraz on October 20, 1819, was born a certain Mirza Mohammad, later to be called the Bab, or "the gate" to truth and the hidden Imam. In 1844, he announced in Shiraz that he was the promised Imam whose message would complete that prefaced in the Qur'an. After the death of Mohammad Shah in 1848, the Babis provoked several badly coordinated revolts and were murderously repressed for four years. On July 9, 1850, the Bab was executed on the orders of Nasirudin Shah, an event that was not unexpectedly followed by a Babi effort to kill the Shah, which was in turn followed by the execution of many leading Babis including the leading and defiant philosopher, poet, and feminist Qurrat-ul-Ain.

Bahaullah, the disciple of the Bab, announced in 1863 his claim to be the Imam predicted by the Bab. He had fled from Iran first to Iraq, then to Kurdistan, and finally to Palestine where he died in 1892. He softened and universalized the appeal of the Bab by declaring Baha'ism to be an inclusive faith that transcended divisions created by geography, nationalism, and culture. Unlike the Bab who declared open hostility to the monarchy, Bahaullah, while declaring himself nonpolitical, committed the allegiance of Baha'is to the Shah. This gesture further ruptured the traditional Islamic bond between God and Sultan, or in this case, between the Islamic Ulama and the monarchy, thus earning for Baha'is the continuous enmity of the traditional clergy.

The extermination of the Baha'is by the Islamic Republic is another chapter in a long history of persecution and denial of the inherent contradiction between the claim that discrimination against minorities is anti-Islamic and the insistence that all Muslims are one nation in danger of being weakened by ethnic fragmentations. And this in a country in which religious and ethnic minorities constitute some 53 percent of the population. The persecution of Baha'is was declared acceptable because they were not "people of the Book" and because they were declared to be spies "just like the Tudeh [Communists]" (Benard and Khalilzad 1984, 133).

I have cut from Haghighi's narrative the story of his growing up into journalism, his studies in India and the Philippines, and his gradual politicization. I have also omitted his stories of the anti-Communist hysteria that followed the 1953 CIA coup when the label of Tudehi *(Commie) was freely used to attack anyone against whom one held a grudge. After working as a youth for the leading magazine of political satire,* Towfigh, *he started with some friends a similar paper called* Dakho. *Like other Baha'is, Haghighi was surprised at the catastrophic changes he saw in what he assumed was a culture and a people he knew. He fled the country after the start of the killing of Baha'is in Shiraz. We asked him why he was here rather than there.*

Why did I come here? The revolution, of course.

While I was away from Iran in India, I believed that our people were maturing into enlightenment, into thinking individuals. But alas, what I saw during the revolution proved that beneath the facade of enlightenment, we had kept our prejudices undisturbed. It was the unexpected eruption of prejudice and the abuse of power that caused my departure from Iran. I saw people using the revolution as an excuse to carry out personal vendettas. Anyone who had a grudge against another found it easy to get him arrested by accusing him of being against the revolution. A traffic officer was shot, for instance, by a taxi driver who had once in the past been ticketed by him. A student shot a teacher for once giving him a failing grade. A grocery was looted by a righteous mob led by someone who had once felt that the grocer was a price-gouger. And so this is exactly what happened in Shiraz.

One January morning immediately after the Shah left, we heard people demonstrating and shouting that the night before, forty people had been murdered in Saadi—a small village where the poet Saadi is buried—near Shiraz. Why had such a massacre taken place? Saadi, like many other small communities, especially around the Caspian Sea, was a place where people of different tribal or religious affiliations had lived peacefully side by side for many years. Now all of a sudden the revolution had become a weapon with which to destroy whomever you did not get along with or wish to have around. In Saadi about 40 percent of the residents were Baha'is. The father in one of these families had died and been buried. Two days later, these wild revolutionaries exhumed the body, burned it, then urinated and defecated on the grave. The clergyman Ayatollah Mahalati himself denounced this act and said that opening a grave and disturbing the dead is forbidden in Islam, no matter what religion the dead person.

Then they went to the house of a Baha'i staff sergeant and raped his wife and daughter. The sergeant got back from work and realized what had happened. While people were still swarming up around his house, he went up on the roof with his son-in-law and started shooting those who entered his yard. Seven people died in the shooting. Then he went down into the house and killed his wife, his daughter, his son-in-law, and himself. The bodies were then brought to the hospital—and that is where I was the reporter for TV and I saw with my own eyes the corpses covered with spit and dirt.

This incident became the excuse for wholesale attacks on communities like Saadi and Haafezi-yeh and other villages where Baha'is lived. In the meantime, under the guise of revenge against Baha'is, many Jewish homes were also set on fire. That night about sixty homeless people slept in our house. I must admit that in the midst of all this violence, there were those who showed bravery and compassion and did not succumb to the lawless mood of the time. Our neighborhood Muslim baker and butcher stood on the roof of our house with two large casks of kerosene in their hands, ready to set fire to the approaching crowd if they drew near. Our house was full of women and children. These same men—the baker and butcher—delivered free of charge to our house huge trays of bread and eggs. Mr. Mahalati[18] managed to quieten the people, but Mr. Dastgheib incited them all over again. These disturbances actually caused fewer casualties than reported. But on the other hand, the military was doing nothing to quiet down or prevent these outbursts. Their thought was that if they let people vent their aggressions in this way, they would then have none to spare for the ruling hierarchy. The minorities thus became a symbol on whom people could vent their dissatisfaction.

The most interesting and unusual aspect of this revolution was that the people had no previous experience in political action, and the entire thing was treated more like a spectacle or joke than a serious change of life and thought. For example, crowds would come onto the streets with *tombak* [drums] under their arms, chanting in rhythm all sorts of one- or two-liners making light of political and social problems. Groups practiced these slogans every night outside the city. I remember a group of musicians accompanying a female singer who was singing slogans as if they were classical melodies. The atmosphere of merriment and sloganeering was the only available diversion during these times when power stations were sabotaged and homes had no electricity. So people would make bonfires around which they would sing hours of slogans to the accompaniment of drums.

In the provinces, the revolution took a different form than it did in Tehran. It seemed more chaotic and irresponsible. But when I went to Tehran I found an entirely different situation. My friends involved with the Mojahedin knew the true meaning of revolution. When they organized a demonstration, they knew it would travel from points X to Y; they knew exactly who would be driving which bus from what stop and who would replace him for what fraction of the way. Not even the Hezbollahis were so organized. When the leftists and the Mojahedin organized a meeting in Shahyad Square and Bazargan and other activists spoke, even I, who had no special leanings to either side, found myself repeating the slogans.

But in the provinces, in Jahrome and Shiraz, this was not the case. In Jahrome, for example, I asked an elderly woman what she thought of the revolution. She said: "They say the Imam is coming and he's very good, and that the 'tooteh' [incorrect pronunciation of "Communist" in Persian, which makes the word Tudeh into *tooteh,* or parrot] is coming, and they are also very good." She not only had no notion of how the names of parties were pronounced, she had no idea what the words meant. In Shiraz I used to frequent the neighborhood around Shah Cheragh [a holy shrine] and talk to the students I saw. I asked one why he was not in school. He said that all the petty bourgeoisie were going to be arrested. I asked him who these were—he said people like teachers, school principals.

I saw the blind leading the blind. During one of the marches in Shiraz—some fifty thousand demonstrators—the crowds shouted slogans following the call of a leader. At one point one of the men with a loudspeaker shouted, "People, don't walk far apart." And the crowd shouted, as if it were a slogan, "People, don't walk far apart." Why did they follow so blindly and so enthusiastically?

Some clergy—such as Mr. Dastgheib—and their cohorts would prepare food, bread, dates, etc., and personally distribute them among the poor, promising them that when the government fell into the hands of the men of the cloth, then everyone would have a house of his own, that water and kerosene would be free, that everyone would be given a stipend of some 350 tomans [about $50] a month as pocket money, and so on. Those who suffered most were those who were promised the most. As in all systems, the rich got away. Even in the Russian Revolution, those with money managed to escape by smuggling themselves out of the country.

By itself, the revolution was good. I had believed in it. But the real reason I left was that I could not remain a silent observer to watching a horse being whipped to death. I decided to leave, expecting fully to return when the system changed. But it didn't. Even now I think that the revolution brought about a necessary awareness in people. It forced people to read, to think, and to study. It purged people of mere facade.

Yahya

Yahya (pseud.), who left Iran in 1985, is an academician I met while he was completing his Ph.D. in the United States. The year he entered Mashhad University was the year that Ali Shariati was fired from his teaching position there. A great admirer of Shariati and a devout opponent to the Shah, Yahya was a young man in his mid-thirties, a believer in the revolution when it started, and even when he first came here. Yahya's class and cultural background made him particularly susceptible to the call of the revolution. I interviewed him in 1992. I did not split the first part of this interview into the category "There" because I wanted to preserve the nexus of class, family, and religion that produced some of the most fervent believers in the Islamic Revolution.

I don't want my name used in any of this. Let me tell you what happened to me. I was born into a lower-middle-class family in which my mother was very religious. My father was a lower-class worker for the government. We always rented and never owned a house. I was twelve when my father was given a subsidized flat by the government. My grandfather had his own business, and his three sons and their new families lived together. But when my father clashed with his father, preferring a white-collar job over his father's business, we left my grandfather's care. My father and uncles had no education—only elementary school. My father's first salary was three hundred tomans (then about $45) a month. Very difficult.

Until I was twelve years old, economic conditions in our family were hard. We lived in a two-room apartment. Five of us had one room and my parents the other. My parents lost many infant children. I can't remember how many. But many died. Five survived.

When my father got government housing and a raise, he could save money and buy a used car. My father, though religious, didn't practice religion—no daily prayers or fasting. My mother, to whom I was very attached, was religious. I saw my father as a harsh dictator. Too much pressure on me as the oldest son. His harshness on me and my mother made us very close. I started to say my prayers when I was very small. So we were all thrilled when the revolution happened because we were all for Khomeini—all except my father, who was for the Shah.

It was hard on the family to be so divided. I supported my education with jobs in various hourly positions around town. In Iran, if our grades were high, we needed to pay no tuition. So my jobs were for paying for extras like buying books. My father was proud of my education—I was the only member of our entire extended family to be admitted into the university.

When the revolution happened I was in Shiraz and a student at Mashhad University, so I saw what happened and I recall it as a great time. Mashhad University was where Ali Shariati taught and where he was fired because of pressure from SAVAK. But his memory was still alive. I remember that Jalal Matini was dean of the college of literature. He published a journal called *Iran Shenasi* [Iranian Studies]. The older students who had attended Shariati's lectures had many stories about him. They told of how the entire college would attend any lecture he gave, that students would not attend any other class if they knew he was speaking, that people sat on the floor and outside the window to hear him speak. He taught sociology. My first contact with revolutionary ideas was through Shariati. I'm giving you this background because when Khomeini finally came with his message of revolution, it was familiar and welcome.

I got my ideas of Islam as a liberating force from Shariati's books rather than from Khomeini's lectures. I thought that both Islams were the same— Shariati's and Khomeini's. I and my friends thought that this was a progressive and revolutionary Islam that we should support and help.

The revolution came in with this unbelievable atmosphere of freedom—all kinds of books published, no restrictions on any ideology, and no censorship. I remember finding Marx's *Das Kapital* and other books that had been banned like those by Golsorkhy [an anti-Shah Marxist poet killed by SAVAK], all on street corners, and so cheap, so cheap. So many magazines and journals, and we were all reading.

This phase, though, lasted only a few months while Bazargan was in power until the Iran-Iraq war started, until the clashes started between the pro-Bazargan intellectuals and the clerics—when things went sour. That's when they took over the American embassy. That was all part of the political game to get rid of Bazargan. Before the revolution, Khomeini talked of freedom from the influence of imperialism. He had said that after the revolution, *akhoonds* [clerics] will go to the mosques and will do what the *akhoonds* are supposed to do—guide and teach but not govern the people. We will leave the country to the young and educated people, he said. I remember those words clearly. I remember him saying that *akhoonds* should not interfere with the executive affairs of the country for two reasons: first, they are not the power, and second, if anything goes wrong the people will blame *akhoonds* and that is bad for

Islam. So for the betterment of Islam, clerics should not interfere with the executive branch.

So the revolution at first was very promising. I remember another famous *akhoond*, Ayatollah Mofatteh, who was teaching at the school of theology, as the first person to open up these issues. He said that in the school of Islamic theology we will teach Marxism and other ideologies along with Islamic teachings. He said, "We will not invite *akhoonds* or Muslims to teach Marxism. We will invite a believing Marxist. We should establish a chair in Marxism and we will invite a well-known Marxist to occupy that chair; and we will also teach Islamic ideologies and we will invite people to listen and choose what they wish to believe."

And I remember too at that time a very interesting discussion going on on TV. Hard to believe now—a debate between two Marxist scholars and two famous Islamic scholars—Ehsan Tabari, a great Marxist theoretician, and another from the guerrilla movement, Fadayaan Khalq. This debate went on for several months, and all of us would tune in at a certain hour to see and hear this discussion. No censorship. All this was just before the war broke out.

I want to give you a sense of the atmosphere after the revolution, of how promising it was to hear such open debate and argument. It really was a great, great time in the history of Iran. But when the clashes started everything changed. Everything changed once the clerics decided to take over power. Anyone they didn't approve of, they accused of associating with the United States. America became the great Satan. The mass of people was of course religious, and the government could play with the masses. This was how the revolution moved away from the initial promises it made to freedom and democracy. And the violence began when the censorship began, when they began to close down the magazines and journals, when they stopped free speech on radio and TV. Bazargan never wished to resort to violence—a man I admired who is still an influential voice of reason. But when the war started, it became a good excuse to suppress everything in the name of security.

A very difficult time. I was twenty-six years old. I was very religious and I was very confused. Assassinations. Taleghani died. Very hard to figure out. All the big thinkers were either assassinated or died. For instance, Taleghani was for me the great hope of the revolution. He was one whom everyone loved. He had an open mind. He was called *Pedar* [Father]. Everyone felt they could talk to him. I followed his wonderful lectures. And we could see the difference between his democratic stance and others. He always emphasized the role of the people—*anjumans* [associations/society]. He believed in *Anjuman i Mardom* (The People's Society), in everything being governed by the people. That was not what happened.

Although Taleghani supported Khomeini generally, he always tried to mediate between the people and Khomeini. He was the only mediator between the *Mojahedin-i-Khalqh* and the government. He tried to compromise extremes.

He would refer to the Mojahedin as "my children." "You are the children of this country." He didn't further animosity toward those who eventually became counterrevolutionary groups. Unlike others, Taleghani didn't polarize positions. Taleghani, who helped write the Islamic constitution, suffered a lot. On one hand he didn't wish to give up his support of Khomeini. On the other, he tried to keep the young supporting the revolution. But he died. Motahedi was also a good man who died. All the big thinkers, ideologues, died. The country was left with *akhoonds* and extremists. That's what went wrong with the revolution.

Then of course the other *akhoonds* accused Bazargan of what they accused everyone else- -of affiliation with the United States. He was tried and sent to prison. Things were happening so fast—assassinations, appointments, resignations, changes—so that the only unifying figure in all this fast change was Khomeini. When the war began and people went to the front, people unified around Khomeini. But the war took years, too many years, too much dissatisfaction, and that was when I came out of the country—1985.

And the end of the war created even more problems for the country. What had the country gained? There were many in the country (I was one) who had believed in Khomeini. I remember his first speech when he came to Tehran, when he arrived in Mehrabad Airport and then went to the cemetery, *Behesht-Zahra* [Zahra's Paradise, the national cemetery]. I remember hearing him ask, "What did the Shah do for us? He just killed our people." And of course he was referring to the hundred thousand or so killed during the revolution. But Khomeini and the war were responsible for millions of Iranians killed, and we never heard a reference to those whom Khomeini led to the slaughter.

Another major problem began with Ayatollah Montazeri. He was again trying to be a kind of Taleghani figure, to compromise. But he didn't succeed. He began to criticize the government for its policies on *hejab,* on violation of human rights, on violence, but it went nowhere. He tried to speak out against censorship. He was supposed to have been Khomeini's successor. People had some hope in him because he was open-minded. But the *akhoonds* are very smart. They knew that if Khomeini died, Montazeri would bring more freedom, so just before Khomeini's death, they convinced him that Montazeri was ineffective. And I think that was the biggest shock and disappointment— the loss of our only hope. Montazeri was the last opposition to the conservative right. But he was too passive and so was overruled and marginalized. Now he is in Qum and under surveillance. No one can see or meet him.

I left in 1985, and yes, my way of looking at Iran changed. When I left Iran, I was a firm believer in the Islamic government. But when I came here, two things made my way of thinking change. One, I was not bombarded with Iranian propaganda. I could be more objective and less emotional. Yet, it took me a few years before I could see and hear differently.

Before the revolution, I hated the Americans in charge of the English Center at the university because they never involved us, never consulted us about employment, raises, exams, hiring, firing. When the revolution began, I worked from twelve to sixteen hours a day, and no matter how hard I worked I felt it was for the cause of the revolution. We planned to help the underprivileged, to help the villagers with the harvest, with practical details. That's what we thought the revolution was about. But after a few years, we saw that even those who had been working in close association with SAVAK were back in power. The Islamic government needed their help to run the government! They actually consulted SAVAK.

We were shocked. Ex-SAVAKIS came to power like actors changing costumes. Now they wore newly long beards and said their prayers and associated with *akhoonds.* We saw how they took advantage of their power. And we wondered what we had fought and worked for.

Now I have lost my faith. I am not a blind follower. But I am in some ways worse off, because now I am lost. I don't know where I belong. If you had asked me some years back, "Are you going back to Iran after completing your Ph.D.?" my answer would have been a definite yes. But now my answer is a definite no. Because I can't work there. Now I question myself and my ability to see. But if time repeated itself and I were in the same position, I would not behave in the same way.

Professor Ali

A librarian at a large American state university, Professor Ali (pseud.) was born in 1936 and left Iran for the United States in 1983. He and Pari belong to the same generation of activists for whom reading and activism were part of growing up politicized. Pari spoke to him in 1990, and I interviewed him again in 1992.

I am of the generation of 28 Mordad [the generation that saw the CIA coup of August 1953 that overthrew Mossadeq and brought the Shah back into power].[19] Although I was in high school at the time, I was politically active. I went to Alborz high school. I wrote articles against the teachers in the school paper and Dr. Mojtaheddi, the principal, flogged me. I was a good student and was not expelled, but I was forbidden to put out the paper anymore. Yet I was interested in politics and in effecting change and wanted to start my own party with two other persons. We even went so far as making up our own manifesto.

When I was in the tenth grade, street fights and demonstrations began. I played the role of mediator. The people from the Tudeh Party would beat up the Pan-Iranists. There were riots and strikes in the school. Dr. Mojtaheddi couldn't get anywhere simply by beating students. Once, he took me to his office and wept. I could write well. I wrote political material that could easily incite the students. The teachers liked it, too.

I graduated from high school just as the coup d'etat of 1953 occurred and all the relative freedoms that we had suddenly disappeared. It was a time of futility and suffocation. I took the university entrance exams in literature hoping that I wouldn't pass, but I did, and so I entered the faculty of letters. I was the youngest in my class. That same year I became classmates with people like Iraj Gorgin [a radio journalist] and Bijan Mofeed [playwright], and also with M. Azad [reporter and essayist] and Sadreddin Elahi and Badrolzaman Ghareeb [other writers]. The second year I was in courses with Mehrdad Bahar [scholar and teacher], who had been recently freed from prison. In that period of intense oppression, I engaged in dialogue and artistic activities with these poets and artists. After completing my studies at the university, I went to England to the School of Oriental Studies.

I have to say that I was never part of the Tudeh Party, but I was a leftist. From the beginning I worked with *Jebhe Melli* [National Front] and then I was with Khalil Malekki [a reformer and Socialist who broke away from the hardline communist Tudeh Party]. After that first year in England, friends contacted me and the political activities of my student days began.

I was one of the founders of the Iranian Students Confederation and I was its first secretary. But the next year, because of the Tudeh Party's intervention, students in the confederation became divided. The following year, the intervention led to a crisis in the confederation. We were the first group of students to establish an Iranian socialist group in Europe, and we published the newspaper *Niroo* [Power]. I shared a house with a friend, Hamid Enayat [a translator and university professor]. Among us there was an agent [SAVAK] from the government of the time, and my fate depended to some extent on what that agent reported back to the state. This agent seldom bathed. He always stank. And they'd throw us out of establishments wherever we went with him, but he didn't seem to understand. He is now a much-quoted and well-respected writer in Europe and the United States.

What forces in childhood made me politically active? Many different elements, I suppose. As a child I was aware that people should defend and have their rights. When I was in the third grade, at night I'd write "night letters" about the injustice among teachers and other problems in school, and during the day I'd secretly post them on the school walls. From childhood I liked reading newspapers. My favorite was *Marde Emrooz* [Contemporary Man], which was considered too advanced for my age. My uncle would buy it, and though he never talked to me about the paper, he'd read it, so I became interested. By the time I was twelve, I'd read the works of Mohammad Masood. My father never protested against my reading such texts, but I was afraid my mother would find out. So I'd blacken the covers of the books to hide the warning that it was unsuitable for readers under the age of fifteen.

In the years '58 and '59, I was an eager reader of the journal *Ashofteh* [Chaotic] by Emad Assar. The social circumstances, the newspapers, street demonstrations, the *Jebhe Melli* [National Front], and the nationalization of the oil industry—all these contributed to the growth of our consciousness and identity in those days. Yet I tried not to enter the Tudeh Party, perhaps because I felt they were getting their orders from the Soviet Union.

The last time I left Iran during the Pahlavi regime was the year 1976. I was certain that because of centralization and corruption, the government wouldn't last more than ten years. In 1978 I returned to Iran. The Writers' Society had been founded, and poetry readings were held at night. But something unusual, new, and religious was also happening. When the revolution occurred I was in America.

I was ready to accept—and did—someone like Ayatollah Shariat Madari or Boroojerdi as the religious leader (*Marjaee Taglid*). But when the first events occurred in Paris, I realized that a religious government was on its way into power and I knew that I couldn't support it. In my opinion, Khomeini never lied. It was we who failed to hear what he said. In Paris he declared very openly that the only party in Iran would be Hezbollah. Though he had referred, as examples, to parties people opposed, he wasn't two-faced. He would either evade questions or say that everything had to be done according to Islamic standards. It was the people who interpreted his statements according to their wishes.

During the elections I went to see Ebrahim Yazdi's[20] son-in-law at the embassy to change my passport and heard the new rule of compulsory voting for the Islamic Republic. It was also at that time that they stoned a woman to death in Kerman. Right then I decided never to vote for Islam. The Left was a sham. No question about that; it was all talk and slogans. Among the Fadayaan Khalqh were some positive elements. But the Tudeh infiltrated them, divided them, and weakened them. The Mojahedin, under the influence of Reza Khanloo, acted somewhat democratically, so when I was in Iran during the election for the presidency, I supported Rajavi, their leader. The Tudeh Party had chosen Hassan Habibi as a candidate.

Khomeini pounded the Writers' Society and the Democratic Front (Matin Daftari and his group). Everyone then became leftist. The regime alienated the urban middle class. Everyone talked about the proletariat and about defending their rights, but I personally thought that the urban middle class had to unify into solidarity to defend themselves against the *akhoonds*.

During the Shah's regime I had been imprisoned for a year and a half because of the incident at the Marmar Palace [the attempted assassination of the Shah]. I was arrested in 1965. I was twenty-nine, in prison in Bagh Shah; then I was transferred to Qalleh, then to another open prison in the city. The value of prison for me and for many others is a chance to sit and think out your life, to assess the meaning of your life up to that point.

When they couldn't find evidence to connect me to the event, they freed me on the condition that I leave Iran. But I was not given official permission to work. Yet I managed to teach Persian literature and pre-Islamic history on an hourly basis at Shiraz University after the head gave me a temporary teaching permit. In 1974 while I was in Shiraz I was told that I either had to leave Iran or go to prison. My activities during my youth had caught up with me—the reports sent by the same stinking spy who is now a known writer; all this made it impossible for me to find work in Iran even after the revolution.

I had considered myself a vital part of Iranian society, and I thought others were like me. We knew we were nonpracticing Muslims. Yet we continued certain religious practices out of habit. For instance, we had a *rowzeh khun* [rhapsodic preacher] who came to our house once a month all through the year—every family I knew had that—and that *rowzeh khun* would sermonize to anyone who was in the house to listen to him. Very few did. Even the servants made fun of him. But we paid him every month. So religion did not play a major part in our lives or in my life. Politics was always much more important to me than religion. Religion was not something to be thought about—it was part of the practice of everyday life, like cleaning your teeth. So I assumed that my generation never gave much thought to religion. I was taken by surprise.

Now Iranians have changed. They have become intellectually religious. They study Sufism. All this religiosity is alien to me. Even the new waves in literature seem to be steeped in a mysticism that is fresh and strong, but again alien to me. After the revolution, in the summer of 1979, I went to Iran and taught at Shiraz University for three years. I felt strangely alienated. We spoke the same language, but didn't. They looked at me strangely. They spoke of things I couldn't understand. Their values had changed. I felt I had lost everything—I wasn't part of that life and I wasn't part of this America. I learned that at Shiraz University the servants had become members of the university council and interfered in the teaching of medicine to the students. Intellectuals were looked at with suspicion. When Rejaii, the prime minister, came to visit, the professors were warned not to use the word "specialist" in his presence lest he be offended. We were told he disliked the word.

Once I was even expelled from the university because I was accused of being pro-American. But I kept on working until Shiraz University was closed. A year after, in 1983, I left Iran and came to the United States. I had a heart attack.

Fereydoun Safizadeh

After describing his childhood in Tabriz, Fereydoun continued to tell of his schooling in the United States, his return to Iran, and his experience of the 1979 revolution. I include only his description of the women's march on International Women's Day.

Between December 1977 and February 1981, I experienced the preparation for a Pinochet-type mass killing of the opposition, the Cinema Rex fire, the September 8 Jaleh Square killings; the nights of shouting *Allah-o-Akbar* [God is Great] from rooftops; the street scenes after the Shah's departure; the chaotic arrival of Ayatollah Khomeini; the dangerous existence of the dual governments of Bazargan and Bakhtiar; the February 9–11 final armed struggle that emptied the armories and delivered the final blow to the Pahlavi monarchy; the bloody killing of Hoveyda and others linked with the old regime; the mood during the *Bahar-i Azadi* [Spring of Freedom]; the violent renunciation of individuals and groups who questioned the setting-up of an Islamic Republic; the November 4, 1979, hostage-taking of the American embassy personnel; and the September 22, 1980, Iraqi bombing of the Iranian cities, including Tabriz where my parents refused to leave the city because my father felt that he had to stay to treat the injured.

Yes, I clearly remember the women's march in 1979 in part directed against Khomeini's edicts and in part marking the International Women's Day. As the gathered women and men began to move from the university west on Shah Reza Avenue, handfuls of young men began yelling obscenities and harassing the marchers and provoking them into confrontations. The attack by the *chomagh be dast ha* (club-wielding lumpen) and all the obscenities that the marchers experienced was only a taste of the repression of women to come.

On the other hand, we should not forget that for the traditional *chadori* women of Iran who did not have access to public space during the Shah's time, the *hejab-e Islami* (Islamic dress code) has been a positive change allowing women a little more freedom to occupy public space. Soon after the 1978 women's march, women without the *hejab-e Islami* were becoming as out-of-place in the streets of revolutionary Iran as Peter Brook's plays were in the bazaars of Shiraz.

Keyvan

I end this section with three of my youngest informants, who were teenagers when the revolution occurred—all three were in Tehran. Keyvan was twenty-three when I spoke to him in 1990. He was in high school in Iran during the revolution, and I include this anecdote as one of the few funny memories of the effect of revolutionary change on daily life. Keyvan now works as an accountant in Philadelphia.

I was twelve years old when the revolution took place. My happiest memory and the happiest moment of my life happened a few years later at Alborz high school in 1982 on one of those days when we were supposed to burn American flags. School changed for us after the revolution. Now all classes had to stand in the yard every morning and listen to boring speeches, first to the principal, then to the Qur'an, then to something else in Arabic, then to some government sort who would analyze the meaning of what had happened in the war or in the world that day. Didn't matter if it was winter or summer. We weren't supposed to laugh or talk—it was a serious crime to laugh during that time. And we had supervisors who would monitor our behavior. I was sixteen then. Classes would begin at 8:00 a.m., and this assembly would start at 7:40 a.m. We prayed for it to go on longer and cut short our first class. Here we were, five thousand students lined up begging for more so that our boring classes would be shorter.

One day, something was about to happen in the *Majlis* [Parliament] and we were to celebrate this officially by burning American flags. They had bought six flags. Our school looked like a castle with turrets; each turret had an American flag hanging down from it. They had installed the flags—one giant flag and five small flags. Small signs and posters hung beneath each American flag saying, "God is Great" and "Khomeini is Great." At the podium, someone started talking and half an hour into the ceremony someone went up to light the flags. We cheered because the assembly had already cut into our first class—literature. It was a boring class and we were all so happy to miss it. The speaker from the *Majlis* began to talk for another half hour. We are by now bored to death. But then they are ready to burn the biggest flag. A man goes up, has forgotten the match, comes down, takes a match, sets it to flame. But by now the oil put on the flag has evaporated and it refuses to light. Two men go up with him and carry oil. Now the lighting of the flag is about to begin and we are all laughing. We are told to hush. Finally the flag is doused with more oil and once again they try. But something funny happens. The flag is made of nylon and droplets start to form that get bigger and bigger and begin to fall. First, one huge, massive drop falls on the posters, then more on the Islamic propaganda, on the postcards, and the drops set everything on fire. The signs of the Qur'an also burn, and now the mullahs and supervisors panic and run to save the signs, and then we are laughing and running and returning to watch and laugh some more.

I am sixteen at this point and in the eleventh grade. My education was interrupted during the revolution. The school year is normally from mid-September to mid-June. In 1978 we had only one or two months of school. When school reopened they decided to condense all the material into a few months. I am glad I stayed there and did not come out to the States. The man who convinced my parents not to send me was Dr. Saleh, who told them the story of the bad effects on his child who was sent to England at the age of four. The child grew nervous, wet his bed, and now at the age of forty has still not reconciled himself to his father's decision. That decided my parents against sending me.

I watched how the schools changed during the revolution. Some of our teachers remained strong. Our geometry teacher still wore a tie—the sign of his connection with the old monarchy—and our class admired the teacher for resisting the Islamic regime's propaganda against Westernization. It was important for everyone to look like the poor and to look sad and perpetually oppressed. I couldn't ever be seen in new clothes. Some of our teachers were brown-nosers who sold themselves to the government. They talked of Khomeini as the greatest leader of the twentieth century and religion became a required course in all schools. The mullah, our teacher, was vulgar, aggressive, and vile-mouthed.

One of his stories was about the rewards awaiting us when we entered heaven; he said we would have sex that lasted five hundred years. And gave details of the kind of sexual ecstasy that would follow. And he was cruel—would hit us. Once he hit a kid so hard that he broke a book against him. We had compulsory, daily prayers at noon. There were strict orders about where we had to keep our eyes trained. School boys weren't allowed to play soccer or basketball any more. The effect of religion was to stop our games and our freedom.

I hate the idea of prayers in schools. I hated it there and now that I am in America, I dread hearing it happen all over again in this country. Prayer became used as a ticket for all things; even admission to college was determined by your religious practice and training.

I left the country when I was sixteen years old. The exit from Iran was done in great secrecy. I couldn't even say goodbye to my best friends.

Ali Behdad

Ali was compelled to leave Iran while he was still in high school; he spoke earlier of his childhood and adolescence.

I left Iran in January of 1979. When I left, the airport was almost closed, had been for several days, and I wasn't sure whether I could actually leave. And I still didn't believe what was happening. There was at that time such a sense of instability that one never knew whether something was going to happen or not.

I've been thinking a lot about the condition of my leaving Iran. The story I usually tell is in fact only half of the story of why and how I left. The story is about that day in September 1978, Black Friday—the day of the massacre in Jaleh Square—a day in which I would normally participate in the demonstrations. I was seventeen. Instead, I had gone with a bunch of leftists to the mountains. This was typical of our leftist activity; we would climb and then get to the peak and then sing all these revolutionary songs and then return. When I came down, there was a curfew. And that day, the Shah imposed martial law. When I returned home, my mother was utterly horrified. My parents thought I had gone to Jaleh Square. The radios were not playing their regular programming, and she thought I'd been killed. She thought I had lied, that I had gone to Jaleh Square, because I always lied about where I went in order to get away. I'd usually say I was visiting a friend.

I always tell this tale as the starting point of why I left. My parents feared I would get killed. Because the schools were closed, they thought I might as well come here to the United States instead of risking death. But this episode only captures half the story. There were all sorts of contradictions going on in me during that time that I have always repressed. One example is that day in September when I was in the mountains. I had a gold Allah chain and wore a shirt that didn't conceal it. When, during the exercises I did with the group before starting the climb, my Allah chain showed through the shirt, I was embarrassed and tried to hide it. My Allah chain was something that upper-middle-class kids would wear as a kind of fashionable jewelry. I think we liked the heroic story of making a revolution, and my embarrassment at my Allah peeping out of my shirt signifies my sense of awkwardness at the contradiction in bourgeois kids like me participating in the revolution.

I tell you this because I mean to say that the story I tell is not always the true story, that there is another story beneath this, and that is the story of my desire for America. That desire was constructed for me as a middle-class child in Tehran through all kinds of mechanisms ranging from the fact that I went to American language schools (the American Institute) and to its cultural extensions—the American Cultural Center, its books and music. And then of course their films and television, which since the 1970s had informed our desires for things associated with America. So although I was outwardly revolutionary and wanted to work for a revolution, I really had this fantasy of coming to America.

And I always hid that narrative. I prefer to recall the heroic story and only recently have I become aware of the complexity of reasons for my exile. And I think this kind of blindness to my desires for coming here lies at the heart of my sense of homesickness and nostalgia.

When did you first become aware of the revolution or of its ideas?
I think I will start with my introduction to Ali Shariati—that's the start of my political consciousness. Before that I remember my brothers returning from university talking about politics. I must have been nine years old. But it was really with my friend Hamid Kaffash that I was introduced to the possibility of change and revolution. And Shariati's *One Followed by an Eternity of Zeroes*—that book opened a new world for me. It intrigued me into revolutionary action, into some kind of a one-dom to get away from the zero I was, to feel special about myself. And this was the time I was becoming sympathetic toward the Mojahedin and had all these arguments with my parents who got really nervous. They, in turn, would ask if I wanted anything, to get me to stop such talk: "Do you need a watch?" they would ask. And of course, in some ways I was craving material things, which also connects to my bourgeois contradictions.

By the time I came to Tehran at thirteen and a half I was already being intro-duced by my friend Masood Jelowkhani to Marxist readings. Jelowkhani was reading Freud and Nietzsche and George Orwell the night before final exams. He would walk around Tehran and talk and teach me about Iranian leftists. That is how I became a hard-core leftist. Jelowkhani was my inspiration. He was one of the people who stayed behind, got involved in chemistry, and was the one, too, who introduced me to the idea of comparative literature.

By then—1977 or so—though the revolution had not in fact begun, the *cherikha* [guerrillas] had started assassinating generals, and we would read their material and identify with them. We read the work of Samad Behrangi, Ahmad Shamlu, and other poets for their allegorical content. We knew that "when the storm comes" or "the sun" represented something clearly political. There were poetry readings in Tehran in the Goethe Institute; a famous book has come out of it. These were nights when all the revolutionary poets came and read their work to a packed hall.

Also, of course, I had brothers at the university at the forefront of this sort of leftist, intellectual, political engagement. My brother Hamid was arrested at a demonstration at Aryamehr University and jailed for a month. This was how the authorities were creating a general system of fear in the late '70s. The earliest memories I have are from the beginning of 1978. I recall the burning of the Cinema Rex, the subsequent trial, and the photographs of the suspects. When the revolution started the schools closed. My school, Kharazmi, was on Shah Reza Avenue across from Tehran University. So from early on, whatever demonstration was in Tehran University, we in the high school joined. That's why my parents wanted me out of the country.

I left Tehran on January 7, 1979.

Soheyl

Here Soheyl speaks of his experience of the revolution, which occurred while he was still in high school. Like many other urban Tehranis, Soheyl knew nothing about the Kurds or Kurdistan or nonurban Iran until, like so many others, he was forced to flee the revolution through that region. He left Iran in 1982.

I was not a participant in the revolution against the Shah because, to tell you the truth, I couldn't understand the meaning and the consequences of people's acts of revolt. I remember going to this big demonstration and hearing, for the first time, people chanting the slogan, "The only party is Hezbollah [the Party of God], and the only leader is Ruhollah [Khomeini's first name]." I came home confused. I thought they were making fun of the Shah. I asked my father what the slogan meant.

He was reluctant to respond. Although he favored the revolution against the Shah, I think the slogan had surprised him, too. Like many, he had assumed that all the clergy wanted was to kick the Shah out, that they would then turn to the intellectuals for the reconstruction of the society. But his disappointment came soon. I was only in high school and didn't know all the things that make up a society, a nation, the history of a nation.

I left Iran in 1982. The army had wanted me for a couple of years and I hadn't responded to the draft notices. They wanted to send me to the front. And that was the main reason I left Iran. But there was something else. Not only did the army want me, I was in trouble with the government, too. After Khomeini came to Iran, I became active in the opposition against his Islamic government, although I had not been active in the opposition against the Shah. I was young and confused, and didn't understand what the Party of God, or Khomeini, or Dr. Shariati, our martyred teacher, represented, and I didn't understand what people were fighting for. But the slogan "Bread, shelter, freedom of choosing your party" was a slogan I could relate to. It was the only one that I understood, and the only slogan opposed by the clergy and stopped under the pretext that it was a Communist Party slogan. And it became clear to me that the clergy were quite organized and determined in their attempt to lead the nation. We were lost. They were not. So after Khomeini came—and by then I was older, too, and had gained a little more experience—I became active, very active against Khomeini, as a leftist. That's why I had to leave. But I'm not a leftist anymore.

I got tired of seeing the depression on the streets, the hopelessness of revolution, the fights. I wanted to breathe a breath of fresh air, and that is why I set out to leave, to get out in secrecy. I can tell you some, but not all, of the specifics of my journey out. I took a long bus ride. I had a Kurdish friend who took me to his home, in Kurdistan. I stayed with them for six weeks and then I left the country via the Turkish border. But the most important part of it, the most valuable part, was the time I lived with the Kurds in the mountains of Kurdistan. I didn't know much about my own country except the few cities by the Caspian Sea I had visited and my birthplace—Qamsar—and Kashan. It was the first time that I encountered a people who were considered Iranian, who had their own culture and language, and who could barely speak Persian; yet they were so different from the Iranians I knew and was used to seeing in Tehran or other places I had visited.

This was a nation that was fighting against the Tehran government, that was proud of its nationality and proud of its ethnic clothes. After living with the Kurds a short while, I began to realize that our people and our government had done nothing for the Kurdish people at all. If they had water pipes in the mountains, they had installed them themselves. If they had a school that taught their children the Kurdish language, they had built and run it themselves. If they had doctors serving their people, they had hired them from foreign countries themselves. In Kurdistan, I saw more French and German doctors than Iranian doctors. Seeing Kurdistan so disillusioned me in regard to the central government that after a month and a half of living with them, I turned into a believer and advocate for the autonomy of the Kurds.

I grew to love Kurdistan. I found it unbelievable that with all the oil money, the Iranian government had failed to teach us in school that there existed several ethnic groups living in Iran in isolation. They failed to teach us who these people were, or to tell us that those of us who live in Tehran must be proud of having such diverse and rich ethnicity in our nation.

The Kurds knew how to enrich their daily life in spite of the harsh environment, in spite of enemy airplanes dropping bombs on their homes, in spite of the war, in spite of their lack of food. They ate cooked tomatoes with bread daily, and once or twice a week they ate rice, and only once while I was there we had meat, and that was on the occasion of the anniversary of the twenty-fifth of Mordad, the day the Kurdish Democratic Party was founded. In spite of these conditions, these people held gatherings of music and poetry every Sunday in the mountains at night. One read poetry, one sang Kurdish songs, and one gave an update report of the news; it was incredible.

To me there was no similarity between these pure people who are becoming extinct, like the Amazon Indians, and the strange characters called Iranians I knew in Tehran. The Kurds had a wonderful system of living and self-defense. The shepherds not only watched over their sheep but watched out for the Iranian army. So, the shepherd would watch over his sheep with a gun hanging from his shoulder. This way of organization reminded me of the Viet Cong: whatever you are, you are a fighter as well, and you are always in touch with others via a radio you carry.

Were you with the Komoleh?
No. I was not with the Kurdish *Komoleh* [Communist groups] but with the Democratic Party of Kurdistan. And to tell you the truth, the Kurdish people didn't pay much attention to the *Komoleh*. They were there, and they were hardliners, but they didn't carry much weight, because they were so out of touch with the system of Kurdish self-organization. For example, even in Tehran the *Komoleh* were a joke because there was a rumor that they had set out to form "The Workers' Communist Party of Iran" in Kurdistan. Marxist ideas of class didn't translate here. One of the Kurds told me, "What are these people talking about? There are no workers in Kurdistan. Who do they think they are going to recruit?"

In Kurdistan there are a few powerful landowners who lend their land to the Kurdish peasants. The peasants are entitled to work on the land and at harvest time take whatever their family needs and give the rest to the landlord. I never heard peasants complain about the system. One told me his father also worked on the same land and now owned a small house. They had houses and a comfortable life. But when the *Komoleh* came and tried to agitate them, saying that they lived under a feudalistic system (the Kurds didn't know what the term meant), and that the peasants should fight and destroy this system because the land should belong to the peasants and so on, the Kurds couldn't relate to these ideas. The landowner already shared what he had with everyone.

The Kurds taught me something about Iranianness. I too think of my family as a tribe. I love that tribe, I love my birthplace, and I belong to it. Here in exile, no matter what I hear on the news, I always put it in the context of Iran. Iran is my center of gravity in the world.

CHAPTER 4

Here: Reconstructing Migration and Exile

The narratives collected in this book—memories fabricated out of the past and woven in the present—suggest the competing and unstable discourses that inform national, exilic, and diasporic identities. Because exile is the space in which we negotiate relationships with imaginary pasts, it becomes the site where new cultural imaginaries, unexpected in-betweens, and group identity formations reproduce some of the fault lines that constitute both the old and new imagined nations. Exilic identity, like all identity, is always mistaken, but it is all we have on which to build a self.[1] The nostalgia provoked by exile is, as Ali Behdad also reminds us, always about homelessness, always about the absent language, the absent parent or friend. But perhaps, more generally, the human condition or any *present* is that of exile because it is premised on the desire for the perpetually absent.

When the hostage crisis occurred, my older son Taimur, then ten years old and in elementary school, found himself subjected to minor taunts from other children. One day, in the spring of 1980, his assigned homework was to draw himself. He was to complete a drawing done of his body traced on brown paper by a classmate. He was to attach to his bodily parts some of his favorite things. I remember his drawings of musical notes, a record, a book, a dollar bill, and an ice cream cone. But slung across his shoulder, his heart, and his stomach, he placed a bright banner on which he wrote the word "IRAN."

I have thought of that drawing many times. And I have wondered at how the word acquired weight and significance for that little boy, at what got displaced onto that sign. I have thought of the connection between the highly charged sign "Iran" and its absent referent. That drawing, the body on which Taimur announced a part of his newly found identity, linked present desire (music, money, ice cream) with symbolic absence—the place "Iran"—a word that bore no relation to a known referent, a place where (as the song went) the streets had no names. For me, the drawing predicated its articulation of identity on absence: in an elementary school in Champaign-Urbana, a child's sense of self is built out of the stitching of identity with difference, desire and lack, with the banner representing an unreachable place that is an uncanny extension of a mother linked forever to a perpetually lost and absent country. It is, in other words, an instance of what Ali Behdad (and Lacan) describe as the identity of desire, conditioned by lack, always "where the subject is *not*, in a beyond" that always points to another (Behdad 1994, 29). It can also be read as a case of what Eva Hoffman calls "the wholeness of childhood's truth's" colliding with the "divisiveness of adult doubts" (272).

The irony of this incident was that neither of my sons knew the extent to which I had severed bonds with the past named on that banner, the extent to which that original affiliation had been rejected, dispersed, and displaced across other countries and other people. Yet for them and for me, the revolution disrupted the clarity of that separation, led to new ways of being, to new familial configurations, new movements of parents, grandparents, aunts, cousins, and friends across continents and into new possibilities in this country. By attempting to record a few disrupted, dislocated narratives, this book of exilic memories is, in a way, a tribute to all our families and their management of that disruption.

Twenty-five years after leaving the last of my unhomely homes in Pakistan, and many Americas later, I began to notice, perhaps because of this project, variations on the management of displacement after the "unimaginable" revolution. I saw that the new diaspora gave rise to new configurations of communities, once again reimagining, collectivizing, and affirming identities in terms of lost origins and new possibilities, reinventing origins and differences, and rejoicing in new liberties framed in loss by establishing newly interdependent groups of Iranians in exile.

In March 1990, I attended a *sofreh* (a ritual meal) in Los Angeles to honor the birthday of an Imam who died sometime in the ninth century—a hybrid gathering around a luncheon spread on the floor. The group consisted of several members of my family and other Iranians who had left Iran after the revolution and had managed to build a life on the combined salaries of all family members, including the children. But I was surprised to see there some of the community I lived among in Dacca (then East Pakistan) in the mid-1950s, now in Los Angeles—dressed in Pakistani clothing, but joined with the exiles and emigrés from Iran to call on the Imams in verse and song to ask for explanation and alleviation of their woe. The most requested and recurring song was *"Ali Gooyam, Ali Jooyam"*—"Ali I call, Ali I search." This was a familiar *rowzeh* (ritual homily or lamentation) from my childhood, but the change from the lyrics I remembered was what interested me. The singer was a rather beautiful Iranian woman dressed in white lace with her hair tinted in the shade most fashionable during the last days of the Pahlavis—blond. She had (or so I thought) added a verse that called Ali *Shah i Velayat* followed by *Janam be Fadayat*—"King of our country / May I sacrifice my life for you." So the song seemed to conflate the divine and the secular, Hazrat Ali, the son-in-law of the Prophet, and Shah Mohammad Reza Pahlavi, and the tears that flowed among this hybrid gathering were for all losses—real and imaginary.[2] The point of such a gathering was to find an excuse to collect in the name of a dead Imam. That cause was displaced and shifted significantly onto grief for Ali—an overdetermined figure in recent postrevolutionary history. But it was also an occasion to express in public ritual what the women perceived as communal trauma. And as I listen to the tape after so many months I hear the singer coax a guest who finds she cannot stop weeping to return to the room, where the singer promises a different narrative, a happy song, not about exile, she says, not about loss. "You will dance to this song," she adds. "Anyone who has wiped her tears over my last song must get up and dance to this one." But some of the weepers cannot stop, no matter how happy the song; it recalls and rewrites another context in another country where the same song had once been sung—the lost nation of Karbala/Burma/East Pakistan/India/Iran.

The Los Angeles community of Iranians, split between familiar royalist, leftist, and ethnic factions, briefly came together for a more immediately traumatic event reported by several of our informants—the funeral of an exile in 1988. A young, dejected, leftist bookseller, Neusha Farrahi, anguished at the accusation that Iranians did nothing to protest the Islamic regime, set himself on fire on September 20, 1988. My friend Pari had known Neusha as a little boy and was devastated at an event that, for her, replayed the tragedy of a country that never seemed to be prepared to face the political or social consequences of gesture or action. The boy, said Pari, didn't calculate the cost of his gesture, and his friends were unprepared to act. The point of the preplanned self-immolation was to make a gesture of protest against the visit of the president of Iran to the United States; the fire was to be doused by his friends, and the event recorded by the national media. Maryam Pirnazar recalled the pathos of the coverage: "The picture of Neusha's charred body was on the cover of the *New York Post* the next day. . . . The *Los Angeles Times* reported the incident with a small inner-story headline: 'Man sets self on fire to protest Iranian's visit.' Other 'serious' newspapers failed to cover that incident, or the many similar antiwar protests which took place around the country." Neusha's gesture turned into gruesome reality, and his hope for national attention vanished under more ironic circumstances: the event lost media coverage that night because it competed with the Emmy awards.[3]

The desire expressed by some exiles is for an original imaginary condition charged with the significance of longing, and that yearning is, by extension, for an irrecoverable primary loss: in the words of Gerard Manley Hopkins to the young girl weeping at falling leaves, "It is Margaret you mourn for." The loss for the exiles to whom I spoke was sometimes more specific— they mourned the executions of friends, brothers, sisters. They mourned for aging, dying parents they could not see, and for a lost generation imprisoned, tortured, and killed either in Khomeini's prisons or in the Iran-Iraq war. The Iranian Kurds who spoke to me mourned a double loss because they knew the problem of displacement from a country whose governments successively suppressed and exterminated their Kurdish populations in the cause of national unity.

The yearning for an imagined Iran crosses all ethnic and religious boundaries: Lily, the educator and writer and a Baha'i politically compelled to live in exile, could barely speak when I asked her if she thought of herself as an exile and if she missed Iran: "I see myself as an exile wherever I am, if it's not Iran." Rebwar Kurdi, who witnessed the destruction of his village by Khomeini's bombs, nonetheless admonishes his child by reminding him that he is an Iranian. "In Iran," he tells his son, "we are always polite to others; we stand when elders come in; we are never rude, we are always kind." This is a father who knows doubt and dispersal, yet chooses to instill unity with an imagined homeland as a cornerstone of childhood's identity. Another Baha'i couple insisted, in spite of their persecution and flight, in spite of historical evidence to the contrary, and in spite of the purging of the Baha'i population of Iran, that until the ayatollahs there had been no persecution of Baha'is in Iran: "We want nothing but Iran and being Iranian. This [the United States] is not a country that satisfies us culturally in terms of daily living. Iranian upbringing [*tarbiat*] and love for family is precious and we do not see it here."

The history of socializing within the community where I live in Champaign-Urbana has remained both the same and different over the twenty years since the revolution. What remains unchanged are the homes transformed into familiar Persian spaces filled with Persian carpets, familiar artifacts, and regular ritualized gatherings of Persian friends around masses of Persian food and conversation spiced with pungent aromas of saffron and memory. What changes is the passion surrounding the topic of the revolution. An evening I recount from 1990, occasioned by the visit of my oldest informant, captures a transitional moment at a time before the collapse of the USSR and before the recent liberalization of the Khatami government.

As always, the conversation follows a certain familiar dancelike strategy. Polite ritualized inquiry about the welfare of family members segues into politics, anecdotes, jokes split along party and gender lines. Like the *nastaliq* script it takes turns and counterturns from left to right and back again to unexpected centers.

Someone older tells a story about Reza Khan (later Reza Shah): it is a charming story about a prediction made by a dervish that someday he would be king. But it is also a story about character, selfhood, and identity, about Reza Khan's reputed simplicity and brusqueness, about the contrast between two codes—that of the king and the dervish and the significance of a word whose meaning the king can't understand although he heard it years ago—*esteghna* (self-sufficiency/independence). The story's repeated punch line is the dervish's insistence to Reza Shah, before and after he becomes king, that his possession of *esteghna* is what makes the dervish self-sufficient and impervious to dependence on property, court, or king. It is also an anecdote whose privileging of dervishlike simplicity and toughness prepares us for the later cultural opposition between the trustworthy and simple Khomeini and the untrustworthy and decadent Pahlavis.

That story is followed by others about encounters with those who experienced the old Shah and the new, meandering into recollections of the revolution, of the ecstasy of the Spring of Freedom, of the fall of the Iranian Left. Several jokes about mullahs. Then someone growls a reminder that a swift visit to the USSR would have exorcised the Left from its fantasies. My son, Kamran, who has just returned from a trip to the USSR, says that the trip was great but the food was awful. "You hear what the boy says? Nobody wanted for bread under the Shah. There was plenty of everything." Someone on the right sighs and laments the lost past, which leads to tactful but pointed stories told by a younger man on the Left about the state of corruption in the Shah's Iran. "Why blame the corruption on the Shah?" says another on the right. "Let me tell you about my experiences with corruption in the United States—about being exploited and robbed by lawyers and landlords all because I was Iranian. Should I blame that on the President of the United States?" A long and bitter story follows. "Yes," says an angrier voice, "it was the United States that destroyed the only man who could save us—Mossadeq—they and the Soviets and the British killed him. The bastards. They did it then for oil and power. They are doing it again. It was the United States who paid the *bazaaris*, the mullahs, the crowds. I was there, I saw it; the CIA set up mercenary mobs. What more proof do you need?" By now the voices are orchestrated into melodies we know by heart: theories of conspiracy, a story that proves beyond the shadow of a doubt that it was the CIA is countered by another that proves it was the British. "The old Mullah Khomeini," someone says, "was a reincarnation of what we find in men like Hitler and Ghaddafi." And now most agree out of polite fatigue at having once again preserved civility from imminent wreckage, that surely such an old man could not create a revolution, surely he was empowered by American power, Thatcherite power, French power, Super Power. The scenario seems clear and the world crises resolved until a lone voice—that of a young historian—interrupts the illusion of unity: "What we have all said is exactly what is wrong with Iranians. Khomeini is no demon. He is us. He has our faces. We made him, allowed him, empowered him." Dinner is served.

At the time I spoke to my narrators in the early and mid-1990s, I asked about their arrival and sense of belonging in the United States. Some echo Faranak's resistance to their new diasporic location, feeling "no passion" for a country whose structures of national and cultural feeling elude them; others echo Rebwar Kurdi's pleasure in political possibility: "living in this part of the world has further deepened my belief in the struggle for equality, justice, and socialism. It has opened new doors, new inspiration." Some unambiguously celebrate the discovery of freedom in everyday life, others seem more ambivalent. Hamid Naficy, when asked about separation from Iran, paused for a long while and then said the following words whose impact I stress spatially in order to do justice to his silences, his pauses, and his repetitions:

> So
>
>   I don't I don't
> I don't think that
> I don't look with
> Pain
> at
> Not being in Iran.

Our memories of the past, whether recollected in tranquility or at moments of danger, are organized and constructed by the effects on memory of other narratives, by screen memory, and by culture—its daily practice, its rituals, its modes of perception and knowledge. Exile, displacement, or migration provoke stresses that intensify cultural fault lines—the need for origins, the rigidifying of boundaries between us and them, or its opposite—the collapsing of distinctions between identities, or the reification of imaginary pasts. That past, or "history," is what one of the most famous of modern Western exiles, James Joyce (as Stephen Dedalus), called the "nightmare from which I am trying to awake." My concern is with the collective amnesia that results from awakening but forgetting the material of nightmare. Benedict Anderson tells us that "all profound changes in consciousness, by their very nature, bring with them characteristic amnesias. Out of such oblivions, in specific historical circumstances, spring narratives" (1991, 204).

In this last section I collect parts of narratives in which most of the interviewees speak of present (diasporic) formations of self and community in the United States. Most are middle-aged women and men whose dislocations have empowered them to start life again: Rebwar Kurdi has found metaphoric "Kurds" everywhere and now identifies with marginalized groups in the United States while he writes about Kurdistan. Barbod is once more a filmmaker, though he had to start by working at a one-hour photo lab and by playing court photographer to wealthy Iranians before he made a film about an Iranian exile's self-immolation. Mehrdad Haghighi started by distributing flyers for supermarkets; in 1990 he was publishing a journal for Iranian-American children, and now, in 2000, he is a writer for Radio Iran in Los Angeles (AM 260) and published a monthly Persian journal, *Hamsayegan.* Homa Sarshar is director and founder of the Center of Iranian Jewish Oral History and is working on the book *Esther's Children: A Portrait of Iranian Jews.* Mandana lost her husband in the process of displacement, worked odd jobs, and now works and acts in Iranian theater. Pari and Professor Ali both suffered through bouts of debilitating depression from which they emerged into light: one works in a department of Oriental studies, the other returned to Iran where she established centers for children's rights. Several are writers and professors at prestigious American universities; at least five of these academicians write (one said "compulsively") about Iran as a way of textualizing and therefore containing displacement and diaspora.

Rebwar Kurdi

Rebwar fled Kurdistan and found refuge in the United States after the forces of the revolution destroyed his hometown. He described his Kurdish childhood and his experience of the revolution in earlier parts of his narrative. Here he speaks of the birth of a new exilic self that has found a space to which he "belongs" in the West. That space includes organizations of transnational labor and ethnic minorities. Whether here or in Iran, Rebwar finds "home" in groups that are fluid, grassroots, and resistant to repressive state powers.

While I share many frustrations of other refugees and immigrants, and while I really miss my family, friends, relatives, people, and country, I do not feel a stranger in North America. I feel that I belong here, too. For me there are two realities when I look at the United States, the United Kingdom, Canada, or other Western countries. To take the example of the United States where we are at the moment, I of course strongly reject the neocolonial domination of the American state, its warmongering, its support of fascist and despotic regimes throughout the world. This is one face of the political realities of this country that many refugees from the developing world are familiar with.

The other part of it, which is not known to many, is the repression of the radical, labor, and communist movements, native peoples, etc., within the United States by the American state. There is a rich tradition of struggle of Americans of all races and ethnic backgrounds, the First Nations, the workers, the intellectuals, etc., who have fought for the cause of democracy, freedom, and socialism.

I do not forget that the occasions for celebrating the International Workers' Day (May 1) and International Women's Day (March 8) originate in the United States. The Lincoln Brigade was composed of thousands of American and Canadian volunteers who went to Spain in 1936 to support the struggle of the Spanish people, and many of them lost their lives. The brigade was the triumph of internationalism and solidarity between peoples set apart by oceans. How can someone caring for freedom feel a stranger in Canada, the land of Norman

Bethune?[4] Or how can an oppressed Kurd feel isolated in North America, where the First Nations continue their struggle for self-rule?

Although now I value the *Shahnameh* as a great literary creation, I feel much closer, emotionally, to the epic of the Wobblies[5] and the Paris Commune. Having lived in North America and Europe for years, I have broadened my concept of freedom and democracy. My knowledge of racism, sexism, and other forms of domination has deepened. Few of us, even those involved in the political struggle in Iran, were aware of sexism or racism in language, in arts, and in the social sciences. I have also had the opportunity here to learn much more about the national liberation movements and the struggle of workers and peasants throughout the world. So, living in this part of the world has further deepened my belief in the struggle for equality, justice, and socialism. It has opened new doors, new inspiration. It is taking new steps from the confines of nationalism to the more colorful world of internationalism.

Barbod

Barbod, the filmmaker who works in Los Angeles, earlier recalled how the revolutionary censors affected not only his documentary record of the revolution, but his decision to leave Iran. He now speaks of the stages of his domestic and professional adjustment to forced migration and exile. Two years after his original interview, I called him on the telephone to ask about his film about Neusha Farrahi, the Iranian who, in February 1987, set himself on fire on the steps of the Federal Building in Los Angeles in protest against the Islamic Republic. This segment includes his response during that conversation.

For these four years that I have been forced to be out of Iran, I have traveled many countries, not out of choice but out of necessity. I have proved to myself that it is not only Iran where I can work but wherever I am in the world.

Yet, I miss being home. I miss sensing, feeling, touching that earth, that weather, and that people. I feel I could be more useful there. But I will not go back in the present situation. I will not cooperate with the present government. I will not try to bring them any sort of glory, honor, or justification for their existence. I'm not criticizing the artists who are still there. I think those who are there and can work and can leave behind a document of the present situation in Iran are all doing great work. I admire their work. But I am against giving the government any sort of honor, any sort of legitimacy.

I had two problems staying in Iran—first, I was from a Baha'i family, and second, I was affiliated with the Left, with the whole range of leftists from the *Fadayaan* to the *Hezb Tudeh* to the *Mojahedin* to the *Komoleh*. I worked with all these people. I have made films for the *Mojahedin* and for the *Fadayaan*.

I have made films and traveled all over the world from the Far East to the Soviet Union. And we probably owe all this to Mr. Khomeini, who forced us abroad. In a sense we have been forced into a compulsory scholarship of running around the world, given to us by the Islamic government.

What specific difficulties have you experienced in exile?
Many difficulties. After all the rewards and awards that came to me as a successful filmmaker at home where I had a very comfortable life, when I

arrived in Los Angeles I had fifty dollars in my pocket and that was all. I had a place to stay for probably one month with a cousin. That was all I had. It was hard to start from scratch.

Nobody is willing to accept you. You are illegal. I didn't have a passport, so I couldn't even get a driving license. It was hard. And your children were away at home, and you don't know what might happen to them. Will they be able to get out of the country? What will become of them because of you? I had arranged to be legally separated from my wife so that the government would not associate them with me, so they could be freed from my taint and not be touched by it. I knew, for instance, that on the third day after I left the country, government agents went to my house to catch me, and I knew that my family had been under surveillance, to see if they had any connection with me.

I had no job and no home. I was not a twenty-one-year-old just out of school. Rather I was a forty-two-year-old who found it difficult to start again. But I did. I started working in a one-hour photo lab at $3.50 an hour. I worked after hours. After filming feature films and after making films that went to festivals and won awards, I started my postrevolutionary life in the United States by filming weddings. And I could hear Iranians saying, "You know who that guy is who's holding the camera? He's that big name so-and-so. Now he has to shoot our wedding for two hundred or three hundred dollars." I was not ashamed of shooting a wedding and earning my living—but you have to understand our culture, the way people talk and the way it can hurt you. It's not so much a question of prestige. But as an Iranian who's earned a name, it's hard for me to hear people say, "Okay, we have a separate table for you over there—separate for the photographers." Art had an honored place in our community, but now that I was here, I was given a separate table. All that hurts.

So here I was, hoping to show what was happening in Iran. And instead I had to work in one-hour photo labs, printing pictures of people going to Venice Beach and having parties, and shooting weddings of people who I know were the real cause of the revolution. These people were probably literally filthy rich people who lived only to show and boast of their wealth, their jewelry, and what they had spent on those lavish weddings—people who lived to show off to one another and who called each other the old titled names of *Teemsar* and *Vazeer* and ex-general and ex-minister and ex-so-and-so and still lived on those dreams of those days when they robbed the country, stole everything they could, and transferred it to foreign banks, and as soon as they saw the situation was turning, they fled. And now they own multimillion-dollar industries here and households and real estate. They don't really give a damn about those people in Iran or their country. And here is the irony of my position: those people are *still* in power. They attend these weddings, displaying expensive jewelry and dresses, while I, who have always been against them and against the unfair distribution of wealth in my country, I have to film them for two hundred dollars.

So those were some of the hard moments. But I quickly found my way to a bigger market. When I was editing one of my films in one of the studios someone said, "Hey who shot this material?" I said, "I did." And they said, "Who edited that?" and I said, "I did." And they said, "Do you want a job?" And that was the beginning of new openings. Since then I have moved up to become a professional cameraman. I have moved up to doing commercials with reasonable pay, and then I have done a series of films about my community. I can now afford to spend some money on the projects that I wanted to do. I can now afford to give some time to the people who are doing work about the community. Fortunately, at this very moment that I'm talking to you, one of my scripts, which is a sort of love story about Iran, has been approved by a major company. I'm hoping to do that film next year, maybe. And if that happens and it becomes a good film, I will be so happy and satisfied.

The most satisfying part of it is that my filmmaking has become a way of opposing the Islamic Republic. They claim that those who have left the country are dead. They say that those who have left the country are all working in gas stations and can achieve nothing. We proved that we are not dead, that we can make films, and we are making films and our films are receiving attention at international film festivals.

All this can be read as a new dawn or a new beginning for the Iranian artists who live in exile, who have recently established themselves in new countries, and who know they are fighting back the only way they can—through their art. As artists, they have not forgotten their country and they are fighting back with art against the Islamic Republic. That gives me much more energy and life to continue.

I got involved in making the film *Guest of Hotel Astoria*, directed by Reza Alamezadeh. We made the film in 1988. It's about Iranians who flee from Iran and find themselves in this hotel in Istanbul from where they try to gain reentry into the world. Iranian filmmakers and artists came from six different countries to make that film. Reza Alamezadeh has another film about censorship—a documentary called *Night of the Revolution*, which he made in Holland. Another is called *A Few Simple Sentences*, a touching film about an immigrant kid who, if he could only speak a few simple sentences, would clear up much. Another of his films I admire is called *Holy Justice*, about the killings done by the Islamic Republic around the world.

How has your family adjusted to living in the United States?
My wife has not adapted to America. She doesn't enjoy living here—she has always found it very difficult and would prefer to return. But even she knows that if tomorrow it were possible to go back, there would be a problem with our children who would find it hard. My wife is not adventurous. She's cautious and wants things to be certain. When I was traveling around different countries, she chose to stay in Iran because she had a job, a house, an extended

family and felt secure. But also, when I had the option of finding political asylum in Germany, she didn't want it. Hoping to return, she wanted to keep her Iranian passport for herself and for the kids. After a two-and-a-half-year separation I rejoined my family who eventually came to Los Angeles to live with me. We have now been living together for two years. This separation, the impact of the revolution, as well as America itself have caused stress on all our personal relations. Although I had lived abroad, my wife had not. She is not a fighter. She worries about the children and how they should be brought up. So the impact was different on the two of us.

My children really enjoy it here, especially my son. At first he adapted by choosing an American name—Andy. He didn't want to be called by his Iranian name. He wished to cut connection with Iran, perhaps because he felt that Iran was responsible for our separations from each other. My son is American Iranian, but my daughter is Iranian American, more inclined toward being Iranian. My son was seven when he came here, so the things he enjoys are all provided by the American way of life rather than the Iranian. He enjoys games, computers, fast-moving things, and a kind of individuality that is common in the United States—while my daughter is more warm, less individualistic. She was thirteen when she came, and that's why she is more Iranian than her brother.

But there are many times when I look at my pictures, when I go back into memory, and I imagine that I'm in the Iranian desert, I'm in Bam with its scent of beautiful flowers and citrus trees and nightingales singing all night, and in front of me those huge ruins. It is the desert I remember when I travel. I wonder if that old woman to whom I talked, from whom I heard those beautiful stories, still lives; or that young shepherd in whose hut I lived for several days who played the flute next to the sea at Maranjab, the meeting point of the desert and the Dead Sea. I feel more than loss or nostalgia; it gives me joy to think about those villages and I hope, one day, I'll be able to return.

Mehrdad Haghighi

Haghighi has already described the purge of Baha'is in Shiraz. Here he describes his flight into exile. This is also a segment that shows the difficulty of separating the story of "here" with the story of "there." The memory of revolution persists in erupting through the boundaries of present experience.

I was on the last plane that left Shiraz for the [Persian] Gulf States and landed at Qattar. After waiting for twelve hours at the airport with my one-year-old son and my wife, we left for Pakistan. I was detained there for ten days. Although my passport identified me as a journalist, they gave me a hard time at the airport. They even tore up my shoulder pads in their body search. This was all in General Zia's time. But when I arrived in London, my identification as a journalist worked to my advantage, so that I was given a visa to the United States with no trouble.

When I arrived in the United States, I had only $800 left of the $1,200 that I was able to bring out of Iran. One of my dear friends took me to his house that night, and the next day at 7:00 a.m., I was at work in his printing press. Four days later, my wife, who is a physical therapist, found a position in a downtown Los Angeles hospital. We rented a house that was very dirty. I took off my shoes to walk up the six flights of stairs with my luggage. When I returned, my shoes were gone. We had no furniture, so I used a cardboard box as my desk. The only money I spent was to buy a radio to prevent me from going insane. Soon we got our work permits and after a hundred days, we got our green cards. I used to put my son in his pram and go around distributing flyers for supermarkets at $3.50 an hour. People warned us that we couldn't take it and that we would want to return to Iran in three months. Instead, we got our green cards. Exactly eight months after our arrival I was able to rent a nice house in which we are still living. For the first time, we enjoyed sleeping in real beds and eating breakfast at a table. Eleven months after arriving here I bought a car.

I had left all I owned in Shiraz, and after my departure the building in which I had my office was burned down because on the ground floor was a liquor store.

I had about eight thousand volumes of books, newspapers, and magazines that I had collected for several years. These were all lost in the fire. My house was plundered. My father was in the house, and he lost his sight. Then he was jailed. The administrator of the mosque near our house took a towel and visited Ayatollah Dastgheib. He said to the Ayatollah, "Either release this man or cut off his head and place it in this towel I have in my hand." Because this man was much respected, he was able to get my father out and to get an exit permit for my father, who then came here for treatment. After my father's departure, they put this same administrator in jail, accusing him of being a Baha'i. My father, still in treatment and unwell, flew back to Iran. Ayatollah Mahalati asked him why he had returned. He said, "This man endangered his life and freedom for me. I will not let him suffer for that. He stood as a guarantor for me. I am here. Let him go." They released the man and put my father in jail. One night Ayatollah Mahalati went to him and said, "You have twelve hours to get out of the country, and I beg you to leave." He gave my father a ticket, and my father went to Spain.

Six of my friends were hanged. The point is not what religion you have. The point of a revolution is to guide and free the people, not to take away their lives and freedom. I saw some awful things. I witnessed the little son of my friend getting up early one morning and saying, "I dreamt that they have killed my father." In fact his father had been put to death in prison that very morning. When they went to visit him in jail, they gave them the body to take away. What legacy have these people left?

Many were put to death. The purpose of a revolution should be to teach a better way of life, not to eliminate the opposition. I can understand penalizing the opposition in a way that is instructive. In India, for instance, a man who had killed the father of a family with small children was sentenced to work for eighteen years on the victim's farm until his children grew up. Wouldn't that be of more benefit to society than simply eliminating people? My problem with religion occurs when it becomes a force for suppression. It was not only the killing of the Baha'is that affected me. I had a friend whose sister was a Mojahid. Why was he executed? I had a friend who was Zoroastrian. Why was he executed? What caused a revolution within me was the description of how some of these friends were subjected to physical and mental torture. When I finally read the last testaments written by these people and saw photographs of their bodies, I broke down. I don't understand why when a woman was guilty, the jailers needed to wring the neck of that woman's small child as well. What makes someone stretch the limits of barbarism to the extent of first pulling out a person's tongue while he is still alive and then executing him?

As you know I am a journalist, and I believe in documenting things. I have kept copies of the last wills and testaments of these people and the letters of my friends and the photos of atrocities. There is a letter written by the sister of Sheedokht Baghaa who was in Evin Prison. When she asked her sister what she would like in jail, the response was, "Bring me contraceptive pills so that I won't carry the fetus of these men." There was so much rape of women in the jails. We need a museum that will hold these documents, so that the world will someday understand the extent of these atrocities.

However, here I am in California, fourteen hundred miles away from Iran. And my voice from this distance resembles the story of the man in a lunatic asylum. Someone went up to him and said, "You don't seem crazy, so why did you end up here?" The man replied, "I believed the whole world was crazy and the whole world considered me mad. Since they were in the majority, they won."

Lily

In earlier sections, Lily spoke of her childhood in Iran, her marriage, and her work for children's literature and for the literacy campaign. In this final short segment, she responds to my question about exile.

Six months after my husband left, I got my passport and the official permit to leave the country. I left our wonderful house with two suitcases of autumn clothing—as if I were to return in three weeks. We were planning to return and work in Iran. Our children were planning to return and work there. Three months after our arrival in the United States, the real persecution of Baha'is started. We were told to stay out and not go back.

Do you consider yourself an emigré or an exile? What do you miss most?
Definitely I think of myself as an exile. Wherever I am, I am an outsider. I wish to be in Iran and I miss Iran. Here, I work. I like what I do. Though I live in the West, whatever I do in education is mostly for the third world because that is my way of feeling nearer to Iran. If for a minute I thought that I would never go back, I would die. I understand very well that if ever we did go back, Iran would not welcome us.

What do I miss? Most of all I miss our people, and I miss our mountains. Being Iranian is so many things. It is language, our books, culture, music, the way people look, the eyes, the eye contact. You know, I lived in Thailand for four years and for a part of that time lots of Iranians used to come to Thailand. They were mostly Hezbollahi people with whom I didn't want to associate, but I would stand many a time in the corner and just watch them because they were young Iranians. Maybe it's very sentimental. Most probably it is. But I have this fear—I am always afraid now to become a chauvinist. I love Iranians just because they are Iranians. And that's not right. I prefer to think of myself as an internationalist. I have just finished a book on that—a book for children called *The World Is My Home, and Mankind My Family.* A person who writes that cannot be a chauvinist. Right? But Iranians and Iran have a special spot in my heart, and I cannot do anything about it.

Homa Sarshar

Earlier Homa Sarshar described her work as a journalist in Iran, the personal and professional effect of revolutionary "purification" on her work, and the conditions that made her leave Iran. Here she speaks of her experience of exile, and of starting life again as a journalist.

When the six of us arrived in the United States we joined my mother and my older brother's family in Los Angeles. My mother had already bought a house here in this area. And she had always wanted, long before the revolution, to come out of the country and stay in the United States. She is the kind of woman who did not like living in Tehran. She is a very liberated woman for her age, and she was not very comfortable in Iran. She's very outspoken and wants to live freely. She also wanted to get a higher education for herself and better education for my sister—the youngest child.

So much bothers me about this revolution. What bothers me and makes me angry is that I think that I had worked hard for over sixteen years, and I had paved the road for myself and for other women. There were only five women journalists in Iran when I started, and just two or three years before the revolution young people began to be interested in this profession. Young girls started to become journalists and to become reporters, and I was beginning to be nationally known. I had training, experience, and finally, a year or two before the revolution, I felt that I was finally doing something good for women and my country, that the field was open to me, and that I had the energy and the opportunity. My sons were grown, I didn't have to worry about them, and I was comfortable. My husband's work was good and the time was good. And then suddenly everything stopped. And I came here and I started all over again. But I think that even if I work twice as hard as I was working in Iran, I'll not reach any of my goals.

This is because of language, because my career depends on language. I am an Iranian journalist. I write in Persian. So no matter how good a journalist I am, I don't have any outlet here.

But living in exile also has its positive side. It gives me some satisfaction because of my children and their education. I know that they can have more opportunities here for a better life. I too have learned a lot here. I have read things I wouldn't have had access to in Iran. I have learned of my own importance and worth, something I would not have learned in Iran. In Iran it is always someone else—your teacher, your parents, your boss, your supervisor, your husband—who is always superior to you.

That culture makes you feel that you are the least important person. Not here. And that is positive. I went back to school, to the University of Southern California, and got my M.A. in communications management in 1981.

How would you describe your perspective as a journalist? Which of your projects are you most proud of?

We have an expression in Persian that says that, when looking at a glass some people see it as half full and others as half empty. I see always the half-empty glass; I see first what's lacking. I am a social critic. That makes me closer to the average Iranian who sees everything but doesn't dare to talk about it. It's good to have someone with the courage to reflect what they conceal in their hearts. And I appreciate all the feedback that I get on my writings, on the issues that I tackle, or about which I talk on the radio. I am told my readers respect my courage. So, it's a kind of closed circle. I dare, they encourage me; I dare more, and they encourage me more and I can become more courageous because of that. I'm a very outspoken journalist, and that position is something I enjoy.

Of the pieces I am most proud of—I wrote a piece in *Rahavard* three years ago on Iranians in Los Angeles. This was a critical reading of how different groups of Iranians live in Los Angeles. The other article I'm proud of is a story about a woman called Meena—a type who represents my generation—about the effects on her of the revolution, her feelings about her husband, her family, her children, her work, and her past. This will be published in *Nimeye Digar* [The Other Half; the feminist journal edited by Afsaneh Najmabadi]; it was broadcast on radio. And it was very well received.

I am also proud of my essay on the singer Haedeh's death. My thesis was that Haedeh did not know how to center her attention on herself, to take care of herself. I see her as a type of Iranian woman, as a Middle Eastern woman who couldn't handle the responsibility of being a mother, a wife, a public figure, and an artist. So she unconsciously sacrificed herself to her roles, but could never reconcile herself to her sacrifice. She was divorced from her husband. She wanted very badly to be a singer, and a good one, so she separated from her husband. Although she became a good singer, she never could forgive her separation from her children. So this was the start of her self-destruction. She started drinking. She started to use drugs and finally this abuse ended in her death. I talked about that in my eulogy on the day of her *Khatm* [memorial]. This article too was well received.

My loss is not living and working in Iran. I have family—aunts and uncles and cousins—living in Iran right now. They don't seem unhappy—not any more unhappy than the Muslims I hear from over there. So life is livable there. Before my brother-in-law came to the United States, he was living with his family in Tehran for eight years after the revolution. He said if it was not for all of us who left, if it was not for loneliness and missing the family, he wouldn't have left Iran because he was living very well and his business was doing well. No one cared about his religion. He came here because all of us were here.

Mandana

The story of Mandana's marriage is probably a case study of the many kinds of stresses placed on marriage by immigration and exile. In the earlier sections, Mandana spoke of the specific effects of family and revolution on her as a woman, as a sister, and as a part-time actress.

Even if you wish to be honest with yourself, the answers to questions about home aren't simple. I can easily say, "Iran is my country, my home, my everything." But the fact is, it isn't. I don't belong there. I don't belong here. Actually I don't know where I belong and who I am.

My husband was an engineer. Of course, before entering the United States, we'd hired a lawyer who ripped us off. Then we were held up in Turkey forever. When leaving Iran, I told him that as long as we had each other, we shouldn't worry about all we had lost. I took a risk and came here, but my husband wasn't willing to take the risk.

For two years I tried to get him over here to the United States. I worked nights at a hard job, trying to get labor certification so I could get him a visa. I went to school for seven hours and then I worked for eight. I hardly slept. This went on for two years. I decided to go to Canada and become a refugee. My husband changed his mind about coming here after a few months. He wanted everything to be finalized and legal first.

I worked in a bakery for two years so that I could, through labor certification, get my husband here legally. I never told him about all the problems I was having here. Unfortunately, he depended on me too much. I think that's why he married me. We were colleagues in the same firm, and everyone talked about how independent I was and how much gumption I had. That is what attracted him in the first place. But he was soon threatened by that same independence.

I felt very guilty being here. And I was under so much pressure. I worked, I went to school, and I was very homesick. I was also sexually under pressure because I missed my husband. Because I hadn't thought about such needs, I didn't understand the sources of my discomfort. I, who had fought and cared so much for women's issues, did not know how to apply my knowledge to my own situation. Finally it was my husband who said it would be better for me to stay in the United States. He said it was safer. A month later he accused me of not wanting to be with him. We finally separated about a year ago. I told him I wanted to stay friends, that I wanted to help him, that I'd filed for residency for both of us, that he could still use the documents. He was embarrassed and thanked me. I even packed my bags to go back to Iran. I told my husband, "I'll come to keep my word, but I can't promise you that I'll be able to live with you."

That was when my parents stopped me. My father, who was religious, conservative, and against divorce, called me and said, "I think that it's best if you don't come back; if you do, both your lives will be destroyed. You did what you could do; your conscience is clear. If you come back, you'll ruin his life too. He may not see it this way now, but he'll thank you some day."

Now my life is different. I had problems with immigration. I had to give up school to continue work in the bakery. So I gave up school and lost my visa. First I enrolled in an English as a Second Language class, then I studied biology. I took classes in art in Santa Monica; I found an office job with an Iranian. I am now in a women's group here. We have lectures, meetings, discussions. On March 8—International Women's Day—I put on a show about women, a play that portrayed women of all classes in Iran, from leftists to Hezbollahis, to an ordinary housewifely woman. Now most of my work is devoted to women, with women's lives. Next week we are putting on an Iranian *Medea*—a modern adaptation by an Italian writer. It's a play about a husband who asks his wife to leave him so that he can marry a rich woman. And everyone advises Medea to do so because it is better for her children. Then Medea goes through a transformation, goes crazy and attacks all the laws that subjugate women, laws that make women into sheep that can be sheared at men's will.

Professor Ali

One of the generation of Iranians whose identities were formed in part by their resistance to the Shah, their support of Mossadeq, and their resentment of the CIA coup of 1953, Professor Ali could only articulate his deep despondency about loss and exile.

Exile? During the years I lived in Europe and later in America, I felt I was living a life in transition, in flux between here and there. I had always hoped to return someday to Iran. I had lived in the United States and had studied and taught here briefly in the 1960s, then returned to Iran in 1972. When I came here after the revolution, however, I felt differently from any other time I had been here. The difference was that now I am in exile. The last few times I was here it was only temporary. This time I knew I could not return to Iran.

I can't understand why I am so deeply attached to Iran even after being away for so long. I try to go out, get friends, work, read, but it is all different.

Since 1981, however, that life of transition has ended. I am here now. But the result has been that I ask myself why I am living at all. Naturally I am very depressed. My family can't bear me any longer. The thought that I would die alone in America was and is very difficult. I am better now. But the sense that I am in exile is always with me. My way of life has always been 100 percent Iranian. By that I mean simply that I had grown up with that culture, with those traditions, and I shared the social and political foundations of thought belonging to those people. I always felt that I understood the sufferings of those people and that my function was to work to see an end to those sufferings. I had that goal in life. But I have no hope of effecting change or of return, and the whole situation seems meaningless.

I went through a very dark stage of depression knowing that I could not go back. I felt cut off from Iran. It feels Kafkaesque. I feel a stranger in this country. But I was shocked after the revolution. All my values and standards and beliefs went to pieces. I lost everything—social, political, familial. Even my own work was lost to the revolution. I became what I still am—a wanderer.

Yahya

In earlier sections, Yahya described his gradual, painful disillusion with the shape of the revolution. He is currently working in the United States. Here he addresses questions about gender roles in his marriage, about negotiating his own identity and those of his children, and about reconciling himself to an imagined Iran with which he can live while working in America.

Intellectually it's hard for me to identify myself. I still am wrestling with whether or not to go back. Once I supported and fought for the revolution. To be an Iranian now means a different thing. Now I tend to associate myself with the Iran before Islam, with the civilization that we once had before Islam. When I think of being an Iranian, I try to think of the Iran that has its roots in a pre-Islamic civilization. That's what I'm trying to teach my eldest son, trying to teach him about what Iran was, what the culture was before Islam. I don't know. Being in this country has changed me.

I think I have exiled myself. I left with the full intention of returning. Now I can't. The biggest question for me is what can I do? What can my children do when I go back? What can I do with literature? What could I teach? Any book might be subject to censorship, might create problems. Everything is changing so fast that I can't predict anything. For instance, you are not allowed to teach Ahmad Shamlu. Imagine that. A student in Iran gets a B.A. or M.A. in Persian literature and he has not read Shamlu or Forough Farokhzad, whose name is never mentioned, or Sadeq Hedayat or Gholam Hosein Saedi, Ibrahim Golestan, or Beizaii. None of these can be taught. You can't teach Naguib Mahfouz either.

My wife has a different approach to the issue. For me the problem is an intellectual problem. For her, she is concerned with her family. She feels that she has no one here, no personal relationships. The intellectual abstractions that concern me don't concern her. But she is concerned about the education that our three sons will have in Iran. With sons, we immediately think of military service and war. So that is a concern for both of us.

She has an M.S. in engineering. She has an idea that as the man in the family, I should have the job. I have encouraged her to go and find a job, told her that I would stay home and take care of the kids, but she worries about what the family at home would say if I stayed home and she went to work. So we have to work at all those new ways of thinking to live in this country.

Pari

Pari speaks first about everyday life in the United States after her arrival during the hostage crisis. The second part of this section is based on a series of conversations we taped, first in May 1992 as we were driving Pari to Chicago to catch a plane to Iran, and then again in 1994 in California. In the car we discussed the story about the immigrant Iranian who left Iran in 1979 as a twelve-year-old, a story that builds up to a climax in a grocery store where the cashier asks the source of his accent. His mother abruptly replies, "We're from Spain." A friend from Kentucky tells of Ramin, the fiddler in his Irish band in 1992, who still says he's from Spain.

The days of the hostage crisis—with endless church bells—were among the hardest days of my life. I remember once in a graduate seminar in 1981 I was asked to introduce myself. I had done so many times before and never found it difficult. But now announcing that I was Iranian was beyond me. Not because I was ashamed. But I knew that all these people who were sitting around the table had some sort of anger at Iranians. So when I started talking about me, I said, "I am a graduate student in early childhood education," and then I stopped. I could go no further. They started to probe me, and then I broke down. This was something they had never seen—someone breaking down in public in the middle of class introductions. The professor was extremely sensitive and kind. It wasn't that people weren't treating me right. But the frenzy of the atmosphere made me feel bad to be around Americans.

And now, wherever I am, even in Iran, if church bells ring, I feel my face draining of all color.

In those days, the student office told me I should live with a friend. They said I might be harassed, or even worse, killed. I was too ashamed to live with anyone, even you, Zohreh, who was so close to me. I simply couldn't share my unhappiness.

When I first came to the United States, I thought I'd live in a furnished apartment. In fact I found myself in an unfurnished apartment that was called "furnished." My experience in Europe had prepared me to think that "furnished" included everything. All I had brought with me had been a few clothes and a trunk. I was sure I would return soon to Iran, so I wished to buy nothing.

A workman came one day to put in storm windows for the winter. He asked if I had a screw driver. I was ashamed that I had nothing. "Don't you have even a knife?" he asked. "No," I said, "I don't think so." Then we started talking about who I was and why I was here. I said I was from Iran and that I was buying things little by little. And he told me of his son who was a lawyer. We then talked about the hostages, about how hard it was on me as an Iranian here and on American families whose family members had been taken as hostages. He showed a lot of empathy. When he left, I went to the bedroom and found that he had left his tools behind. So I picked them up and ran after him as fast as I could. I got to him as he was driving away. "You have left your stuff," I cried out after him. He got really red and said he had left it on purpose. It broke my heart. How kind and nice he was, and at the same time I was embarrassed. I said, "No, no. You have to take it. I am going away," I said, "and I won't need it." So finally, he gave me one of his tools and took the rest back.

In 1981 we were at Thanksgiving with a family of American lawyers. They knew we were Iranian. One said very proudly, "Iranians are shits. We should get the hostages out and exterminate the entire land." Maryam [my daughter] and I simply put our heads down. And when I looked up and met Maryam's eyes we knew we had to leave that table. We didn't say a word to each other, but we knew that we could not have dinner with people who believed that the entire country must be bombed for fifty-two people. [*I remember bumper stickers that said "Nuke Iran."*] It was so painful. And it was Thanksgiving.

The vastness of this culture always overwhelmed me. The university, for instance, was so big. I thought, "I am lost." Tehran University, where I took my master's degree in education, had only a small department in one building. And here I was in a huge place where the library was in one building and my classes in others. I was afraid of parking lots because they had so much space for cars.

When I lived with my daughter in Champaign, we always pretended to have more than we did. Although I lived at poverty level, I pretended very hard that I was middle class and could afford what a middle-class woman could afford in Iran. I think many Iranians do that. We are very class-conscious. Sometimes I tell myself that value is in the mind, but yet when I go to someone's house who covers the table with a lot of food, I suspect I respect them more [*she laughs*].

When I lived in University Housing, Maryam and I found it therapeutic to have a lot of plants and to multiply them. But then the plants became so numerous that we had to sell them. It was common for students to put out a table and sell anything one wanted—a garage sale. But I was ashamed. I would say to Maryam, "Why don't you just give it to them? How can you ask for money, when we haven't spent any money on it?" But Maryam would laugh and say, "Okay, I'm not going to share any of the money with you." For the life of me, I couldn't go out and sell my junk to others. Yet, funnily enough, when I became a salesperson in Los Angeles, I became a top salesperson. I can sell anything for someone else, but I can't promote my own stuff.

I get stressed living here even for a short time. I am not at home here. And the reason I stay in Iran is because I am more comfortable there among my own people. I am somebody there. My work is respected by Iranians. But when I come to this culture, I am one of millions of immigrants and nobodies. Even if they do know me, they don't respect third-world work.

When I look back on my time in Illinois and in California, I feel I have failed. My studying at Illinois went nowhere. I worked here as a salesperson and my background and appearance helped me succeed. But the best part of California was putting together an Iranian women's group. I found women in the mall who couldn't speak English, and I put together a support group. We met regularly and had a banquet every season so that the younger generation could get to know each other.

But I had to go back to Iran to take care of my mother. And I could work there. Although I had to struggle with the government rather than with department store management, I have succeeded in doing worthwhile work. I thought I would build a shelter for women and children, a clinic with classes in the evening. I now run classes that help women and children to learn about legal issues and children's rights. In 1994 I started an organization called the National Association in Support of Children's Rights in Iran. This is a grassroots organization that has caught fire and has resulted not only in women's marches on the street in 1997, but in a change in national law. No longer do men have automatic rights to children after a divorce. And we are trying to raise the age of female consent in marriage from the current age of eight to eighteen. As a child of divorce, as a child who has experienced a stepmother, as a child who has known insecurity, as a child who once mistrusted everyone, I really enjoy my current work as organizer of such groups, as leader of therapy groups, as someone who is helping the status of children in Iran.

Afsaneh Najmabadi

In earlier sections Afsaneh talked of her childhood, her education, her politics and her return for the revolution. Here she describes her arrival at the age of twenty-one in the United States in 1966 and the start of her schooling at Radcliffe and Harvard. Although this section, unlike the others, is not about arrival in the United States after the revolution, it is a revealing story about the evolution of one woman into an activist and a scholar after leaving home for studies in the United States.

I had to go to Washington because, though I had scored very high in the sciences, my English was pretty poor. Radcliffe required that I take a summer course in English, which was arranged for me at one of these language schools in Washington, D.C. I left Iran in June 1966 and spent two months in one of those language courses in D.C.

I must tell you the bizarre story of my arrival in the United States, because it took a combination of complete naiveté and luck to have survived such an arrival. I didn't know anyone in the United States. When I had gone to the Ministry of Education in Tehran to get a student passport, I had seen this huge sign on the wall saying, "If you're going abroad as a student and you don't have anybody there, inform the local consulate of the details of your arrival and it will meet you and help you." I believed this sign. So as soon as I got my ticket, I sent a telegram to the student section of the Iranian consulate in Washington, D.C., giving them the details of my arrival at the airport, and I expected somebody to meet me there. And of course, nobody did.

My plane arrived in Washington, D.C., on a Friday night—past midnight. The airport was almost shut down. And nobody to meet me. And there I was with these two huge suitcases and very little English because most of my English was scientific English. Although I could write a sophisticated physics paper in English, I couldn't say something as simple as "Hi, I'm lost." So there I was stranded at 1:00 a.m. in Dulles Airport looking around, waiting for consulate people to take care of me. I gradually started getting worried. Then a black man, a janitor, walked toward me, very sweet, and said, "You're lost. What's wrong?" I told him that nobody was here to pick me up and I needed to go to Washington. He said, "Where is the address in Washington? Can you take a taxi to it?" I said, "I only have this school address." The only thing I had was the address of a language school at which I was supposed to show up on Monday morning. That's all I had. I had no notion of what I would do. So he said, "But it's Friday night. This school is not open till Monday. What are you going to do between now and then?" I said, "I don't know." So he said, "I live in Washington. I'll drive you there and I'll see what I can do for you." Suddenly in the middle of the highway I—having no idea how many miles out of Washington the airport was—I panicked. And the man was so sweet—he realized I had panicked. So he kept showing me the highway signs, "Look, it says, 'To Washington.' I'm taking you to Washington. I'm not taking you anywhere else." He was so sweet.

Not knowing where to take me, he said, "Look, I have some Egyptian friends. I'll take you to their house." So he took me there, thinking that maybe they would understand my language, or they would know people who would understand my language. By that time I was shaking in complete panic. So he took me to this Egyptian family and when the door opened, there right in front of me was this huge picture of Gamal Abdul Nasser. It was the connection with something familiar—Nasser. And I burst into tears. The family knew Arabic and English, but by this time my English had entirely disappeared. Through some friends of friends who knew some Iranians, they contacted the man who was in charge of Student Affairs at the consulate, who then came sometime well after 2:00 a.m. to take me to a party at the Iranian consulate. This is the story of my arrival in America.

When I got to Radcliffe—and there again, I'm telling you, I'm just very lucky—they accepted all my transfer grades, and I found myself a junior in my very first year at Radcliffe. The resident family in the dormitory were the Duncans—Anne and David—and Anne knew Persian because her parents had been missionaries in Iran. So it was another one of those lucky coincidences that smoothed my breaking into dormitory life in America. She was extremely kind and happy to practice her Persian. But she also taught me the etiquette of college life in America in a way that was never insulting or rude.

The most difficult part of life for me was language, ordinary communication. I would sit around a table and I wouldn't understand anything people said. They spoke with New York accents and Southern accents, and none of it sounded like English. And though I excelled in all courses that didn't require human communication—like physics—I failed elementary dormitory communication. That made me retreat into work and away from people. The two friends I made there who tried so hard to pull me out of my shell are still good friends today. My memory of that first year is of very difficult physics courses and Russian. And then, to my great disappointment, I discovered I had requirements in humanities that I had to satisfy—courses in social sciences, history, and government.

I then went to Harvard graduate school after which, from 1969 on, my life drastically changed. I was, so to speak, born again into politics—this through a friend involved with a group of Arabs and Israelis who were trying to create solidarity committees with Palestinians. This was a time of teach-ins. I went to one meeting at MIT where Chomsky was speaking, as usual, critically of Israeli policies. The meeting was packed with Israelis and Jews attacking Chomsky. A few days later, there was this two-day teach-in on Palestine at Harvard and MIT. I went both days. That was sort of a turning point for me, because there I met a whole number of people who became the most intimate friends in my life, and I got involved in all kinds of activities—Palestine solidarity activities, antiwar activities—through this network of political friends and activists. This is also where I met Kanan, whom I fell in love with instantly and pursued immediately and then lived with. I remember him intensely arguing, circled by some twenty people, talking in defense of Palestinians in this really passionate, attractive way.

Kanan and I lived together, and by 1972, I knew I had to drop physics. In 1974 we moved to England. We lived there from '74 to '83. We moved to England because both of us were finished with academic life here. Kanan got his master's in architecture and urban planning. I was doing a thesis on elementary particle physics—theoretical physics—trying to work out mathematical models for an explanation of symmetry in particle physics. Kanan got accepted into the London School of Economics to earn an urban planning degree for one year, and I got into a program at SOAS doing anthropology—the School of Oriental and African Studies at London University. There I did one year studying the anthropology of the Middle East with Richard Tapper. Our move was also politically motivated. We got involved in various political formations. Both of us, for instance, were involved in the antiwar movement, within which, at the time, the Socialist Workers' Party had a very strong presence.

Now, I teach at Barnard College, I write, I edit *Nimeye Digar,* the Persian language feminist journal we founded with a group of Iranian women in London in 1982. My most recent work, *The Story of the Daughters of Quchan: Gender and National Memory in Iranian History,* I see as an act of recalling and restoring to history a forgotten tale about the sale of daughters to pay taxes to a king.

Mehrnaz Saeed-Vafa

In earlier sections, Mehrnaz Saeed-Vafa spoke of the estrangement of growing up female in a divided culture and family, of her entry into film, and of her work before and during the revolution. I asked if she felt she was an émigré or an exile.

I experienced feelings of exile a long time ago, long before I came to the United States, when I was a teenager in Iran: when I realized that values were so confusing, when I wasn't sure what being a woman meant, when I wasn't sure whether womanhood was defined by education, or by wifehood, or by talent, or by seduction, or by sexuality. These questions were made more confusing by the confusion in my own home, so that by the time the revolution happened, I could really understand why women were going to the opposite extreme. It was a way to address the feelings of alienation and exile some of us already felt within the country. As the person/woman/Iranian I have evolved into, there are three levels to my alienation. The first is one common to all immigrants: We leave our country, feel separated and foreign. Second, because I am a woman, I experience a different set of hardships that make me feel more of an exile. I know that I am an exile in my own country because I am not a man; if I return, they will ask me why I am not married, how old I am, why I want to live alone, and so on. My gender is a big barrier. And finally, apart from being an Iranian, the person I have become is very suspicious and skeptical—another kind of exilic condition. I grew to know and understand many kinds of hypocrisy—hypocrisy in religion, in relationships, and in family values. So because of my personal and family history, I have become separated from and skeptical toward what I once was part of—Iranian tradition. This sense of separation—from the land, its culture, its confusion—has created in me a deep sense of alienation.

What do I miss in Iran? First of all, and most powerful, is the language. Then a sense of history, of living with my own past. Here in the United States, of course, I make connections with students and friends, with the field I teach; my bonds are international and human in a general sort of way. What

I miss is using my potential to produce things that are and will be much more meaningful in Iran, more so than in the United States. What I miss is a way of relating to people that I don't and can't have here. Here it is hard to see myself as part of American history, whereas I can see myself as part of Iranian history. To be honest, what I really miss are the streets, all the buildings that were part of my childhood and youth. I just miss them. I want to go and see those places even if they are all destroyed and gone. So if there is a magic in one's childhood and youth, it's all those memories. My roots are not in contemporary Tehran. My roots go far back—those roots were cut, damaged, severed somewhere and sometime. I don't suffer the illusion that I will be reconnected with my sources the moment I return. Coming to the United States gave me a distance, and that distance helped me to appreciate where I came from, to simultaneously question and appreciate my attachment to Iran, my longing to return. I don't know what the function of my longing is or where this longing will take me.

What connects me to Iran, to the students I taught there, was something far deeper and stronger than I experience elsewhere—though I enjoy my teaching here. I come from the same culture and language—I have suffered as a child, a youth, as a teenager, and as a grown woman in and out of marriage, so that my problems are similar to what other Iranian women go through.

You see, it's not everyday life that I miss. Whether I'm here or there, in everyday life I have to work, I have to do certain routine things. In both places I have friends, too. But the attraction for me is to really feel a connection that I miss, a connection with being a part of Iran's history. Of course there are things in Iran that I appreciate. Part of the tradition that I find undesirable is still within me, is part of me. Spiritually I feel I can only function in that land, connected to that culture. So perhaps I have to be physically in that land in order to function. On another plane, what might embrace me and what I long for is a connection to the living and the dead, to the present and the past, to people who have left a mark on me, whose traditions and history I have inherited. The sense of connection to a past that made me is what I want. The past that made me began long before I was born—in the women in my family, my mother and grandmother and all those who made them. If I could make a vital connection with those living and dead people of my past, if that connection could embrace me, that would be something.

The kinds of films I made in Iran after the revolution were generally small films on such subjects as addiction, life in a village; I also wrote scripts and articles that people liked. When I left Iran, I had had no conflict with the government. My conflicts were mostly internal. I was worn out after all the years of fighting with my father. Just as I was on the verge of success, the revolution happened both in the outside world and in my own life. Of course, there were major restrictions and rules for making films that were stifling—all that has now changed. Then, they feared and objected to music in films; they wanted every character in my films to be seen at prayer at least once. They accused me of not complying with my contract and with their expectations. When I experienced such harassment, I decided not to make films anymore. I didn't wish to start a film that I then couldn't finish. I was part of a generation of filmmakers just on the edge of being discovered. I wasn't one of the established filmmakers like Mehrjui or Behzai.

That's why I want now to return. I hear that women are allowed to make films and if I am allowed, I would prefer to work there. Now, after thirteen years, all Western films, American and Western European films, are banned. So people have to see Iranian films. That's a great support to indigenous filmmakers. Even if a film is not a box-office hit, they are willing to produce it if they believe it has worthwhile values.

This condition is unique. Nowhere in the world could I have such opportunities. Here no one will give me the money to make a film about the subjects I wish to work with. No one is interested in the experience of Iranians. After the hostage crisis, that's not a popular subject. Here they tell me they don't wish to involve themselves in a film that requires them to engage the Iranian government. That's why I would much prefer to work in Iran. What does freedom in the United States mean if I am not free to make the kinds of films I wish to make? I am very happy teaching here, but I cannot make films.

My dream is to make films in Iran that would satisfy the public there, to teach in a place where the women can benefit from my experience. I never had a role model. But I could be a role model to the women in Iran who could see how a single woman can produce and be useful and successful. My life will sooner or later be over. I don't care much about my life, but I care about film. Film is, I believe, important to the history of a country, and it is there that I could produce what is more important. Perhaps that is the key to my longing for Iran. Although I might say that it is Iran that needs my work, it is really I who need to work there.

Tahereh

In earlier sections, Tahereh talked of her conservative background, her marriages, her education, and her return to celebrate the revolution. Her journey to the United States began in the early 1970s when she came to New York expecting to go to Columbia University. After returning to Iran for a B.A., she came to the University of Illinois to get a Ph.D. in social psychology. This portion of her narrative picks up after her return to the United States following the turn in the revolution.

And while I was in the States working toward my degree, my brothers and sisters in Tehran were getting arrested. In late 1982 I finally finished my studies. So did my husband. I got my degree, but we had to leave because we didn't have a green card. I sent my passport to the Iranian embassy to get it renewed, but my request was rejected because they said I was an antirevolutionary. I don't know why I was identified and others more active were not. Some say because I had talked about women's issues, because I had given different lectures against their policies about women.

My husband and I were stuck, yet we didn't have any legal status to work. We had a friend in California who had a company, who asked us to come to California. He thought he could hire my husband and that we could both get green cards through his job. Since my husband had some accounting training in Iran and had worked for the Ministry of Finance, he had some kind of credentials for us as a means to get this green card. So that's why we moved to Los Angeles, where I worked at all sorts of odd jobs. I worked, for instance, at Sears, as a cashier, and my husband for a while sold used cars. By the time we got our green card, I was so detached from academia that I didn't even know how to look for an academic job.

We filled in at the Los Angeles county school district during a time of shortage for teachers. For two years we taught at elementary schools, which was a very different experience and very helpful financially. We saved some money, and then gradually we found ourselves and started looking for a house.

I comment on her remarkable strength and resilience.
Looking back at my life, I realize I always had resources of strength. I could have become like one of my aunts. They can't imagine how I live the kind of life I do. And so I always feel proud of myself. My family who now are proud of me would feel embarrassed by these stories. They don't wish to have me repeat any of this. But I think my stories about growing up in Iran should be repeated. It shows what women in my social stratum went through—women like me, who felt I could do things my mother couldn't do. And the consequences of feeling that strength: it shows I had another vision. Something—maybe the books I read—instilled in me another possibility.

In 1991, Tahereh made the following comments.
Yet, I feel like I'm stuck here. I feel a dual marginality. I'm marginalized by my own people, because I'm alienated from them. Although I have tried to keep in touch and follow events, I feel distanced from Iran. I have tried to keep in touch. Tried to follow the events, tried to read, but still I know that I have changed a lot, and they have changed a lot, and we have been away from each other. So therefore I'm a stranger to them and they're strangers here. So that's the hybrid life. I don't think I can consider myself just an American. Even in academia, I feel like they want me because I'm exotic. I'm a Middle-Easterner. They don't take me as a social scientist. And I still have problems with the language. Especially when it comes to writing. It's more difficult to express myself in writing that is not just technical writing but writing with style, a literary style and a personal style as I have in Persian.

I feel I'm always translating my thinking into another language, and I have to fight for every word, every right word, and that's why I'm not as productive writing in English as I would like to be. Even learning Persian was a struggle for me in the beginning—I didn't know any Persian until age six. I spoke Turkish-Azari at home because I am an Azari from Azarbaijan. We used to speak Azari to my parents. English is actually my third language. I can function in English, but that's not enough. I can't enjoy reading, writing, or hearing a poem in English, for instance, the way I can enjoy the same in Persian.

What does it mean to be an Iranian emigré in a country of emigrés?
Being Iranian in America means shared common experiences, especially when it comes to the last ten years. It's so hard to be understood by non-Iranians. We can share and communicate and understand as exiles—even the experience of exile. The experience of unwanted immigration to another country can be shared by many other cultures. But the common experience of what happened during the revolution and what happened after the revolution—that's what makes us distinctive, and distinguishes between an American and an Iranian. First of all, when I talk to an Iranian, we know where we are coming from, what experience, what background, what aspirations, what failures,

what disappointments, what pains and joys. So being Iranian to me means speaking Persian and reading all the writers we love. Being Iranian also means understanding the rule of the clergy whom we might hate, understanding the abuse of religion, the power of religion, the pain of ignorance, the pain of manipulation.

In August 2000, Tahereh wanted me to edit the position she had adopted in her earlier narrative.

Now I feel much less marginalized and more at home. I find my feelings even toward Iran have changed after visiting there in 1993 and 1994. I found a changed Iran, and I feel less alienated in both societies. I am much more comfortable and at peace with my multiple identities. Perhaps my visit in 1991–92 to the Republic of Azarbaijan was a turning point that revived and reinforced my Azari identity. Rather than seeing, as I once did, these splittings as reasons for confusion and anxiety, I now see all these identities as advantages.

Hamid Naficy

In earlier sections, Hamid Naficy, who currently teaches at Rice University in Houston, Texas, has told of his childhood in Isfahan and of his work in Tehran's open university. He left Iran in 1978 on sabbatical leave and expected to return after a year. He starts with a meditation on the word "exile" and continues to reflect on deterritorialization and reterritorialization in the postnational, postrevolutionary world. I choose to follow his narrative with that of Ramin Sobhan because Sobhan's reification of a pre-Islamic Iran illustrates a problem Naficy theorizes.

Iranians are sensitive about the term "exile" because most understand it to mean *Tab'eed*, or political exile, which has negative connotations. And I'm not exiled in that sense of the term. But there's another sense of exile for which the Iranian word *ghorbat* [the feeling, regardless of circumstance, of estrangement] is perhaps more approximate. If we use that variation of the term, we could say that I am in exile. But I have problems with all that because these meanings of "exile" imply that I was living at some age in an authentic, stable, unified country and that I was united with it and then suddenly something happened and I became separated, disunited, fragmented, and exiled. Both the unity of the former and the disunity of the latter are illusory, however.

During my own life major transformations have occurred in the way we experience space and time. Since the 1950s we have entered a different world. It is a world where we may live in geographically-bounded terrains called countries, but ideologically and symbolically we are crossing those boundaries with greater facility and rapidity.

In a sense I think Westernization in Iran and my own contact with the West were, in effect, the beginning of my exile. And I mean this as a positive thing, because this sort of exile introduces you to new ideas. It puts you in touch with other ways of producing meanings and it makes you aware of the pitfalls of the chauvinistic nationalism to which you might have been subjected prior to the distance of exile. Exile allows you more room for self-criticism and self-construction, as it were. When you have more discourses available, you have more elbow room to move around in. And so I see exile as a largely positive experience.

I did not become aware of these issues until years later. In fact, until I began to write an autobiographical essay and my Ph.D. dissertation, I really hadn't thought about these issues seriously. Because of physical travel, because of global interconnection through media, news, and popular culture, people are becoming so hybridized that everybody is exiled in one way or another. Everyone operates in situations and in environments that are not necessarily of their own making but are of their choosing. Obviously, not everybody chooses. Some people are forced to flee El Salvador or Iran or whatever to go somewhere else because they can't live where they are. But in the end when they reach their destination, they may be able to choose the kind of amalgamation of cultures that they want to belong to. So I don't look with pain at not being in Iran.

One of the characteristics of exile is deterritorialization, and by that I mean the full range of displacements that it engenders. One, of course, is physical separation from home, from the past, from the family, and so forth. But the other has to do with certain losses and shifts in status. You have a job, you have a particular status back home. You move across borders and things are changed. You can't go back. You don't have access to the money or property or whatever you once had, so you have to live a different lifestyle. Your status changes. Your job changes. Your human relationships change. Most importantly, the language you use every day is not there anymore. So both physically and symbolically, everything that you construct your world with is transformed. What I mean by deterritorialization, then, is the physical, symbolic, and ideological terrains that have shifted as though by tectonic force.

So for me it has been financially very hard. In terms of status it has also been very hard. I had a fairly high-level job that was secure in Iran. But it just so happened that exile also coincided with another sort of mid-life crisis that was driven by exile itself. So I decided to go back and finish up my doctorate in the mid-'80s. And that meant that I was no longer a professional person working and earning money.

I was a student again. And so this shift in status was hard, has been hard, is very hard financially right now until I finish and get an honest-to-goodness job. But it's also been very enriching for me personally. This is another aspect of deterritorialization—that you can actually put yourself in a position or be placed in a position to reterritorialize yourself again. And this time you can do it more consciously than you did the first time when you were a kid and when your family created an environment around you that enveloped you and helped to create you.

This reterritorialization is by necessity a more conscious process. And for me, going to school has been very influential in coming to terms with interpreting what is happening to me. Writing and theorizing about it has been my way of dealing with my own personal changes and with exile. I think people who are involved in creative work are also involved in self-narrativization, which helps us to fashion ourselves through the narratives we create. So, my effort at autobiography in *Emergences* [Naficy 1989] was a conscious effort to do just that. The territory I have found is an in-between territory. It's a space, if you will, perhaps more than a territory. It's in-between and betwixt—a liminal space and I'm a liminar, as it were.

I spend a lot of time thinking about Iran, because I'm writing my dissertation about exile and about Iranians in Los Angeles and their cultural productions. And I'm also organizing this festival of Iranian cinema, so these days I am around Iran and Iranians constantly. I'm on the board of editors of three journals, *Quarterly Review of Film and Video, Emergences,* and *Jusur.*

The liminalities of exile eventually will awaken Iranians, not necessarily to become "American," but to start to pay attention to this culture and to unpack their bags. And to realize that unpacking their bags does not instantly turn them into redneck Americans.

I think of myself as an Iranian American. My two children, seven and ten, think of themselves as hybrids, as Iranian Americans. Even though they don't know Persian, they know Iranian culture whose world view permeates the household. We talk about the past. We have letters from our families. The children write or send stuff to Iran—paintings and drawings and other things to them, and we go to Iranian films sometimes. I just want to keep them on the edges of the culture so that it's not completely alien for them.

What I miss about Iran is a sense of being very comfortable with the language and with the cultural codes to the degree that using them is completely un-conscious. It is as though your contact with the world is utterly effortless, and it's as though that contact comes from some internal well—spontaneously—while all my contacts in English always go through a filter of some sort, so that there is a bit of self-awareness, always a bit of distance between me and this culture.

I am not a master of this culture or a product of this culture as I am a master of and a product of my original culture. There is a certain double pleasure in mastering and being mastered by culture and language. I don't have that double pleasure of identification with language and being. But of course if I go to Iran now I would be in the same position there as I am here. I would not have the kind of ease with being master and mastered by the culture because language, society, and culture in Iran are constantly changing as they do anywhere else. So there is some unbelonging, a lack of fit, wherever I go.

The danger, of course, is to create from a position in exile an imaginary thing called "Iran"—which is precisely what, in my studies, I feel Iranians have done in Los Angeles: they have created an imaginary Iran and they have fetishized it at a particular time in history and they keep circulating these fetishes in their newspapers and magazines and television programs, while the thing itself, Iran itself, is undergoing developments and evolving in ways that they don't know anything about. Although politically it's a dangerous thing to do, maybe psychologically it's necessary to have some unchanging construction somewhere.

What they fetishize is an idealized pre-Islamic Iran, the one that the Shah tried to reconstruct, or a prerevolutionary Iran. That spectacle he tried to create has become reality for some people. Of course, that's one of the characteristics of this postmodern age—the inability to tell the difference between the image and the thing itself. The simulation becomes the real. The other fetish they have created is of the present Iran under the Islamic Republic as a desolate cemetery, the "devastated homeland" filled with savagery and violence. While these constructions bear some truth, yet like all fetishes, they also suppress other complexities and other truths.

I have become Americanized through my children. Simply through sharing their American nursery rhymes and books, a whole cultural encyclopedia has become available to me. It wasn't available to me before. I couldn't draw upon Daffy Duck. So yes, this is the Americanization of Hamid Naficy, but I'm also doing the opposite. I'm making Americans aware of what Iranians are about. And I'm hoping that, more importantly, I'm making Iranians aware of what Iranian culture is about and what they are about. And, and I guess what I'm trying to do is to create a space where a reexamination of one's identity could be made possible. Therefore, I organized a number of film shows at UCLA this year in which films that younger Iranians had made here in exile were screened. The reason I did that was because I wanted first of all to show that Iranian filmmakers were not limited to one or two well-known feature film directors. Second, I wanted to show that younger Iranians were also making films here, that they too were dealing with their own crises of personal identity, of national identity, and of ethnic identity. I hope that by seeing these films, younger Iranians are supported and encouraged, and that other Iranians become a little bit more aware of the real issues that are going on in their lives.

I hope to create a cultural space in which alternatives to fetishized images of Iran and of the past can be discussed with an audience who is asked to actually engage with those issues and to create something out of them. Some of these films, for example, address problems of what it is to be an immigrant or an exile. I'm hoping that in this cultural space I can make possible an open engagement with problems of life after the revolution and with problems of life in America. We can't create or live in an Iran of our imagination, an Iran that's frozen and put away. We have to keep creating ourselves, just as we have to be open to new creations of our country.

Ramin Sobhan

Pari and I visit Ramin Sobhan (pseud.)—a scholar, teacher, and writer—in his Los Angeles office from which the sound of Persian music emerges. He is tall, handsome, and stately, with dark hair and a goatee. Unlike others who started with a story about the past, Ramin Sobhan started with a narration of national and cultural identity. Voicing an ancient idea of the nation-state, replete with ideas of racial purity, cultural unity, and sanctity of origins, Sobhan believes in the cultural superiority of Persians over other people, particularly over the Arabs toward whom he felt a ferocious hostility. Like de Gobineau, he argues for the superiority of "blood" and for the recognition of the "natural" inequality among the races. He identifies the essence of Iranian identity as the Shahnameh*—a work he chooses to see as the originary, unified source of history, culture, and wisdom. Firdowsi's Persian epic, translated as* The Book of Kings *10 A.D., celebrates Persian myths and legends of national heroism. Attributing unity to Iranian culture by grounding that identity in a single book satisfies the need for reification, and it doubles even as it is the predicate for the process of recomposing the past.*[6]

On a second meeting, conducted by Pari four years after the first, Sobhan lost his composure describing a childhood whose moments of authoritarian terror he had chosen to repress in our first meeting. In May 1994, he told a story of childhood anguish and anger. One day, when he was nine years old, Sobhan was unexpectedly called home from school to find himself standing before the accusing, mantled figure of his father seated next to a blazing fire. His father, a mojtahid,[7] *asked the boy: "Do you know what it means to be a thief? Do you know the punishment for stealing?" The little boy, stricken into silence, finding himself accused of the sin of stealing five tomans, watched as his father took a knife, slowly sterilized it in the fire, and placed it on the boy's wrist ready to cut off his hand. His mother's cries at seeing what the father was about to do interrupted the proceedings. As she forced the child out of the way and out of the house, he heard her say, "What was wrong with the milk I fed our son that you can now hurt the child I nursed? Cut my hand in place of his." Some weeks later, the boy was again called out of school and asked to run home. He met his mother on the street without a* chador, *her*

hair flowing uncombed, shouting for the boy to run home. There, before the
same fire, he found his mantled father who, without a word of apology, told
his son that he had just discovered the missing five tomans. The father then
gave Sobhan the money as a gift. Years later, he wrote a short story about this
incident titled, "How I Came into a Lot of Money."

The patterns of authoritarianism evident in the father's sadism get trans-
lated, first, into Sobhan's sense of perpetual exile from the inadequate and cor-
rupt cultures he inhabits, and then focused into specific anger against stereo-
typed Arabs, whom he blames for the fragmentation of homogenous Persian
civilization. His exilic reconstructions of self, race, culture, and nation are all
forged in resentment against what he sees as the imperialism of Islam and of
Arab culture. That is why I include his narrative in this final section. I begin
by assuring him that this interview will be anonymous if he so wishes.

No, *Khanum* [lady]. Write my name, because my good name is not something
I wish to take to the grave with me or give to the *morde-shoor* [washer-of-the-
corpse]. I come from Iran, and all my life's effort is to live with that country
and its people. And I do. If I have left Iran and am following an unhappy
ugly migration, it is only so that someday I can return. I am a gypsy. We
have a country that didn't originate today or yesterday or ten years ago or one
hundred or a thousand years ago. In the words of Mr. Khanlari, the venerable
Iranian scholar, we originated from the fountains of Time itself. If you visit
the Ancient Treasures of Iran [*Ganj Khani*] in the Iran Bastan [Museum], you
will see that the treasure piece that greets you, welcomes you to the Treasure
House—if the devils [he means the Islamic clergy, though he uses the word
Ahriman, the evil force in Zoroastrianism] haven't destroyed it—speaks of
eighty-five thousand years ago. Our ancestors, eighty-five thousand years ago,
had a valued existence. They had an artistic life; they were craftsmen and
tool makers; they made hunting instruments. Our Aryan ancestors were not
migrants from another place nor did they bring another culture with them.
No. They were themselves cultured. The first of the Iranian migrations was
the migration of the Aryans.

When they reached Iran, they found a valuable culture already there. And
they stayed there. A merging of ancient Aryans and Iranians took place. What
we are today comes from such a powerful culture. It is a culture of which—
unfortunately—we still do not have a single, unified interpretation. The migration of these people cannot be recorded in historical time. I believe they
migrated during an "archeological" time. There are indications of an extended
Ice Age that covered the birthplace of us Aryans. Because of this expansive
freezing, the people had to migrate. And an Iranian—or I should say—an Aryan
who was cultured and uniquely learned, is among these migrators. He was
the one who left us songs [poetry, *Suroud*]; he is the one whose learning and

ideas were immortalized in the vessel of song or *Chakameh* [a kind of Persian verse; loosely translated as an elegy or ode]; and he was Zoroaster. Zoroaster has been traced to ten thousand years ago. I think this is wrong. He belonged to the age of migratory people who began city-dwelling. Or, I should say, people who were hunters and were to become farmers. It is during this period of transition that the Ice Age began. So, when extensive ice covered the whole area, our ancestors were forced to migrate, and this was the first of our seven migrations. I have described this in one of my many publications, in a book called *The Seven Great Iranian Migrations*.

As far as I know, among the migratory people who have come to America, Iranians are among those having the highest levels of education, university education. But from my viewpoint, all this is worthless. Would that they had culture instead of knowledge! The peasant in our country has no learning, but he has culture; that's why he's kept the *Shahnameh*. Our university professor, because he's had no culture, has destroyed the *Shahnameh*. Why? Because he's gone to see what others have written, or what foreigners have written. The Iranian peasant has lived with the *Shahnameh*; he's derived his child's name from the *Shahnameh*. There is a man in Iran who is one of the narrators [*nagghal*, those who recite] of the *Shahnameh* by the name of Abbas Naneh-Hombi. This man, often in his own talk, in a most beautiful manner, from the depth of his heart, swears on the *Shahnameh*. What kind of wondrous book is this that one can swear upon? On the other hand, ask the more than a million Iranians who live in America, "Who among you has ever read the *Shahnameh*?" Maybe you think there are many. I don't believe that the number would reach the number of fingers on one hand. If this is the case, do we, who do not know our own identity, deserve to be called Iranian? Never.

The *Shahnameh* is the Iranian's identity card, the Iranian's report card, the biography of Iran and the Iranian. If someone knows the *Shahnameh*, then he's an Iranian. If he doesn't, then he isn't an Iranian. Or, to go even further, the Russian scholar Mr. Bertells, the German scholar Mr. Wolf, the French scholar Mr. Moun, the Iranian scholar Mr. Khaleghi Motlagh—those who have spent time studying the *Shahnameh*—they are all Iranians. And if someone hasn't found his way to the *Shahnameh*, in my viewpoint, he isn't an Iranian. Because he doesn't know his identity card. The *Shahnameh* is the record, the biography, and the identity card of Iran and every Iranian.

If you don't know your father or mother, you can do whatever you wish. If you know your father and mother, you won't do certain things because you have an inherited identity, because you know this is not worthy of your family's honor. I first read the *Shahnameh* when I was in the fifth grade, in the same year I became acquainted with the gypsy family and Mithraism. My religion? I am a follower of *Mehr* [the Sun]. The most ancient religion or inner perspective is being a worshiper of Mehr. Others have called worshiping Mehr, Mithraism. And unfortunately, or maybe fortunately, they do not have a correct understanding of the Iranian worshiping of Mehr. Worshiping Mehr in Iran was an underground movement.

The story of *Shahnameh* is exactly like the history of city-dwelling or civilization. It tells the story of man's birth and the creation of the world. It spans the story of the creation of the world to the defeat of the Iranians by the Arabs during the Sassanid dynasty.

Culture is the people's life, body, and soul. From our cultural viewpoint, this system has twelve foundations. Only one of the foundations of culture is knowledge. Another of the foundations of culture is blood. And I am not afraid to say that I am a racist. I am a racist, and I believe in racial superiority. I believe that no two people are equal. The world is a battleground for worth, and only worthy people can enter this battle. I don't believe in equality and brotherhood. Not at all. I am a racist and I believe in racial superiority, and I think those who don't acknowledge it are afraid. Because at no time can one person agree that he's equal to another. Whoever says so is deluding himself. Because no one internally can think of himself as equal. Therefore, I don't want to delude myself into thinking that all races are equal. This is not true either in human beings or in animals. So what if they call me racist? So nothing.

See, *Khanum*, Hitler was a German. He was a man who rose from that culture. Hitler insulted the Iranians. He called us barbarians. An Iranian, an important scholar, Professor Aryapars, wrote a letter to him [Hitler] and said, "You haven't understood who the Iranians are. When you want to boast about yourself, you say you are an Aryan. Where did the Aryan come from? You have to know that your origins are from Iran."

You think: What did Hitler, with his SS, do to this man? Skin him? Or send him to the ovens? No, Hitler sent two of his SS officers to Professor Aryapars to bring him with honor to the palace. And Hitler said to him, "I read your letter, and I apologize." Today, the world has not reached the right judgment about someone like Hitler. And the reason is obvious. Because the mass media, television, radio, the newspapers are in the hands of the Jews in the world. They have money and so they write history. If one day the Aryans conquer the world, they will undoubtedly write the history of the world.

Why do you exonerate the Germans and yet condemn the Islamic Revolution?
I didn't say what the Germans did was good. If you remember, I said I can't even behead a chicken. But, if I was the head of an army facing the Arabs, I would say, don't even spare their children. When Islam, for the second time, invaded my country, how many youths died every day? During this period, with the brainwashing our children went through, how much more has religion grown, and how has it led to our regression? And regression not just in our own country. Fourteen hundred years ago, Islam came to the dry, burning country of the Arabs. Maybe for them, Islam was one of the greatest rewards of God.

This greatest mercy of God, for that dry country, was like rain. But for my country it came like the torrent of death.

I believe whoever wants to know Iran and Iranians should read the *Shahnameh* at least once. If the rulers of our country had read even one small legend of the *Shahnameh* once, only once, we wouldn't have reached the dark days that we have now reached.

Ali Behdad

In earlier sections, Ali told of his childhood in Sabzevar, his education in Tehran, and his involvement in the early days of the revolution. He left Iran at seventeen, the year of the hostage crisis, and found himself in a high school in Lincoln, Nebraska. Here he talks of the stages in which exile constructed a renewed sense of national and cultural identity.

When I left Iran during the revolution, I found myself in Lincoln, Nebraska, where I attended a Catholic high school. I don't know what that tells you about Iranian middle-class choices. In order to come to the United States you have to have admission from a university or high school. There was this institution in Tehran that, back then, if you paid them seven or eight thousand tomans, would get you an admission and the I-20 form. There were a lot of kids who ended up in bizarre universities. So I got into Pious X and didn't know that "X" meant ten and thought of Malcolm X and assumed that was the kind of school I was to attend. My parents sent me out because the schools were closed; they were worried, and I wanted to come.

And so I arrived in Nebraska and went to this little house filled with many Iranians. I said, "I don't want to be here. Look, I came from Iran to learn English, and I don't want to be with Iranians." So they got me an American family with whom I stayed, a Catholic family. They in fact helped me to graduate in one semester—the school had wanted me to stay and do all sorts of religion courses. And then came the hostage crisis and I couldn't leave. So I went to the University of Nebraska for a year and a half.

High school was very alienating. We were treated terribly by Catholic kids. They were basically Midwestern kids who had never seen Iranians. And the Iranian kids were wild and crazy. No one wanted to go out with the Iranians. I had to shave my mustache as soon as I arrived; that was my sign of the revolution, but you weren't allowed to have facial hair in this high school. I took an English course with a Sister Amata who got me excited about literature.

I was at the University of Nebraska during the hostage crisis. I open my book, *Belated Travelers*, with one of my memories of this time. Let me read it to you. It was a terrible experience of being cornered:

> Many times during my reflections on the beginnings of this intellectual journey, the study of the culture and political implications of the Western representation of Orientals, the violent memory of one cold autumn night in 1979 has returned to me. While working on a writing assignment in my dormitory room on the campus of a midwestern university in the United States late one night, I was startled by the belligerent voices of two fellow resident students shouting anti-Iranian slogans at my door. Soon their violent words were accompanied by the sound of darts sinking into my door. Imprisoned and claustrophobic—thus reenacting feelings I had often felt during those 444 days of the hostage crisis—I silently waited trapped inside my room until the campus police arrived. During those harrowing minutes, well before I had learned much about Orientalism, I could not but feel scapegoated by the power of representation and stereotypes that had transformed me into a metonymy of what the Middle East signifies in the collective imaginary of the United States: incomprehensible terrorism and fanaticism. Although I finally managed to repress the terrifying memory of that experience—well after my American students had forgotten the hostage crisis—I could not overlook the way my identity as an "Oriental" in the United States had been interpellated by the violence of popular representation of the Middle East and Islam. Thus, through my experience I came to realize early on to a large degree how the cultural confrontation between the West and the Middle East is of a discursive nature. It should not be surprising that I later became interested in the genealogy of those representations and tried to understand the history that had helped to construe me as a threatening, threatened Other. This book emerges from that personal interrogation, and in some ways its writing "exorcises" the violent image-repertoire that has haunted me. (Behdad 1994, vii—viii)

That was an important memory I had to write about, because it is part of the cultural imaginary of what it means to be Iranian. So that was my Nebraska experience. Terrible depressing experience.

It was only when I got to Michigan that I began to feel at home. After Berkeley I went to New York City and worked in restaurants and lived with my friend Masood Ghandahari, which was again tough but interesting. We did that for a year, and then I started graduate school at Michigan (Ann Arbor). I loved Ann Arbor. What made it different? My social life was better. I was respected more, and it's amazing how acceptance makes a difference to you. All of a sudden I was very popular, had no problem going out, and women were all over me. I know this sounds silly, but it's not. It's very profound—the effect of rejection and then becoming desirable.

I think the shift was this: in Nebraska and Berkeley, I apologized for my Iranianness in explaining my identity. That was something I didn't think about back then. But in graduate school my Iranianness is what made me popular, albeit in an exoticist way. I was also theoretically sophisticated, and that made me a "star" student, because in Berkeley I had done a lot of theory, or at least I got the jargon. So I was ahead of a lot of other students in the early '80s. I knew Lacan, I knew Freud, and I had read my Marx and Foucault when I was a kid.

For so long I did not have a sense of national identity. You know that the Iranians of my generation who came to the United States have a particular kind of shame. I told you about personal shame. But let me tell you about political shame. I came a few months before the hostage crisis. And soon the hostage crisis happened. And I, a seventeen- or eighteen-year-old kid away from my family, was trapped in this country in a very bizarre way. To be Iranian was marked for people of my generation in this country by the hostage crisis, the way we were ashamed of our Iranianness. I did not cook anything Iranian until about four or five years ago. I didn't have any Iranian things as I now do anywhere in my apartment. It was not until two or three years ago that I celebrated *Norooz* and put out the *Haft Seen*. Those are elements of culture that were being repressed. When I wanted to go out and socialize with people during the hostage crisis I would say I was Afghani, I was Italian—anything so as not to say I was Iranian. I was ashamed to own my Iranianness—something that now I am recuperating in Los Angeles. That's why it's important for me to be here.

You are asking about my cultural identity. And that is not a stance but rather memory traces—the stories from childhood, the details I associate with eating, what I associate with the everyday. *Irani boodan* [being Iranian] in Los Angeles means being able to go to Super Jordan and being able to buy all the fresh *sabzi* [herbs] that I need and return and eat them with feta cheese and *noon* [bread]. *Irani boodan* means being able to socialize and speak bilingually with people. Those are the everyday things that constitute cultural identity. Memory tracings are like markings of culture on you, the way those practices interpellate you as an individual with a certain taste.

Also, a lot of the people you interview come from the middle classes. I've become very conscious of that through my marriage to Laura, a Chicana. I've simultaneously become critical of and have learned about my class. I've become critical of our tendencies. So *Irani boodan* to me also means these kinds of silly practices—making people fascinated with BMWs and surfaces and clothes and superficial relations. And those are things I don't like and want not to emulate.

I like Los Angeles. Here I am sort of proud of my Iranianness. Yes, it's a kind of arrival. It's also an identity. It's great to have people coming over and enjoying themselves, a big shift from having darts thrown at your door. Los Angeles has given me a way of reconciling with my sense of homelessness. I really feel homeless in a very profound way because of a lack of family, a lack of contact with home, because of a total absence of home that exile is about. In L.A. you see Iranians all over. And people know about Iranians. You don't have to explain anymore, something that I had to do even in an accepting place like Ann Arbor. Everybody has at least eaten some Persian food in Westwood. And the school has many Iranians, who now are so happy there is an Iranian professor here. So these kids will come up to me and say, "Oh my God, I didn't know there was an Iranian who did literature!"

So it's been good for me and for the students to have this sense of community. I have grad students in Comp. Lit., for example, who are Iranians who work with me. Also L.A. gives this sense of home. If I want Persian videos or music, I go around the corner and buy a tape. So it's a different sense of arrival. And now Iranianness has become a kind of political project for me in a way that it had never been. What I mean is that I feel political, especially living with a woman who is also a person of color from a much more displaced community, a much more disempowered community, a much more violated community in many ways.

I want to educate and work against racism within the Iranian community— a tremendous amount of racism exists in our community. A lot of Iranian students in UCLA are bound up with many of the racist attitudes of their society. And I feel a responsibility as an intellectual to make them aware of other possibilities, to criticize the community in ways that it hasn't been so far. It has been a community that has been caught within its own materialist drives, and though I personally don't believe that one person can change a community, yet I hope to mediate and serve as a catalyst for some changes. That's my hope—to politicize the Persian community.

One of the sad things, for instance, I encounter among the Iranian community in Los Angeles is the fact that they buy into this sort of government immigration discourse—that is to say that they blame Latinos for the misery of California's economy. They blame African Americans for their laziness, and for crime in the street. And that, from these people who up to ten years ago were the object of the kind of violence I experienced. They have now become—what's the Iranian proverb?—the pot that is hotter than its soup. Their classism too adds to this. So one of my projects is to make at least some people aware of these problems: "Look, you're an immigrant yourself; why do we have to blame economic problems on another immigrant community? Why this hatred?"

Is Iranian exile similar to any other exile?
I think Iranian exile is like Cuban exile. It is politically conservative for the most part, and it's economically privileged for the most part. Even those who are not doing well had a history of doing well. They came from the middle class. But after reading *Irangeles* [the book of photographs, interviews, and essays edited by Ron Kelley, Jonathan Friedlander, and Anita Colby] I'm skeptical of any generalization I make. The book tells you not to assume generalizations; it gives you a sense of diaspora in ways that are accurate.

Also, that book confirms the class bias among Iranians in Ron Kelley's chapter called "Wealth and Illusions of Wealth."

My homesickness and nostalgia form a kind of black spot. It's a black spot that is unnameable. My life in the United States has been a kind of in-betweenness that constitutes the black spot so deep within me. I still want to get back. I haven't completely unraveled this myself. It's interesting that I always use the word "melancholia" as opposed to "mourning." Freud makes a distinction between melancholia as the unnameable and mourning where you know what it is you have lost, say, your father. You mourn it and then go beyond it. But in melancholia you can't name it, you feel this unease, this dis-ease.

This brings us back to the earliest part of our talk. It's almost hard for me to say what I feel nostalgic for. I feel nostalgic for the possibility of walking with my friend Masood and talking with him, I feel nostalgic for walking on Pahlavi Avenue and looking in stores, I feel nostalgic for going to Shah Reza across from Tehran University and seeing all the bookstores next to one another. I feel nostalgic for my parents and my friends. It's funny but I feel nostalgic, almost, for the memories that I am starting to lose. Nostalgia is always about an absence; it's about that sense of homelessness. I feel nostalgic for someplace I can call home. And I think my search in exile for a sense of home has a lot to do with trying to overcome that sense of nostalgia.

And for me on a personal level I sense the pain that I as a young boy felt and still feel that I could not see my parents. I didn't see my mother until nine years after I left Iran, and I didn't see my father until ten years after I left Iran. I still haven't seen my youngest brother. I haven't seen any of my nieces and nephews, and we have eight. I see a lot of Iranians in Los Angeles who are much more "normal" than me. I don't mean to say that I am totally abnormal, but having their parents around, they have an easier way of flowing between Iranianness and Americanness. And so much of my conflict comes from the fact that there is in my life this fundamental absence. I haven't grown out of my childhood in Iran. I think of Eva Hoffman's *Lost in Translation*, in the sense that if I go back even once to Iran I might perhaps be cured of my nostalgia. But until then, I still have that sense of loss.

Zia Ashraf Nasr

The reification of the past is a way for some exiles to forget the present. The oldest of my interviewees, whose remarkable memory and narrative powers filled days of tapes with vivid and detailed stories of childhood and maturity in Iran, had only this to say about life in exile.

Now I am in this country.

When I was here in the 1950s I tried to build a little Iran around me, but I don't do that now. Because now I can't think of the present Iran. I only think of the old Iran and hope that Iran will return to the way it was—a place where we could all work toward something. The present Iran is not the country I love. I don't see the present Iran as my own. Yes, I feel in exile from the new Iran, from the old Iran, and from America. We who have a strong love for our country really suffer from this loss. Sometimes I sit and think and ask myself again and again—who am I? Where am I from? I don't see myself as part of this nation. And I don't like the present Iran.

I am a person without a country.

Susan Bazargan

Susan, who came to the United States for graduate study and chose not to return to Iran after the revolution, who now teaches English literature at Eastern Illinois University, translated twelve of the Persian tapes and read most of this manuscript in an earlier incarnation. When I asked if I could include her story, she said she would prefer not to be interviewed; she preferred, she said, to provide her own essay on exile written after she read this manuscript. Hers, therefore, is a narrative written in a different mode: the self-reflexive musings of an Iranian academician in the United States who chooses to opt for a form other than the spontaneously oral. I choose it as the last selection as a response to the narratives that precede it.

Persian Letters

Letter One

The difference between here and there is the letter "t." A sign, a floating signifier—that is one place to begin discussing exile. Having lived away from Iran for the last twenty years, I find my imaginary wanderings to "home" and back taking more and more the shape of letters. As missives from home, letters arrive bearing heavy stamps, images with unfamiliar referents. But letters also carry me back to the Persian alphabet—the *aleph-ba*. I cross from English to Farsi, "t" transforming into the small "teh" and the large "teh." In elementary school in Tehran, I wrote endless pages of "mashgh" both at school and home to master the Persian script. And so I would write words like "toot" (white mulberry—its sweetness and fragrance float in memory), which started with the small "t" and ended with the large "t," over and over again, using a reed pen and an inkpot. The lowly pencil could not do the job—it did not allow the fingers to impose the needed pressure on paper to form the delicate bends and twists, the tangents and swerves of Farsi letters. Fountain pens were allowed only after third grade and ball point pens were forbidden. And so in first grade, my fingers guided the tortuous dance of letters on paper as I practiced the intricacies of Persian calligraphy. A minor crisis occurred when the tip of the reed pen broke; it had to be taken up to the teacher who sharpened it with a special knife. At home, a few times without my parents' knowledge, I used a razor blade to sharpen the pens myself. I had to be extra cautious not to cut myself. The inkpot posed another problem. The ink would spill—on my hands, on the finished homework, on my clothes, even once on brand-new furniture my parents had bought—after months of saving—for *Norooz*. My physicist father brought all sorts of chemicals home from the lab to clean the damned spot, but to no avail. Writing was not an easy task, I realized; it could cut; it could spill over and stain. But writing also produced "calli-graphy"— calli, kallos, beauty. And so it was in the arduous, repeated task of dipping unreliable reed pens into ink and writing that I learned to connect the body with a site, a location, a blank page and letters.

Letter Two

One-thousand-and-one nights. Night is another locale of exile. Day organized by work carries the rhythms of the adopted culture. But the night is free, one's own time, time to roam and remember. The Chinese-box narrative framework of the one-thousand-and-one-nights tales I read as a child structures my own story. One begins at the beginning but then realizes that her narrative unfolds as a series of physical and psychological displacements, one tale containing another that contains (and is contained in) multiple others. I remember the relief I felt as a child—reading late at night yet another tale of Sinbad the sailor—when the "first," originary narrator would finally reappear in the story and bring it to a closure. I knew then that Sinbad was home and safe and I could go to sleep. Exile is the impossibility of recovering that first narrator and the safety of home. In insomnia lies exile. Having lost the first narrator, one understands the lesson of Scheherazade—that survival of the self lies in one's ability to compose endless narratives of the self.

Nocturnal returns to home can also take the shape of disturbing dreams. My recurring one includes the figure of a servant, a woman who calls me because she has not been paid. In the dream I realize I owe her many months of wages, but it is not clear when the debt started. "How much do I owe you?" There is no response. My debt to my past accumulates, and I cannot settle it since I cannot locate its origins or its amount.

The loss of origins is also the loss of authority, of master narratives. Growing up in Iran, one was always conscious of the gaze of the authorial Other—the "they" who watched us, foreign or domestic. Exilic freedom implies a freedom from the faceless face of they. Hence the exilic, existential angst. For the displaced individual, the question of "Why am I here?" informs daily life and shapes one's relation to others. With remarkable accuracy, the coveted green card marks one's in-between state. The card bestows permanent residency on its owner, but it also registers her as an "alien." Hence a life of interesting contradictions—at the cost of unbelonging, one's real and fictional homes extend from East to West, from here to there.

Letter Three

Flight. "There" is only a flight away. I was introduced to one image of flight when I first started reading *Kalileh and Dimneh* at school. The origin of these ancient animal fables is India. The third-century A.D. Panchatantra is one text in which one finds stories of the two jackals, Kalileh and Dimneh, living in the kingdom of animals. But this is not gentle La Fontaine. Kalileh and Dimneh, who exchange stories all through the collection, are worldly, ambitious creatures—crafty, often devious, and always eloquent. One story Dimneh tells describes the flight of a turtle. The turtle lives with two ducks in a pond and becomes fast friends with them. When the time comes for the ducks to fly away, the turtle mourns and begs to be taken with them. The ducks finally come up with a plan. They find a long stick; each duck holds one end in his beak; the turtle hangs on the middle with his mouth, and so the three lift off. Before departure, the ducks make the turtle promise one thing: not to open his mouth on any account. The plan is a success until people begin to notice the curious trio in flight. Surprised, they cry, "Look, the turtle is flying! How hilarious!" The cries of amazement continue until the turtle, unable to contain himself, shouts: "It's none of your damned business!" As a child I grieved over the fate of the turtle and imagined his last moments when he fell—that final free-fall. But I also learned the moral of the story: silence, despite public harassment, is necessary in precarious times and situations. Iranians in exile have often chosen silence, especially during those media events that once more demonize them as hostage-takers and terrorists. But the image of the turtle's flight says more to me. Listening to some Iranians tell the story of their flight from home—traveling on mules and motorcycles, many with small children—I find their journey as incredible as that of a hanging turtle in flight. But Iranians, for the most part, are resilient, enterprising survivors, and having arrived, they can, finally, speak.

Letter Four

What is "Iranian" about being an Iranian?

Being Iranian is to make the body the site of several cultures and their accompanying rituals. In exile, the body becomes acutely conscious of itself and the protective layers of cultural fabric that now seem ill-fitting. One has arrived at the party dressed in the wrong clothes. But the self-consciousness provokes inquiries into "Iranianness": in exile one finally learns about home.

Iranian life begins and ends in ceremonies that mediate the relation between self and other, rituals that over time have become ingrained in the body—audible in language, in voice and tonality, visible in bodily gestures, expressions, and eye contact. Hence the joke: "From one farsang away (a farsang is roughly six kilometers), you can tell the guy is an Iranian." The mediation between self and other is of extreme significance since acknowledgment of the other is at the crux of Iranian life. To be noticed, one does not have to take drastic measures. It is this perpetual attention to the other, to a degree unknown in American culture, that shapes the principles of Iranian social life—hospitality, charity, and the preservation of the family and its reputation.

From the rudimentary bargaining over the price of cucumbers to the elaborate body language and phrases used when one enters a room as a guest, Iranian social life is consumed in well-rehearsed, extended negotiations. One might perceive these familiar dramas as a source of safety and belonging or as an entangled web of unnecessary confinement. But the Iranian love for "low" and "high" bargaining tells us something else about the people. Having learned the difficult art of negotiation with invaders and immigrants populating the country from the time of the ancient Persians to the present, generations of Iranians have produced and preserved a culture that is heterogeneous and eclectic.

Letter Five

The Iran I remember was a country of people from different ethnicities, languages, and religions. A ride in a taxicab, that microcosm of Iranian urban society, could reveal such diversity. (A taxicab in Tehran functions most of the time like a public minibus, the route improvised by the driver as he picks up passengers at random stops.) The automobile itself was made in the West and assembled in Iran. On the cab's dashboard, one could see evidence of the Iranian faith in words—various signs written in beautiful Arabic script, mostly Islamic messages such as "In the name of Allah, the merciful." But the radio, always on, played classical Persian music, the lyrics of the songs based on Persian poetry, words of Hafiz, Saadi, Molavi, and others, first recited and then sung. Words from the *Rubaiyat* might fill the air: "And, as the Cock crew, those who stood before / The Tavern shouted—'Open then the Door! / You know how little while we have to stay, / And, once departed, may return no more.' " No one seemed bothered by the contradictions. Among the passengers one might see a carefully veiled woman sitting next to one dressed in jeans and a designer T-shirt. The cab driver gossiped with the passengers, who might be Azari, Kurdish, or Armenian. Efforts were made to keep the male passengers in front and the women in the back. If by chance an argument arose, the driver would invite all to calm down and "send a Salavaat," a praise to God and his prophet Mohammad. The chant usually worked.

Letter Six

In the domestic arena, too, diversity was the rule rather than the exception. My father came from Tabriz, the center of the province of Azarbaijan. His mother tongue was Turkish, or Azari, and he spoke Persian with a bit of an accent. My mother was from Tehran, and Persian was the main language spoken at our home. But when my father's relatives visited, it was the long, drawn-out vowels of Turkish that resounded in our living room. But never for a moment did my family's bilingualism seem odd, significant, or even interesting. The shift from one language, one "ethnicity" to another, was effortless, as natural as serving tea to my aunts and cousins. The family's religion was Islam, and my father's sister wore the veil, but my mother did not. Yet the difference in religious orthodoxy did not create animosity between the families. It was a difference both sides respected. My friends across the street were Baha'i; another neighbor was Jewish, and some of my classmates spoke Armenian and celebrated Christmas. In all my years in Iranian public schools, I do not recall even one incident involving what might be called religious or ethnic persecution or harassment directed toward the "minorities" (I did not learn the word until I came to the United States). Dressed in our ugly, gray uniforms, following Ferdowsi's advice—"seek knowledge from cradle to the grave"—we walked to school together six days a week, studied hard, played little, and knew that life for our parents was a daily struggle.

My family belonged to the slowly developing Iranian middle class, among them educators and some government employees. My father was a university professor, and my mother taught English in high school. After finishing high school in Tabriz, my father had passed a special national exam that enabled him to study in France. He was among the first young Iranian men to do so, thanks to a government-funded program established by Reza Shah to send Iranian males to Europe for higher education. When my father and his peers returned to Iran, they were hired as the first faculty of what later became Tehran University.

My mother first learned English at the Iran Bethel school in Tehran, a progressive high school for young women established by American missionaries in Tehran. (American missionaries first came to Iran in the late nineteenth century and settled in Urumiyeh, Azarbaijan, populated by a relatively large Christian Armenian community. Later on, in Tehran, the missionaries set up high schools for boys and girls.) She then attended the Teachers College at Tehran University. My family, for better or worse, was "Westernized." And yet, fundamentally, our "Iranianness" remained intact. Family dynamics were governed by Iranian values, rituals, and measures. My father taught physics and chemistry, but he recited Persian poetry from memory and had a great passion for Persian classical music.

Letter Seven

As a child my own sense of "West" came first in the form of bright colors, found in the "Little Golden Books" for children I discovered in the Iran-America cultural center's library in Tehran. Children's books in Persian were unavailable. So with some schooling, I taught myself how to read English; I still remember the profound joy of reading *Little House on the Prairie*. Much later in life, when my entrance exam scores failed to qualify me to follow in my father's footsteps and study physics in Tehran University, he grudgingly agreed to send me abroad.

When I arrived in America, I spoke fluent English and thought myself adequately Westernized. And yet, I quickly realized the depth of my alienation. Presiding over the American melting pot were discriminating chefs. The acquisition of the new culture, I learned, would be painful, its possession virtually impossible. In the late '60s, as a college student, I learned the paradox of being a foreigner in this country: to be part of the culture, I had to remain outside the culture. Publicly, as long as I identified myself as an Iranian student—an exotic cultural object—I was welcome, supported, even sought after. But in the late '70s, when after being away from the States for nine years I returned to do graduate studies, a drastic shift in my public persona occurred. I was now associated with hostage-takers and terrorists. But of the two equally false public identities, I preferred the second. The reasons for exclusion were now blatantly clear rather than insinuated. But I was told to keep a low profile; I watched my Iranian friend dye her hair an ugly blond and heard of other friends changing their names into Italian-sounding ones. I did not take such measures. If I had been transformed into the Other—exotic in the late '60s, demonic in the late '70s—I had to resist the concept of America as Other, at least in my imagination. My divided identities, separated by one decade, mirrored another dichotomy, the two sharply-divided projections of America itself: the land of the free, the land of opportunity; the great imperialist and oppressor. The commonplace analysis, that America's first identity was only guaranteed by the second, seemed too facile to me.

To seek partial refuge from this hall of mirrors, I joined the university community, one enclave of American society that, in my experience, is at least interested in inquiring into the question of dichotomies and the dynamics of oppression. My decision not to return to Iran was based on saving my partial visibility. The veil, imposed on women by the new regime, in both a material and abstract sense, would have obliterated even my "low profile." Taking a cue from the word itself—"profile" comes from "pro," forward, and "filare," to spin, draw a line—I decided to move forward and spin my own lines, write my Ph.D. dissertation. I had the emotional and moral support of my children (aged three, seven, and nine), the resources of the university, and my own desire and will to do so. Perhaps my refusal to join the trenches in Iran was a form of betrayal. I had not "served my country." But by now, the concept of country, of nationality, had become extremely problematic for me. How could I serve that which I could not locate?

Letter Eight

In 1721, Montesquieu published *The Persian Letters*, a critique of European society presented in a series of letters written by two fictitious Persian travelers to France, Usbek, and Rica. The Persians are "innocent observers" used as mask for Montesquieu to satirize European conventions and institutions. But the book also offers an image of Persia as a land of seraglios, eunuchs, and unending harems, that spurious representation typically found in travel books of the eighteenth century, Montesquieu's main source of information on Iran. For too long, the Orient has been used as mask, as a convex mirror, as a playground for the Western imagination. At the dawn of the twenty-first century, Iranians can finally tell their own stories. They can write their own letters.

CHAPTER 5

Epilogue

Whereas some of the narratives above orchestrate history, displacement, and exile with melancholic loss, others have used that loss as the scaffolding for possibility (even as identity itself is premised on lack) and find ways to fill in that lack with compensatory possibilities. The narratives collected here provide a sense of identity and history as palimpsest—remembered, reified, and refashioned in the present. My strategy throughout has attempted to represent the narratives surrounding exile. Ideally, these stories will complicate the current state of cultural criticism about Iran, will get around the "un-get-aroundable fact that all ethnographical descriptions . . . are the describer's descriptions, and not those of the described" (Geertz 1973, 145), and therefore serve as a means to liberate both speakers and readers from the past as silence, stereotype, or nightmare.

Michael M. J. Fischer and Mehdi Abedi describe Iranian culture as "woven on a geographically situated loom, one beam end set in Iran and one set abroad in America and Europe" (1990, 254). They distinguish between the suspended paralysis of the exile (*avareh*) who lives in a world of memory, and the fertile mobility of the migrant (*muhajir*) whose assimilation nevertheless cannot "project into a future that gives the present significance" (255). The most famous Iranian poet and writer to elaborate on distinctions between exile and migration was Gholam Hossein Saedi, who died in exile in 1985. Although he understood the titles given to his condition—political and existential exile (*tabeed* and *ghorbat*)—he preferred the word *barsakhi* (purgatorial despair/limbo) for the state in which he found himself. Unlike the immigrant who has chosen to join the diasporic community and gradually blend into the larger alien culture, the exile, he says, has no choice and therefore cares only about his loneliness:

> The exile . . . is a vagabond who cannot gather the scattered parts of his being. . . . For a long time, he clings to his past identity . . . clinging to the memories of his country, clinging to the memories of his friends and companions, companions of struggle, companions in ideology, clinging to a few verses by Hafez, or to stories he remembers; sometimes clinging to using a few idiomatic expressions to spice up his speech, or to telling a joke and making others laugh. (Saedi 1993, 33)

Unlike the exile, the Iranian migrants are not, in Saedi's words, confused and crippled: "Death never stalked them with its long, sharp scythe, with its machine guns and semiautomatics. Neither the former regime nor the present one ever bothered them" (32). Saedi's anxious and alcohol-driven exile lives in fatigue and hunger; his worst sickness is fear and dread of expulsion from the host country, and even of such mundane happenings as a ring at the door or the glance of an unarmed policeman (33). He defines his exilic state as that of a dead person pretending to be alive. Imprisoned by both regimes, Saedi died, or drank himself to death, in Paris in 1985.

The purpose of my work has been to offer alternative narratives to those reified by any single source or by images in mass media. I assume, along with Adorno and Horkheimer, that all reification is a forgetting, and that what it forgets can be partially recovered in the inexplicable, fluid, and unstable memory of another, in an other's story that recalls the matrix that produced all the others. In collecting these stories, my intention is not to valorize or sentimentalize the idea of origins, be it contained in the concepts of "home," "religion," "nation," "language," or "motherland." Along with Adorno, I believe in a healthy dose of suspicion toward the "nature" of past attachments: "It is part of morality not to be at home in one's home" (Adorno 1974, 39). Homes, families, clans, nations, and languages can be safe havens or prisons, or both. Said and Auerbach, both writers in exile, quote the twelfth-century monk Hugo of St. Victor who wrote:

> The man who finds his homeland sweet is still a tender beginner; he to whom every soil is as his native one is already strong; but he is perfect to whom the entire world is as a foreign land. The tender soul has fixed his love on one spot in the world; the strong man has extended his love to all places; the perfect man has extinguished his. (Hugo of St. Victor, 1961)

The voices in this book, however, are not those of "perfect" men or women. All share with other emigrés and exiles certain patterns of narrations that attempt to negotiate new ways of remembering the past and living in the present. Although some exiles come uniquely equipped to make a virtue out of their duality and double vision, others resist dialogue with an alternative culture and retreat into a monolithic defense of a unified imaginary past. "Most people," writes Said, "are principally aware of one culture, one setting, one home; exiles are aware of at least two, and this plurality of vision gives rise to an awareness of simultaneous dimensions, an awareness that—to borrow a phrase from music—is contrapuntal" (Said 1984, 55).

But exiles also construct a fantasy community that has much to do with fear and desire that derive from the contingencies of the past, and from the instabilities of memory and of history. And this too has been a part of my project—to narrate the materials from which they construct the fabric of their lives and their new culture, and to show the move from "being" to "feeling" Iranian in the United States.[1] Ali Behdad, who called himself an exile when I spoke to him in 1994, now in 1999, after returning to Iran for several visits, says that he no longer feels like an exile but an immigrant. Living in Los Angeles, he says, is now a choice even as his homelessness is a choice. In 1999, he wrote to say:

> Ironically I feel more at home in L.A., one of the most "unhomely" places on earth than being in Iran! But perhaps L.A. is the only place an ex-exile like me would be able to live happily! As an immigrant, I only feel at home where there is a plurality of identities, where I am one of the many possible identities. L.A. allows me to become American in a different way than the assimilationist model. I feel my Iranianness has been at once consolidated and diluted. Consolidated because I am comfortable with it—for example, I am now married to an Iranian and regularly go to Iran and do things the Iranian way—and more diluted because it has been constantly changed and challenged by other immigrant identities I encounter and socialize with in L.A. It is perhaps for this reason that I did not feel entirely at home when I went back to Iran. Perhaps, as my old therapist observed, "I have finally found a home in homelessness." Home is no longer fixed, and I am no longer fixated on a nostalgic object—Iran.

The state of exile has always been subject to debate. Exile, in the words of the Palestinian exile Edward Said, is a state of terminal loss, of an "unhealable rift forced between a human being and a native place, between the self and its true home" (1984, 49). Said echoes the tragic Greek paradigm of exile as loss. Socrates, we know, chose hemlock over exile,[2] but Ovid's Rome, Dante's Florence, Joyce's Dublin, Kundera's Prague, and Rushdie's Bombay suggest the possibility of other paradigms picked up more recently by Joseph Brodsky, Nurrudin Farah, and Anton Shammas—that exile can also be celebrated as "the whetstone" (Shammas's term) on which to sharpen talent: "Maybe one should be grateful to the State of Israel for expelling that Palestinian writer," muses Shammas (1990, 85). And Farah says (echoing Joyce) that to write inspired fiction about Somalia, "I had to leave the country" (1990, 67). Joseph Brodsky suggests that since it is tyranny that gives rise to modern exile, one might celebrate the freedom of the democracy to which one flees, but quickly adds "the disheartening idea that the freed man is not the free man" (Brodsky 1990, 109).

The Iranians to whom I spoke were only the most recent among those who share exilic sensibility. Iranian literature, religion, and identity have incorporated prolonged lamentations for that from which the subject has been separated. Therefore, my use of the term "exile" does not refer only to physical separation from a country. It is also the cultural and psychic exile that the alienated feel within a country. Although at its most ahistorical exile is charged with the "uncanny" recollection of another exile from our original "imaginary" home, a country that never was, it takes shape in the specifics of a history and culture.

Memory replays tensions even as the exile struggles to produce meaning out of the unsettled space between the self and absent other, between childhood's singularity and its loss, between Iran and the United States. That production of meaning takes on different cultural forms when, for instance, it is informed by Sufi yearning for mystical union with God or prelapsarian unity, or when, on another (loosely Lacanian) register, we can read such loss as the fall from childhood's imaginary plenitude into the symbolic or social state of adulthood. Whereas the imaginary may share a common currency in most cultures, the symbolic, because it is determined by history, is more culture-specific. So, too, desire may be unconscious, but it is determined by the Other, by the Law of the Father (the symbolic) that structures desire. Iranian culture provides a multiplicity of such structures, with each concentric layer more inaccessible than the other, each providing another alterity, another signifier for constituting the idealized self. In several of our conversations, we wondered what it was in the larger culture that gave a particular spin to Iranian melancholia in exile.

The more ragged the seams of the nation, the more intense the desire for restoration and reconstitution in exile. This truism appears not only my selection of voices, but also in the illuminating and luminous book by Roy Mottahedeh that he calls "the story of all of us in the last part of the twentieth century"—*The Mantle of the Prophet*. Framed by a meeting between the author and the central figure, Ali Hashemi, the book uses Hashemi's memories as an entry into a core vision of Persian and Islamic epistemology that fed the current Islamic Revolution. Hashemi recalls a life cloistered within literal and figurative gardens, and within layers of families—the immediate, the extended, and the imaginary (*Sayyid*) family of the prophet; a life defined within certain charged and familiar geographic centers—the shrine whose mirrored surfaces reflected identically-clothed mourners, a house whose divisions mirrored each other architecturally even as they served to split the family by gender and occupation, and a world triangulated into the mosque, the bazaar, and the school. In fact, Mottahedeh's book is itself an example of an exercise in a particular type of masculinist Iranian imagining marked by cultural traces. It narrates the central and real figure of Ali Hashemi as the product of a vast and nameable cultural location constructed by a naturalized fall away from the feminine into its seamless links with such earlier (masculine) Persian poets and philosophers as the eleventh-century Abu Ali Ibn Sina (known in the West as Avicenna), the early twentieth-century Ahmad Kasravi, the twelfth-century Sohravardi, and the more recent Ali Shariati and Ayatollah Khomeini.

In Mottahedeh's provocative book, the problematic space between individual desire and symbolic order is negotiated through a series of poetic and mystical metaphors that, in pursuit of an idealized oneness, elides political vexations, collapses the human into the masculine, the individual into the cosmic, and in the course of articulating universal mystery, constructs a subject protected and enclosed by mirrored structures. It is precisely those structures of desire and alterity that set the stage for inarticulate loss, and that both create and alleviate the anxieties of division and of belonging.

Mottahedeh's book, as well as the ultimate Book (the *Shahnameh*) that served as the key to Sobhan's identity, and the Holy Book (the Qur'an) that is the source of Nuri's anxiety, and the book I am writing, are all part of the narratives through which we create and evade anxieties about belonging, home, and nation. These stories suggest a sense of nation and identity as processes of becoming, as occupied zones of fear and longing between here and there, with the uncertain "here" always in a state of invasion by an imagined "there." Diasporic identity, in spite of a lost past, in spite of exilic searches for origins, oneness, and authenticity, is necessarily a "traveling identity,"[3] one that disturbs the boundaries of location, power, and politics in the process of migratory transformation. Although some of our migrants and exiles seem possessed by an unquenchable need to return to a center and others tell of a more joyfully uncentered journey, each constructs a slightly different nomadic narrative of seeking to find "home" in spaces that were at once home and not home. Just as some of us learn to live with the daily doubt that "it is so and it is not so" (the opening to every Persian tale), a sense of living in two simultaneous spaces—perhaps three if we include cyberspace—that nonetheless requires daily reaffirmations of the fictions that we build into a life.

One of the purposes of this book has been to link narratives of displaced Iranians to those of other diasporic communities; to contextualize reified representations of Iran; to open up current representations of Iranian culture through gendered voices from different ethnic, religious, and class backgrounds; and to resist a fundamentalist ideology that perceives cultural memory and the past itself as threats to its present. The narratives of Iranians gathered in this book, therefore, shore a multiplicity of fragments, histories, and cultures against the ruins of memory, against the irrevocable losses of the past and its fictions, and thereby complicate our understanding of who constitutes this newest patch in the fabric of American culture. In our need to both create and evade anxieties about belonging, home, and nation, we constantly build personal narratives whose creation, like the making of the ultimate Book, or any book, becomes part of our perpetual search for unity, identity, and meaning. These narratives are part of that search.

Notes

Preface

1. In contemplating the figures most appropriate for this project, I have been helped by Gayatri Chakravorty Spivak's questions about "texting" as weaving as in textile, of texts that shuttle between two points (the weaver's movement) as they elaborate and embroider ("Acting Bits/Identity Talk," 1992). There are, of course, no two points between which this text shuttles, as there are no fixed points on which to premise diasporic or Iranian identity other than "there" and "here," or "home" and "unhome."

2. The tape Pari later made of this terrified woman's story was inaudible and therefore untranslatable. That was also true of the tape I made during an interview with the chief Iranian Rabbi of Los Angeles.

3. Those readers who wish to amplify this book with sociological data on Iranian diaspora should turn to the work of Mehdi Bozorgmehr and George Sabbagh and to *Encyclopedia Iranica*.

4. See Edmund Wilson 1978 [1929], 223–43.

5. See Homi K. Bhabha's "Culture's In-Between" (1996, 55–60) for his reflections on the "partial" relations between already contaminated migrating cultures, of the Otherness of the self, and on borderline spaces between cultural differences that constitute modernity. See also the poems and stories in Karim and Khorrami's (1991) anthology of Iranian-American writing that rely on "the experience of in-betweenness."

Chapter 1

Epigraph: See Walter Benjamin 1969, 178.

1. David Lloyd (1987, 60). See also Hobsbawm (1991), Bhabha (1990), Kedourie (1993), Breuilly (1982), and Anderson (1991).

2. Here I am thinking of the classic cases of the Armenian, Jewish, and Palestinian diasporas in which uprooting was the result of forced expulsion. See Tololyan (1991), Safran (1991), and Clifford (1994) for elaborations on the changing meanings of this term.

3. I recall here various evocations of home and homelessness from Adorno (1974) who claimed the greater morality was not to feel at home in one's home, to the Sufis who see mystical thought and exercise as the yearning for the return to the ultimate home, to Edward Said's (1983) distinction between "filiation" and "affiliation," to Homi Bhabha's *The Location of Culture:* "To be unhomed is not to be homeless . . . the recesses of the domestic space become sites for history's most intricate invasions. In that displacement, the borders between home and world become confused" (1994, 9). See also Rosemary George who contends that "home is a way of establishing difference," that home, gender, sexuality, race, and class work as "ideological determinants of the subject," and that "the politics of location come into play in the attempt to weave together a subject-status that is sustained by the experience of the place one knows as Home or by resistance to places that are patently 'not home' " (1996, 2). See also Avtar Brah's essay "The homing of diaspora, the diasporising of home" in *Cartographies of Diaspora* (1996, 190ff).

4. For an account of this visit, see my essay "Returning to Iran" (1998b, 3).

5. In arguing the gendered construction of modernity, Afsaneh Najmabadi's work in progress *Female Suns and Male Lions: The Gendered Tropes of Iranian Modernity* breaks down the unified emblem of the Iranian "lion and sun" by explaining that the Lion as Nation (*millat*) was scripted as male whereas the Sun as Homeland (*vatan*) was scripted as female. In reaching beyond the historic limits of the nation-state, diasporic culture, though transnational, isn't merely antinationalist (see Clifford 1994); it builds new communities still connected, if not to nation, then to the idea of a homeland.

6. In a country populated by foreigners, I find it easier to face such essentialist questions as: "Are you *really* Iranian, Pakistani, or American?" My answer to the visiting Pakistani speaker who last asked me that was, "None of the above, all of the above, and the relation between all three."

7. See *The Nation,* July 15/22, 1991, for various musings on the idea of patriotism in practice and in theory.

8. See Haeri's informative reading of the differences between the stability of men's and the instability of women's legal and social identities in Islamic Iran. The determining factor in such status, she writes, is not only the unequally gendered law of inheritance, but rather the state of female sexuality—whether she is virgin, married, divorced, or widowed (1989, 28).

9. See Eliz Sanasarian (1995, 20–21).

10. See Guppy (1988, 61).

11. See Hamid Naficy's (1993) reading of films, periodicals, radio programs, music videos, and television in Los Angeles. He contrasts representations of exilic nostalgia and fetishized representations of a purified past with their commercials that rely on an advertising economy fueled by voracious consumerism. The presence of such established Persian communities as "Irangeles" in Westwood area of Los Angeles buffers immigrants against the anxieties of dislocation and encourages them to preserve cultural separateness from both the hegemonic culture and other disempowered minorities.

12. See Spivak (1988, 154–75) for a provocative reading of Marxist schemes of "value," and of the complicity between Western consumer prosperity and third-world exploitation.

13. Homi Bhabha uses Frantz Fanon's line on "occult instability" to provoke his reflections on the duality of cultural identity formation: the linear, unifying line of traditional history (the pedagogic), and the persistent enactment of loss demanded by change, disrup-

tion, and the counterprocess of subject formation (the performative); see "DissemiNation," pp. 303–4 in Bhabha (1990).

14. In their essay on diaspora and Jewish identity, the Boyarins (1993) valorize diaspora as an historical and theoretical model for a way of being and as an alternative to exclusivist nationalisms. Robin Cohen consolidates a list of features common to diaspora: "(1) dispersal from an original homeland, often traumatically; (2) alternatively, the expansion from a homeland in search of work, in pursuit of trade or to further colonial ambitions; (3) a collective memory and myth about the homeland; (4) an idealization of the supposed ancestral home; (5) a return movement; (6) a strong ethnic group consciousness sustained over a long time; (7) a troubled relationship with host societies; (8) a sense of solidarity with co-ethnic members in other countries; and (9) the possibility of a distinctive creative, enriching life in tolerant host countries" (1997, 180).

15. I am indebted to conversations with Mohamad Tavakoli for help with such categories.

16. Except for two who happened not to mention the subject, all my informants mentioned writers who had been censored, harassed, and, in the case of poets like Golsorkhy, killed by the Shah's regime. Several mentioned writers who had chosen Paris as their place of exile—Alavi, Gholam Hosein Saedi, and Ali Afrashteh—and of others, like Samad Behrangi, who had died exiled in their own country. Nineteenth-century European travelers noted with some surprise the cross-class proclivity of the Iranian for Persian poetry, memorized and recited by illiterate peasant, student, and king. It was not unusual for men to choose a part-time profession as coffee- or tea-house poet, reciting for hours tales from the *Shahnameh* and other poems. There is no comparable tradition of public recitation in the modern Western world; the thought of grown men reciting *Beowulf*, or *Paradise Lost*, or the *Iliad* or the *Odyssey* by the hour with an eager audience day after day would be the only viable hypothetical comparison. Or perhaps, it is in less print-saturated worlds, say India, that epic recitation still remains a vital form of cultural formation. Furthermore, the conflation of poetry with the divine word, of the book with the Book, is apparent in the status of such poets as the thirteenth-century Hafez. It is common cultural practice in towns and villages to ask a question (as one does of the *I-Ching*) of the book of Hafez's poetry, to open it randomly on a page that contains the divinely accurate answer. This practice is called *Faal-i-Hafez*. Tribal and village women were often encouraged to read, but not to write, and the most common texts for them to read and memorize would be the poetry of Ferdowsi and Hafez.

17. See "The Crisis of Secular Politics and the Rise of Political Islam in Iran," where Ali Mirsepassi Ashtiani (1994) discusses the formation of workers' unions, the participation in new political parties, and the sudden increase in presses (from ninety-three before 1940 to almost six hundred after Reza Shah); by the summer of 1942, he tells us, a group of labor organizations formed the Council of United Workers. The larger Union of Iranian Workers and Toilers organized branches in 346 modern industries—a sign of the increased involvement of citizens and workers in political culture (Ashtiani 1994, 53).

18. See Arendt (1965).

19. For illustrations of some of these stamps see Fischer and Abedi (1990) and Abrahamian (1993). In addition to the fine books Michael M. J. Fischer has written on Iran, his essay "Becoming Mollah: Reflections on Iranian Clerics in a Revolutionary Age" (1980a) draws attention to the constellation of figures that produced the charisma of

Khomeini—tropes of the martyr, the lone hero who, unlike other more moderate Ulama, spoke out consistently against the Shah's tyranny, even at the risk of exile and execution. He contrasts Khomeini's populist, confrontational, hyperbolic style with the reasonable scholarly discourse of Shariatmadari or Taleqani. See also Ashtiani's (1994) more recent essay on three currents—conservative, liberal, and radical—that evolved in the Islamic political movements of the 1960s and 1970s.

20. See Naghmeh Sohrabi's (1993) "Soc.Culture.Iranian" for the multiple forms of communal contestation and belonging provided for Iranians on the internet. See also Ella Shohat's (1999) "By the Bitstream of Babylon: Cyberfrontiers and Diasporic Vistas."

Chapter 2

1. The construction of this palanquin is described later in her narrative.

2. Among other questions, I asked if she played games and if boys and girls played together. "Yes, we played in the streets. Near our house was a small square. When we left the *Maktab* we were allowed to play in the square because it was close to our home. We'd play *Gorgam-be-Hava* [Wolf-in-the-Sky]. One person would go to the sky [*Hava*] and couldn't be caught. Another would become *gorg* [wolf] and catch the others. If she caught another person, then she would become *gorg*. This was the kind of game we played in the old days. The other game that the boys played was *Alak-Dolak* [a game with two sticks, a ball, and a base]. The girls played *Ghayem Bashak* [Hide-and-Seek] or *Gorgam-be-Hava*. We were allowed to play with the boys who were our age (we were about five years old then)."

3. Afsaneh Najmabadi's great-grandfather was a contemporary and friend of Pari's uncle Yahya Dowlatabadi before the Constitutional Revolution of 1906–9. The Bab's disciples, Sobh Azal and Bahaullah, were exiled to Turkey where they were visited by Afghani and Yahya Dowlatabadi; the main core of the Constitutional Revolution, Pari claims, was formed outside Iran. Siddiqeh's brother Yahya Dowlatabadi wrote an important book on the Constitutional Revolution in the guise of autobiography, *Hayat Yahya* (Life of Yahya). After the Pahlavi dynasty came to power, Yahya couldn't accept its dictates and chose exile. For a time, he was supervisor of students in Belgium. Because there was friction between the two brothers, Sobh Azal and Bahaullah, the former was sent to Cypress, the latter to Palestine. The Azali movement died when Sobh Azal was poisoned in Accra; the Baha'is in Palestine survived, Abbas Effendi became a seer in Accra, and Baha'ism became an international religion.

4. Samad Behrangi, poet and writer of such well-known political allegories as *The Little Black Fish*, drowned in the river Aras that borders Azarbaijan in 1968. Because he was born into peasant poverty, believed that all art needed to be socially engaged, and grew into an influential social critic and innovative educator, Behrangi has been seen as the prototype of the populist intellectual (*raushanfekr-i mardomi*) (Dorraj 1990, 128).

5. Space forbids me from including genealogies for all my informants. Afsaneh's will serve as a sample genealogy: "The family legend among the Najmabadis starts with an ironsmith named Baqer who lived in the village of Najmabad near Qazvin. Baqer had two sons later known as Mullah Ibrahim and Mullah Mahdi, neither of whom chose to become ironsmiths. They left Najmabad for Najaf and started a line of religious scholars— the Najmabadis. Later, they returned and settled in Tehran. Mullah Mahdi and his wife,

Khanum Bihbihani, had a son who became the famous Hajj Sheikh Hadi Najmabadi, prominent as both a religious leader and as a freethinker. He had two wives and was known to be absolutely just in his treatment of both—so goes the family legend. With one of these wives he had a son Hajj Sheikh Mahdi who had three wives. He fathered Nur al-Huda Najmabadi who was my paternal grandmother. She married Hajj Sheikh Sadiq Najmabadi, a son of Aga Hasan and Maryam Khanum. Aga Hasan was the son of Mullah Ibrahim, one of the two original brothers who had gone to Najaf."

6. See Lila Abu-Lughod (1993), particularly chap. 4, "Patrilateral Parallel-Cousin Marriage," for a different but related account of the fetishizing of virginity in a Bedouin community. Pari, Kambys, and others also had stories I have omitted about the importance of virginity in measuring a girl's value.

7. See Etienne Balibar's (1991) "Is There a 'Neo-Racism' "? and Avtar Brah (1996) for their reflections on new configurations of old forms. Brah, for instance, considers the new racialization of South Asian religions in postwar Britain.

8. Faridudin Attar was a twelfth-century mystic poet whose most famous work was the epic *The Conference of the Birds,* the story of how the birds search for Simurgh (the phoenixlike magical bird in the *Shahnameh*) in order to make it king only to discover that they as a group constitute that for which they search—Simurgh is literally "thirty birds." In the *Shahnameh,* Simurgh saves the white-haired child Zal, one of the four great ancient heroes, abandoned by Sam his father. Zal becomes the father of the hero Rustam.

9. See Kelley, Friedlander, and Colby (1993, 141–48).

Chapter 3

Epigraph: See William Wordsworth 1954.

1. See Fischer (1980a, 180ff) for a reading of the economic and political causes of the revolution.

2. See Eliz Sanasarian (1995, 243–65).

3. Some parts of this section are elaborated on in my essay "Eluding the Feminist, Overthrowing the Modern" (Sullivan 1998a).

4. Shariati, *Bazgasht bih Khvish,* p. 316, quoted in Mohamad Tavakoli (1988, 124).

5. Ali Shariati, *Fatima Is Fatima,* (1980a, 105 and 108).

6. According to Irfani (1983, 128), Fatima as model inspired other real-life Fatimas such as Fatima Amini, the schoolteacher from Mashhad, who joined the Mujahedin-i-Khalq guerrillas and led their first demonstration against the regime. Her arrest and torture by SAVAK in 1974 preceded her death in prison in 1975.

7. Oriana Fallaci (1976, 272).

8. See William R. Darrow (1985, 307–20) for a valuable reading of the ambivalent discourse of women's rights in the Islamic Constitution and its sources in earlier writings by Shariati and Motahari. Shariati faults not Western women in general but rather their commodification. In spite of their power to effect social change, women, he claims, allow their desires to be so manipulated that they become vulnerable pawns in capitalist consumption and leisure.

9. My source is the section entitled "Women's Organizations in Iran," in Tabari and Yeganeh (1982). This useful book includes documents on the question of women from

Khomeini to the Tudeh Party. It also lists positions taken by thirteen major and ten smaller women's organizations on the revolution.

10. Haleh Afshar, "Khomeini's Teachings and Their Implications for Iranian Women," in Tabari and Yeganeh (1982, 83ff). Afshar quotes specific sections from Khomeini's *Towzih al-Masa'il:* massaleh 2374, 2376, and 2459.

11. See Annabelle Sreberny Mohammadi and Ali Mohammadi's reading of rumor as the "collective construction of reality" (1994, 131–32) and more generally their fine study of the role of traditional channels of communications and media in undermining the Pahlavi regime.

12. Taha Hejazi, "The Day the Iamam Returns," quoted in Amir Taheri (1987, 224).

13. See my analysis of this event in my essay (Sullivan 1998a).

14. Kianuri, the secretary-general of the Tudeh Party, had been in exile in the Soviet Union for thirty years. He returned to celebrate the revolution but was imprisoned in February 1983. A few months later, he appeared on television to make a public confession and apology. Kianuri is cousin to Zia Ashraf Nasr.

15. The enlightened reformer who had been a friend of Sheikh Hadi, Afsaneh's grandfather, and of Mirza Hadi, Pari's grandfather.

16. See my comment on this narrative in my essay in *Remaking Women* (Sullivan 1998a).

17. Iranians were asked to answer the question, "Islamic Republic, yes or no?" Kurdish political organizations argued that this was undemocratic.

18. Ayatollah Mahalati, the leading theologian in Shiraz, was as respected by the people as Ayatollah Taleghani and Shariat Madari were in Tehran and Qum. Both were noted for their enlightened, liberal, democratic piety. Both warned that it was against the principles of Islam to repress dissent and protest among the people. See Fischer (1980b). Both died some two years after the revolution. Ayatollah Dastgheib, a pro-Khomeini cleric, was a radical reactionary who died in the suicide-embrace of a young Mojahid woman.

19. Pari tells me that this also implies an optimistic generation who believed that the possibility for change lay in our hands. After the fall of Mossadeq, this generation lost its voice.

20. Khomeini's deputy minister for revolutionary affairs and then foreign minister in 1979.

Chapter 4

1. See Frances Bartkowski's (1995) elegant introduction to *Travelers, Immigrants, Inmates,* which moves from the Lacanian grounding of identity to more specific current global problems of mistaken identity and identity wars. More generally, see Stuart Hall's (1994) important reading of cultural identity in diaspora as both "being"—a constructed oneness continuous with a shared past—and "becoming" as a process of transformation and difference, positioned by history and circumstance. See also Ian Hacking's *Rewriting the Soul* where he triangulates Foucault's two poles of development with the science of memory-as-narrative, or "memoro-politics": "We constitute our souls by making up our lives, that is, by weaving stories about our past, by what we call memories. The tales we tell of ourselves and to ourselves are not a matter of recording what we have done and how

we have felt. They must mesh with the rest of the world and with other people's stories . . . but their real role is in the creation of a life, a character, a self" (1995, 250–1).

2. When Tahereh read this chapter, she said I misremembered the original song, that Ali had always been "Shah" implying that his kind of kingship was the only morally proper kingship. I therefore find interesting my postrevolutionary inflection to that song, a sort of screen memory that (as Freud wrote) recomposes an original event along new narrative lines.

3. See Kelley (1991).

4. Bethune (born in 1890) was a Canadian surgeon, political activist, and inventor. He went to Spain in 1936 to help the Spanish freedom fighters and in 1938 joined the medical team of the People's Liberation Army of China. In Canada, he struggled for a socialized medical service and made several innovations in medical practice and instruments. He died in China in 1939.

5. The Wobblies, or the Industrial Workers of the World, was a radical labor union established in Chicago in 1905. It aimed at gaining workers' control of the means of production and was the only labor organization to oppose U.S. participation in World War I. It was subjected to harassment and suppressed by the mid-1920s.

6. See Adorno, Frenkel-Brunswik, Levinson, and Sanford (1950) for an analysis of the symptoms and syndromes of the authoritarian.

7. Students of theology lived and studied in colleges called *madresseh*. Their studies ranged from mathematics to philosophy, law, and theology. Those who stayed for the first stage of training left with the title of Mullah. Those who stayed for further study and were qualified to interpret the *Sharia* (Islamic Law) and the Qur'an received the title *Mojtahid*.

Epilogue

1. See Anny Bakalian (1993) for her analysis of diasporic passages away from a politicized diasporic "being" to more local and ethnic "feeling"; and see Khachig Tololyan (1996) for his reading of this move.

2. See William Gass, "The Philosophical Significance of Exile," in Glad (1990, 1–4) for Gass's address to the conference of writers in exile in Vienna, December 1987, and for responses from three of the sixteen writers.

3. I am referring to Said's (1983) "Traveling Theory" in *The World, The Text and the Critic*; and Clifford's "Notes on Travel and Theory" in *Inscriptions 5: Traveling Theories, Traveling Theorists* (Clifford and Dhareswar 1989). See also Clifford's (1992) "Traveling Cultures" in *Cultural Studies*.

Select Bibliography

Abu-Lughod, Lila. 1987. *Veiled Sentiments*. Berkeley: University of California Press.

——. 1993. *Writing Women's Worlds: Bedouin Stories*. Berkeley: University of California Press.

——, ed. 1998. *Remaking Women: Feminism and Modernity in the Middle East*. Princeton, N.J.: Princeton University Press.

Abrahamian, Ervand. 1968. "The Crowd in Iranian Politics: 1905–1953." *Past and Present* 41: 184–210.

——. 1973. "Kasravi: The Integrative Nationalist of Iran." *Middle East Studies* (October): 271–95.

——. 1982. *Iran between Two Revolutions*. Princeton, N.J.: Princeton University Press.

——. 1989. *The Iranian Mojahedin*. New Haven: Yale University Press.

——. 1993. *Khomeinism: Essays on the Islamic Republic*. Berkeley: University of California Press.

Adorno, Theodor. 1974. *Minima Moralia: Reflections from a Damaged Life*. Translated by E. F. N. Jephcott. London: New Left.

——, Else Frenkel-Brunswik, Daniel Levinson, and R. Nevitt Sanford. 1950. *The Authoritarian Personality*. New York: Harper.

Afary, Janet. 1989. "On the Origins of Feminism in Early Twentieth-Century Iran." *Journal of Women's History* (Fall) 1(2): 65–87.

Afkhami, Mahnaz, ed. 1995. *Faith and Freedom: Women's Human Rights in the Muslim World*. Syracuse: Syracuse University Press.

——, and Erica Friedl, eds. 1994. *In the Eye of the Storm: Women in Post-Revolutionary Iran*. London: I. B. Tauris.

Afshar, Haleh. 1982. "Khomeini's Teachings and Their Implications for Iranian Women." In *In the Shadow of Islam: The Women's Movement in Iran*. Edited by Azar Tabari and Nahid Yeganeh. London: Zed Press.

——, ed. 1985. *Iran: A Revolution in Turmoil* Albany: SUNY Press.

——, ed. 1987. *Women, State, and Ideology*. Albany: SUNY Press.

Ahmad, Aijaz. 1992. *In Theory: Classes, Nations, Literatures*. London: Verso.

Ahmad, Eqbal. 1979. "The Iranian Revolution: A Landmark for the Future." *Race and Class* 21: 3–11.

Akhavi, Shahrough. 1980. *Religion and Politics in Contemporary Iran: Clergy-State Relations in the Pahlavi Period.* Albany: SUNY Press.

Albert, David. 1980. *Tell the American People: Perspectives on the Iranian Revolution.* Philadelphia: Movement for a New Society.

Al-e-Ahmad, Jalal. 1982. *Gharbzadegi.* Translated by John Green and Ahmad Alizadeh. Lexington, Ky.: Mazda.

Alishan, Leonardo. 1985. "Ahmad Shamlu: The Rebel Poet in Search of an Audience." *Iranian Studies* 18: 375–422.

Anderson, Benedict. 1991. *Imagined Communities.* London: Verso.

Arberry, A. J. 1960. *Shiraz: Persian City of Saints and Poets.* Norman: University of Oklahoma Press.

Arendt, Hannah. 1965. *On Revolution.* New York: Viking Press.

Arjomand, Said Amir, ed. 1984a. *From Nationalism to Revolutionary Iran.* Albany: SUNY Press.

———. 1984b. *The Shadow of God and the Hidden Imam.* Chicago: University of Chicago Press.

———. 1988. *Authority and Political Culture in Shi'ism.* Albany: SUNY Press.

Arlen, Michel J. 1970. *Exiles.* New York: Farrar, Straus & Giroux.

Ashtiani, Ali Mirsepassi. 1994. "The Crisis of Secular Politics and the Rise of Political Islam in Iran," *Social Text* (Spring): 51–84.

Auerbach, Erich. 1953. *Mimesis: The Representation of Reality in Western Literature.* Translated by Willard Trask. Princeton, N.J.: Princeton University Press.

Azari, Farah. 1983. *Women of Iran: The Conflict with Fundamentalist Islam.* London: Ithaca Press.

Bakalian, Anny. 1993. *Armenian-Americans: From Being to Feeling Armenian.* New Brunswick, N.J.: Transaction Press.

Bakhash, Shaul. 1984. *The Reign of the Ayatollahs.* New York: Basic Books.

Balibar, Etienne. 1991. "Is There a 'Neo-Racism'?" In *Race, Nation, Class: Ambiguous Identities.* Edited by Etienne Balibar and Immanuel Wallerstein. London and New York: Verso.

Bani-Sadr, Abol Hassan. 1991. *My Turn to Speak.* Translated by William Ford. Washington, D.C.: Brassey's.

Barahani, Reza. 1977. *The Crowned Cannibals.* New York: Vintage.

Bartkowski, Frances. 1995. *Travelers, Immigrants, Inmates: Essays in Estrangement.* Minneapolis: University of Minnesota Press.

Bashiriyeh, Hossein. 1984. *The State and Revolution in Iran: 1962–1982.* New York: St. Martin's Press.

Bayaat, Mangol. 1982. *Mysticism and Dissent.* New York: Syracuse University Press.

Behdad, Ali. 1994. *Belated Travelers: Orientalism in the Age of Colonial Dissolution.* Durham and London: Duke University Press.

Behnam, M. Reza. 1986. *Cultural Foundations of Iranian Politics.* Salt Lake City: University of Utah Press.

Behrangi, Samad. 1984. *The Little Black Fish and Other Modern Persian Stories.* Translated by Eric and Mary Hooglund. Washington, D.C.: Three Continents Press.

Benard, Cheryl, and Zalmay Khalilzad. 1984. *"The Government of God"—Iran's Islamic Republic.* New York: Columbia University Press.

Benjamin, Walter. 1969. "Theses on the Philosophy of History." *Illuminations.* Edited by Hannah Arendt. Translated by Harry Zohn. New York: Schocken.

Bhabha, Homi K., ed. 1990. *Nation and Narration.* London: Routledge.

——. 1994. *The Location of Culture.* London: Routledge.

——. 1996. "Culture's In-Between." Pp. 55–60 in *Questions of Cultural Identity.* Edited by Stuart Hall and Paul du Gay. London: Sage.

Bill, James A. 1988. *The Eagle and the Lion: The Tragedy of American-Iranian Relations.* New Haven: Yale University Press.

Binder, Leonard. 1962. *Iran: Political Development in a Changing Society.* Berkeley: University of California Press.

Bourdieu, Pierre. 1991. *Language and Symbolic Power.* Cambridge: Harvard University Press.

Boyarin, Daniel, and Jonathan Boyarin. 1993. "Diaspora: Generation and the Ground of Jewish Identity." *Critical Inquiry* 19(4): 693–725.

Bozorgmehr, Mehdi. 1996. "Diaspora in the Postrevolutionary Period." Pp. 380–83 in *Encyclopedia Iranica,* vol. VII. Edited by Ehsan Yarshatar. Costa Mesta, Calif.: Mazda Press.

——, and Georges Sabbagh. 1998. "High Status Immigrants: A Statistical Profile of Iranians in the United States." *Iranian Studies* 3–4 (November): 5–36.

Brah, Avtar. 1996. *Cartographies of Diaspora: Contesting Identities.* London and New York: Routledge.

Brennan, Timothy. 1989. *Salman Rushdie and the Third World: Myths of the Nation.* New York: St. Martin's Press.

Breuilly, John. 1982. *Nationalism and the State.* New York: St. Martin's Press.

Brodsky, Joseph. 1990. "The Condition We Call 'Exile'." Pp. 100–30 in *Literature in Exile.* Edited by John Glad. Durham, N.C.: Duke University Press.

Browne, Edward G. 1910a. *The Persian Constitutional Movement.* From the Proceedings of the British Academy. London: Cambridge University Press.

——. *The Persian Revolution: 1905–1909.* 1910b. London: Cambridge University Press.

Chaliand, Gerard, ed. 1980. *People without a Country: The Kurds and Kurdistan.* London: Zed Press.

Chatterjee, Partha. 1995. *The Nation and Its Fragments: Studies in Colonial and Post-Colonial Histories.* Princeton, N.J.: Princeton University Press.

Chow, Ray. 1993. *Writing Diaspora: Tactics of Intervention in Contemporary Cultural Studies.* Bloomington: Indiana University Press.

Cohen, Robin. 1997. *Global Diasporas: An Introduction.* Seattle: University of Washington Press.

Cottam, Richard W. 1988. *Iran and the United States: A Cold War Case Study.* Pittsburgh: University of Pittsburgh Press.

Clifford, James. 1992. "Traveling Cultures." Pp. 96–112 in *Cultural Studies.* Edited by Larry Grossberg, Cary Nelson, and Paula Treichler. New York: Routledge.

——. 1994. "Diasporas." *Cultural Anthropology* 9(3): 302–38.

——, and George Marcus, eds. 1986. *Writing Culture: The Poetics and Politics of Ethnography.* Berkeley: University of California Press.

——, and Vivek Dhareswar, eds. 1989. *Inscriptions 5: Traveling Theories, Traveling Theorists.* Santa Cruz: University of California Press.

Dabashi, Hamid, ed. 1992. *Parviz Sayyad's Theater of Diaspora. Two Plays: The Ass and the Rex Cinema Trial*. Costa Mesta: Mazda.

Darrow, William R. 1985. "Woman's Place and the Place of Women in the Iranian Revolution." In *Women, Religion and Social Change*. Edited by Yvonne Y. Haddad and Ellison B. Findly. Albany: SUNY Press.

De Certeau, Michel. 1984. *The Practice of Everyday Life*. Translated by Steven Rendall. Berkeley: University of California Press.

Dorraj, Manochehr. 1990. *From Zarathustra to Khomeini: Populism and Dissent in Iran*. Boulder and London: Lynne Rienner Publishers.

Esfandiari, Haleh. 1997. *Reconstructed Lives: Women and Iran's Islamic Revolution*. Washington, D.C.: The Woodrow Wilson Center Press.

Fallaci, Oriana. 1976. *Interviews with History*. Boston: Houghton Mifflin.

Fanon, Frantz. 1963. *The Wretched of the Earth*. Translated by Constance Farrington. New York: Grove.

Farah, Nuruddin. 1990. "In Praise of Exile." Pp. 64–77 in *Literature in Exile*. Edited by John Glad. Durham, N.C.: Duke University Press.

Farhang, Mansur. 1981. *U.S. Imperialism: The Spanish-American War to the Iranian Revolution*. Boston: South End Press.

Fathi, Asghar, ed. 1985. *Women and the Family in Iran*. Leiden: E. J. Brill.

——, ed. 1991. *Iranian Refugees and Exiles Since Khomeini*. Costa Mesta, Calif.: Mazda.

Fischer, Michael M. J. 1980a. "Becoming Mollah: Reflections on Iranian Clerics in a Revolutionary Age." *Iranian Studies* 13: 83–177.

——. 1980b. *Iran: From Religious Dispute to Revolution*. Cambridge: Harvard University Press.

——, and Mehdi Abedi. 1990. *Debating Muslims: Cultural Dialogues in Postmodernity and Tradition*. Madison: University of Wisconsin Press.

Freud, Sigmund. 1996. *The Complete Psychological Works*. 7 vols. Translated by James Strachey. London: Hogarth Press.

Friedl, Erika. 1991. *Women of Deh Koh: Lives in an Iranian Village*. New York: Penguin.

Gasiorowski, Mark J. 1991. *U.S. Foreign Policy and the Shah: Building a Client State in Iran*. Ithaca: Cornell University Press.

Geertz, Clifford. 1968. *Islam Observed*. New Haven: Yale University Press.

——. 1973. *The Interpretation of Cultures*. New York: Basic Books.

George, Rosemary Marangoly. 1996. *The Politics of Home: Postcolonial Relocations and Twentieth-Century Fictions*. Cambridge: Cambridge University Press.

Giddens, A. 1985. *The Nation-State and Violence*. Cambridge, U.K.: Polity.

Gilroy, Paul. 1987. *"There Ain't No Black in the Union Jack": The Cultural Politics of Race and Nation*. Chicago: University of Chicago Press.

——. 1993. *The Black Atlantic: Modernity and Double Consciousness*. Cambridge: Harvard University Press.

Glad, John, ed. 1990. *Literature in Exile*. Durham, N.C.: Duke University Press.

Goode, James F. 1997. *The U.S. and Iran: In the Shadow of Mussadiq*. New York: St. Martin's Press.

Grossberg, Larry, Cary Nelson, and Paula Treichler, eds. 1992. *Cultural Studies*. New York: Routledge.

Guppy, Susha. 1988. *The Blindfold Horse.* Boston: Beacon Press.

Hacking, Ian. 1995. *Rewriting the Soul: Multiple Personality and the Sciences of Memory.* Princeton, N.J.: Princeton University Press.

Haeri, Shahla. 1989. *Law of Desire: Temporary Marriage in Shiah Islam.* New York: Syracuse University Press.

Hall, Stewart. 1994. "Cultural Identity and Diaspora." In *Colonial Discourse and Postcolonial Theory.* Edited by Patrick Williams and Laura Chrisman. New York: Columbia University Press.

Hillmann, Michael Craig. 1985. "Preface." *Iranian Studies* 18: 131–36.

Hobsbawm, Eric J. 1991. *Nations and Nationalism since 1780: Programs, Myth, Reality.* 2d ed. Cambridge: Cambridge University Press.

Hoffman, Eva. 1989. *Lost in Translation: A Life in a New Language.* New York: Penguin.

Hohn, Hans. 1952. *Nationalism in the Middle East.* Washington, D.C.: Middle East Institute.

Hugo of St. Victor. 1961. *Didascalicon.* Translated by Jerome Taylor. New York: Columbia University Press.

Irfani, Suroosh. 1983. *Revolutionary Islam in Iran: Popular Liberation or Religious Dictatorship?* London: Zed Books.

Kamalipour, Yahya R., ed. 1995. *The U.S. Media and the Middle East: Image and Perception.* Westport, Conn.: Greenwood Press.

Kandiyoti, Deniz, ed. 1991. *Women, Islam and the State.* Philadelphia: Temple University Press.

Karim, Persis M., and Mohammad Mehdi Khorrami. 1991. *A World Between: Poems, Short Stories, and Essays by Iranian-Americans.* New York: George Braziller.

Karimi-Hakkak, Ahmad. 1985. Review-essay on Jamalzadeh in *Iranian Studies* 18: 423–26.

Katouzian, Homa. 1981. *The Political Economy of Modern Iran: Despotism and Pseudo Modernism, 1926–1979.* New York: New York University Press.

Kazemi, Farhad. 1984. "The *Fada'iyan-e Islam:* Fanaticism, Politics and Terror." Pp. 158–76 in *From Nationalism to Revolutionary Islam.* Edited by Said Amir Arjomand. Albany: SUNY Press.

Kazmi, Yedollah. 1990. "On Being Educated in the West: The Disruption of the Self as a Narrative and Authenticity and Inauthenticity of Self." *Studies in Philosophy and Education* 10: 281–95.

Keddie, Nikki. 1981. *Roots of Revolution.* New Haven: Yale University Press.

Kedourie, Elie. 1992. *Politics in the Middle East.* Oxford: Oxford University Press.

——. 1993. *Nationalism.* 4th ed. Oxford: Oxford University Press.

Kelley, Ron. 1991. "Iranian Political Demonstrations in Los Angeles, USA: A Photographic Essay." In *Iranian Refugees and Exiles Since Khomeini.* Edited by Asghar Fathi. Costa Mesa, Calif.: Mazda.

——, Jonathan Friedlander, and Anita Colby. 1993. *Irangeles: Iranians in Los Angeles.* Berkeley: University of California Press.

Khan, Mohammad Zafrulla, trans. 1970. *The Koran.* Arabic text with a new translation. New York: Praeger Publications.

Khomeini, Ayatollah Ruhollah. 1964. *Towzih al-Masa'il* [Interpretation of Problems]. Qum: Elmiyyeh.

———. 1979. *Islamic Government*. Translated by Joint Publications Research Service. New York: Manor Books.

———. 1984. *A Clarification of Questions: An Unabridged Translation of Resaleh Towzih al-Masa'il*. Translated by Borujerdi. Boulder, Colo.: Westview Press.

Kohn, Hans. 1944. *The Idea of Nationalism*. New York: Macmillan.

Levinas, Emmanuel. 1986. "The Trace of the Other." In *Deconstruction in Context*. Edited by Mark C. Taylor. Chicago: University of Chicago Press.

Limbert, J. 1987. *Iran: At War with History*. Boulder, Colo.: Westview Press.

Lloyd, David. 1987. *Nationalism and Minor Literature: James Clarence Mangan and the Emergence of Irish Cultural Nationalism*. Berkeley: University of California Press.

Lytle, Mark Hamilton. 1987. *The Origins of the Iranian-American Alliance 1941– 1953*. London and New York: Holmes & Meier.

Martin, Biddy, and Chandra Talpade Mohanty. 1986. "Feminist Politics: What's Home Got to Do with It?" Pp. 191–212 in *Feminist Studies/Critical Studies*. Edited by Teresa de Lauretis. Bloomington: Indiana University Press.

Martin, Vanessa. 1989. *Islam and Modernism: The Iranian Revolution of 1906*. New York: Syracuse University Press.

Milani, Farzaneh. 1992. *Veils and Words: The Emerging Voices of Iranian Women Writers*. Syracuse: Syracuse University Press.

Moaddel, Mansoor. 1993. *Class, Politics, and Ideology in the Iranian Revolution*. New York: Columbia University Press.

Moayyad, Heshmat, ed. 1991. *Stories from Iran: A Chicago Anthology 1921–1991*. Washington, D.C.: Mage Publishers.

Moghadam, Valentine, ed. 1993. *Modernising Women: Gender and Social Change in the Middle East*. Boulder, Colo.: Lynne Rienner Publishers.

———, ed. 1994. *Gender and National Identity: Women and Politics in Muslim Societies*. London: Zed Books.

Moghissi, Haideh. 1994. *Populism and Feminism in Iran: Women's Struggle in a Male-Defined Revolutionary Movement*. New York: St. Martin's Press.

Mohammadi, Annabelle Sreberny, and Ali Mohammadi. 1994. *Small Media, Big Revolution: Communication, Culture, and the Iranian Revolution*. Minneapolis: University of Minnesota Press.

Motahari, Ayatollah Mortaza. 1974. *Masaleh-e Hejab* [The Problem of the Veil]. Tehran: Anjuman-i Islami-i Pizishkan.

Mottahedeh, Roy. 1985. *The Mantle of the Prophet: Religion and Politics in Iran*. New York: Pantheon.

Naficy, Hamid. 1989. "Autobiography, Film Spectatorship, and Cultural Negotiation." *Emergences* 1 (Fall): 29–54.

———. 1993. *The Making of Exile Culture: Iranian Television in Los Angeles*. Minneapolis: University of Minnesota Press.

———. 1995. "Mediating the Other: American Pop Culture Representations of Postrevolutionary Iran." Pp. 73–90 in *The U.S. Media and the Middle East: Image and Perception*. Edited by Yahya R. Kamalipour. Westport, Conn.: Greenwood Press.

———, ed. 1999. *Home, Exile, Homeland: Film, Media, and the Politics of Place*. New York and London: Routledge.

Najmabadi, Afsaneh. 1991. "Hazards of Modernity and Morality: Women, State and Ideology in Contemporary Iran." Pp. 48–76 in *Women, Islam and the State*. Edited by Deniz Kandiyoti. Philadelphia: Temple University Press.

——. 1992. "Without a Place to Rest the Sole of My Foot." *Emergences* (Fall): 84–102.

——. 1998a. *Sedighe Dowlatabadi: Letters, Writings, and Remembrances* (in Persian). Edited by Mahdokht Sanati and Afsaneh Najmabadi. 3 Vols. New York: Nigarish va Nigarish-i-Zan.

——. 1998b. *The Story of the Daughters of Quchan: Gender and National Memory in Iranian History*. Syracuse: Syracuse University Press.

——. Forthcoming. "Feminism in an Islamic Republic." In *Gender, Islam, and Social Class*. Edited by Yvonne Haddad and John Esposito. Oxford: Oxford University Press.

Naraghi, Ehsan. 1994. *From Palace to Prison: Inside the Iranian Revolution*. Translated from French by Nilou Mobasser. London: I. B. Tauris.

Nashat, Guity, ed. 1983. *Women and Revolution in Iran*. Boulder, Colo.: Westview Press.

Nuri, Shaykh Fadl Allah. 1988. "Book of Admonition to the Heedless and Guidance for the Ignorant," translated by Hamid Dabashi. Pp. 354–70 in Said Amir Arjomand's *Authority and Political Culture in Shi'ism*. New York: SUNY Press.

Paidar, Parvin. 1995. *Women and the Political Process in Twentieth-Century Iran*. Cambridge: Cambridge University Press.

Parker, Kenneth. 1993. "Home is Where the Heart . . . Lies." *Transition* 59: 65–77.

Parsa, Misagh. 1989. *Social Origins of the Iranian Revolution*. New Brunswick: Rutgers University Press.

Pratt, Minnie Bruce. 1988. "Identity: Skin Blood Heart." In *Yours in Struggle: Three Feminist Perspectives on Anti-Semiticism and Racism*. Edited by Elly Bulkin, Minnie Bruce Pratt, and Barbara Smith. Ithaca, N.Y.: Firebrand Books.

Radhakrishnan, R. 1996. *Diasporic Mediations: Between Home and Location*. Minneapolis: University of Minnesota Press.

Rahnema, Ali. 1998. *An Islamic Utopian: A Political Biography of Ali Shariati*. London: I. B. Tauris.

Reeves, Minou. *Female Warriors af Allah: Women and the Islamic Revolution*. New York: E. P. Dutton, 1989.

Rosaldo, Renato. 1989. "Imperialist Nostalgia." *Representations* 26 (Spring): 107–22.

Rushdie, Salman. 1991. *Imaginary Homelands*. New York: Viking.

Saedi, Gholam Hossein. 1993. "Avatars of Exile," *Aleph Ba*. Translated by Saideh Pakravan. *Chanteh: The Iranian Cross-Cultural Quarterly* (Spring): 31–35.

Safran, William. 1991. "Diasporas in Modern Societies: Myths of Homeland and Return." *Diaspora* 1: 83–99.

Sahebjam, Freidoune. 1994. *The Stoning of Soraya M.* Translated by Richard Seaver. Boston: Little, Brown.

Said, Edward. 1981. *Covering Islam: How the Media and the Experts Determine How We See the Rest of the World*. New York: Pantheon.

——. 1983. *The World, the Text, and the Critic*. Cambridge: Harvard University Press.

——. 1984. "The Mind of Winter: Reflections on Life in Exile." *Harper's* (September): 49–55.

——. 1993. *Culture and Imperialism*. New York: Alfred A. Knopf.

Sanasarian, Eliz. 1982. *The Women's Rights Movement in Iran.* New York: Praeger.

———. 1995. "State Dominance and Communal Perseverance: The Armenian Diaspora in the Islamic Republic of Iran, 1979–1989." *Diaspora* 4(3): 243–65.

Shammas, Anton. 1990. "Exile from a Democracy." Pp. 84–99 in *Literature in Exile.* Edited by John Glad. Durham, N.C.: Duke University Press.

Shariati, Ali. 1979a. *On the Sociology of Islam.* Translated by Hamid Algar. Berkeley: Mizan Press.

———. 1979b. *One Followed by an Eternity of Zeros.* Translated by Ali Asghar Ghassemy. Tehran: Hoseiniyeh Ershad.

———. 1980a. *Fatima Is Fatima.* Translated by Laleh Bakhtiar. Tehran: Hamdami Foundation.

———. 1980b. *Marxism and Other Western Fallacies: An Islamic Critique.* Translated by R. Campbell. Berkeley: Mizan Press.

Sheffer, Gabriel, ed. 1986. *Modern Diasporas in International Politics.* New York: St. Martin's Press.

Shohat, Ella. 1999. "By the Bitstream of Babylon: Cyberfrontiers and Diasporic Vistas." In *Home, Exile, Homeland: Film, Media, and the Politics of Place.* Edited by Hamid Naficy. New York and London: Routledge.

Shuster, Morgan. 1912. *The Strangling of Persia.* New York: Century.

Sick, Gary. 1985. *All Fall Down: America's Tragic Encounter with Iran.* New York: Random House.

Sohrabi, Naghmeh. 1993. "Soc.Culture.Iranian." *Chanteh: The Iranian Cross-Cultural Quarterly* 5 (Fall): 24–26.

Spellberg, D. A. 1994. *Politics, Gender, and the Islamic Past: The Legacy of 'A'isha bint Abi Bakr.* New York: Columbia University Press.

Spivak, Gayatri Chakravorty. 1988. *In Other Worlds.* New York: Routledge.

———. 1992. "Acting Bits/Identity Talk." *Critical Inquiry* (Summer): 770–803.

———. "Diasporas Old and New: Women in the Transnational." *Textual Practice* 10(2): 245–69.

Starn, Randolph. 1989. "Introduction." *Representations* 26 (Spring): 1–8.

Stewart, Susan. 1984. *On Longing: Narratives of the Miniature, the Gigantic, the Souvenir, the Collection.* Baltimore: Johns Hopkins University Press.

Sullivan, Zohreh T. 1992. "Born in the U.S.A., or the Story of Two Kinds of Fish," *Chanteh* (Fall): 12–16.

———. 1993. *Narratives of Empire: The Fictions of Rudyard Kipling.* Cambridge: Cambridge University Press.

———. 1998a. "Eluding the Feminist, Overthrowing the Modern?: Transformations in 20th Century Iran." Pp. 215–42 in *Remaking Women: Gender and Modernity in the Middle East.* Edited by Lila Abu-Lughod. Princeton, N.J.: Princeton University Press.

———. 1998b. "Returning to Tehran." *Suitcase: A Journal of Transnational Traffic* 3 (Summer): 28–48.

Tabari, Azar, and Nahid Yeganeh. 1982. *In the Shadow of Islam: The Women's Movement in Iran.* London: Zed Press.

Tabori, Paul. 1972. *The Anatomy of Exile.* London: Harrap.

Taheri, Amir. 1987. *The Spirit of Allah: Khomeini and the Islamic Revolution.* Bethesda, Md.: Adler & Adler.

Tavakoli, Mohamad. 1988. "The Constitutional Revolution of 1905–1906 and the Islamic Revolution of 1978–1979." Ph.D. Dissertation. The University of Chicago.

———. 1992. "Refashioning Iran." *Iranian Studies* 23: 77–101.

Terdiman, Richard. 1985. "Deconstructing Memory: On Representing the Past and Theorizing Culture in France since the Revolution." *Diacritics* (Winter): 13–36.

Tohidi, Nayereh. 1993. "Immigrant Iranians and Gender Relations." In *Irangeles: Iranians in Los Angeles.* Edited by Ron Kelley, Jonathan Friedlander, and Anita Colby. Berkeley: University of California Press.

———. 1994. "Modernity, Islamization, and Women in Iran." In *Gender and National Identity: Women and Politics in Muslim Societies.* Edited by Valentine Moghadam. London: Zed Books.

———. 1996. *Feminism, Demokracy ve Islamgarayi* (Feminism, Democracy and Islamism in Iran). Los Angeles: Ketabsara.

———, and Herbert Bodman, eds. 1998. *Women in Muslim Society: Diversity within Unity.* Boulder, Colo.: Lynne Rienner.

Tololyan, Khachig. 1991. "The Nation-State and Its Others." *Diaspora* 1(1): 3–8.

———. 1996. "Rethinking *Diaspora(s):* Stateless Power in the Transnational Moment." *Diaspora* 5(1): 3–36.

Walcott, Derek. 1974. "The Muse of History." In *Is Massa Day Dead? Black Moods in the Caribbean.* Edited by Orde Coombes. New York: Doubleday.

Wilson, Edmund. 1978 [1929]. *The Wound and the Bow: Seven Studies in Literature.* New York: Farrar, Straus, Giroux.

Wright, Robin. 1985. *Sacred Rage: The Wrath of Militant Islam.* New York: Simon & Schuster.

Wordsworth, William. 1954. *The Prelude.* Edited with an introduction by Carlos Baker. New York: Rinehart & Co.

———. 1989. *In the Name of God: The Khomeini Decade.* New York: Simon & Schuster.

Zarrin, Ali. 1999. "Made You Mine, America." In *A World Between: Poems, Short Stories, and Essays by Iranian-Americans.* Edited by Persis M. Karim and Mohammad Medhi Khorrami. New York: George Braziller.

Zonis, Marvin. 1971. *The Political Elite of Iran.* Princeton, N.J.: Princeton University Press.

Index